D1552664

Managing Pension and Retirement Plans

MANAGING PENSION AND RETIREMENT PLANS

A Guide for Employers, Administrators, and Other Fiduciaries

August J. Baker
Dennis E. Logue
Jack S. Rader

OXFORD
UNIVERSITY PRESS

2005

658.3253
B16m

OXFORD
UNIVERSITY PRESS

Oxford   New York
Auckland   Bangkok   Buenos Aires   Cape Town   Chennai
Dar es Salaam   Delhi   Hong Kong   Istanbul   Karachi   Kolkata
Kuala Lumpur   Madrid   Melbourne   Mexico City   Mumbai   Nairobi
São Paulo   Shanghai   Taipei   Tokyo   Toronto

Copyright © 2005 by Oxford University Press, Inc.

Published by Oxford University Press, Inc.
198 Madison Avenue, New York, New York 10016

www.oup.com

Oxford is a registered trademark of Oxford University Press

All rights reserved. No part of this publication may be reproduced,
stored in a retrieval system, or transmitted, in any form or by any means,
electronic, mechanical, photocopying, recording, or otherwise,
without the prior permission of Oxford University Press.

Library of Congress Cataloging-in-Publication Data
Baker, August J.
Managing pension and retirement plans : a guide for employers, administrators,
and other fiduciaries / August Baker, Dennis Logue, and Jack Rader.
    p.   cm.
Includes bibliographical references and index.
ISBN 0-19-516590-X
1. Pension trusts—Managment.   2. Pension trusts—Investments.   I. Logue,
Dennis E.   II. Rader, Jack S., 1949–   III. title.
HD7105.4.B35 2005
658.3'253—dc22   2004009737

9 8 7 6 5 4 3 2 1

Printed in the United States of America
on acid-free paper

Preface

THE SHIFTING LANDSCAPE

This book evolved from an earlier work on pension plans that was published in 1998.[1] At that time, we were nearing all-time highs in the U.S. equity markets. Employers in Defined Benefit (DB) pension plans had seen the asset pools that they managed grow much more rapidly than the liabilities they were established to fund—so much so that many plan sponsors made little or no contributions for the better part of the 1990s—an extended vacation from what had historically been a significant expenditure. Furthermore, earnings on pension assets of public corporations added substantially to company earnings for many firms. This, in turn, had a positive effect on executive compensation schemes and may have made the stocks of these companies more attractive to investors.

Employees who worked for sponsors offering Defined Contribution (DC) plans were in love with their pension schemes. Many employees had small fortunes in the DC asset pools they owned—they were wealthy! Planned retirement ages were being moved forward; people were thinking seriously about retiring at 55 instead of 65. Visions of luxurious retirement lifestyles danced in people's heads. And the common wisdom—everywhere, it seemed—was that Defined Contribution pension plans were the only pension plans that made any sense whatsoever.

Then came March 2000. The equity markets turned down. Way down. By the end of August 2002, the Wilshire 5000 index had fallen by nearly 38% from its previous high, and the NASDAQ index had fallen by 74%.

Many employees saw their DC asset pools shrink by huge amounts. Some unfortunate people who had virtually all of their pensions in their employer's stock watched in horror as their employer's stock became worthless. They lost everything—100% of their savings vanished. Among other things, these unexpected results led people to reassess the value of Defined Contribution structures as the advantages (to employees) of defined benefit plans became more apparent.

University Libraries
Carnegie Mellon University
Pittsburgh PA 15213-3890

Defined Benefit plans also suffered. Employers with overfunded plans suddenly had plans that were underfunded. Contributions were needed to correct this underfunding. Making things worse, the economy weakened and, along with the weak economy, corporate profits and cash flow took a nosedive, making unanticipated pension contributions a hardship for many corporations. The sponsors of public pension plans experienced a similar funding challenge as tax receipts fell and government budgets came under significant financial pressure. As a final blow, interest rates fell, thus raising the economic value of pension plan liabilities.

With all this, it became clear, once again, that pension fund decisions and management matter—a lot. These are complex issues that deserve a lot of attention and a lot of effort. Pension fund management is not the "no-brainer" that some had come to think. Further, the fraud and misstatement of earnings that subsequently came to light lend urgency to pension fund decision making and management. We need informed fiduciaries in fact as well as in name.

Partially in response to this tumultuous environment, and partially in response to some significant advances in financial and pension decision making, we decided that a new book is required. In this volume, we present an economic and financial view on how pension plans can create value for their sponsors. We hope that it will be useful for those who are involved in decision making, policy, management, and advising pension funds and the sponsors of pension funds. This is not a book of sound bites, nor is it intended to be a book that oversimplifies some very challenging and complex issues. To the contrary, it is intended to pull together what the reader needs to know to make informed judgments about everything that matters in the world of pensions. We think we have succeeded; we hope you agree.

THE CONTEXT OF PENSION PLAN MANAGEMENT

The U.S. population is getting older. At present, for every person of retirement age, there are five working-age people. Over the next thirty years, this ratio will decrease to three workers per retiree.[2] Most retirees will be eligible for Social Security income, but many Americans are skeptical about Social Security. Only about 13% of Americans expect Social Security to be their largest source of income during retirement.[3] As a supplement to Social Security income, many people participate in employment-based retirement plans, collectively known as "pension plans."[4] There are many different varieties of pension plans that are currently being offered. At one extreme are the traditional DB plans, which pay retirees a fixed income as long as they live. At the other extreme are the more "modern" DC plans, such as 401(k) plans, which provide retirees with assets built up over time in investment accounts.

We will discuss both of these plan types—and several others—in this book. What the plans all have in common is that they are based in the employment relationship. A person becomes eligible for them through working, and their ultimate value depends on the terms of the person's employment. For example, the value of the plan may depend on how many years the person works for their employer, or what their salary was during their employment.

It is usually the employer who establishes and sponsors a pension plan. Virtually any employer can sponsor a pension plan of some kind or another. Private for-profit companies can and do sponsor plans. State and local governments also sponsor significant plans, as do public school systems and nonprofit organizations. Labor unions can and do sponsor pension plans as well.

In the aggregate, these pension plans have built up significant assets and are continually growing. At the end of 2003, pension plans held about $7.4 trillion in assets. State, local, and federal government plans held about 45% of this total. The remainder was distributed across the various nongovernmental "private" plans.[5]

Plan participants are, of course, keenly interested in these plans: the success of their plan can determine their standard of living during retirement. It can also determine whether they can retire as early as they would like. Investors in general are interested in these plans because of the plans' significant clout in the financial markets and because private pension obligations and funding come from firms that have publicly traded bonds and stock. In addition, employers are keenly interested in these plans. A pension plan can help an employer attract, retain, and motivate a competent workforce. Moreover, the employer's financial health can depend significantly on the financial health of its pension plan.

The list of interested parties does not end there. Many government agencies take an interest in pensions. On the federal level, the Treasury Department and the Department of Labor are two prominent examples, and on the state level, as well as on the federal level, there is substantial regulation and governmental oversight of pension plans. For a pension plan, complying with all the relevant laws, regulations, and fiduciary obligations can be a significant undertaking.

Finally, the news media and the general public are also interested parties. When a sizable pension plan fails, for example, there will be a lot of public discussion about it. Pension plans are important to the financial well-being of our older citizens and are key determinants of their standard of living in retirement. This subject matter can elicit strong reactions.

THE PURPOSE OF THIS BOOK

In the middle of all the interested parties are the people who establish and manage pension plans, the people who make sometimes difficult and always complex decisions regarding pension plans. Our primary purpose in writing this book is to provide a text that can be helpful to these decision makers. We hope to provide some clarity on the underlying economics and finance of pension plans. We also hope to provide some practical advice; for example, on pension plan investment strategies. In general, pension plan managers make many decisions that have high stakes, and we hope this book will help them make good choices.

This book will also be of interest to all who come in close contact with public and private pension plans. Chief financial officers, of course, should find it of interest. Pension plan administrators, investment managers, consultants, and members of corporate boards of directors and public pension trustees will also find much of value here, as will pension actuaries, accountants, and even those who comment on the pension scene for one reason or another. Some of the material may seem a bit challenging for those who are not trained in economics or finance. Although pension fund management is challenging, we hope the analysis is not excessively daunting. Where we have had to assume a level of technical expertise that some readers may not have (e.g., in discussing risk management and the proper use of derivatives), we do so knowing that there are other resources available to the interested reader. We ask your understanding: pension management is not easy, so the topics do not always lend themselves to simple assertions or rules of thumb.

ADVISORY SERVICES

To advise and assist the plan sponsor in structuring plans with the right features and in making other pension decisions, there exist a plethora of consultants. Benefits consultants help sponsors determine the proper replacement rate and the appropriate plan design for particular employers. They advise with respect to compliance with pension law, and they also help set up various plans for different sectors of the sponsor's business.

Tax lawyers advise regarding the plan's compliance with IRS rules and regulations. Similarly, actuaries tell the defined benefit sponsor how much it needs to set aside each period to comply with the law and to have enough money to pay retirees.

There are consultants who help plan sponsors find and monitor the performance of external money managers and the dealer/brokers who provide research and execute investment trades. These consultants further assist in developing investment strategies for both internally and externally managed funds.

Thus, the pension plan supports and has access to advice, counsel, and service from many service industries. Pension plans are "big business," and they interact with other big businesses that work on their behalf. The risk, of course, is that a wonderful pension plan design developed in isolation of the employer's other interests can prove to be a mistake within the larger organizational context. Thus, sponsors have to focus on the long-term goals of the organization and make sure consultants are aware of these goals.

ORGANIZATION OF THE BOOK

The book is divided into five parts. Part I, Fundamentals, covers what pension plans do and how they do it. It starts with an introduction to the two major plan types: Defined Benefit plans and Defined Contribution plans. It also includes an overview of fiduciary principles and regulatory compliance. Part II focuses on Defined Benefit plans. Part III focuses on Defined Contribution plans and "hybrid" plans. Part IV goes beyond the fundamentals to discuss measuring, evaluating, and improving investment performance. Part V contains some useful insights on managing the decision-making process, strategies, and people.

ACKNOWLEDGMENTS

We are grateful to the many readers who offered helpful and constructive criticism of this book and of our 1998 book. These include Rebecca Duseau of Adamas Partners, Roger Murray of Columbia University (Emeritus), Charles Elson of the University of Delaware, and Fran Ayres of the Price College School of Accounting. Thanks also to Paul Donnelly for his encouragement. Most of all, thanks to Caroline Apovian, Marcella Logue, and Mary Rader for their patience and support.

Contents

16   Managing Pension Fund Risk   194

17   Risk Management Strategies Using Derivative Securities   213

PART V   Management Issues: Decisions, Strategies, and People

18   Selecting and Managing Asset Managers   237

19   Managing Costs   248

20   People and the Psychology of Pension Fund Decisions   256

21   The Pension Plan as Shareholder   267

22   The Path to Better Pension Plan Management   278

        Appendix A   A Guide for the Prudent Fiduciary   289

        Appendix B   Global Investing for Pension Funds   291

        Appendix C   Example of a Multiemployer Hybrid
                     Pension Plan   296

        Appendix D   Measuring Returns   297

        Appendix E   Adjusting for Risk   305

        Appendix F   An Example of an Equity Swap Hedge   307

        Appendix G   Manager Selection   309

        Notes   315

        Works Cited   325

        Index   337

Managing Pension and Retirement Plans

PART I

Fundamentals

1

An Introduction to Pension Plans

This chapter provides an overview of the two major types of pension plan: Defined Benefit (DB) plans and Defined Contribution (DC) plans. The chapter introduces both plan types, and it also introduces terminology that will be used throughout the rest of the book. The discussion of DB plans will focus on how benefits accrue over an employee's career. The discussion of DC plans will differentiate among the several varieties of this plan type.

As noted in the Preface, pension plans are heavily regulated. Suffice it to say that for any plan feature discussed here, there is a vast amount of regulations. Discussion of these regulations is deferred to later chapters. For now, the focus is on the attributes and operation of the plans themselves, not on the rules that govern them.

DEFINED BENEFIT PLANS

DB plans are plans in which a person's retirement benefit is specified by the plan itself. A DB plan includes a benefit formula that specifies how much each covered employee will receive when the employee retires. With a DB plan, retirement benefits are typically made in the form of an annuity: retirees receive periodic benefits for as long as they live. The benefit formula says how much these periodic payments will be. For example, a benefit formula might indicate that a particular employee will receive $12,000 per year in retirement as long as he or she lives.

Different plans use different benefit formulas. Many plans use a benefit formula that takes into account the number of years a person works for the employer. The more years of service a person has, the greater his or her pension income will be. In some plans, this is the only input into the benefit formula. For example, a plan's benefit formula might be

$$\text{Annual Pension} = \$1,000 \times \text{years of service.}$$

3

In this case, with each year of service to the employer, an employee's annual retirement payment increases by $1,000. Someone with twelve years of experience receives $12,000 per year. Someone with thirty-five years of experience receives $35,000 per year.

Many benefit formulas also take into account how highly paid a person is while working for the employer. The higher a person's salary, the greater the annual pension payment he or she will receive. Of course, this raises the question of which salary to use. An employee who spends thirty-five years with an employer will often have thirty-five different annual salaries. The early salaries will be quite low compared to the later salaries.

One possibility is that the benefit formula could be based on the person's average salary. For someone with thirty-five years of service, the retirement benefit would be based on the average of the thirty-five salaries. In fact, through the early 1970s, many plans did use the average as the measure of salary. In the late 1970s and early 1980s, however, many plans switched to using a measure of final salary. Inflation prompted this change: averaging salaries over many years came to make little sense. Final salary can be measured in several ways. It could be simply the salary in the very last year of employment, or it could be the average of the person's salaries in the final three to five years. There is also the issue as to whether or not nonsalary compensation, for example, annual bonuses, is taken into consideration. Indeed, at this time, many highly compensated executives do have final pay plans that include nonsalary compensation.

Notice that this final salary is the final salary with a particular employer. If the person stays with an employer up to retirement, then final salary is also the person's final, preretirement salary, but for people who change employers during their career, "final salary" is the person's final salary with the given employer. If a person works for several employers with final-pay DB plans, then each DB plan will be evaluated at a different salary. Each DB benefit will be based on the person's final salary with the particular corresponding employer.

In principle, final salary could be the only input into the benefit formula. In this case, the benefit formula might be

$$\text{Annual Pension} = \tfrac{1}{4} \times \text{final salary.}$$

With this formula, each employee receives 25% of his or her final salary, and it doesn't matter how long a person works for an employer. Regardless of years of service, a final salary of $60,000 merits an annual retirement benefit of $15,000.

Such benefit formulas are rare, however. More commonly, benefit formulas are based both on years of service and on final salary. An example of a modern benefit formula is

$$\text{Annual Pension} = 1.5\% \times \text{years of service} \times \text{final salary.}$$

With this benefit formula, the more years of service, the greater the percentage of final salary that a person will receive. Ten years of service merits 15% of the final salary; twenty years merits 30% of this salary.

One important implication of such a benefit formula is that benefits are "back-loaded." That is, a significant part of the benefit accrual occurs at the end of a person's service with an employer, assuming, of course, a history of rising salaries. The result is that if a person moves from employer to employer during their career, he or she may never build up a significant pension benefit. It is by staying many years with one employer that an employee can build up the most significant pension benefit.

To see this in an example, compare a person's pension benefit in two cases: a person spends thirty years with one employer, or a person spends fifteen years with one employer and fifteen years with a second employer. Suppose that all employers offer the same benefit formula of 1.5% × years of service × final salary. To focus on the backloading, suppose also that salary growth is the same in the two cases. Suppose that salary in year fifteen is $48,000 and salary in year thirty is $100,000. This corresponds to salary growth of about 5% per year.

In the first case, the thirty years of service with this one employer mean a pension benefit of 45% of final salary. Final salary is $100,000, so the annual pension benefit is $45,000:

$$\text{Annual Pension} = 1.5\% \times 30 \text{ years of service} \\ \times \text{ final salary of } \$100,000 = \$45,000$$

In the second case, at retirement the individual receives pension checks from two employers. The total pension benefit is simply the sum of the pension benefits for the two employers. For the first employer, there are fifteen years of service, so the individual merits 22.5% of final salary, which in this case is $48,000. The result is that the pension benefit from the first employer is $10,800.

$$\text{Annual Pension} = 1.5\% \times 15 \text{ years of service} \\ \times \text{ final salary of } \$48,000 = \$10,800$$

For the second employer, the individual also has fifteen years of service, so he or she again receives 22.5% of final salary. This time final salary is $100,000, so the pension benefit is $22,500.

$$\text{Annual Pension} = 1.5\% \times 15 \text{ years of service} \\ \times \text{ final salary of } \$100,000 = \$22,500$$

In total then, the job-changer receives $33,300 per year in retirement: $10,800 from the first employer and $22,500 from the second employer.

Thus, in this example, the individual's pension benefit declines from $45,000 to $33,300, a 26% decrease, simply because the person works for two employers rather than one. This decline is the result of backloading: much of the pension accrual occurs at the back end of a career with an employer. It is only by staying with the employer to the end of one's career that the pension benefit is maximized.

Another way to see the backloading effect is to consider what happens when an individual stays an extra year with an employer. There are two effects. First, the employee accrues an additional 1.5% of final salary. Second, all prior accruals are revalued at the individual's new higher salary. As long as the employee stays with an employer, he or she keeps getting an additional 1.5%, and all prior accruals keep being revalued upward as salary increases. In contrast, when an individual leaves the employer, the accruals to that point are fixed. They are valued at the person's salary at that point in time and are not adjusted upward in the future.

DB plans also have vesting provisions. An employee's vesting percentage is the percentage of the accrued benefit that the person has a right to receive in retirement. Fifty percent vesting means a right to 50% of the accrued benefit. One hundred percent vesting means a right to all of the accrued benefit. There are two general types of vesting provision: with cliff vesting, employees go from 0% to 100% vesting on a particular date; for example, the fifth anniversary of the date of hire. The alternative is gradual vesting; for example, 20% per year for the first five years.

Together, the benefit formula and the vesting provisions indicate how much a specific employee can receive on retirement. To get an estimate of total payouts, it is necessary to aggregate across all employees. It is also necessary to incorporate some actuarial assumptions. For example, it is necessary to estimate how many years of service employees will have, how fast salaries will increase during their years of service, and how long people will live after retiring.

Given these estimated future payouts, the next question is how to fund the plan. In principle the employer could pay the pension payments as they come due. That is, the pension payments could come out of annual income in the year the payments are due. In practice, most plans are funded at least to some extent in advance, some because there is a legal obligation to do so. Employers contribute more money to their pension plans than is necessary for current disbursements, and the plan builds up assets in a pension fund.

DB plans may thus be overfunded (in which case they have more assets than are needed to pay accrued benefits), adequately funded, or underfunded. Over time, unfunded benefits must be funded either through additional contributions from the sponsor or through investment returns. The funding status of a pension plan partially describes, at a specific point in time, the financial health of the plan as well as the ability of the plan to bear risk.

Funding involves a lot more than just putting cash into the plan. In particular, decisions have to be made about how to invest the plan assets. Future chapters will have much more to say about this decision. For now, note that for DB plans, the pension recipient is entitled to the promised pension even though the asset pool and future investment returns may be insufficient to pay it. The plan sponsor earns the reward of exceptionally good investment performance—but also bears the risk of poor planning and poor investment results.

DEFINED CONTRIBUTION PLANS

In a DC plan, there is no benefit formula—there is no formula indicating how much a person will receive in retirement. In addition, benefits are not typically paid in the form of an annuity. Instead, when a person retires they get access to an investment account that has held funds on the person's behalf. The value of the account at retirement depends on two factors: the contributions that were made to the individual's account and the investment returns that were earned on the account.

In some cases it is the employer who makes the contributions on an employee's behalf. In other cases the employee makes the contribution to his or her own account. In either case, the contributions may be regular (occurring systematically through an individual's career), but they may also be quite sporadic (occurring some years but not others). In some cases, the employee has some control over how the contributions will be invested; in other cases, the employee has little control. In either event, it is the employee who directly bears the risk of the investment strategy. If the investments perform well, the individual will receive more in retirement than expected. If the investments perform poorly, the individual may have to work longer than expected or enjoy a lower standard of living in retirement than expected.

As with DB plans, DC plans can have vesting provisions. Thus, an employee may have a positive balance in his or her individual account, but no right to actually receive funds from the account. The employee only gets the right to receive retirement funds from the account when he or she becomes vested. These vesting provisions, however, apply only to those contributions that are made by the employer. Contributions made by the employee are fully and immediately vested.

DC plans are not backloaded like final-pay DB plans. In fact, aside from the vesting provisions there is typically no systematic relationship between retirement benefits and the number of years an employee spends with one employer. The result is that many DC plans are highly portable. An individual can build up a significant value for retirement even when switching employers every few years.

There are many different varieties of DC plan. This section briefly introduces four of the varieties. First there are the so-called "money purchase" pension plans. These are plans in which the employer contributions are fixed by formula. For example, a plan may specify that each year the employer will contribute 10% of each participant's salary. An employee who makes $50,000 per year will receive a $5,000 contribution. An employee who makes $75,000 per year will receive a $7,500 contribution.

A second variety of DC plan is the profit-sharing plan. A profit-sharing plan is a plan in which the employer can vary the amount it contributes to the plan depending on its profits. The employer contributes a lot in years in which it does well. It contributes little or nothing in years in which it does poorly. Typically, the employer determines how much it will contribute in total, and then the contributions are allocated across the participants depending on the participants' salaries. For example, if an individual's salary is 1/100 of the total wage bill, then the person may receive 1/100 of the annual contribution.

A third variety of DC plan is the Employee Stock Ownership Plan (ESOP). An ESOP is a DC plan that is designed to be invested "primarily" in the company stock. In practice, the word "primarily" here means that at least 51% of the plan assets should be held in company stock. With an ESOP, the assets available to an individual at retirement depend on how well the employer does; specifically, it depends on the performance of the employer's stock.

The fourth variety of DC plan is the 401(k) plan. The 401(k) plan has become the most popular type of private DC plan. By 1998, 401(k) plans comprised 74% of all private DC plan assets.[1] A 401(k) may be funded by the sponsor, the employee, or both. Through these plans, employees may elect to take current compensation and defer it, putting it instead into tax-qualified accounts. Public school systems and charitable nonprofit organizations have their own version of the 401(k), known as the as the 403(b). State and local governments have another version, known as Section 457 plans.

In many 401(k) plans, the employee participates in the investment decision by choosing to allocate money to asset classes such as equities or fixed-income investments, and sometimes by choosing the specific investment fund or funds within each asset class. Thus, the employee plays a role in determining the risk profile of the investment fund. This is attractive, as it allows employees to meet their own unique needs and preferences, but it can also be risky, as good asset allocation requires knowledge.

SUMMARY

This chapter has provided an introduction to the two basic pension plan types. DB plans are plans in which the employee receives an annuity at retirement and in which the payment level depends on a formula specified by the plan. With some DB plans, a significant retirement income depends on many years of service with one employer and a high final salary with that employer. Because benefit payments do not depend directly on investment returns, the employer bears the risk of the plan's investment strategy.

DC plans are individual account plans in which a person's retirement benefit depends on contributions and on investment returns. The most popular type of private DC plan is the 401(k) plan in which employees can choose to either receive money currently or have it contributed to their account. In some DC plans, such as many 401(k) plans, the employee has significant control over the investment strategy for his or her individual account. In other DC plans, such as ESOPs, the plan managers choose the investment strategy. Because the benefit payments depend directly on the plan's investment strategy, the employee bears the risk of the plan's investment strategy.

2

What Pension Plans Do

Pension plan management starts by understanding why employers have pension plans in the first place. This chapter discusses the five basic justifications for pension plans:

1. They have significant tax advantages.
2. They help people save for retirement.
3. They help employers recruit the type of workers they want.
4. They can be used as severance pay, to help restructure the workforce.
5. They can increase productivity.

This chapter will discuss these advantages in turn. Before looking at these current advantages, it is at least interesting to note that a significant historical reason for the growth in pension plans was the existence of government-mandated wage and price controls during World War II and the Korean War. If not for these controls, pension plans in the United States might not have grown nearly as rapidly as they have. Employers needed employees, but they could not attract them by offering higher wages in the form of current income. Accordingly, many employers raised total compensation by adding pension plans to the compensation package. Pensions did not count as wages under the various wage-price control laws. The wage and price controls thus forced employers to learn about pension plans and the advantages of offering them.

TAX ADVANTAGES

If a pension plan meets a series of regulatory requirements, it is a "qualified" plan. Qualified plans offer several significant tax advantages. The primary tax advantage is that with a qualified plan, income taxes can be deferred for many years. To see precisely where the advantage lies, consider a corporation that has had a good year. At the end of the year, it is considering paying an additional

$100,000 to its employees. It is considering either giving taxable bonuses or contributing the money to a qualified retirement plan.

With either choice, the company will be able to deduct the $100,000 payment from its taxable income. If the company is in a 35% tax bracket, then by making the $100,000 payment, it will "save" $35,000 in income taxes. That is, the after-tax cost of the additional payment will be $65,000: the $100,000 payment minus the $35,000 in tax savings.

If the payment is made as a bonus, then the income will be taxable to the employees. From the perspective of the Internal Revenue Service (IRS), the $100,000 is taken out of the company's taxable income and put into the employee's taxable income. If the employees face marginal tax rates of 35% or more, the IRS loses no income when the company pays the additional $100,000 in bonuses.

The situation is different, however, if the company contributes the $100,000 to a qualified retirement plan. In that case, the corporation is still able to deduct the $100,000 from its taxable income. However, the $100,000 is not included in the employees' taxable income for that year, and interest earned on the contribution will also be tax-free through the years. In fact, the employees will not pay tax until they receive distributions from the plan in retirement. It is in this sense that qualified retirement plans allow the deferral of taxable income.

Over time, the value of tax deferral can be substantial. Consider a person whose employer makes annual contributions to a qualified pension plan on the person's behalf. Suppose the employer contributes $8,000 a year for thirty years, at which time the person retires. The plan earns 10% per year. Beause the plan is qualified, the person pays no tax on either the $8,000 contributions or the annual interest. At the end of thirty years, the fund has grown to $1,315,952. If the person withdraws it in one lump sum at retirement, the person pays taxes then. At a 30% tax rate, the individual receives $921,167 after taxes. In contrast, suppose the $8,000 were paid as taxable income to the employee. Then, after tax, the contribution is only $5,600 per year. The person may invest it, but he or she will pay taxes on the interest earned. If the after-tax interest rate is 7%, the fund grows to only $528,980 after thirty years. This is only 57% of the after-tax accrual in the qualified plan.[1]

This tax deferral is the primary tax advantage available to pension plans. A second tax advantage is that some people will face a lower marginal tax rate in retirement than while they were working. As a result, not only are taxes deferred but the tax rate may be lower when the taxes are finally paid. Because of the tax code, employers can use pension plans to increase the after-tax compensation they pay their employees. This is an immediate justification for pension plans. Of course, it raises a deeper question of why the government encourages pension plans. One reason is that pension plans may reduce the political pressure on the government to provide all retirement income by expanding Social Security.[2]

STRUCTURED RETIREMENT PLANNING

A second reason that employers sponsor pension plans is that some employees value them (for more than just the tax benefits). Certainly, when people look for jobs, or when they choose among job offers, one of their considerations will be the retirement plans offered by alternative jobs. One job may not pay well, but it may offer a very substantial retirement income, and this could sway a job-seeker's choice. Employers of course recognize this and tout their retirement plans when trying to recruit workers. At first glance, it may seem that employees could always save on their own, so there might be little value to pension plans. In fact, many people are not very good at saving: they may understand the importance of saving, but left on their own they will not save as much as they would like.[3] Employees value pension plans, then, to help them achieve their savings goals. The pension plan helps people save because it effectively segregates part of their income. Part of their income does not go into their checking account—it goes instead into a separate retirement account. This can be of substantial value to employees. It provides the structure necessary to help them achieve their long-term goals.

Thus, consider someone who is choosing between two jobs: a moderate-paying job with a generous DB plan and a high-paying job with no pension plan. In theory, this person could take the second job and save a portion of income each month until retirement. The person may prefer the first job, however, because with the first job he or she is able to commit in advance to a savings program over time. The DB job offers more security because it auto-matically takes care of the savings problem. In taking the DB job, the person is taking both a salary and a structured savings plan.

DC plans are also valued for providing structured savings. A job with a money purchase pension plan, for example, might provide that 5% of each year's salary is put aside in an investment account for retirement. A profit-sharing plan also provides some structure: when a person accepts a profit-sharing plan, he or she is also thereby accepting a structure whereby in good years, money will be put aside for retirement.

With a 401(k) plan, an individual chooses how much of his or her salary to defer. To some extent this puts the onus on the employee to save, but 401(k) plans also offer structure to the extent that an individual signs up in advance to have a certain percentage of each paycheck deferred. When an individual chooses to defer, say, 5% of each paycheck, this can act as a commitment. The 5% is deferred each paycheck and never reaches the person's checking account. Again, this helps the individual reach his or her savings goal.

Note that the structured savings attribute is typically stronger for DB plans than for DC plans. With DC plans, there is no guarantee that the assets accu-mulated at retirement will be sufficient to last through the end of the employee's life. Many DB plans, however, offer payments for as long as an employee lives. This can be a significant advantage for DB plans.

SELECTING DESIRED WORKERS

Not all workers will value pension plans the same. Because of this, employers can use pension plans to select the sorts of workers they want.[4] To see precisely how this works, it is useful to consider a simplified model.

Consider a world in which there are two kinds of people. People in group A assign a high value to the future consequences of the actions they currently take. They are less likely to skip work on the pretext that they are sick because they value their reputation as reliable. They want to be seen as "low cost," so they take care of the equipment they use. They work hard so they will get promoted. People in group B, however, are the opposite of group A people. They call in sick without reason. They do not take care of the equipment they use, nor do they work especially hard.

Group A people exhibit qualities that identify them as high-quality, productive people. They are also the sort of people who are actively concerned about their own future, and specifically with their own retirement. They are desirable workers, and they are also the sort of people who will value pension benefits (both because of their tax savings and because of the structure they provide).

Group B people exhibit qualities that identify them as low-quality workers or workers who are more likely to take inappropriate risks. In particular, they may not be desirable workers where productivity and reliability are important. Consistent with the way they assign a low value to the future consequences of the actions they currently take, they place a low value on savings relative to current consumption. They are not likely to see future pension benefits as valuable.

Now consider two employers, Employer X and Employer Y. Employer X offers a pension plan that is quite generous, whereas Employer Y offers somewhat higher wages but no pension plan. Type A people will assign a high present value to the pension benefits offered by Employer X and thus may find X's total compensation more attractive than Y's. Type B people will see little value in the future pension benefits and thus will be attracted to the higher current wages at Y.

In a world with competition, type A people will receive the value of their higher marginal work product. This is what employers will have to pay to attract and retain them. Employers that want high-quality type A employees have two options. They can either monitor the workers they have and attempt to pay more to the more productive workers (incurring potentially high costs), or they can use a pension plan as a low-cost sorting device to attract and keep these high-quality workers.

SEVERANCE PAY: RESTRUCTURING THE WORKFORCE

Sometimes employers want to bring more youth to their workplace. They want to bring younger workers in, or they want to promote younger workers to positions of greater responsibility. When this occurs, employers want their older employees to retire: they want those jobs empty so that they can fill them with younger people. On a fundamental level, pensions—along with the social security system—allow employers to do this. Without retirement income, it would be problematic for employers to replace older employees: it would be problematic ethically, it could be illegal, and it would also damage the employer's reputation.

Thus, on a general level, pensions help employers make the transition from one generation to another. This is true for both DB and DC plans. Providing retirement assets helps an employer replace older employees.

In addition, DB plans in particular can be used to provide incentives for employees to choose to retire at chosen points in time. For example, some DB plans base benefits on years of service, but they effectively stop counting after a certain number of years. For example, the benefit formula may say that an employee receives 1.5% of final pay for each of service—up to a maximum of thirty years of service. In this case, after thirty years of employment, the individual is entitled to 45% of final pay. If the individual works beyond thirty years, he or she will not move beyond this 45% level, and each additional year worked is a year in which retirement benefits earned are not received. Such a plan provides an incentive for employees to voluntarily retire after the thirtieth year of employment. It adds still more employer control over employee retirement decisions.

PRODUCTIVITY

Pension plans can also increase employee productivity. Different types of pension plan achieve this end in different ways. In the case of ESOPs, for example, employee productivity is thought to be enhanced because the ESOP helps align the interests of employees and owners. With an ESOP, a person's retirement income depends on the performance of company stock. Therefore, the employee, like other owners, wants the company stock price to be high. In theory, the employee may therefore work harder and smarter to help support the stock price.

The same reasoning applies to any pension plan that holds a significant portion of assets in company stock. DB plans are restricted from holding significant quantities of company stock, but in addition to ESOPS, there are other varieties of DC plans that can and do hold company stock. For example, some 401(k) plans hold significant quantities of employer stock. The use of company stock in pension plans will be discussed in Chapter 12. There are disadvantages to be sure, but the primary advantage is this potential productivity effect.

Profit-sharing plans can also increase productivity. If the employer consistently contributes a portion of profits to the plan, then again employees are in a position similar to owners. They want higher company profits, and they may work harder or smarter as a result. In this case incentives are aligned around current profits as opposed to the long-run company stock price, as in the case of ESOPs.

DB plans can also increase productivity, but the mechanism is somewhat different than with DC plans. The primary way that DB plans increase productivity is through backloading. As noted in Chapter 1, because of backloading, workers will have higher pension payments if they stay with one employer as opposed to moving from employer to employer in their career. As a result, employees can lose significant retirement benefits if they change firms or are laid off or fired. This gives employees an incentive to stay with the firm and to work efficiently. They want to work hard so that the employer does well so that the company will not have to lay people off. They also want to keep their effort up so that they are not fired. In short, the DB pension benefit can be a carrot at the end of a successful career with an employer. The awareness of this carrot can increase productivity throughout a person's career.

Backloading can also increase productivity through its effect on seniority. For some employers, there is significant specific human capital that employees build up on the job. These employers are damaged by high turnover and want their employees to stay on the job. They can use several techniques to do this, most notably a rising wage profile and a backloaded pension plan. The total productivity of the employer's workforce is enhanced because the more senior, more productive workers are retained.

CONCLUSION

There are many things that pension plans do for employers and employees that are more qualitative than quantitative. Which of these features an employer wants to emphasize must be made manifest in the choice of type and design of the pension plan. These issues are discussed in the next several chapters.

3

Designing the Best Pension Plan

There are two layers of designing pension plans. The first is determining what plan structure is best: will the plan offer defined benefits or defined contributions, or will it be a hybrid plan that exhibits characteristics of both? To make the right choice, sponsors and the other parties involved in the decision-making process must understand the differences in the attributes of these structures regarding funding, sponsor liability, benefit assurance, and the differences in who bears the risks and rewards of investment performance.

Once this choice is made, there is a second layer of choices. Sponsors can choose among numerous features that can improve the fit of the plan, given both the sponsor's and employees' needs.

These two choices—plan structure and plan features—are extremely important. It is essential that senior management be involved in these decisions. Thus, boards of directors or government officials as well as senior management and the finance and human resources teams must accept a leadership role in forming and structuring pension plans.

The level of benefits, the nature of the implicit contracts, and likely employee responses to pension parameters demand careful analysis because of the effect—desirable or otherwise—that pensions have on employee incentives and behavior. Review by tax experts is also necessary to ensure that none of the plan's provisions results in the loss of tax advantages for the sponsor or the employee. Finally, board-level approval and, ultimately, oversight is necessary so that the pension plan and all its features can be reconciled at the highest levels with the means and willingness to finance the plan. Without the involvement of the organization's leaders, it becomes all too easy to make seemingly innocuous adjustments in plan provisions that have significant and unfortunate financial implications.

DEFINING THE BENEFIT, THE CONTRIBUTION, OR BOTH

Whether a DB plan is more attractive than a DC plan is not a straightforward issue. Although the tax incentives of DC plans and DB plans are pretty much the same, DC plans differ from DB plans in important respects.

Specifically, the ability to structure contracts that motivate desirable behavior, such as longevity and loyalty, is much weaker for DC plans because they cannot easily be backloaded and because they typically are portable. However, employees who want to obtain retirement income insurance will not find DC plans attractive unless funding is quite high. Employees who value portability and the option of changing employers without incurring high costs in forfeited pension benefits will find DC plans attractive. In general, attractive aspects of each type of plan from the sponsor's perspective may not be attractive to employees, and vice versa. Thus, sponsors and employees may not always agree that one form is more suitable than the other. There are some features, however, on which all will agree. For example, both sponsors and employees can be better off if plan administrative costs are lowered. As discussed below, DB administrative costs can be significantly higher for DB plans, especially for small DB plans.

In general, which scheme is better for a sponsor? It depends on what the sponsor wants to accomplish and is permitted to do by regulatory and labor market forces. From the viewpoint of an employee, the optimal plan is a function of the employee's attitude toward risk and mobility.

Funding and Investment Performance

A significant difference between the two plans is funding. A DC plan is, by definition, always fully funded if promised contributions have been made. The asset value equals the employer's liability. A DB plan may or may not be fully funded. An employer must make contributions to a DC plan as it has promised. An employer may, however, make less than actuarially adequate contributions to a DB plan in the early years and then either hope for exceptional investment performance or plan on heavier contributions in later years.

For private single-employer and multiemployer DB plans, both the level of funding and the source of funding are guided by legislation that is technically consistent. It is, however, philosophically separate. The Employee Retirement Income Security Act (ERISA), originally designed to strengthen private pension plans, encourages more, rather than less, funding to make plans safe. For private pensions, IRS legislation—the intent of which is raising revenues—tends to hold funding down to enhance tax collections, because pension contributions are tax deductible. In recent years, the band of permissible funding has grown fairly small. For public pensions, there is no equivalent to ERISA, and thus no blanket mandate forcing adequate funding. There is, however, a plethora of state rules and regulations and union contracts governing funding for public pensions.

The level of funding for DB plans is also affected by the investment performance of the pool of assets owned by the plan. Thus, a key difference between the two types of plans has to do with who bears the risk of, and stands to benefit from, investment performance. Given that the sponsor of a DB plan must in-crease funding if investments do not perform as expected, why not shift to a DC plan? One reason is that DB plans are more efficient than individuals in risk bearing and insurance. Thus, there is a surplus to be divided. Another reason to stay with a DB plan is that DC plans carry an implied obligation to educate employees about investing. The risk of not doing so is that the courts may shift the investment risk back to the sponsor.

The trade-off, then, is between funding costs on one hand and investment performance on the other. Some sponsors may believe they can reduce the total contributions made to employee pensions by offering DB plans in an attempt to profit from investment performance. Other sponsors may be willing to make higher funding payments over time to shift the risks and benefits of investment performance to employees by offering DC plans. Regardless of which view they take, however, sponsors must remember that employees also have preferences. There is no reason to believe that employees will be indifferent to the differences between $1 of DB plan funding and $1 of DC plan funding. Some employees may find the burden of investment risk (and mortality risk) unattractive if a sponsor shifts from a DB plan to a DC plan. In return for bearing the risk of adverse investment performance on their retirement security, they may demand higher levels of funding for DC plans or higher wages.

Is investment risk important? In the late 1990s, many self-appointed author-ities and employees were convinced that investment risk was not a material concern. After all, stocks and other investments were providing handsome re-turns, and DC plan balances were so high for many employees that early re-tirements and wonderful plans for retirement were common topics of discussion. Following the market peak of March 2000 and the dramatic fall of equity val-ues,[1] however, the risk of adverse performance has come back as a source of concern.

Employee Mobility

DB plans, as earlier noted, are currently heavily backloaded as a result of the strong tendency among employers to offer final pay plans. That is, the benefit levels have much less to do with early-career salary experience and much more to do with late-career salary experience. Of course, this discourages employee mobility and provides an incentive to work hard and long for a single employer because, by achieving a high ending salary, the employee is rewarded twice: first by the salary and second by the pension benefit based on the high salary. However, such backloading can reduce the attractiveness of the plan to new employees by raising the cost of leaving the organization.

Consider an employee who switches jobs in midcareer and anticipates getting identical 10% annual pay increases in the old and new jobs, and who anticipates the application of the same pension formula. Taking into account the advantage of the higher salary, one study indicated that a 3% higher starting wage in the new job followed by identical percentage wage increases will leave the employee with about the same current value of benefits. That is, a 3% higher starting wage will offset over time the loss of the backloading portion of pension benefits from the first job.[2] (This does not take into consideration the net nonpecuniary benefits of a new job.)

Vesting requirements are another aspect of mobility. ERISA's vesting requirements are discussed in Chapter 5. Public plan vesting is not covered under national legislation, so vesting requirements can be quite different and may depend on state legislation and union agreements.

Under DB plans, workers lose all or part of their pension benefits if they take a job with a different employer before they are fully vested. Thus, vesting requirements also tend to discourage workers from changing jobs during the vesting period. From the sponsor's perspective, vesting requirements may be beneficial because they may keep turnover and associated replacement hiring and training costs low, and because they allow employers to recapture the implied pension contribution should employees leave sooner than an employer would like. In addition, vesting requirements allow employers to fire unsatisfactory short-term workers without having to make long-term commitments to them. Thus, from an employer's perspective, vesting helps to retain employees that the employer wants to keep and provides strong incentives to get rid of low-productivity employees quickly before they vest.

DC plans frequently, though not always, vest immediately (although contributions may not be made for the first three years of employment) and are frequently independent of the number of years of service to an employer and of employee age. This is a disadvantage to employers because a DC plan does nothing to discourage valuable employees from leaving; however, this portability feature is attractive to employees.

Employer-Specific Knowledge

Although there is no definitive theory or robust empirical study that indicates why one type of plan is favored over the other, one school of thought suggests that the choice has to do with the amount of employer-specific human capital that a plan sponsor determines is optimal or, more generally, acceptable. Consider, for instance, university professors, most of whom have DC plans. What professors do requires very little employer-specific human capital. Intricate knowledge of the university's organization or technological base is not necessary to perform the jobs of teaching and research. Rather, the professor's set of skills—those necessary in teaching and research—are presumably valuable at virtually any university. Therefore, there is no general reason for a university to set up a pension plan that rewards length of service or a large investment in organization-specific skills.

Many public and private organizations, however, really do need employees to possess a great deal of employer-specific knowledge for decisions to be made correctly. Such organizations can reward long-time employees—those who have invested in building a lot of employer-specific human capital—through back-end-loaded DB pension plans. In this context, back-end loading of pension plans is a reward for not contributing to turnover and for enabling an employer to economize on the searching and training costs of replacement employees, rather than a penalty for job hopping.

There is evidence that the shifting job mix of our economy accounts for a good portion of the trend to DC plans.[3] This evidence is consistent with the view that as manufacturing growth declines, the need for pension plans that reward employees for building employer-specific human capital diminishes.

Plan Costs

Another important factor in the choice of plan type is the financial and other costs the employer will bear in providing the pension benefit. In general, the marginal costs of the plan chosen should be equal to or less than the marginal benefits to the sponsor and, ultimately, the shareholders/taxpayers in whose interest the sponsor is presumably acting.

Administrative Costs

The cost of administering a DB plan for a large firm is about 40% greater than the cost of administering a DC plan. Moreover, this cost differential widens substantially as the number of participants decreases. With fifteen participants, the administrative costs of a DB plan were about twice the cost of a DC plan.[4]

Funding Costs

Another perspective on cost comes from investment theory. Accepted theory tells us—and practice confirms—that people have different discount rates for investments that are more or less risky. On average, people will have higher discount rates for investments they view as risky. Consider, from the employee's perspective, pension plans as investments. A basic difference between a DC plan and a DB plan is who bears the risk of adverse investment performance and inadequate accumulation of future wealth. Faced with the choice of either a DB plan or a DC plan, knowledgeable employees may view the DB plan as less risky and hence use a lower discount rate when evaluating it. If sponsors can deliver good investment management at relatively low cost, DB plans may have a cost advantage over DC plans. In other words, employers offering DC plans may have to make higher contributions to offset the risk premium demanded by employees because of the added risk. For defined benefits to have a high present value, the sponsor and workers must agree that the sponsor is credit worthy and will still be around when workers retire, and that employee turnover will be low.[5]

The Hidden Value in DB Plans

Total costs must be evaluated within the context of the benefits gained as a result of the course of action that gives rise to the costs. Although they may have higher administrative costs, DB plans offer the sponsor many valuable options. For example, DB plans offer the sponsor the latitude to manage the demographics of its work force. Frequently, sponsors can adjust benefit formulas on an ad hoc basis to encourage early retirement (e.g., increase benefits ex post to offset unanticipated inflation) or some other behavior it deems necessary. Sponsors also may use pension schemes to reward high-quality or "fast track" workers. If these workers are low discounters, they are likely to see back-end-loaded DB plans as an economic reward for their superior performance. Employers may also be able to use DB plans to fund postretirement benefits if the investment performance of the underlying asset pool is good enough. These types of options may be sufficiently valuable to offset the more obvious pension costs.

Variability of Sponsor Cash Flows

Finally, companies with highly variable cash flows may be able to reduce their operating leverage (the variability in operating cash flow that comes about because of variable revenues and the mix of variable costs and fixed costs) by opting for DC plans that are related to profit, not wages. For this to work, the plan must be structured as a profit-sharing plan. In a profit-sharing plan, contributions are a percentage of profits. If there are no profits, there are no contributions. Thus, contributions can be adjusted to compensate for variations in cash flow. When profits are high, dollar contributions would be high; similarly, when profits are low, contributions would be low.[6]

Choosing the Basic Plan

DB plans are not necessarily as unattractive as some authorities have argued. This form of pension offers employers and employees numerous benefits as well as costs.

Organizations that value longevity, firm-specific knowledge, the option of restructuring the workforce, the opportunity to motivate certain types of behavior, and the potential to lower total funding by capturing the results of favorable investment performance should give careful consideration to DB plans. Organizations that do not value these things, that can not afford to pay for them, or that have highly variable cash flows should consider DC plans. Organizations that find elements of both options attractive and unattractive may want to consider the hybrid plans that have evolved in recent years. Hybrid plans are discussed in Chapter 13.

Fairness

Some writers argue that DC plans promote fairness primarily because they do not penalize workers for moving from one firm to another. Whereas these plans allow for greater labor mobility, it is far from obvious that greater labor mobility is fair to all concerned. This preference for a specific element of social policy obscures an important issue.

Pension plans serve both employers and employees. They are part of the contracting between employees and employers. Employees trade their human capital for wages and retirement benefits paid by employers who desire the skills and knowledge that employees possess. In a market-driven economy, fairness is determined by the contracting that takes place between the two parties. Is it fair to shift mortality and investment risk to employees? Is it fair to take valuable options away from employers without giving anything in return? The process of attracting, motivating, and rewarding competent employees is quite complex. Indeed, it is sufficiently complex that rules that limit the range of mutually agreeable choices available to employees and employers are as likely to reduce fairness as to increase it.

DETERMINING PENSION PLAN FEATURES

Once the basic type of plan has been chosen, plan features must be defined. It is important to note that pension schemes do not exist in a vacuum: they are part of the organization's total compensation package. Thus, they have to cover every possible employee behavior that a sponsor may wish to influence. Other forms of contracting may be more efficient or effective. Regardless of sponsor preferences, the labor market will constrain sponsor choice of pension scheme.

Once the choice of what type of pension plan to establish has been made— whether it is to be a DB plan, a DC plan, or a hybrid—attention must be turned to designing plan features. Among the features that warrant careful attention are benefit levels, integration with Social Security, and vesting.

Benefit Levels

The first important feature to be determined is the benefit level or the target replacement rate. This is the proportion of wages an employee's pension benefits are intended to provide or "replace" on retirement. It is important to employees because it represents what they will live on in retirement. It is also important to employers because it is a key component in attracting and retaining workers, and in getting them to leave when it's time.

The optimal replacement rate must be based in part on the rates of competing employers. This rate may also be computed by estimating what fraction of pre-retirement income would be necessary for the employee to continue to enjoy the same lifestyle in retirement, allowing for reduced expenditures on items such as clothing, entertainment, commuting, and taxes. Finally, this rate may be determined in an acceptable funding/investment framework.

For a DB plan (or the floor of a combined plan), the replacement rate becomes operational through the benefit formula to which the sponsor and employees agree. The number of years worked, the percentage multiplier (or flat dollar amount), explicit inflation indexing, and related factors are all components that must, in total, be consistent with the target replacement rate. Backloading via a heavy weighting on the final years of service may or may not be desirable. For DC plans, the concept of replacement rates is nebulous, at best. Targets may be set, but because the assets in these plans tend to be managed by the beneficiaries, and because the sponsor is not willing to guarantee the amount of the benefit, alternative replacement rates are virtually impossible to evaluate.

Though many considerations go into its computation after counting Social Security, DB plans seem to have target total replacement rates in the vicinity of 50%–70% for long-term private-sector employees. The targets are higher— 70%–90% for public-sector retirees.[7] The following data are useful in seeing how these replacement rates come about:

- 58% of private plans (medium and large employers) base benefits on terminal earnings
- 37% of private plans use a flat percentage per year of service (the most common rate lies between 1.50% and 1.74%)
- 62% of private plans vary the percentage earned per year of service
- State and local government plans virtually all use terminal-earnings formulas
- 78% of public plans use a flat percentage per year of service (the most common rate is 2.00%–2.24%).[8]

Social Security Integration

Sponsors must decide whether the target replacement rate will take into account or exclude Social Security payments. This is known as Social Security integration. In essence, Social Security integration means that pension plan payments move inversely to Social Security payments. Sponsors that integrate argue that their contribution to the Social Security system on their employees' behalf should be taken into account when deciding how large their direct pension obligation should be.

Private pension plan integration with Social Security is a very complex area.[9] All else remaining the same, however, an integrated plan requires less funding and is thus less costly at a given replacement rate than a plan that excludes Social Security. Employees may, of course, find the plan less attractive and raise other compensation demands, or they may find it less costly to move to another firm than if the plan were not integrated.

Social Security payments can be integrated directly into DB plans; integration does not have to be done at the early, contributory stage. There are two methods: the offset approach and the excess approach.[10]

In offset plans, the computed pension payment can be reduced under current law by up to 37.5% of the Social Security payment. Thus, if an employee had a final three-year average pay of $40,000, with forty years on the job, and the employer offered 1.5% times the above, the computed annual pension benefit would be $24,000. The replacement rate would be 60%. If Social Security payments were to be $10,000 per year, the sponsor's pension payment would be $24,000 less 37.5% of $10,000, or $20,250. Note that the recipient would get $20,250 from the sponsor's pension payment plus the $10,000 Social Security payment, or $30,250. Everything considered, the replacement rate would be 75.6%. Of course, the employer would factor into the decision on the benefit percentage that is originally chosen the fact that the entire Social Security payment cannot be deducted from the computed pension benefit.

Excess plans produce benefits only above a specified amount. The pension benefit is computed only on excess income, the amount by which income exceeds the Social Security wage base or some fraction thereof. A variant of the excess plan is the step-rate excess plan. In the step-rate plan, full benefits are paid on excess income as well, but benefits might still be paid on the base income, though at a lower rate.

For DC plans, the only way to integrate potential Social Security payments is to allow for Social Security contribution percentages in the DC arrangements. For instance, a nonintegrated DC percentage may be stated as 12% of salary per year. An integrated contribution, however, could be 12% of salary in excess of the Social Security wage base that goes into the DC plan, along with the difference between 12% and the Social Security tax rate on wages up to the Social Security wage base. For example, if the Social Security wage base was $89,000, the plan would contribute 12% of salary in excess of $89,000 and the difference between 12% and the Social Security tax rate on the first $89,000 of income. So if the salary was $100,000, and the Social Security tax rate was 8%, then the employer contributions to the pension fund would be $4,880: 4% of the first $89,000 in salary and 12% of the remaining $11,000.

The choice of whether to integrate or not can be very significant in terms of sponsor costs and in terms of the replacement rates realized by retirees. Concerning the latter, a nonintegrated plan tends to provide more protection against inflation to workers than an integrated plan because pension benefits are not reduced as Social Security benefits rise. Of course, many sponsors with integrated plans as well as those with nonintegrated plans have voluntarily made upward adjustments on an ad hoc basis in the past to compensate for inflation. Whether they will do so in the future is anyone's guess. However, because Social Security payments themselves are indexed (adjusted for inflation), those employers who do not integrate at least put themselves in a position in which they cannot cut their own benefits in an inflationary environment. It should also be noted that such employers need not increase their benefits in the event that Social Security benefits are reduced.

Roughly 50% of private DB plan participants participate in integrated plans. In contrast, only about 5% of public-sector employees who participate in DB plans participate in integrated plans.[11]

Vesting

With most private DB pension plans, employees are fully vested after five to seven years with the sponsor. Public pension plans, as would be expected in the absence of ERISA-like legislation, have a wider variety of vesting schedules. Ten-year cliff vesting is as common as five-year vesting (except for some federal employees); twenty-year vesting is used by the military. With most DC plans, vesting occurs when funding occurs. Although legislation limits the range of vesting possibilities for private pension plans, the vesting choice still affects employee incentives, labor mobility, and sponsor cost.

Qualifying Requirements

Pension plan sponsors generally specify age and service requirements before an employee can qualify for a pension fund. Typically these might be that the employee be twenty-one years old and have two years on the job. These sorts of requirements simply allow sponsors to avoid setting up administrative accounts and putting money aside for very short-term employees. These requirements are highly regulated for private plans.

Retirement Provisions

Retirement provisions include early retirement options, normal retirement age, spousal death benefits, and a host of other features that individually may not seem financially substantial. In terms of attracting and keeping good employees and motivating desired behavior, however, they may be both useful and costly. They are thus worth careful scrutiny when designing pension plans.

Funding Status

Funding status is not a question for DC plans because they are, by definition, fully funded. However, funding status is an important element of plan operation for DB plans. For private plans, ERISA and the Pension Benefit Guarantee Corporation (PBGC) provide rules governing acceptable levels of underfunding, and the IRS provides rules that discourage excessive overfunding. Public pensions have no comparable set of rules within which to determine what the sponsor finds to be acceptable.

Funding status is a policy parameter. Nonetheless, it may be thought of as a plan feature in some regards. In general, underfunding may be a desirable feature from the employer's perspective because it may keep wages lower than they might otherwise be. With an underfunded plan, employees may be reluctant to press for wage increases that would further weaken the sponsor's financial health. In addition, an underfunded plan may bond workers to organizations because the value of the pension benefit is more directly tied to the success of the firm. Of course, if the underfunding is severe, younger workers may find the cost of leaving the organization lower than it might otherwise be because their future pensions are extremely risky and thus have a lower value.

CONCLUSION

Pension schemes make sense for many organizations. The U.S. pension system has worked well as an employee motivator and as a provider of a special form of social insurance for employees. Many decisions about pension plans have significant workforce and financial implications. Because pensions are part of the total compensation package, they are useful in attracting and selecting employees and may motivate what the sponsor believes to be desirable behavior. To be useful, however, they also must be desirable from the employee's perspective. Addressing these issues requires close collaboration among treasury managers under the careful supervision of top management and the employees for whom the plan is designed. Optimal pension plan design will have to meet the needs—conflicting at times—of employers and employees. Optimal design also is, and will continue to be, affected by the forces that shape the labor markets and by public policy.

DC plans, DB plans, and the hybrid variations all offer economies of scale with regard to information and management. All are efficient means of saving for retirement. All have subtle and not so subtle advantages and disadvantages with respect to financial implications and employee incentives.

Sponsors who wish to encourage longevity and retirement when it is most convenient for them may find DB plans attractive. Some employees, however, may find the immediate vesting and mobility of DC plans attractive. Similarly, although sponsors may desire to shift investment risk to beneficiaries by offering DC plans, employees may have a preference for a known benefit stream and the possible protection DB plans may offer against inflation and the failure of Social Security to keep pace. For private plans, the risk of an unsatisfactory pension is less because of funding standards and, as a last resort, because of the PBGC. DB plans cannot be customized to meet individual employee needs, however. DC plans are easy to understand and value, whereas DB plans are more complex. Investment expertise is required for both, but it may be more efficiently delivered through a DB plan.

Finally, in evaluating the advantages and disadvantages of DC plans and DB plans, remember that the U.S. equity markets were unusually robust from 1982 to 1999. DC plans are much less appealing following the 2000 to 2002 period, during which the equity market fell by 40%. Employee morale and satisfaction are likely much lower than they were only a few years earlier.

With all of these sometimes conflicting factors, a multidimensional plan (e.g., a DB plan coupled with a DC plan) has a certain appeal in allowing employers to structure appropriate incentives while accepting the preferences of those in the labor force. Ultimately, choice of pension plan structure depends jointly on the nature of the industry/organization and the preferences of employees in that industry.

4

The Prudent Pension Fiduciary:
A Pragmatic View

When pension plans fail to deliver the promised benefits, completely or in part, the harm done can be catastrophic. Consider DB plans of US Airways, Anchor Glass, WHX Corporation, and Polaroid, all now administered by the PBGC. Although the PBGC pays benefits to retirees, in many instances, retirees receive substantially less than had been promised.[1] Worse still, consider that when Enron collapsed in late 2001, and its stock became worthless, thousands of employees saw their retirement go up in smoke. At this writing, the courts have barely begun to evaluate who was responsible, how it happened, and how employee retirements should have been protected. Regardless of what eventually is decided, this event was catastrophic for many and offers an appropriate backdrop for a discussion of the fiduciary obligations of those who sponsor and manage pension funds.

Because pension plans are important to employees, and because of the socioeconomic role they play—to governments as well as to companies and individuals—pension plans are regulated. In the United States, ERISA governs corporate or private plans and multiemployer plans. State and local law covers non-ERISA plans. A central element of pension regulation is that decision makers have fiduciary responsibilities to behave prudently. Prudent behavior is expected to reduce the risk that promised benefits will not materialize or to protect the value of pension asset pools. Virtually all operating pension decisions must consider the intent of the regulations that require prudence. This chapter provides the framework necessary to make decisions that are both good and prudent.[2]

FIDUCIARY RESPONSIBILITY DEFINED

A fiduciary is a juridical person—that is, a real person or legal "person" such as a bank or insurance company—that manages business affairs on behalf of another. As such, a fiduciary is an agent who enjoys a special relationship of trust and responsibility with the principal (either a person or an organization) that entrusted assets to the control of the fiduciary. Conflicts of interest must be resolved in favor of the principal or beneficiary; only when all other things are the same can a fiduciary act on self-interest.

Fiduciaries are charged with the duties of care and loyalty. Care in this context means that fiduciaries must give extensive consideration, using generally available and widely used methods of analysis and modes of behavior, before committing the principal's resources to a particular course of action. With respect to pension plans, this aspect of fiduciary duty deals in large part with prudent investment decision making. Loyalty in this context means that the fiduciary must act in the best interest of the principal who assigned the fiduciary responsibility, even if this is not the best course of action for the fiduciary. This aspect of fiduciary standards is concerned with conflicts of interest that may arise between the financial beneficiary of the investment fund and the fiduciary. Appendix A provides a quick guide to responsible fiduciary behavior.

For someone who manages funds for private pension plans, there is an even more stringent standard of care. Under ERISA, that person must be a prudent expert. This means, in general, that there is an affirmative obligation to use those methods of analysis and modes of behavior that other experts employ to manage the funds with which the fiduciary has been entrusted. The managers of public pension plans are also fiduciaries. The explicit obligations of these fiduciaries differ from state to state because public plans are not covered by ERISA; instead, they are subject in general to state trust law. Standards of behavior are generally less stringent than those under ERISA. However, an increasing number of states are legislating standards similar to those of ERISA.

The broad requirements of fiduciary responsibility apply more or less to plan trustees, corporate boards, chief investment officers, plan administrators, and internal money managers. They also apply to outside money managers and any others who render advice for a fee. Moreover, the requirements for being prudent apply not only to the governance, oversight, and investment aspects of a pension plan but also to the everyday management aspects of a plan. For example, all of the actuarial and accounting work must meet the standards of prudence.

In this chapter we first offer an overview of the obligations that must be satisfied by a prudent fiduciary. Next, we discuss what this means from a practical perspective: What sorts of analysis and behavior are most likely to pass the test of prudence? What must a person who is a fiduciary do to remain within the limits of prudence? We begin with ERISA and what ERISA means for private pension plan fiduciaries and for fiduciaries of public plans subject to ERISA-like legislation. After this, we turn to the fiduciary issues that are unique to public plans.

Although private plans are governed by ERISA and public plans are governed by state trust laws, the responsibilities of those charged with administering them are quite similar. Thus, we shall not draw any fine distinctions between those who are agents of shareholders and those who are agents of taxpayers. This chapter constitutes the underlying principle for the rest of the book. It tells the reader why the material in the following chapters is important and how each aspect of pension plan management fits with the others. As we will see, the prudent fiduciary develops overall investment policy, selects managers, monitors performance, keeps the books straight, and does what is possible to enhance investment performance and the likelihood that promised or expected benefits will materialize.

THE PRUDENT INVESTOR

In 1830, the case of *Harvard v. Amory*[3] set the precedent for what is now commonly known as the Prudent Investor law (originally termed the "Prudent Man law"). The decision stated that

> All that can be required of a trustee to invest is that he shall conduct himself faithfully and exercise sound discretion. He is to observe how men of prudence, discretion, and intelligence manage their own affairs, not in regard to speculation, but in regard to the permanent disposition of their funds, considering the probable income, as well as the probable safety of the capital to be invested.

More than a century later this broad statement was modified, but not much. In 1940, the Trust Division of the American Bankers Association adopted a slightly modified version of this language to establish the Model Prudent Man Investment Act. It reads:

> In acquiring, investing, reinvesting, exchanging, retaining, selling, and managing the property for the benefit of another, a fiduciary shall exercise the judgment and care, under the circumstances then prevailing, which men of prudence, discretion, and intelligence exercise in the management of their own funds, considering the probable outcome, as well as the probable safety of their capital.

ERISA Rules

In 1974, ERISA, which considerably strengthened employees' claims on promised pension benefits, was passed to stop perceived abuses of private pensions by sponsors and others involved in managing plans and plan assets. It specifically stated that a private pension fund manager has fiduciary responsibilities to the pension fund and is therefore required to use the prudent investor standard in making investment decisions.

The fiduciary obligations specified in ERISA cover six areas of pension fund management and administration.[4] The fiduciary duty of care entails four of these. The first obligation of the duty of care is the prudent expert requirement, which is more stringent than the prudent investor standard. In the language of ERISA, the fiduciary must exercise the "care, skill, prudence and diligence under the circumstances then prevailing that a prudent man acting in a like capacity and familiar with such matters would use in the conduct of an enterprise of a like character with like aims."[5]

Second, ERISA requires that plan assets be diversified. This rule is bent a great deal in ESOPs, stock bonus plans, and sometimes 401(k) plans that invest heavily in the stock of the sponsoring employer. Apart from these situations, the requirement means that the plan must hold a variety of securities and may hold a variety of asset classes, including real estate and even collectibles. Importantly, ERISA standards allow individual assets to be viewed as a part of a diversified portfolio. That is, a particular investment may be allowable no matter how risky it is so long as it adds little to total portfolio risk. In contrast, many states still require that each asset be able to stand alone as a prudent investment; thus, for these states there is no meaningful diversification standard. An unintended consequence of setting standards on an asset-by-asset basis is that it is possible to end up with a portfolio that is poorly diversified, taking too much risk for too little expected return.

The third ERISA requirement of the duty of care is the documents rule, which states that a plan must be administered in accordance with its governing documents—for example, the plan sponsor's investment guidelines—so long as those documents do not conflict with other ERISA rules. (Consider, for instance, investment guidelines issued by a plan sponsor stating that plan assets should be held entirely in, say, modern art. These would not provide safety to the pension manager from ERISA's prudence and diversification requirements.) As long as the investment guidelines themselves are financially sensible, they must be followed. Among other things, this requirement strongly suggests that a plan sponsor have a set of written investment guidelines.

The fourth obligation of the duty of care is an indication of ownership rule that states that, with few exceptions, documents relating to asset ownership must be within the jurisdiction of U.S. courts. Basically, this means that U.S.-based trustees must be used by U.S. pension plans.

The fiduciary duty of loyalty has two aspects. The first is that a pension plan must be administered solely in the interest of the beneficiaries. This means that when there is a conflict between the welfare of the fiduciary and the welfare of the pension plan, the choice that is made must not be disadvantageous to the plan or its beneficiaries. Second, the plan must be administered for the exclusive purpose of providing benefits to participants and beneficiaries and defraying reasonable administrative expenses. This means, for example, that a plan must not buy stock in a company so that the chairman of the stock-purchasing firm can get a seat on the board of directors of the portfolio company.

The Prudent Investor Law

Since ERISA was drafted, the vagueness of the prudence language has led to confusion and concern about making appropriate investment decisions and proper decisions regarding other aspects of fund management. The practical, economic definition of prudence has evolved with changes in both financial theory and the capital markets. Court opinions also have contributed to an environment in which prudence is not fixed but evolves. The result is that the interpretation of the Prudent Investor laws changes over time, and that it is the responsibility of the fiduciary to update his or her knowledge continuously regarding these changes.

In 1992, The American Law Institute drafted a new standard Prudent Investor law that, as of the end of 2002, thirty-eight states, including the states with the largest public pension plans—California and New York—had adopted for the trust funds administered in those states as well as for state and local pension plans. The new "Prudent Investor Rule" urges courts to adopt a flexible standard of review in the context of modern financial theory. It provides the following specific standards:

- Any and all investments must be considered as part of the portfolio and not be judged on an individual basis.
- No investment should be considered inherently prudent or imprudent.
- In the majority of cases, trust assets must be diversified.
- Inflationary effects must be given consideration in investment decisions. That is, the focus must be on real values. (This is a significant departure from the original notion that the primary risk to protect against was the erosion of nominal principal.)
- Investment skill must be demonstrated by the fiduciaries, or else the investment management should be delegated to a qualified party; this is the "prudent expert" position.

Although the restatement of the Prudent Investor law helps to clarify some of the vagaries in many states, the dynamic nature of financial markets and investing theory presents a challenge to fiduciaries to stay current with both— as well as with current legal theory. Furthermore, although the requirements for behaving as a prudent fiduciary may appear to be benign, they are not. Taken as a whole, they can be hard to follow and may create situations in which the law and economic rationality are, or at least seem to be, at odds. Resolving such conflicts in a prudent manner can pose a difficult challenge for even an experienced fiduciary.

PRUDENCE AND FINANCIAL THEORY

For over one hundred years after the *Harvard v. Amory* decision, stocks were considered too risky an investment for any prudent trustee. Today, modern portfolio theory and the accumulated experience of most investors across many countries would indicate that failing to invest a portion of a pension portfolio in stocks is imprudent. The rates of return on stocks have been very high relative to those on bonds, and stocks have provided better long-run inflation protection.

Indeed, even now, finance theory is altering the concept of prudent behavior. For instance, despite the general public's view that the use of derivative securities (such as puts, calls, futures, and swaps) is very risky, a case can be made that not using derivatives is riskier still in some instances. For example, in light of the widespread use of derivatives as a means of reducing risk and achieving cost-effective diversification, fiduciaries may now be required to understand and use derivatives in certain circumstances, while avoiding derivatives in circumstances where they are not suitable.[6] Of course, many derivatives are primarily speculative in nature and, as such, should clearly be avoided by fiduciaries unless the advantages of their use are substantial. At the same time, some derivative instruments are prudent investments within the context of a specific investment strategy, providing definable costs or risk-reducing benefits to a portfolio. As a result, a fiduciary may be liable to the beneficiaries for not taking advantage of all that the financial markets offer. These and other dramatic changes and innovations in financial theory are constantly changing the definition of the role of a trustee.

Prudence and the Courts

Prudent expert behavior on the part of a fiduciary mandates that the fiduciary be up-to-date on mainstream innovations in investment and financial theory and associated empirical findings. It does not require a manager to believe and embrace these innovations, it simply requires that the manager know about them and have good reason for incorporating them or ignoring them in making investment decisions. From an economic perspective, it means that a fiduciary should have some view regarding how asset prices are determined and how and why they move, and should understand clearly how to exploit that view for the investment benefit of the pension plan. Given current widespread use of derivatives such as futures and options to help implement various investment strategies and hedges, and given also the perpetual evolution of financial products, the educational implications for fiduciaries can be substantial. They must invest much time in training and education.

Despite the fast pace of new financial developments that pension fiduciaries must understand, they cannot ignore historical context and precedent, as these can provide the basis for allegations of imprudent behavior. In other words, the manager must be forward looking, but must not ignore prior legal and economic views.

Regulation and legal precedent can have perverse consequences. Empirical evidence suggests that enforcement of the single security version of the prudent investor law in fiduciary situations has resulted in a tilting of the affected portfolios toward the "high-quality, prudent sector of the equity market."[7] However, because returns are generally linked with risk, too little risk typically leads to low relative returns. Thus, holding portfolios that are heavily weighted toward "prudent" stocks may be inadvertently taking too little risk and thus inadvertently getting too little return. Low relative returns will require higher contributions and may, ironically, reduce the security of plan benefits. Nonetheless, many fiduciaries may fear being found "imprudent" if they invest or authorize investment in "imprudent" securities with promising returns.

DUE DILIGENCE

Under the Prudent Investor law, the fiduciary must meet certain standards of due diligence. Although what constitutes sufficient due diligence is not always completely obvious, there are particular steps that fiduciaries can take to ensure that they are reasonably protected from serious litigation risk as well as from poor financial results.

The Department of Labor has made it clear that a written investment policy on the part of a plan sponsor helps to ensure that a rational and prudent investment strategy is carried out. The written investment policy also provides the fiduciaries with a written document that can support an individual investment in the context of a broader strategy. Such a policy should be given to any money managers and pension consultants the plan sponsor employs.

A fiduciary is responsible for answering the following questions when considering a particular investment:

1. Does it meet the diversification and minimum quality standards, if there are any, set forth in the overall plan?
2. Does it assist the plan in meeting its overall investment strategy objective? How does it expect to do this?
3. Is the investment cost-effective, and are the costs of implementing the investment reasonable?
4. Does it offer an appropriate expected reward-to-risk ratio within the context of the overall portfolio?

It is essential to note that these standards also apply when choosing an investment manager: fiduciary responsibility cannot be avoided by delegation. The decision to use an outside manager to carry out an investment strategy does not reduce the need for care, skill, and caution in the selection process. A manager should be evaluated on his or her administrative costs, transaction fees, overall performance in the context of his or her chosen investment strategy, and willingness to conform to the specified investment policy. When choosing an investment manager, a benchmark should be selected to assist in the ongoing assessment of performance. Benchmarks are discussed in detail in Chapter 14, but suffice it to say that an appropriate benchmark is the standard against which various actions may be deemed to be prudent—or not.

Documentation and monitoring are both critical to prudent decision making and to due diligence. For example, fiduciaries should evaluate investment strategies and managers regularly and should document the analysis and the decision to retain or terminate either. This activity forms the basis for a formal ongoing program analysis that, if properly established and executed, ensures prudent monitoring and provides evidence that monitoring is ongoing. The monitoring process is described in detail in Chapter 15.

EXCLUSIVE BENEFIT RULE

Apart from the prudent investor aspect of pension management, there are other rules that are vague and challenging but that sponsors must obey. One such rule is the exclusive benefit rule.[8] ERISA requires that fiduciaries carry out their duties for the exclusive benefit of participants and beneficiaries. This means they are restricted from doing anything that is in conflict with the interests of the beneficiaries. However, numerous conflicts arise in managing pension plans. An obvious conflict is posed by the implicit consolidation of a plan and sponsor liabilities. Economically targeted investments, socially responsible investing (investing in socially desirable activities or avoiding investing in tobacco or gambling stocks, for example), asset reversions from plan terminations, and directed commissions are also situations in which those who manage the plan or its assets may have interests that diverge from those of regular plan beneficiaries. Resolving these conflicts in the interest of beneficiaries, noble as it sounds, is, however, an elusive concept.

Consolidation of Liabilities

The intent of the exclusive benefit rule is to ensure that companies that provide private pension plans for their employees manage those plans in the employees' best interest. (It is not clear, however, who wins if there is a conflict between retired and present employees.) At the same time, ERISA established that pension fund liabilities are the most senior debt obligation of the firm, ranking immediately behind tax obligations. As a result, despite the accounting separation of the pension fund liabilities, the "economic model of the firm" considers the total liabilities and assets of the firm to include the assets and the liabilities of the pension plan itself. These two issues—the exclusive benefit rule and the consolidation of liabilities—lead to inherent conflicts of interest.

A case cited by Copeland clearly demonstrates the sort of conflict of interest that can arise in private pension fund management. In 1982 International Harvester switched $250 million, out of a total of $1.35 billion in pension assets, from stocks to bonds. The intent of this switch was to diminish the volatility of future pension contribution requirements on the part of the company. Such moves may make the pension plan seem safer, but they can also lead to the need for larger contributions in the future, because stocks are likely to produce higher returns than bonds. What may appear to be in the best interest of the plan beneficiaries may be negatively affecting the future wealth of the firm. This may eventually cause problems for the beneficiaries of the plan because lower future profits may hamper future investment and the firm's long-run ability to compete and provide employment.

It is worth noting that although private fund managers have a strict primary obligation to the beneficiaries, they also have implicit obligations to their managers (bosses), which can be directly or indirectly enforced by the threat of job loss. Thus, those who manage pension plans may face pension regulations that run counter to what is best for their careers.

Under state law similar conflicts may arise. One case noted by Fischel and Langbein dealt with the New York City Municipal Unions pension plans during New York City's fiscal crisis in the early 1970s. The pension plans bought very risky municipal debt to help the city stave off insolvency. Not only can one question the wisdom of a tax-exempt fund buying tax-exempt bonds, but the bonds were so risky that the pension plans' safety was compromised. Older workers sued the pension plans, contending that the investment helped the city, not them. In fact, the investment hurt them because of the increase in risk and the increased chance of the pension plan's going bust while benefits were still owed. The court found that younger workers benefited from the investment because it increased the city's chances of long-run solvency. The courts allowed the investment, but the argument for exclusive benefit to beneficiaries was stretched. The court, in effect, sided with current employees and went against retired and soon-to-be retired employees. "Exclusive benefit" remains an elusive concept.

Economically Targeted Investments

Further complexity is added by the debate over economically targeted invest-ments (ETIs). ETIs are "capital projects that are designed to provide economic benefit to the economies of the geographic regions in which they occur."[9] This suggests that a pension plan investment designed to benefit a certain geographic region or type of worker would be "prudent," so long as no direct economic benefits to the plan were sacrificed.

Advocates of ETIs point to success stories: for example, municipal pension funds lent money to New York City during its fiscal crises in 1975.[10] There is some limited evidence, however, that on average the risk-adjusted returns as-sociated with ETIs are typically low.[11] As a result, there is considerable debate as to their prudence.

Public pension plans have made greater use of ETIs than private plans. One explanation for this is that public plan beneficiaries are more likely to benefit from ETI investments (e.g., a teacher pension plan investing in real estate de-velopment in communities in which more schools will be needed). A second explanation is that private plan sponsors are reluctant to invest in ETIs because of the exclusive benefit rule. The exclusive benefit rule does not play as large a rule in public plan decision making, and this may explain their greater use there. It is true that the Department of Labor has tried to encourage ETIs for private plans, but even this has caused controversy.[12]

Socially Responsible Investing

Another investment issue that arises periodically is the idea of socially respon-sible investing. Socially responsible investing involves constructing portfolios that may include specific companies because of special criteria in addition to projected investment returns, and may exclude companies that make or produce things that some portion of the investing public views as morally wrong.

For example, when apartheid was still the law of the land in South Africa, many portfolios, particularly the endowment funds of colleges and universities and public employee pension plans, eliminated the stocks of companies doing business in South Africa. There also are institutional investors that exclude gam-bling, tobacco, and alcoholic beverage companies from their portfolios; some that exclude weapons producers and nuclear power suppliers; and some that exclude companies with poor labor relations or that are not family friendly.

The issue for pension plan managers is whether, under existing law, pension portfolios that consist of only "socially responsible" companies, however de-fined, are acceptable within the law. By definition, because of their refusal to consider the entire universe of common stock investment opportunities, such portfolios are not as well diversified as they might otherwise be. Further, spon-sors of such portfolios have goals other than the exclusive benefit of the pension plan beneficiaries. On these grounds, one could also argue that the prudent fiduciary of a DB pension plan should not use social criteria to select securities.

The evidence, although not extensive, does not show that socially responsible

mutual funds have produced lower risk-adjusted returns than conventional mutual funds. In other words, these portfolios have not been punished for systematically narrowing their investment universes, though the time period during
which performance has been scrutinized is short. Admittedly, this tells us little
directly about the investment performance of public or private pension plans
that employ social criteria relative to those eschewing such criteria, but the
evidence we have at least indicates that it may be possible to run a socially
responsible portfolio without financial sacrifice. Thus, although there may be
legal problems connected to socially responsible pension funds, so long as there
are no deleterious financial consequences, a limited amount of such behavior is
likely to be tolerated because it incurs no significant financial damage.

Plan Terminations

There are other examples in which prudence and the exclusive benefit rule can
produce unexpected conflict. In the mid-1980s, many corporations found themselves with heavily overfunded pension plans as a result of the sharp rise in
stock prices that occurred after 1982. Under ERISA rules, they could not simply
withdraw the amount by which the plans were overfunded; however, they could
reduce or eliminate future contributions until the surplus was exhausted. To
capture this overfunding, corporations had to terminate their existing pension
plans. Thus, many companies terminated plans to capture the excess assets and
used a portion of the total assets from the terminated pension plan to buy annuities from insurance companies that would give workers the pensions they had
been promised. A number of companies that chose to recapture the pension plan
overfunding in this way conducted bid processes among annuity providers to
select the insurance company that would handle the terminations.

Many companies chose Executive Life Insurance Company, the insurance
subsidiary of First Executive Corporation, because it was the lowest-cost provider. It also had, through 1987 at least, a top credit rating from A.M. Best, an
insurance company credit-rating agency, and from Standard & Poor's (S&P's),
as well as a very good rating from Moody's. Unfortunately, Executive Life
Insurance Company was seized by the California Insurance Commission in
1991, and for a variety of reasons was unable to meet 100% of its pension plan
annuity obligations.

Lawsuits flew. They were filed by aggrieved former workers, unions, and the
Department of Labor. These suits alleged that the companies that purchased
Executive Life Insurance Company pension termination annuities had behaved
imprudently and ignored the exclusive benefit rule. They behaved imprudently,
the suits alleged, because although Executive Life had top ratings, its investment
portfolio contained "too many" junk bonds. Moreover, the suits alleged that these
companies violated the exclusive benefit rule because they chose the low bidder,
Executive Life, and passed the savings along to their shareholders. Although
most of these suits were settled on reasonably favorable terms for the companies
that terminated their pension plans, the story shows how ambiguous the interpretation of prudence and the exclusive benefit rule can be.

Directed Commissions

The exclusive benefit rule is germane to "soft dollars" as well. Soft dollars arise in connection with directed commissions. Soft dollars are credits granted to a money management firm or other service provider from a broker in return for trades that are directed to the broker. Soft dollars can be used to pay for a particular investment service such as research.

The pitfall for fiduciaries with soft dollars is that the soft dollar credits may not be used for the benefit of the plan, and even when they are, the practice reduces accountability and disguises transfers of value between parties. As a result, directed commissions make it possible for some money management firms or pension plan sponsors to use the soft-dollar credits to obtain some service that is not useful for the pension plan. For example, a manager might rationalize that because the security trading commissions are being spent anyway, why not get a product or service for them that could be useful in some other area of the sponsor's organization? Or why not buy some research that the investment manager wants even though the research may not apply to the plan?

Although this rationale might seem reasonable, it ignores the economic reality that the benefits that are generated from directing trades to one broker or another are rightfully an asset of the fund and hence belong to the fund's beneficiaries. Further, it may result in commissions and other trading costs being higher than they should be, to the detriment of the fund. Finally, it may be unlawful. All things considered, the misuse of soft dollars that arise from directed commissions violates the exclusive benefit rule and should be avoided. Thus, if soft-dollar arrangements are used, policy should specify that the benefits arising from these arrangements must go directly to the pension plan to be used for the benefit of plan beneficiaries. Further, the decision to direct or allow directed commissions should be documented in internal memos and through explicit written instructions and limitations on investment managers' behavior.

PUBLIC PENSION PLANS

Prudent behavior has historically been different for public pension plans. The rules governing public pension plans regarding prudence and other aspects of the fiduciary relationship are set in the states, not by the Department of Labor through ERISA. In general, state courts have been more tolerant of ETIs, more tolerant of social investing, and more tolerant of low levels of diversification than federal regulators. Moreover, until recently, state courts have generally considered the prudence (or riskiness) of individual securities to be germane and have not given much weight to the fact that a very risky individual security can actually reduce the risk of the entire portfolio.

All of these considerations, however, seem poised for change as states adopt rules that conform more or less to those laid out by ERISA. Accordingly, over time we expect a greater convergence between state and federal rules regarding the behavior of the prudent fiduciary. Within this framework, the following discussion considers public plans and prudent management.

As a result of the rapid growth in plan assets and the total number of plan participants throughout the United States, the issues that define exactly what prudent behavior is for public pension fiduciaries have become more important in recent years. With the advances in investment theory and the changes in the regulatory landscape, these issues also are much more complex.

For public pension sponsors, as for private pension ones, prudent behavior is defined in part by legislation and what the courts say it is, and in part by informed management practice. Conceptually, it seems reasonable that public pension sponsors and plan administrators can and probably should mimic some of the economically sensible legal constraints imposed or suggested by ERISA— diversification, viewing investments in a portfolio context, and so forth. However, there is no universally agreed on definition of prudent behavior within the context of the public pension, as the rules and regulations vary from place to place. In addition, public pensions face a number of unique constraints that private pensions generally do not have to consider.

Public pensions have to exist within the fabric of the political process and respond to the use of undue influence to accomplish political rather than economic or plan goals. Inappropriate political influence can create problems or incentives that may be counter to the interests of plan beneficiaries. In particular, this can lead to imprudent results—such as hiring the wrong managers or hiring too many managers or appropriating fund assets for general spending. In addition, the financial health of the plan may be threatened as politicians approve popular increases in postretirement benefits (hidden pay raises) without considering their effect on the funding status and health of the plan. Finally, the pay-as-you-go mentality that is so politically popular is counter to what many consider rational economic funding of plan obligations.

Public pensions are also subject to uneven but occasionally intense (frequently naive) public scrutiny. Perhaps even more than private pensions, public pensions are in the public eye, and as such the decisions they make—and the consequences of those decisions—are fair game for newspaper reporters and politicians. This would not be especially troubling if the information presented were fair and balanced and the people who received the information were knowledgeable about investing (even good stocks do go down). However, this is not typically the case. To the contrary, misinformed public opinion can lead to harmful legislation, such as legal lists of suitable investments and other restrictions that may reduce portfolio diversification.

The central concern for sponsors for public pension plan fiduciaries, then, is to develop effective ways of encouraging and delivering prudent plan governance and administration despite the factors at work in politics and newspapers. One "higher standard" that the public pension fiduciary must accept is the burden of educating the all the parties involved in plan decisions—legislators, trustees, employers, union representatives, and so forth—as well as potential critics of the fund and its management.

There is more that can be done, however. In its 1994 report on the Virginia Retirement System, the Joint Legislative Audit and Review Commission made several recommendations that are consistent with better fiduciary practice. We have drawn from this report in providing the following suggestions for all public pension plan decision makers.

1. Appoint qualified trustees who have an appropriate level of investment knowledge and judgment (rather than simply seeking representatives of various constituencies).
2. Provide sufficient statutory authority and responsibility (as opposed to implied authority) to manage the plan.
3. Select a qualified chief investment officer.
4. Make a commitment to sound actuarial funding with special attention to

   • the effect of cost of living adjustments (COLAs),
   • sound economics and accounting assumptions, and
   • openness and full disclosure.

5. Discourage the use of extensive "legal lists."
6. Develop written policy statements, with special attention to asset allocation policies.
7. Anticipate and reduce the potential for adverse political influence.

If these recommendations are followed, the issues of prudent fiduciary management that still face public pension plans are not very different from those facing private plans. Because of this, we add the following.

   • It is prudent to apply current investment theory and follow sound practice in such areas as diversification and risk management.
   • It is prudent to attend to the interests of employees even in the absence of ERISA-like legislation.
   • It is prudent to evaluate carefully the value of the services or performance that the fund is getting from its managers, consultants, and others in light of their costs.
   • It is certainly not prudent to follow investment strategies that are poorly understood or that have no theoretical support.
   • It is prudent to be loyal and do one's duty to plan beneficiaries.

DEFINED CONTRIBUTION PLANS

Most of the rules governing the behavior of pension plan sponsors and managers were written with the DB plan in mind. Superficially, at least, this seems to make sense, because the assets and liabilities of DC plans always match, and because in increasingly popular self-directed plans beneficiaries select their own investment vehicles from a menu of selections offered by employers. However, the plan sponsor is not completely free of responsibility. Although not responsible for actual investment decisions, the plan's sponsor, as a fiduciary, still has the responsibility to ensure that

- the beneficiaries have the ability to invest in the appropriate asset classes;
- the investment managers who are available to beneficiaries are themselves chosen prudently;
- there is a routine level of monitoring and evaluating of investment performance, with investment-manager changes made when appropriate; and
- the costs are reasonable and controlled, as most investment expenses are the direct expense of the beneficiary.[13]

Thus, although DC plans reduce the risks the organization bears in providing beneficiaries with a "guaranteed" level of retirement income, they do not eliminate the fiduciary responsibilities that plan managers and trustees incur.

As DC plans have grown in prominence, so has DC plan litigation.[14] Many cases have arisen around changes in DC plans; for example, changes in service providers, changes in investment options, or changes in plan design. Sponsors must be careful about making changes and disclosing these changes to participants.[15]

There has been a great deal of debate about the level of guidance that the sponsor of a DC plan should provide the beneficiaries on issues such as asset allocation and general investing principles. The DOL's 404(c) regulations require that a sponsor structure the product as offering to supply an appropriate offering of asset classes along with a myriad of other administrative disclosures. If a sponsor complies, that sponsor theoretically is protected from an individual who suffers losses because of poor individual decisions about what proportion of each of the funds to invest in. However, these regulations are not intended to protect a sponsor that includes a high-cost, poorly performing fund or one that defrauds its investors.

Among other things, the 404(c) regulations establish the need for and limit the amount of education that a sponsor should provide to limit its fiduciary liability. The intent of 404(c) regulations is to discourage sponsors from acting as investment advisors while encouraging them to provide broad-based guidelines for making informed investment decisions. As an example, if a sponsor educates its beneficiaries on the benefits of diversification, it should be careful not to dictate directly how best to effect a diversification strategy. If the DOL determines that the education provided constitutes an investment advisory role, then companies will be held to the full fiduciary requirements and 404(c) has not limited any of their liability. Once again, there are many unresolved issues.

Over the last two decades, the number of DC plans has exploded, and the issues surrounding the responsibilities of the sponsor have come under increased scrutiny. The fiduciary requirements of due diligence and monitoring are mandated for sponsors of both DC and DB plans. It is not enough that DC plan sponsors offer numerous investment choices. They must also monitor the ongoing suitability of these choices and make changes when the existing money managers falter.[16] Further, plan costs imply a fiduciary duty.

CONCLUSION

Pension plan fiduciaries have a clear obligation to invest prudently and for the exclusive benefit of the beneficiaries of the plan. Moreover, they must administer the plan in an economically sensible fashion, not spending excessively on activities that bring relatively little benefit to the plan. However, the definition of both prudence and "exclusive benefit" are the source of considerable legal and regulatory debate and uncertainty. What is clear is that fiduciaries are required to be familiar with the issues surrounding their investment strategies and their specific implementation. Fiduciaries should be familiar with

- the specifics of any investment, including reading the prospectus for new securities, and the recent financial experience of portfolio companies;
- the current financial theory supporting the application of a particular investment strategy;
- the operations and investment strategies of peer pension investors;
- the legal ramifications from the use of different financial instruments;
- the estimated risk-to-reward ratios for any given total portfolio composition;
- the monitoring of any activity that is delegated outside the immediate authority of the fiduciary; and
- the decision-making process and its documentation, the data used, the philosophies followed, the competence of involved parties, and the policies used to reduce conflicts of interest.

ERISA for private plans and new rules for state and local plans have placed ever-increasing responsibilities on fiduciaries to gain greater depth of expertise, to become much more careful in the monitoring of organizations providing advice or discretionary authority over plan assets, and to be much more aware about who the true beneficiaries of any decision are.

In conclusion, it is critical to understand that no body of regulations or rules can do more than specify appropriate (or inappropriate) behavior. Rules cannot ensure ethical behavior, nor can they ensure informed, competent decision making. The foundations of fiduciary behavior—and we are writing for those who really care—are ethical behavior and competence in decision making. Intend to do the right thing; get all the information necessary; and have the knowledge needed to evaluate it.

5

An Overview of Compliance
for Pension Plans

One of the most important tasks for a pension plan manager is to ensure that the pension plan is complying with the numerous rules and regulations that govern pension plans. The rules and regulations are complex, and they change year by year as new laws are passed, as new regulations are issued, and as new court cases are decided. Because of this almost constantly shifting landscape, those who make pension plan decisions face a nontrivial challenge in trying to stay current. Fortunately, there is an industry of consultants and attorneys who are available to assist pension plan managers with compliance. Unfortunately, compliance issues frequently divert decision-making attention from the frequently more important issues that affect the economic well-being of the various stakeholders in pension plans.

This chapter presents an overview and interpretation of the major laws and regulations to which pension plans—both private and public—must adhere. State and local (public) plans are not covered under ERISA, so their regulation is not as unified as is the regulation of private plans. Therefore, this chapter focuses on the functions of pension plan compliance and generally takes the perspective of private plans.

The chapter is designed to be an easy-to-understand starting point of the "big picture" necessary for compliance. Pension fund decision makers who are new to their positions can use this chapter for an orientation.[1] Note that the material on prudence in Chapter 4 is the foundation of many of the compliance issues facing pension plans.

The bulk of this chapter is devoted to three primary areas of compliance: the first addresses obligations related to reporting and disclosure; second, the chapter provides an overview of the funding requirements for DB plans; and third, there are the requirements that a private pension plan must satisfy to count as a "qualified" plan under the tax code. The chapter concludes with a discussion of the Sarbanes-Oxley Act of 2002 (SOX). Although not a pension plan act per se, SOX has implications of which pension decision makers should be aware.

REPORTING AND DISCLOSURE

ERISA requires private plans to issue reports both to the government and to plan participants and beneficiaries. This section covers three of the required reports:

summary plan description (SPD),
annual report (Form 5500), and
summary annual report.

These reporting requirements are emphasized in ERISA. Indeed, ERISA specifies that any person willfully violating these requirements can be fined or imprisoned or both.[2]

Summary Plan Description

ERISA requires that administrators provide a SPD to participants and beneficiaries. The purpose of the SPD is to "reasonably apprise" participants and beneficiaries "of their rights and obligations under the plan."[3]

ERISA emphasizes that the SPD should be written so that it is easily understandable to an average plan participant. As a result, managers should take into account the comprehension and education of typical employees. Managers should also be careful if a significant portion of their employees are literate only in a non-English language. In that case, the plan may have to provide a notice in the non-English language offering assistance in understanding the plan.[4]

The content of the SPD varies somewhat depending on the type of plan.[5] It includes general information such as

- the name of the plan (and, if different, the name by which the plan is commonly known by participants),
- the name and address of the plan sponsor,
- contact information for the plan administrator, and
- the name and address for service of legal process.

The SPD also describes the terms of the plan:

- the plan type (e.g., DB or DC),
- eligibility under the plan,
- any joint and survivor benefits provided,
- circumstances which may result in loss of benefits,
- terms of any PBGC provision for the plan, and
- procedures governing claims for benefits.

The SPD must also include a statement of the rights and protections for participants under ERISA. For example, it should inform participants that they are entitled to prudent actions by plan fiduciaries. Labor regulations provide the following model description for inclusion in the SPD:

In addition to creating rights for plan participants ERISA imposes duties upon the people who are responsible for the operation of the employee benefit plan. The people who operate your plan, called "fiduciaries" of the plan, have a duty to do so prudently and in the interest of you and other plan participants and beneficiaries. No one, including your employer, your union, or any other person, may fire you or otherwise discriminate against you in any way to prevent you from obtaining a benefit or exercising your rights under ERISA.[6]

Annual Report

The annual report, also known as the Form 5500, summarizes the plan's operation over a given year. It is filed with the government, specifically the Department of Labor. There is a basic Form 5500, and there are also numerous schedules that may have to be completed depending on the size and the type of plan. ERISA[7] requires that the annual report include financial statements, which could include:

- a statement of the assets and liabilities of the plan for the current year and the prior year,
- a statement of receipts and disbursements during the year,
- a schedule of assets held for investment purposes,
- a schedule of each transaction involving an interested party, and
- a schedule of significant transactions (e.g., transactions involving more than 3% of the plan's assets).

In addition, a DB plan may have to include an actuarial statement each year. Most large plans must have an accountant audit the plan and provide a report to be included as part of the annual report. This accountant's report states which financial statements have been audited and the accountant's opinion on those statements.[8]

Summary Annual Report

ERISA requires pension plans to provide a summary annual report to participants and beneficiaries each year.[9] The Department of Labor has provided a template for this report.[10] The first section covers basic financial information, including

- plan expenses (both administrative expenses and benefits paid),
- the net asset value of the plan (both at the beginning and at the end of the year),
- employer contributions,
- employee contributions, and
- earnings on investments.

The summary annual report also contains a section on whether the plan has met the minimum funding standards of ERISA (discussed below). Finally, there is a section telling recipients how to get additional information (such as a copy of the Form 5500).

FUNDING

From an employer's perspective, a DB pension plan represents a promise to make cash payments (to retirees) far in the future. In this sense, a pension plan is similar to a long-term debt obligation. With long-term debt, an employer is promising to make payments far in the future—in this case to bondholders.

With long-term debt, an employer may fund the debt payments at the time they are due. Suppose an employer promises to pay $1 million to bondholders in ten years. The employer need not put money aside now to fund the future debt payments. Instead, the employer could wait and use operating income in the tenth year to pay the lenders. Or the employer could borrow again from other lenders after ten years to pay the original lenders.

Pension plans are different. Private pension plans in the United States and many public pension plans are required to fund all or a significant part of their obligations in advance. Thus, if a DB plan promises to pay $1 million in ten years, the employer may be required to put money aside now to help make the future payment.[11]

The funding rules are complex, and there are a number of actuarial methods which can be used to fulfill them.[12] Funding is tracked by means of a "funding standard account." Each year, this account is charged with additional costs. It is credited with employer contributions. The account also receives numerous other adjustments as well. For example, if the plan assets appreciated more than had been assumed, these "experience gains" would be credited to the account. Experience gains (and experience losses) are usually not fully allocated year-by-year to the funding standard account. Instead, the allocations are smoothed: an investment gain might be allocated over a five-year period.[13]

There are more stringent funding requirements for plans that have asset values significantly less than their "current liability."[14] The current liability is essentially the liability if the plan were terminated. For valuing this liability, plans were originally required to use a discount rate tied to thirty-year Treasury bonds. In 2001, however, the Treasury Department announced that it would stop issuing these bonds. This has created an opening for Congress to legislate a new discount rate. The controversy has been heated as interest rates have fallen and the PBGC has announced record deficits.[15]

TAX QUALIFICATION

Public pension plans do not have to qualify for tax exemption per se as private pension plans do. Thus, the issues pertaining to "qualified plans" are of relevance primarily to private plans.

This section provides an overview of some of the requirements a pension plan must meet to qualify for the tax benefits described in Chapter 2. Specifically, this section covers three qualification requirements:

- coverage,
- vesting, and
- nondiscrimination.

Eligibility

When a plan is established, the sponsor must determine which employees are eligible to participate in the plan. In making this choice, the sponsor is constrained by the Internal Revenue Code. For example, a plan could not say that employees had to be over thirty-five years old before being eligible for the pension plan. At most, a plan can require that employees be twenty-one years old before being eligible. The exception is certain educational institutions, where the pension plan can require that employees be twenty-six years old to participate.

Likewise, a plan could not require for eligibility that employees have ten years of service with the employer. In general, the plan can require at most one year of service before eligibility. Some plans can require two years of service if the plan's vesting is rapid enough.[16] Of course, the code has precise rules for counting how many years of service a person has. The rules cover part-time workers, seasonal industries, and breaks in service such as maternity or paternity leave.[17]

A plan cannot specify any maximum age. A plan could not say, for example, that workers over age sixty-five years can no longer participate in a plan. Such a maximum age condition is specifically prohibited by the Internal Revenue Code.[18]

DB plans face an additional participation requirement. Most DB plans have to benefit at least fifty employees or 40% of the company's workforce, whichever is less.[19]

Vesting

Pension plan sponsors can choose the vesting provisions for the plan, but as with eligibility, the Internal Revenue Code severely constrains this choice. First, contributions by the employee to the plan must be fully vested immediately.

For employer contributions, the vesting requirements differ depending on whether the contribution is a "matching contribution" (i.e., a contribution that the employer makes to match a contribution by the employee[20]). For employer contributions that are not matches, vesting must be at least as rapid as two options:

- 100% vesting after the fifth year of service, or
- graded vesting, with at least 20% after year 3, 40% after year 4, and so forth until 100% vesting after year 7.

The Economic Growth and Tax Relief Reconciliation Act of 2001 (EGTRRA) specified faster vesting for employer contributions that are matches. Specifically, there must either be 100% vesting after three years, or graded vesting from 20% after year 2 to 100% after year 6.[21] EGTRRA includes a "sunset provision," under which its provisions will no longer apply after January 1, 2011.[22]

As noted above, there are faster vesting requirements if a plan has an eligibility requirement of more than one year of service.[23] There are also additional vesting restrictions for plans that are "top-heavy." Top-heavy plans are those in which the accrued benefit for key employees exceeds 60% of the total accrued benefit of the plan.[24]

Nondiscrimination

To qualify for tax advantages, a pension plan cannot simply be a means for highly compensated employees (HCEs) to reduce their taxes. A qualified plan serves both HCEs and non–highly compensated employees (NHCEs): it does not "discriminate" against the NHCEs.

The nondiscrimination requirements are complex. The regulations start by defining which employees are HCEs.[25] Essentially, employees are HCEs by virtue either of their ownership level or their salary. For ownership, the threshold is 5%: an employee who owns more than 5% of the company is an HCE. For salary, the employer can choose between two measures. One measure says that employees earning more than a set amount ($90,000 in 2002) are HCEs. The alternative measure says that the highest-paid 20% of employees are HCEs.

Once it is determined who are the HCEs and who are the NHCEs, there are two types of nondiscrimination requirements that must be met: nondiscrimination in coverage, and nondiscrimination in benefits and other features.

Nondiscrimination in Coverage

For current employees, a plan satisfies the nondiscrimination in coverage requirements if it satisfies one of two tests: either the Ratio Percentage Test or the Average Benefit Test.[26] The Ratio Percentage Test requires that if the plan benefits 100% of its HCEs, it must benefit at least 70% of the NHCEs. In general, if it benefits $X\%$ of its HCEs, it must benefit $0.7 \times X$ of its NHCEs.

To satisfy the Average Benefit Test, a plan must meet two subtests. First, it must pass a Nondiscriminatory Classification Test, which includes a weaker version of the Ratio Percentage Test.[27] Second, it must pass an Average Benefit Percentage Test. This test is based on a measure of the generosity of benefits. In essence it requires that the benefits going to the NHCEs be at least 70% of the benefits going to the HCEs.[28]

Nondiscrimination in Benefits and Other Features

In addition to coverage, a plan must also be nondiscriminatory in three additional ways.[29] First, all benefits, rights, and features provided under the plan must be made available in a nondiscriminatory way.[30] Second, plan amendments and plan terminations cannot discriminate in favor of HCEs.[31] Third, plans must be nondiscriminatory in the amount of contributions or benefits they provide. There are two general tests which a plan can meet: one for nondiscrimination in contributions and the other for nondiscrimination in benefits.[32] There are also different safe harbors available for different types of plan. Plans are permitted to take into account an employee's salary in determining that employee's benefit or contribution. For example, a DC plan would satisfy a safe harbor if it allocated to each employee 5% of that employee's annual compensation.[33] In addition, plans are permitted to take into account any differences in Social Security benefits provided to HCEs and NHCEs.[34]

THE SARBANES-OXLEY ACT OF 2002

The bankruptcies of Enron in 2001 and WorldCom in 2002 led to SOX,[35] which covers a lot of territory. First of all, it addresses the accounting profession: it establishes a Public Company Accounting Oversight Board, and it restricts the services that auditors can provide.

For public companies, SOX also requires that the principal executive officer and principal financial officer certify the companies' annual and quarterly reports. These executives must certify that the financial statements "fairly present" the company's financial condition.[36] They must also certify that they have designed internal controls to ensure that material information relating to the company is provided to them.[37]

In addition, SOX requires publicly traded companies to have an audit committee that oversees the accounting firms employed by the company. The committee is to be composed of independent members of the board of directors.[38] The committee is to establish procedures for handling complaints and concerns about the company's accounting and internal accounting controls.

As will be discussed in Chapter 10, DB pension accounting can be significant in its effect on a company's financial statements. Thus, SOX certainly affects pension plans through its regulations on accounting.

In addition, SOX directly addresses pension plans in one respect that arose from the Enron debacle. Enron's problems first surfaced on October 16, 2001. On that date, the company announced that it would be taking a $1 billion charge for its third quarter.[39] Ten days later, on October 26, 2001, the Enron 401(k) plan entered a long-planned "blackout" period, in which employees would not be able to change their investments, including their Enron stock. This blackout period lasted about 10 days. There was much publicity about this restriction on employees, and it was contrasted with sales of Enron stock that were made by Enron executives'.[40]

Congress responded through SOX by prohibiting directors and officers from trading company stock during any blackout period that affects significant numbers of employees.[41] If there is a violation of this, the corporation can recover any profits realized from the prohibited trades. If the corporation fails to act, then any shareholder can sue on behalf of the corporation.[42] This regulation confirms again that pension plans are often judged in terms of whether the rank-and-file employees are being treated fairly compared with highly compensated employees and officers.

CONCLUSION

Compliance is complex and time-consuming. It is one reason frequently given by sponsors for their switch from DB to DC plans—any argue that the cost of compliance is too high.

Compliance begins with an understanding of the basics of fiduciary duty as provided in Chapter 4. It requires a working knowledge of the various laws and regulations that govern pension plans, be they public or private. Compliance is necessary, but it is not sufficient. Unfortunately, there are plans that believe compliance is equivalent to good management—it is not. Of much more importance to the long-run economic health of a plan, its sponsor or sponsors, and its beneficiaries are issues such as investment policy, asset allocation, risk management, and related decisions.

6

Establishing Pension
Investment Policy

Policy is an essential element of any set of complex activities. For pension plans, investment policy is critical to facilitate planning, decision-making, implementation, and monitoring. The stakes of pension investment policy—employee security and incentives, the consequences of adverse investment performance, the rights to surplus assets, and so forth—are too high to delegate entirely to lower-level managers or to external consultants and money managers. Trustees, pension boards, top management, and those who represent the interests of shareholders, taxpayers, and employees must play a role in setting, monitoring compliance with, and reviewing pension investment policy.

Sound policy means providing written guidelines for all important decisions concerning the plan, its assets, and its management over time and in different financial markets. Policy should communicate the scope and objectives of the plan unequivocally to all stakeholders, plan managers, consultants, and others. This chapter reviews the key elements of investment policy as they relate to asset pools of pension plans and the goals of funding the pension liability in a cost-efficient manner for DB plans and of accumulation of wealth and providing retirement income for DC plans. The chapter begins by discussing risk and return. It ends by comparing active and passive investing.

STRATEGIC PARAMETERS OF INVESTMENT POLICY

Whether an asset pool is held in a DB or DC plan, investment policy must define what risk the "owner" of the asset pool can tolerate and what return is necessary to achieve the owner's funding, contribution, and benefit objectives. In addition, any constraining factors that are relevant should be identified. For DB plans and employer-directed DC plans, the sponsor must take the lead in formulating investment policies. For employee-directed DC plans, the employee has ultimate responsibility for investment policy, although various decisions the sponsor makes will affect the amount of freedom employees have.

The strategic elements of investment policy include diversification, exposure to market risk, procedures for adapting to changing markets or circumstances, preferences for active or passive investment management, what investment styles are appropriate, what levels of management fees are appropriate, and whether the use of derivatives is permitted and if so for what purposes, as well as numerous operational issues including the strategic asset allocation for the plan. We discuss these issues initially in the context of DB plans. However, the fundamental elements of investment policy described in this section form the basis for participant-directed and sponsor-directed DC plans as well.

Risk and Return

A pension plan's tolerance for risk and consequently its ability to choose a realistic return target are affected by several factors. For a DB plan, the most important of these factors are the underlying financial strength of the sponsor, the funding status of the plan, and the nature of the plan's liability (e.g., the plan's exposure to inflation through its wage-based benefit formula). For a DC plan (we will assume an employee-directed one), the main factors are funding policy, time to retirement, employee income and wealth, access to borrowing, and individual preference.

Risk Tolerance

The importance of specifying the plan's tolerance for risk cannot be overstated: the capital markets allocate return according to risk taken; therefore, no meaningful return targets can be established until the sponsor (or beneficiary) determines the plan's risk-bearing capacity. In general, a financially strong investor (e.g., a municipality with a significant amount of available taxing power) and a well-funded plan may have a fairly high tolerance for risk. Similarly, a plan that is exposed either to inflation because of its benefit formula or to a long time horizon may have to bear substantial risk to earn a real rate of return high enough to offset inflationary pressures. Paradoxically, plans that can bear a lot of risk may not have to, and plans that are at risk may have to bear more; for example, to try to reduce the level of underfunding.

Return volatility and asset volatility are acceptable measures of risk for individual DC pensions. These measures are not sufficient for DB plans because they ignore the interaction between plan liabilities and assets. They also ignore the interaction between the plan and its sponsor. Thus, in addition to setting acceptable levels of investment risk, DB plans must specify an acceptable level of surplus volatility (the volatility of changes in the value of plan assets relative to changes in the value of plan liabilities). Viewing risk as surplus volatility focuses attention on the sensitivity of plan assets and liabilities to factors such as interest rates, rather than erroneously assuming that these factors are unrelated to plan risk.

Similarly, policies should recognize the dynamics of plan performance and of the sponsor's financial performance as they affect future plan contributions. For example, a sponsor in a highly cyclical industry may not be able to make up funding shortfalls if there is unusually poor investment performance during a period in which the sponsor is losing money.

With regard to risk, policy, then, is a matter of defining what is at risk and then defining what level of volatility is acceptable. If low investment risk is desired, this should be stated (useful quantitative measures include beta and duration) and acceptable exposures to the various asset classes should be explicitly defined. If very low surplus volatility is desired, this must be stated as policy so that the asset allocation can emphasize duration-matching strategies. If the sponsor's financial health is itself quite cyclical, this must be translated in a policy that prohibits further exposure to the same cyclical factors and directs investments into assets that are likely to perform well when the sponsor is likely to do poorly.

Return

A plan's return target follows naturally from policies defining acceptable risk exposures for the plan. Return targets, in essence, must both address plan beneficiary interests in receiving the benefits the beneficiaries feel they are due and address the sponsor's interest in achieving a low present value of future contributions.

The key constraint on return policy, of course, is that return targets must be consistent with what the capital markets will provide given the risk tolerance of the plan and how return is provided—through income, capital growth, or both. Return targets typically are set in both total return and income or yield versus capital change. The higher the total return target, the more risk the plan is agreeing to take. The higher the income target, the lower the long-term total investment return is likely to be.

Plan Constraints

Other circumstances can be of varying importance. For example, liquidity needs may be relatively more important to DB plans that have older employees near to retirement or that have a large number of people currently receiving benefits, as well as to hybrid plans such as cash balance plans that offer portability on employee termination. Similarly, IRS regulations governing the deductibility of sponsor contributions and contracts between the sponsor and the plan affect policy with regard to the timing and size of contributions. Compliance with ERISA and other regulations as well as with legislative mandates that public pension funds undertake actions such as socially responsible investing also serve as constraining factors. All of these circumstances and constraints must be evaluated to determine their effect on the amount of risk the plan should take and on its return objectives.

Diversification, Market Risk, and Change

Pension investment policy should reflect principles of sound investment theory and practice. Some of the more important of these include a consideration of diversification and market risk, and how to adapt to change.

Diversification

It is commonly accepted in the investment community that diversification is a desirable goal. Diversification is achieved by allocating plan assets across asset classes (such as stocks and bonds), within asset classes (such as holding both large capitalization stocks and small capitalization stocks, or investing in several industries), and across regions and countries (such as holding international stocks and bonds). For private plans, diversification is required by ERISA at the portfolio level; for public plans, states historically provide diversification guidelines on an asset-by-asset basis, although this has changed somewhat in recent years.

The fundamental issue is that diversification is desirable because markets will not reward investors for risks that can be diversified away and because regulators require diversification. Thus, pension plan policy should specify minimum acceptable levels of diversification and permit concentrated undiversified exposures only under certain circumstances.

Market Risk

Pension plan investment policy should be specific regarding how much market risk the plan will take. In the framework of what has come to be known as modern portfolio theory, this consists of determining what portfolio of risky assets is appropriate given the plan's tolerance for risk and its return objectives. Modern portfolio theory is closely aligned with the concept of diversification in that market risk is risk that cannot be diversified away and therefore can be avoided only by reducing targeted expected returns. Alternatively, plans that need or wish to achieve high targeted expected returns will have to take on a relatively high amount of exposure to the market and, thus, to the volatility characteristic of the returns and values of risky assets.

Defining an acceptable level of market risk is the crux of the asset allocation decision. In general, plans allocating a large proportion of total assets to stocks are taking a high amount of market risk. Correspondingly, the volatility of plan returns and asset values for these plans will be high compared with the volatility of plans with less exposure to stocks.

Adapting to Change

Among the few certainties in investing are the two truths that markets change and that the factors unique to any given pension plan change over time. Thus, pension plan policy should anticipate changes that may occur and should provide guidance on adapting to change when necessary.

Market change occurs simply when a market or an asset class performs unusually well or unusually poorly relative to other asset classes or to historical norms. The net result of this performance is to change the plan's actual asset allocation, resulting in an overweighting in certain classes. One possible adaptation to this change is simply to do nothing—the presumption in this case is that, on average, over time, asset classes will do pretty much what we expect them to do, and asset weights will correspondingly be, on average, where we wish them to be. An alternative policy is to rebalance the plan's portfolio by selling off overperforming asset classes and increasing exposure to underperforming asset classes.

Similarly, over long periods of time, the plan's or sponsor's circumstances are likely to change. As a result, the plan's definition of acceptable levels of risk and return targets should change to reflect the new circumstances. The nature of this change cannot be generalized; suffice it to say that policy must be dynamic, and changes to policy should be anticipated and thoughtfully considered rather than made ad hoc.

Active or Passive Management?

Another key policy decision is whether to invest actively (in an attempt to beat the market) or passively (by attempting to be the market). A large part of the money management community holds itself out as capable of beating the market and relies on plan sponsors, employees investing DC assets, and others to provide the assets (and pay the fees) that they use in this attempt. Sponsors and employees who choose to use or not to use these managers should understand the issues involved.

Active investing essentially requires a belief that a market, sector, or asset may be mispriced and that investors will eventually recognize any underpricing (or overpricing) that exists and thereby bid up (or down) the prices of misvalued assets. In opposition to the view of active investing are the proponents of the efficient market hypothesis (EMH). In an efficient market, all the information available about a given asset is already reflected in the price of that asset; new information arrives randomly and, therefore, cannot be forecasted. When new information arrives, prices adjust rapidly, so there is no opportunity for earning excess returns.

Passive investment strategies presume that financial markets are efficient and cannot be easily beaten. Thus, in the passive management view, money spent trying to beat the market will be money wasted and will simply serve to reduce returns without providing any offsetting benefits. Active investment strategies, however, presume that markets—at least some markets, or some markets some of the time—are inefficient enough to provide excess returns to those who can obtain superior information or who have superior insight. To proponents of active management, these inefficiencies are exploitable opportunities that justify the expenditure of both time and money.

Passive investment strategies emphasize constructing passive portfolios that achieve exposures to asset classes that match the pension fund's risk tolerance and return objectives. In passively managed plans, the only investment decision of significance is the strategic asset allocation decision. In other words, which asset classes, or which indices, does the plan want to track? How much of the plan should be invested passively in U.S. equities versus foreign equities, U.S. and foreign bonds, and so forth. Some recent research indicates that indexing to an index such as the S&P 500 exposes the investor to high transactions costs with new listings and delistings. These costs can include the jump in price that occurs when a stock is added to the index and the decline that occurs when a stock is taken out.[1] Funds that choose to index should select broad indexes that are likely to have low turnover (few changes in composition), to reduce costs and negative price effects.

The case for passive management is supported by its low costs—passive management trades little and spends virtually no money on research—and a large number of studies indicating that professional money managers and the active management strategies they pursue regularly fail to beat appropriate benchmarks even before their fees are taken into account.

Active investment styles are likely to start with the strategic asset allocation as a point of departure, but they will not hesitate to change the asset mix or make concentrated bets within an asset class, often dramatically, in pursuit of higher returns. Active management is an information-driven philosophy that is predicated on the belief that mispriced securities can be repeatedly identified or that market trends can be successfully forecast. Thus, active management, at its extreme, uses either market-timing or security selection.

In market-timing the idea is to be 100% invested in a market segment when it is going to do well and to be 100% invested in some other segment of the market (perhaps Treasury bills) when the target asset class is expected to do poorly. Security selection involves shopping for mispriced assets in the hope that positions can be taken that, when the market recognizes the mispricing and corrects it, will result in positive excess returns.

There is disagreement among researchers and practitioners about which view is correct. Empirical research supports the efficient market hypothesis and yet takes issue with it.[2] There are practitioners who must believe in inefficiency—after all, it is their business—and there are practitioners who sincerely believe in inefficiency, who believe they can or do beat the market on a risk-adjusted basis. There also are practitioners who advocate efficient markets and, thus, passive management.

We will not settle the debate in this book. In fairness to the active management constituency, it does seem that some markets are likely to be more efficient than others, that the efficiency with which a market processes information may wax and wane, and that investors may, for possibly rational reasons (e.g., in response to regulation), "overreact" from time to time, leaving unusually profitable opportunities around for those who may find them. That said, the question investors are left with is whether investors can identify managers (or strategies) that will beat a passive portfolio of comparable risk in the future.

The bottom line is that the decision maker—the plan sponsor, the trustee, the plan administrator, or the employee—must develop a clear set of beliefs about market efficiency. On the basis of these beliefs, the decision maker may then decide whether all, or a portion, or no plan assets should be actively managed. Investment policy should reflect the beliefs that pension boards, senior management, and other fiduciaries involved in a particular plan have about the value of active or passive management. This is not a trivial issue: many theoreticians believe active management increases investment risk. That it costs more is clear; the question is whether the added costs are more than offset by higher risk-adjusted returns. In addition, investment policy should carefully define the investment styles to which the plan is willing to allocate money, so that managers know how they are to manage the money they are given. Policy should also specifically direct managers to follow the style they say they will follow. These policy parameters are essential if the fund is to communicate with and hold its managers accountable for investment management decisions.

Enhanced Indexing

In recent years, a strategy known as enhanced indexing has become widely used.[3] The goal of indexing is to match the return of a benchmark index. The goal of active management is to beat the benchmark index. The goals of enhanced indexing are to consistently outperform a benchmark index by a moderate amount and to control tracking error and the risk of significant underperformance. Thus, enhanced indexing involves both active management techniques to beat the index and techniques used in indexing in order to track the index.

Enhanced indexing attempts to use active management to generate excess returns and to control risk (in part via methods used in indexing). Enhanced indexing is not a free lunch, as excess returns come from exposure to risk.

Consider, for example, the various stock-selection-based enhanced indexing strategies. They can be characterized by broadly diversified portfolios, reliance on a stock selection process, a requirement that the manager have a way of identifying stocks within the index that are likely to either perform better than or worse than the overall index, and the use of risk-control techniques such as limits on the allowable under- or overweighting of individual stocks and limits on portfolio exposures to factor and industry or sector weights.

There are also synthetic enhanced index strategies. These strategies do not try to select stocks within the index being tracked. Instead, they use futures, options, or stock index swaps to establish a position in the index. Synthetic strategies are based on a belief that individual stocks are efficiently priced, but that there are pricing inefficiencies and structural factors that exist outside the individual stocks and that can be exploited, leading to the index return plus something more.

Risk control is a central feature of both selection-based and synthetic enhanced indexing strategies. It is achieved by diversification and limits on the risk exposures taken—sector and industry weights, fundamental factors, and so forth are subject to limits. Proponents of enhanced indexing argue that, regardless of an investor's beliefs on market efficiency, the focus on risk control in these strategies can improve the likelihood of success and reduce the risk of significant underperformance. Opponents argue that enhanced indexing is simply marketing.

Investment Style

The money management industry that serves pension funds and other investors is especially adept at product differentiation. Thus, pension plan policy might also address what are considered stylistic issues. Unfortunately, there is little agreement among practitioners as to what the phrase "investment style" means. Academics have come to define style as an essentially passive preference or expertise in some market sector, usually a subset of a larger investment class. For example, small capitalization stocks are a subset of the stock universe, and thus, investing in them rather than in the stock market as a whole offers a particular investment style. We use this preference for a subset as our definition. The various styles that are offered may be pursued passively (perhaps style specialization is warranted because of information or scale economies) or actively (perhaps by pursuing security selection within a market sector).

There are at least five distinct active equity disciplines, philosophies, or styles; they are growth, income, value, market capitalization, and quality (special situations, turnarounds). International or foreign equities offer a sixth style and can, of course, be broken down into the same categories, as can developed and emerging markets. Active bond management styles can be broken down into a true trading approach, in which the managers are free to select bonds that are believed to be under- or overvalued. Another style is to use a structured bond portfolio in which the manager adjusts the portfolio in response to changing market conditions (e.g., extending the portfolio's duration when interest rates are expected to fall). As with equities, with trading or structured bond portfolios, there are domestic and international versions. If we then add in special categories of investment assets such as leveraged buyout funds, real estate funds, venture capital funds, and perhaps even commodities and managed futures (not to mention market-neutral strategies), a pension sponsor faces the daunting task of evaluating not only the relatively straightforward active versus passive conundrum but also which, if any, of the many investment philosophies might be appropriate for the DB fund or for DC portfolios. Empirical evidence, quantitative modeling, and informed intuition are all helpful in identifying the investment styles that are likely to be appropriate in the future.

Management Fees

Active management fees typically run around fifty basis points, whereas passive fees for funds that hold portfolios that correlate highly with broad-based market indexes (such as the S&P 500 Stock Index) may be two to ten basis points. Mutual funds and other funds used in employee-directed DC plans have somewhat higher fees, with typical active equity fund expense ratios averaging around one hundred basis points and index funds charging twenty to forty basis points.

Fee differentials can be substantial over long periods of time, and as long-term investors, pension plans should be sensitive to the erosion of value that is associated with higher fees. Sensible policy requires fees that are not excessive and that are justified in terms of the benefits the plan receives. Sponsors of DB plans should care about fees because excessive fees will require higher contributions. Sponsors of DC plans should also care about fees because excessive fees will erode accumulations. Finally, sponsors should be concerned that fees that are too high will indicate that the appropriate due diligence was not performed.

Derivatives

One element of policy that has become important since the 1980s is establishing guidelines for the use of derivatives. In spite of a spate of bad publicity resulting from the huge investment losses incurred by such diverse organizations as Orange County, Procter and Gamble, and other investors/derivatives users, derivatives have a legitimate role to play in pension fund management. However, derivatives can be misused, particularly by those who do not understand the nature of the contracts into which they are entering or the way in which positions resulting from these contracts can create exposures to unusually high or magnified levels of risk.

In general, ERISA guidelines and other regulatory constraints discourage using derivatives for speculative purposes. Thus, pension plan policy must require an understanding of the payoff structures and risk/return profiles of the contracts that are being used; the policy must also specify whether it is appropriate to use derivatives in hedging or return-enhancement risk-management activities. Policy should be clear on when and for what purposes derivatives may be used and how derivative exposures will be monitored (keeping in mind that for hedging strategies using derivatives, it is the net exposure that must be monitored).

Operational Policy Issues

There are a number of operational policy areas that should be addressed in the plan's written policy statement. These directly address how the plan will do certain things.

Asset Allocation. Strategic asset allocation is the cornerstone of the operational side of investment policy. As such, it should be clearly defined in terms of broad exposures to the major asset classes as well as in terms acceptable deviations from target weights and of maximum cumulative exposures to subclasses such as small capitalization stocks, nondomestic issuers, and venture capital or special situations. Acceptable levels of asset quality and the responses required for maintaining quality levels should be defined (e.g., whether all fixed-income investments should be investment grade, and what should be done if a security's quality rating falls below the acceptable level). The allocation among active and passive management should be defined.

Rebalancing. When and under what circumstances asset rebalancing will occur or will be permitted must be specified. For example, will trading be undertaken for the sole purpose of restoring the target asset allocations if market action results in a departure from target weights outside of a 5% range (absolute)? How often should such rebalancing occur—once a year under normal circumstances? May rebalancing be achieved through futures or options contracting? May some managers attempt tactical or insured asset allocation? If so, when and how?

Asset Management. Policy should be clear about what assets will be managed by external money managers and in what amounts within each investment category. The criteria for selecting external money managers should be explicit and may include factors such as what assets to include under a particular manager's control, the manager's years in business, and compliance with performance-reporting guidelines such as the Association for Investment Management and Research (AIMR) Global Investment Performance Standards. Further, it should be clear how and how frequently the fund's money managers will be evaluated and how and for what reasons managers will be dismissed (e.g., failure to conform to policy).

Use of Soft Dollars. Should services or products required by the fund be purchased for cash or through directed commissions? Some plans have moved away from using soft dollars (i.e., credits granted in return for directing trades to a specific broker/dealer), believing they are not an efficient way to purchase research and additional services and that managers should be trying to trade at the best available price. Others have established policies to make better use of soft dollars. Still others have implemented commission-recapture programs that return commission dollars to the plan. Regardless of the sponsor's preferences, the fund should articulate its position on the use of soft dollars or directed commissions. There are two issues that plan policy should address: whether directed commissions are permitted, and if they are permitted, who controls them and the benefits provided.

Proxy Voting. Pension funds should direct their equity money managers on how they should vote on issues brought by portfolio companies to their shareholders. This is a fiduciary obligation to the beneficiaries of the pension plans. Accordingly, funds should always direct that its proxy votes be cast in favor of those proposals that are most likely to increase the stock price of the affected companies.

CONCLUSION

Pension investment policy should be articulated in a written set of guidelines designed to resolve many complex, and at times contradictory, issues. These written policies can serve as a guide for prudent decision making. Policy must start at the top: good policy or not, whatever investment policies are in place (as well as those that are not) will affect the financial performance of both sponsors and the pension plans they provide.

The most important of the strategic policies of a pension plan to be determined is that of the plan's (or portfolio's) tolerance for risk. This cannot be overemphasized. Many asset managers get caught up in the quest for return, forgetting that the capital markets allocate return on the basis of the exposure taken to risk. This can be catastrophic, as can be taking too little risk and overburdening the sponsor in having to make up the foregone return or, in the case of the individual employee, finding that too little has been accumulated to permit the type of retirement envisioned in earlier days. Policy should guide decision makers in dealing with these matters by specifying clearly how much risk is acceptable or necessary.

7

The Asset Allocation Decision

A pension plan's investment policy is put in place by allocating plan assets among available investment asset classes. This chapter starts by discussing asset allocation generally. It then presents aggregate data on how pension funds actually allocate assets. Finally, the chapter discusses the primary asset classes and their investment characteristics.

ASSET CLASSES

Broadly, the major asset classes consist of equities (foreign and domestic publicly traded stock in developed countries), bonds (foreign and domestic publicly traded bonds and private placements), cash (short-term, interest-bearing instruments), and private market equity investments such as venture capital and real estate. This list can be augmented with more exotic asset categories such as common stock investments in the firms of developing countries, investments in hedge funds, and commodities (including gold, farmland, commercial forest land, and managed futures pools). Each of these assets has been found by at least one analyst to be a worthwhile addition to institutional portfolios. Although it is an intriguing area, this chapter does not dwell on allocations to each of these asset categories for a pension portfolio; instead, for the most part this chapter considers the asset allocation decision on a broader scale.

To be useful, the concept of an asset class requires that a small number of asset classes are able to explain a substantial proportion of the variance in returns. In addition, the classes used should have security-specific returns that are uncorrelated, have beta values that are measurable, and have returns that are measurable. There should be a low-cost index fund that could be formed within each class. Finally, the user should be able to represent the overall market through the combination of asset classes thus defined.[1]

To start, it is useful to compare returns of common equity, bonds, and inflation over a long period. For the period from 1900 to 2000, U.S. equity returned about 12% per year, U.S. bonds returned about 5% per year, and U.S. inflation averaged about 3% per year.[2] These long-run figures provide the basic insight that stocks have historically outperformed bonds. However, matching that insight on returns is a matching insight on risk: stocks have also been riskier than bonds over the long term. For 1900 to 2000, the standard deviation of equity has been about 20%.

Table 7.1 focuses on the United States experience over the last twenty-two years, from 1980 to 2002. The period considered in table 7.1 ends with the two-year bear market of 2001 and 2002. Even including this bear market, however, common stock returned about 16% per year.

For the United States, over the period 1926–2002, the stocks of large companies[3]

- provided an average annual return of 12.2% with a standard deviation of 20.5%,
- had a high annual return of 54.0% (in 1933) and a low annual return of −43.3% (in 1931),
- had a high five-year return of 28.6% (annual) (1995–1999) and a low five-year return of −12.5% (1928–1932), and
- had a high ten-year return of 20.1% (1949–1958) and a low ten-year return of −0.9% (1929–1938).

Short-run returns may not match long-run averages, or long-run expectations. Returns from year to year can be quite variable. Indeed, in a sufficiently short time frame, low-risk assets could outperform high-risk assets, and in any single year, any of the asset classes could be the best (or worst) in providing returns. For example, in the ten-year period between 1993 and 2002, large capitalization stocks outperformed bonds each of the first seven years. In the bear-market final three years, however, bonds significantly outperformed stocks, with annual returns of 11.6%, 8.4%, and 10.3%, compared with stock returns of −9.1%, −11.9%, and −22.0%.[4]

Table 7.1 United States Asset Class Performance: 1980–2002

Asset Class	Average Annual Rate of Return (arithmetic mean; %)	Standard Deviation of Returns (%)
Large-company stocks	15.9	15.1
Small-company stocks	16.2	17.9
Corporate bonds	10.9	9.7
Government bonds	9.9	7.2
Treasury bills	7.4	3.4

Source: Reilly and Wright (forthcoming). Large-company stocks measured by the S&P 500. Small-company stocks measured by Ibbotson Small Cap. Corporate bonds and government bonds measured by corresponding Lehman Brothers index. For Treasury bills, six-month bills are used.

Table 7.2 Public Pension Plan Asset Allocations (Fiscal Year 2000)

	Amount (billions)	Percentage of Total (dollar weighted)
Short-term securities	$34.9	2.2
Domestic stocks	$713.7	45.0
Domestic bonds	$414.0	26.1
Real estate mortgages	$12.7	0.8
Real estate equities	$63.4	4.0
International equities	$242.7	15.3
International fixed-income	$28.5	1.8
Other	$76.1	4.8
Total	$1,586.1	100

Source: Harris (2002).

Pension managers should be familiar with the historical data on asset-class returns, but a couple of qualifications are also necessary. First, the return-generating factors, such as technology and relative price levels, need not be the same in the future as they have been in the past. Returns and risks change over time, and they may differ from period to period.

Second, a more complete picture of the asset classes would include the co-variance between each pair of classes and a breakdown of the income versus capital change components of the total returns shown. There are several sources of this data (e.g., Ibbotson Associates), so we will not replicate the data here. Suffice it to say that the more familiar one is with the data, the easier it is to use them in making asset allocation decisions.

A Look at Pension Fund Assets

In what asset classes do pension funds invest? Tables 7.2 through 7.4 offer some answers. Table 7.2 shows asset allocations for public plans, table 7.3 covers private DB plans, and table 7.4 covers private DC plans.

From the data shown in the tables, it is clear that pensions invest heavily in stocks and bonds. Stocks make up about 60% of plan assets for public plans,

Table 7.3 Pension Asset Allocations for Private Trusteed Defined Benefit Plans (Third Quarter 2002)

	Total Assets (billions)	Percentage of Total
Equity	$655	41.8
Bonds	$435	27.8
Cash items	$158	10.1
Other	$319	20.4

Source: Data from Employee Benefit Research Institute (2003, p. 9).

Table 7.4 Asset Allocation for Defined Contribution Plans

Company stock fund	35.2%
Stable value fund	12.8%
Actively managed domestic equity	18.9%
Actively managed international equity	2.2%
Indexed domestic equity	10.7%
Indexed international equity	0.2%
Actively managed domestic bond fund	2.3%
Indexed domestic bond fund	0.6%
Technology sector fund	0.2%
Balanced stock/bond fund	6.8%
Cash equivalents	5.1%
Other	4.9%

Source: Profit Sharing and 401(k) Council of America (2003).

and bonds make up 25% to 30% of plan assets for both public plans and private DB plans. DC plans seem to have a greater percentage invested in equities. The striking difference for DC plans is the heavy weighting on company stock. In 2001, over one third of DC plan assets were held in company stock. We will discuss this phenomenon in Chapter 12.

Many plans are also using derivatives to enhance returns, reduce risk, or both. Further, as described in Appendix B, many pensions are increasing their allocations to international securities.

Primary Asset Classes

Why should a pension plan invest in stocks? Or in bonds? Why consider real estate? To answer these and related questions, it is necessary to understand the characteristics of the major asset classes used by pension funds.

Stocks

Common stocks represent the basic risk capital of an economy. As such, their returns are high, on average, and volatile. Some, but not all, of the volatility of individual stocks can be reduced by diversification. Thus, the high returns characteristic of stocks take the form of a premium for bearing the remaining risk.

There are two main reasons to invest in stocks. First, expected capital appreciation is generally high, so over long periods, exposure to stocks should result in the growth of plan assets. This may result in reducing future sponsor contributions or increasing payouts to beneficiaries. Second, the equity risk premium associated with stocks has historically been an effective counter to the effects of inflation. Over long periods, even modest inflation rates can destroy significant real value. The equity risk premium can offset this. This is not to say that stocks do well in times of unanticipated high or increasing inflation: they often do not. The reality is that stock returns lag behind inflation by several years. Nor can it be said that stocks are a good short-term inflation hedge: the inflation-adjusted correlation of large capitalization stock returns with inflation has been −0.21, whereas that of small capitalization stocks has been −0.08.[5] Such correlations would not permit short-term hedging. However, on average, over long periods of time, the equity risk premium earned from exposure to stocks has been sufficient to offset the effects of inflation and still provide a real rate of return.

Some analysts have said that it is a puzzle that the equity risk premium has been as high as it has been historically; that is, why has the return on stocks been approximately double the return on bonds?[6] Arnott and Bernstein argue that the long-term equity risk premium is about half the observed rate, and they say it could even be zero.[7] However, Ibbotson and Chen argue that the equity risk premium is about 6%.[8]

As Mehra observes, the equity premium may be defined as the observed, realized premium of stocks over bonds. This premium appears to have stayed fairly consistent over long time periods. The expected short-term premium, however, can be quite volatile. In discussing the equity risk premium, then, it is essential to define whether one is trying to estimate the long-term premium or a shorter-term premium.[9]

There is a conventional wisdom that holds that stocks are not risky in the long run. This is because the dispersion of annual rates of return is lower for long time periods than for short time periods. That is, rates of return over ten-year periods are less dispersed than rates of return over three-year periods. However, some authorities have argued that it is a fallacy that stocks are less risky in the long run. For example, Bodie argues that if stocks are less risky over long periods, the price of a put option on an index such as the S&P 500 (an index that can be used to insure against a loss in large company stocks) should be lower for a longer time to expiration. However, he suggests this is not the case.[10] Paul Samuelson observes also that simply predicting future success on the basis of historical success may not capture the true riskiness of stocks. Although a long time provides more time to recover from poor performance, it also provides more time to encounter poor performance.[11] Intuition suggests that high returns, however, come from exposure to high risk, so we caution against naively taking the view that time somehow eliminates the possibility of adverse outcomes.

The volatility of individual stocks appears to have risen substantially from the 1960s to the 1990s. To eliminate nonmarket risk (idiosyncratic risk) and achieve diversification, an investor must hold many more stocks than before. The benchmark used to be 15 to 20 stocks to achieve diversification. The higher current volatility indicates that portfolios with as many as 50 stocks may still have significant levels of nonmarket risk.[12]

Bonds

Bonds and other fixed-income investments are the most important alternative to stocks. A distinguishable characteristic of bonds is that they produce an income stream defined by the indenture agreement or contract. This income stream has two very attractive aspects for pension plans. First, it addresses any income or liquidity needs the plan has by producing income that can be used to meet plan spending requirements. Second, the sensitivity of bonds to interest rates and inflation can be used to match (or manage) the interest rate sensitivity of DB plan liabilities and thus to reduce or eliminate the volatility of the plan surplus.

One cautionary note is appropriate for bonds. The recent performance record for bonds since the early 1980s probably overstates a reasonable long-run expectation. This is because interest rates in the United States were quite high in the early 1980s (in 1981, the long Treasury bond rate was nearly 14%) but fell steadily (with occasional spikes) through 1993 (when the long Treasury bond rate was around 6.6%). In a declining interest rate environment, bonds do especially well, producing capital gains as well as interest income. However, in periods of accelerating inflation, bond investors suffer a great deal. Furthermore, when long-term interest rates are volatile (such as from 1993 through 1996), there are wide swings in bond returns. Finally, with very low interest rates (as from 2001 to early 2003), one should be very careful not to extrapolate high future returns.

Cash

Most pension funds hold some cash. More accurately, they invest in high-grade, short-term debt securities (typically with maturities of less than one year)—Treasury bills, commercial paper, and so forth. They invest this way to obtain liquidity and as a temporary parking place for funds that are destined to be invested in longer-term assets.

In many respects, cash is a residual. Pension plans for companies or organizations with young workforces and few retirees need little cash and should be careful about letting cash balances build up, as cash returns generally just match inflation instead of beating it. Pension plans for organizations with older workforces and many retirees may need more liquidity, but they may be able to address this need through income-producing assets such as bonds.

Cash offers the lowest return, on average, of any of the asset classes. Thus, it creates a drag on portfolio returns that is justifiable only if there is a pressing need for liquidity that cannot be met by investment income or contributions. Managers of portions of the pension plan's assets must be monitored to make certain they are not maintaining excessive cash balances. Overall, the reduction in returns attributable to cash can be minimized by using derivatives to create effective exposures to other asset classes.

Real Estate

The case for real estate in a pension portfolio is built on improving portfolio diversification and an apparently strong track record of high-return, low-volatility performance. For the period 1979 to 1998, the annual return on the National Council of Real Estate Investment Fiduciaries (NCREIF) Property Index (a direct real estate equity investment index) was 9.0%.[13]

Real estate differs from publicly traded stocks and bonds in that it is generally illiquid. This lack of liquidity may mean that the realizable value of real estate is substantially below its appraisal value. Further, there is a nontrivial problem in measuring and assessing real estate returns and volatilities. Because there are relatively few market transactions to use in computing returns and standard deviations, appraisals frequently are used in data series. Appraisals introduce a smoothing bias that may make it seem as though historical returns are higher and volatilities lower than they actually may have been. Moreover, real estate transaction costs are high relative to those of stocks and bonds; these costs are not incorporated into most data series that purport to measure real estate performance.

There are some other issues to consider when investing in real estate. Real estate is quite heterogeneous. Some real properties, if their leases are indexed to inflation, offer inflation-hedging possibilities. Other properties, with long-term, fixed-payment leases, look and behave a lot like bonds. Properties in some areas can be appreciating rapidly at the same time that those in other areas are depreciating. Because the market for real estate is quite segmented, diversification across region, economic exposure, and property type is especially important.

Real estate offers a variety of cash-flow and interest-rate sensitivities, degrees of equity participations, and leverage. Thus, it offers pension funds the opportunity to customize their overall asset pool to meet the structure of the liabilities of the funds better. Investments in real estate may be made through direct participations, comingled real estate funds (CREFs), or real estate investment trusts (REITs). The first requires an expertise few pension funds have, and CREFs can be surprisingly illiquid as investors frequently must wait a considerable time to exit positions. REITs offer a viable alternative, with the advantage of greater liquidity because they are actively traded on securities markets. REITs suffered from excessive borrowing and subsequent poor performance in the 1970s, but they have come back into favor with many investors.

International Securities

There is evidence that adding international stocks and bonds to a basic domestic stock/bond/cash portfolio provides a better risk/return profile. There also is evidence that correlations among various markets have increased substantially in recent years. This indicates that the attractive diversification benefits of the 1970s and 1980s may have dissipated, at least somewhat. Exposures to international securities also introduce an exchange rate effect.

International investing may offer more opportunities for excess returns through active investment management because some foreign markets are less informationally or institutionally efficient than U.S. markets. Managers who believe these opportunities exist may search for those markets that offer potentially higher risk-adjusted returns. However, pension funds should beware of the possibility of stress events such as the Russian financial crisis of 1998. An unforeseen event in foreign security or currency markets can lead to changing asset valuations that are many standard deviations away from typical experience. (Appendix B offers further discussion on international investing.)

Derivatives

Financial contracts that derive their value from the value of an underlying asset, index, or formula may not be an asset class per se, but they are clearly an important and distinct part of the investment landscape. Although pension plans have not used derivatives extensively in the past, more plans are doing so, and more will do so in the future.

The most attractive aspect of calls, puts, futures, swaps, and other more exotic contracts is that these contracts offer plan sponsors a variety of ways to adjust the risk/return profiles of their portfolios in a cost-efficient manner. This is because an increased or decreased exposure to other asset classes (or other risks) can be attained fairly inexpensively through derivative contracting, whereas obtaining the same change in exposure through buying or selling the actual stocks and bonds themselves generally will be much more costly.

There are three unfortunate aspects of derivative securities. First, they are very difficult to understand unless one is well versed in the specifics of their payoff structures and valuation. These structures and valuation methods can require a high degree of technical expertise to properly evaluate. Second, large losses incurred by such diverse entities as Long Term Capital Management, Barings Bank, Procter and Gamble, and Orange County, California, have made derivatives politically unattractive. Third, when evaluated independent of the total portfolios of which they are a part, they can easily appear to be imprudent investments because of their high volatility. All these features make many investors reluctant to consider using derivative securities when they should. (Chapter 17 provides a more detailed examination of derivatives and how they should be used in managing pension fund assets.)

Treasury Inflation-Protected Securities

In 1997, the U.S. Treasury began issuing Treasury Inflation-Protected Securities (TIPS). TIPS are structured so that the return a TIPS investor receives is tied to the inflation rate—specifically, the return is tied to the Consumer Price Index. In 2001 a private-sector group, The Treasury's Borrowing Advisory Committee, recommended that the government stop issuing TIPS. The group argued that TIPS were a costly means for the government to borrow. However, other bond dealers and institutional investors argued for continuing the program.[14]

As of 2003, the Treasury seems committed to continue issuing TIPS. It is expected to issue about $20 billion in TIPS in 2003 and $30 billion in 2004.[15] Work by Malkiel indicates that the correlation between TIPS and the S&P 500 is zero to negative, meaning that TIPS should be an excellent diversifier. In addition, Malkiel's work indicates that when inflation accelerates, TIPS are negatively correlated to bonds, whereas bonds and stocks are positively correlated. If inflation accelerates, stocks and bonds are likely to perform poorly, and TIPS should perform well.[16]

Hedge Funds

Many pension funds have been attracted to so-called "hedge funds" in search for high returns. The definition of hedge fund is somewhat controversial. Originally, "hedge fund" referred to privately organized funds that used leverage to reduce exposure to market movements. Now, however, the term refers more broadly to any privately organized fund that uses leverage to a significant extent. Thus, hedge funds today may be significantly exposed to market risk.[17]

One of the advantages of hedge funds is that they are privately organized, and hence, they have less reporting requirements. Hedge funds are thus able to keep their operations and their holdings private—they do not have to share their ideas with the public. For pension funds, however, this can lead to conflict if pension managers attempt to determine how their hedge fund investments are being used. In addition, public pension funds in particular may have strict reporting requirements—potentially negating the privacy desired by the hedge fund.

Estimating returns and risk for hedge funds is problematic both because of hedge fund privacy and because of the variety of different investment methodologies within the umbrella of hedge funds. One study found that during the 1990s, hedge funds returned about 14.2% per year, compared with 18.8% for the S&P 500 index. Of course, this period included the year 1998, which was a difficult year for hedge funds and included the near collapse of LongTerm Capital Management.[18]

CONCLUSION

The broad asset allocation decision—what portion of a pension fund's assets should be allocated to stocks, to bonds, and to cash—is the single most important investment policy parameter that senior management, trustees, and other members of the sponsor's leadership team must determine. The decision requires an understanding of what each asset class brings to the fund, knowledge of how each has performed historically, and expectations for how each might perform in the future. It requires that the decision makers understand the primary alternatives to a simple buy-and-hold implementation of whatever allocation is chosen and how these alternatives are likely to perform under various types of markets. It also requires a commitment to review the asset mix of the total asset pool regularly to see whether it still conforms to the asset weights that have been chosen.

PART II

Defined Benefit Plans

8

The Integrated Approach to Managing Defined Benefit Plans

A DB plan is a complex organism that involves a sponsor, a group of beneficiaries, a liability, and an asset pool. Management of any one component is likely to affect the others. As a result, DB decision makers must attempt to integrate across all components to ensure optimal results (see figure 8.1)

Investment policy is, as are most policies, rooted in philosophical concepts. Should sponsor assets and plan assets be managed as if they were separate? Can the asset pool be managed effectively without considering the liability? In this chapter, we answer these questions.

This chapter has two sections. The first examines the policy implications of managing a DB plan as a separate entity or as an entity that is integrated into the sponsoring organization. The second section shows how the pension liability affects investment policy and how differing views on the nature of the labor market lead to different investment policies.

PENSION PLANS AND THEIR SPONSORS: SEPARATE OR INTEGRATED?

Should management of the pension plan be integrated with the management of the sponsoring organization? Some pension funds are run as entities completely separate from the sponsoring organization; others are managed as if an integral part of the sponsor. The implications are significant.

In DB plans, beneficiaries expect that plan sponsors will make up any shortfalls in pension assets. If assets are less than liabilities, the sponsor is expected to contribute enough cash to the plan to eliminate the gap. One could therefore argue that the pension plan and the sponsor are integrated and should be managed that way. This view is not without its critics, however. Some analysts argue that the economic exposures of a sponsoring organization ought not be considered when deciding on pension plan policy. To use a balance sheet analogy, they argue that the balance sheet of the plan and that of the sponsor should be completely separate. Not uncommonly, the proponents of a separate-balance-

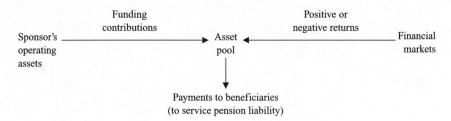

Figure 8.1 DB Plans Are a System

sheet approach worry that there may be a misappropriation of pension assets or similar breach of fiduciary duty if the two are not separated.

Evidence on Integrating the Management of Pension Plans with Sponsors

The interaction between the sponsor and the pension plan can most easily be seen by examining private plans. Before ERISA, private pension funds and their sponsoring corporations were more distinct. A firm could terminate its pension plan, and it was just "too bad" if the pension assets were insufficient.

What prevented most firms from behaving in this manner—that is, promising benefits and then not delivering them—was that sooner or later, potential employees would insist on compensation for any loss in expected pension benefits. In short, plan sponsors could recontract with employees only once, and then employees would catch on and not let the sponsors get away with it again. The incremental compensation costs could exceed the amount saved by reneging on the original pension promise. Accordingly, very few firms abused employees in this way.

Several firms did do so, however—notably the old Studebaker Corporation, which left thousands of retirees high and dry. This instance was such a major abuse that, coupled with much union pressure, it led to the passage of the ERISA and the establishment of the PBGC. Under ERISA, unfunded pension claims have a status in bankruptcy equal to that of tax liens. Although this claim on sponsor assets is limited to a portion of net worth, what is relevant here is that the pension plan can lay claim to other assets of the corporation. If pension plans have this claim in bankruptcy, it is not difficult to make the case that, conceptually at least, there is a claim on or interaction with the sponsor's assets on an ongoing basis. Further, in the absence of ERISA, formal and informal contracting and employee welfare concerns can at least partially extend this concept to public funds.[1]

There is strong evidence that private pension plan sponsors behave as if the pension plan is part of the overall corporation. This has important implications for pension fund asset management and funding decisions. For instance, the actual allocation of pension plan assets between stocks and bonds has been related to the riskiness of the sponsoring corporation and the corporation's own tax status. In addition, the level of funding of the plan has been connected to the financial strength of the firm: the stronger the firm, the greater the funding.[2] No doubt this is in part because of the tax deductibility of pension contributions: because the pension fund would have to be funded sooner or later, strong corporations chose to do it earlier so as to capture the tax deduction associated with pension contributions.

In general, however, these findings indicate that corporate managers make pension plan decisions within the broader context of the financial position and policies of the entire corporation; that is, the operating aspects of the business influence pension decisions such as how much to contribute to the plan. One can infer that other decisions—for example, the type and amount of assets to hold in the pension fund's asset pool—also are integrated.

It is also apparent that investors view the pension plan as an integral part of the corporation. For instance, the total market value of a corporation—its bonds and stocks—is diminished when it has unfunded pension obligations.[3] In addition, the value of a firm's common stock reflects the firm's unfunded pension obligation and is lower than it would be if the firm had no unfunded pension obligation.[4]

Ownership of Excess Assets

Who can claim "ownership" of any excess of plan assets over plan liabilities? One view is that the sponsor is the owner of excess assets. After all, if a plan were terminated, the sponsor would claim the residual after satisfying all the plan liabilities (including any taxes). Ownership rights can be claimed in other ways as well. If the sponsor "owns" excess assets, this supports an integrated approach to pension management.

In general, an "owner" is the person who receives the rewards from risks taken. In a DB plan, beneficiaries have a fixed claim. They do not gain from strong investment performance except to the extent that a large surplus makes their claim less risky. In contrast, a large surplus could lead to much lower sponsor contributions. In this case, however, the surplus is likely to be reduced over time, increasing the plan's risk. Thus, for both public and private plans, the economic link between excess assets and contributions indicates that the better claim to excess assets is that of the sponsor.

By similar reasoning, an organization's investment policy governing pension fund diversification might consider the pension plan plus the claim the plan holds on the sponsor's cash flows and assets. The combined exposure could be viewed as a well-diversified portfolio, even if the pension portfolio, when considered alone, is not. Pursuing such ideas on asset choice might, in extreme cases, actually lead a sponsor to hold in its pension portfolio all bonds or all stocks, depending on the riskiness of the plan sponsor itself. These extreme prescriptions for portfolios could leave very risky sponsors holding a portfolio of risky pension plan assets, say all stocks, and leave safe sponsors holding very safe pension plan assets, such as bonds.

According to the view that excess assets belong to the sponsor rather than to the beneficiaries, the sponsor's attitude toward the surplus will, to a very large extent, determine the plan's risk tolerance and, hence, guide its selection of return targets. For example, if plan sponsors behave as if their shareholders or taxpayers own excess plan assets, they may be willing to assume more risk in the pension plan than they would otherwise to pursue a higher return and, subsequently, lower future contributions.

However, sponsors who believe the pension plan ought to be managed solely for the welfare of the participants may try to minimize the chance that the promised benefits will not materialize. They may aggressively pursue return, though, in the hopes of being able to grant higher benefits to beneficiaries later.

Setting pension plan policy with respect to who "owns" the surplus is challenging. The nature of the regulations to which pension plans are subject is different from that to which the sponsor may be subject. Further, the economic interests of the sponsor and plan beneficiaries are not likely to be the same. Sponsors want lower and predictable funding costs, and beneficiaries want higher benefits and a high likelihood of those benefits materializing.[5] Resolution of this conflict can be achieved only through informed mutual agreement or, more appropriately, through contracting a pension deal that addresses these issues. To resolve these issues, it is necessary to understand the nature of the pension liability and something of the interaction between plan liabilities and assets. This in turn helps define the appropriate relationship between the sponsor's financial well-being and the financial health of the pension plan.

PENSION LIABILITIES AND INVESTMENT POLICY

The term "funding adequacy" refers to the extent to which pension assets are sufficient to cover or offset pension liabilities. If, as noted earlier, the market value of plan assets is less than the present value of plan liabilities, the plan is said to be underfunded; if the market value exceeds the present value of plan liabilities, the plan is said to be overfunded. The adequacy of funding is affected by two broad sets of policy-level decisions made by plan sponsors: the policies governing contributions from the sponsor and the policies governing the investment of plan assets. The latter are addressed in detail later in Chapter 9. The former are addressed here.

In DC plans, the value of the pension liability always equals the value of the pension plan assets. That is the nature of the DC plan. The rewards of superior investment results and the risks of inferior results theoretically are borne entirely by the plan beneficiary. Moreover, because pension assets accumulate as money is contributed to the plan, and they rise or fall as the value of pension assets rises or falls, the assets may or may not be sufficient to cover planned retirement expenditure. If plan accumulations are not sufficient, individuals must adjust their retirement plans—the plan liabilities—without recourse to the sponsor. Accordingly, there is no mystery about the measurement of the pension liability in a DC plan.

Understanding and measuring pension liability for a DB plan, in contrast, poses several conceptual as well as many practical problems. These problems must be understood to set sensible policy.

Funding Adequacy

A central element of investment policy is the adequacy of plan funding—the degree to which pension assets are sufficient to meet plan liabilities. How well funded are pension plans in general?

Pension plan funding varies over time depending on both investment returns (which affect pension assets) and interest rates (which affect the discount rate used for valuing pension liabilities). At the end of 1999, DB plans for the plans for the companies in the S&P 500 were overfunded in aggregate by $251 billion. As a result of falling interest rates and the declining stock market, by the end of 2002, the plans were underfunded by $206 billion.[6] State retirement plans have also shown declines. For state retirement systems, the ratio of assets to liabilities declined from 116% in 2000 to 107% in 2001.[7]

One encounters different estimates of over- or underfunding, and one reason for the discrepancy is that there are several measures of a pension plan's liability. Pension liabilities may be alternatively measured as

- the present value of vested benefits (those earned by employees who will retain them even if they leave the organization),
- the present value of earned benefits vested and not vested,
- the present value of earned benefits also taking into account estimated salary increases, and
- the present value of all future benefits, including the effect of future years of employment.[8]

Liability estimates, then, can depend on a variety of inputs: employee turnover, salary increases, life expectancies, growth in the number and demographics of the pool of eligible employees, and so forth. The second measure above is referred to as the Accumulated Benefit Obligation, or ABO. The third measure is the Projected Benefit Obligation, or PBO.

In setting investment policy, it is necessary to understand how regulation affects funding adequacy. Public DB plans are not required to have a large pool of assets supporting their DB pension obligations. They are not bound by ERISA to protect their pension obligations with a reservoir of capital. They can make payments on a pay-as-you-go basis unless, of course, some state or local statute or union contract precludes such behavior. State or local statutes requiring a specific level of funding are rare, however, because it is in the interest of mobile taxpayers who can move from state to state to avoid advance-funding pension plans to keep current taxes low. If anything, a contractual or legal requirement that there be a reservoir of assets out of which pension obligations may be paid would arise most likely either as a consequence of collective bargaining arrangements between government entities and the relevant public employee unions, or from politically motivated concerns having to do with the welfare of public employees.

Because corporate pension plans and multiemployer plans that are governed by the Taft–Hartley Act are subject to the ERISA statutes, they are not permitted to run their pension plans on a pay-as-you-go basis. That is, they cannot rely on their current pension contributions to meet current obligations. Rather, there must be a pool of assets to which contributions are made and from which obligations are drawn. For this pool to be sufficient to fund the total pension liability (the fourth of the measures above), it would, under most circumstances, be many times the size of the current obligation.

To determine whether the asset pool is sufficient to ensure the safety and the security of timely pension payments now and in the future, the size of the asset reservoir should be measured so that it can be compared with the present value of the liability. Fortunately, the value of most pension assets can easily be measured, and the measured values should be fairly close to true values—even for assets for which the values of which can be hard to measure. Differences between measured values and true values could arise only because of the difficulty of estimating the value of illiquid pension assets, such as real estate or complex derivatives. Even here, however, the gap between true and estimated value should never be too great. Further, it is clear that the financial health of a pension plan is jointly affected by the amount of assets owned by the plan relative to the magnitude of the plan's liability, whatever it is.

Plan Liabilities and Labor Contracts

Plan liabilities are related to the nature of the employment contract between the plan sponsor and the employee. Labor contracts may be considered within the context of either spot or multiperiod implicit contractual markets. If sponsor and employee agree that their relationship can best be viewed as a spot contract, then the true pension liability should equal only the present value of vested, accrued pension payments as of the date of the valuation. The pension liability is that which must be paid to the employee when he or she retires if the employee immediately leaves for other employment. However, if the unspoken or implicit contract between the sponsor and the employee is mutually understood to be long term in nature, then the appropriate measure of the pension liability is the current value of accrued benefits plus those that will be accrued in the future as the employee continues to work for the sponsor and as the sponsor continues to raise the employee's salary by giving promotions, merit raises, and cost-of-living adjustments. Similarly, if the sponsor sees itself as a going concern and has no agreement with employees that would allow it to alter its previous plan, then a liability measure reflecting this ongoing relationship is justified. Again, this is not a straightforward issue.

If an employee receives total compensation in every period equal to the exact marginal value of his or her effort over the period—that is, if wages plus pension accrual equal marginal value product—then the arrangement is consistent with a spot labor market. After each period, neither the worker nor the firm owes the other anything. Because the firm can terminate the pension plan at nearly any time, its pension liabilities are really only those that have already been accrued.[9] This is certainly the case when employees have DC pension plans, and it is also consistent with cash balance plans, in which wages plus the amount contributed to the plan equal the value delivered by the employee. In these plans, there is no trace of an implicit contract in the employment arrangement.

In a multiperiod labor market, the books are not cleared after each period. There is a carryover from period to period, and both employee and employer trust each other to "make good" later on today's under- or overcompensation. As the relationship goes forward, one or the other party may owe the other something at the close of each period. Even when there is no explicit contract extending over several periods, there is nonetheless an implicit one. Both worker and employer implicitly understand that in any period the books may not balance, but over the course of a career they will, much as over a long enough time period, accrual accounting and cash accounting tend to converge.

If the implicit contract theory is valid, one would expect to see salary plus accrued pension benefits that are less than the marginal value of employees' services early in their careers, with a reversal later in their careers. In other words, the combined cash wage plus pension accrual in the early years of a career are less than the value of the employee's labor, but in the later years of a career, total compensation exceeds the value of the period's labor.

Support for the validity of the implicit contract theory comes from several sources. First, as discussed in Chapter 1, final-pay DB plans are backloaded: expected pension benefits rise much more rapidly later in a career than earlier. This means that expected pension benefits will rise with wage increases resulting from promotion, merit, and importantly, inflation. Accordingly, pensions at the start of the retirement period tend to become fixed in real terms, though legally they are fixed only in nominal terms. Implicit contract theory can explain why plan sponsors would be so generous as to promise the kind of automatic inflation protection that arises from final-pay plans. Moreover, this theory explains why plan sponsors have in the past voluntarily enhanced the benefit payment of those who have already retired. At the same time, the theory also suggests that employees "lend" the sponsor money early in their careers; they take less than their marginal product early on with the expectation of recouping, with interest, their "banked" effort. In effect employees become unsecured bondholders of the sponsor; thus, not only are they hesitant to quit, but they are also hesitant to shirk on the job for fear of getting fired and losing some portion of the bond's value.

A second support for the implicit contract theory is the finding that wages are not inversely related to pension accruals.[10] That is, higher wages did not lead to lower pension accruals, and vice versa, when other elements of the labor contract were the same. In the spot contract theory, wages and pension accruals would be strongly negatively related, because given productivity implies a specific level of total compensation; higher cash wages would require lower pension accruals.

In addition to providing guidance in determining exactly what the liability to be funded is, there are also structural implications for the spot and implicit contracting theories. If the nature of the labor market—employer demand and employee supply—is such that long-term relationships are not valued or anticipated, DC plans are likely to be appropriate. If long-term relationships are valued, DB plans will be appropriate.

Funding Policies and the Value of the Pension Liability

As a policy parameter, the value of the liability matters because it affects the nature of the pension plan's portfolio and the timing of and optimal level of funding. The funding status of the pension plan is an important variable in setting policy because it provides information on the financial health of the plan and insights into the plan's ability to bear risk and into future contributions the sponsor must make. As noted, determining the funding status of a plan, however, is subject to a number of choices the analyst may make with regard to what will be determined to be its liability and how it should be measured.

The weight of the evidence indicates that the correct liability measure for DB plans is that of implicit contract theory—that is, the correct liability to use in setting long-term policy should be the present value of all future benefits. This measure of the liability assumes that the pension fund is a going concern, whereas a measure such as ABO assumes that the pension fund should be concerned with the liability it would incur if it terminated today. The implicit contract-based liability is much greater, obviously, than the spot contract liability; indeed, it could be as much as three times the measure of pension liabilities that has been explicitly sanctioned by the accounting profession: the PBO.[11]

Computing the Liability of a Defined Benefit Plan

The total liability in a DB plan can be computed only after assumptions regarding the following items can be made:

1. At what rate will a worker's salary grow?
2. For how many years beyond the present will the worker work?
3. How long will the worker live after retirement?
4. What discount rate ought to be used to bring these projected payments back to current value?

An example will make this clear.

Example

Ms. Landers is fifty years old, has been on the job for ten years, and now earns $50,000 per year. She expects to work for the same employer until the age of seventy years, for a total of thirty years of service. At that time, her life expectancy will be fifteen years. She further expects her actual salary to increase by 5% per year. Her company provides a pension benefit equal to 2% of her final salary multiplied by the number of years of service and makes no adjustment for the Social Security payments received. Finally, the discount rate that will be used in estimating the present value of the pension liability is 6%. (Of course, as in all other aspects of the application of financial theory, the discount rate should reflect the riskiness of the projected stream of payments. In the case of pension payouts, there should be relatively little systematic risk. Thus, the appropriate discount rate should be close to the risk-free rate.)

The Spot Contract Liability. Using the spot contract theory, the pension liability would be the present value of an annuity that begins in twenty years and will last for fifteen years after that. The size of the future annuity would be $0.02 \times$ \$50,000 $\times$ 10 years, or \$10,000 per year. This takes no account of Ms. Landers's likely future efforts on behalf of the plan sponsor or of future raises.

The present value (PV) is

$$PV = (1/1.06)^{20}\sum_{t=1}^{15} \$10,000/(1.06)^t = \$30,283.$$

If the spot contract view of the world is correct, one way to compute the un-funded pension obligation would be to subtract this amount from Ms. Landers's pro rata share of the total pension plan's assets measured at current values. For real organizations, actuaries would actually aggregate over all vested employees to compute the total liability, then compare this to the market value of all plan assets.

The Implicit Contract Liability. If the implicit contract view of the obligation is valid, however, the spot contract theory does not reflect the true obligation ac-curately. The analyst must assess the future salary and the future employment profile of the employee to get a true measure of the plan's liability.

Table 8.1 shows future salary projections and the estimated present values of pension benefits as of the date of retirement and as of the present date. It also shows how annual pension cost might be computed. The "normal cost" is simply the amount by which present value of benefits increases from year to year. The benefit increase reflects the fact that salary is rising, one more year has been worked, and Ms. Landers is one year closer to retirement.

Under the implicit contract theory, the expected pension liability as of the present time, year 0, seen in the "Current Year" column, is \$241,051. It increases each year as the employee becomes one year closer to pension time, so the reverse telescope of present value computation gets shorter. The expected pen-sion liability does not rise because of expected future salary increases or lon-gevity, because these expectations are already built into the computation.

Sponsor Contributions and the Unfunded Liability. Unfunded liabilities will per-sist unless there is market action (net of interest rate effects that affect liabilities) that increases the value of plan assets, the sponsor increases funding, or both. For starters, note that one of the truly strange things about computing unfunded liabilities is that, as Ezra so aptly pointed out in 1980, the magnitude of the unfunded pension liability will change depending on the method a plan sponsor has adopted to fund the plan. The various methods each have a different profile regarding when cash gets injected into the fund.

What becomes truly complicated is in computing the unfunded pension lia-bility. At year 0, let us assume that \$30,283 is Ms. Landers's pro rata portion of the pension plan assets. If that is true, and if it can safely be assumed that the combined increase in the value of the asset and the sponsor's contribution were to equal \$6,793 in year 1, \$7,941 in year 2, \$9,262 in year 3, and so forth, the computed unfunded pension obligation will be zero. The true pension assets in this case are considered to be the actual pension plan assets, plus the expected

Table 8.1 Pension Liability

Current Year	Length of Service	Multiplier (%)	Salary	Accrued Annual Retirement Benefits	Total Value of Benefits at Retirement[a]	Present Value of Accrued Benefits to be Received at Retirement	Normal Cost[b]	Pension Liability[c]
0	10	2	$50,000	$10,000	$97,122	$30,283	0	$241,051
1	11	2	$52,500	$11,550	$112,176	$37,076	$6,793	$255,515
2	12	2	$55,125	$13,230	$128,493	$45,017	$7,941	$270,845
3	13	2	$57,881	$15,049	$146,161	$54,279	$9,262	$287,096
4	14	2	$60,775	$17,017	$165,274	$65,060	$10,781	$304,322
5	15	2	$63,814	$19,144	$185,933	$77,584	$12,524	$322,581
6	16	2	$67,005	$21,442	$208,245	$92,107	$14,524	$341,936
7	17	2	$70,355	$23,921	$232,324	$108,922	$16,815	$362,452
8	18	2	$73,873	$26,594	$258,289	$128,362	$19,439	$384,199
9	19	2	$77,566	$29,475	$286,271	$150,804	$22,442	$407,251
10	20	2	$81,445	$32,578	$316,405	$176,679	$25,875	$431,686
11	21	2	$85,517	$35,917	$348,836	$206,476	$29,797	$457,588
12	22	2	$89,793	$39,509	$383,720	$240,750	$34,275	$485,043
13	23	2	$94,282	$43,370	$421,220	$280,135	$39,385	$514,145
14	24	2	$98,997	$47,518	$461,510	$325,346	$45,211	$544,994
15	25	2	$103,946	$51,973	$504,777	$377,199	$51,852	$577,694
16	26	2	$109,144	$56,755	$551,216	$436,615	$59,416	$612,355
17	27	2	$114,601	$61,884	$601,038	$504,643	$68,028	$649,097
18	28	2	$120,331	$67,385	$654,463	$582,470	$77,827	$688,043
19	29	2	$126,348	$73,282	$711,729	$671,442	$88,972	$729,325
20	30	2	$132,665	$79,599	$773,085	$773,085	$101,642	$773,085

[a]Using the current year's salary to compute the liability at the end of the year. At the end of the current year (0), the $50,000 salary generates a benefit of $10,000 (calculated as 2% × 10 years × $50,000). The value of fifteen years of $10,000 retirement payments is $97,122 at the beginning of the retirement period twenty years hence. The present value of $97,122 is $30,283, the liability roughly analogous to the ABO.

[b]Annual costs to a pension plan for the benefits accrued by employees.

[c]If it is highly likely that the employee will be with the organization for the next twenty years, an alternative liability computation uses the expected salary twenty years hence ($132,665) to determine an annual benefit of $79,599. The value of this benefit at the end of the current year is $241,051. In future years, this benefit measure increases as retirement draws closer.

changes in value, plus the amount the sponsor has committed to put into the plan.

Now let us suppose that instead the sponsor adopts the following funding schedule: the sponsor will contribute nothing in year 1 but will contribute $14,734 (the sum of the normal costs for the first two years) in year 2, and thereafter what has just been specified. Also, let us assume there will be no asset growth in either year 1 or year 2. In this case, the plan will show an unfunded liability in year 1 of $6,793, even though the funding will take place later, just as the other funding will take place. So an unfunded liability arises when the annual contribution plus appreciation is less than the computed normal cost (the change in the value of the liability). The plan would also show an increase in the unfunded pension liability if promised benefits were enhanced before contributions to cover those benefits were made.

Funding Approaches and Assumptions

There are generally four approaches to funding a pension plan.[12] In all of these, there is a "normal cost" component—the portion of the contribution allocated to the current year—and a "past service cost" component—the portion of the contribution allocated to past years that have not yet been funded. DB plans use a variety of actuarial cost methods, and they differ in their allocation of costs over the worker's service life—level payments or varying amounts—and in the length of time over which costs are allocated. There are two broad classifications of actuarial methods: accrued benefit and projected benefit cost methods. (Caution should be taken to avoid confusing the concept of accounting costs with the cash needed to fund the plan.)

In general, actuarial cost methods break down the cost of a plan into the normal cost and the supplemental cost. The normal cost is the annual cost attributable to a given year of the plan's operation. The supplemental cost arises when there is a liability for past service or for prior underfunding. Thus, the total annual cost equals what a sponsor must set aside for the year's work plus what the sponsor must set aside for prior work.

Because each funding method produces different rates of pension plan funding, the magnitude of a measured unfunded pension obligation, and hence the appropriate level of the desired contribution, will change depending on the method chosen. Sponsors can change methods and assumptions (e.g., discount rates), thus altering the estimate of unfunded liabilities. Note that for private plans the IRS has a strong interest in keeping contributions as low as possible, because the higher the tax-deductible contributions, the less tax is collected. The intent of ERISA is to increase the safety of pension plans, and safety is enhanced by higher levels of funding. This conflict in the goals of the two agencies could ultimately lead to some strange legislative initiatives as Congress tries to walk a fine line between collecting more taxes and making pension plans safe.

Interest Rate Assumption

In addition to funding or contribution schemes, changes in the assumed interest rate (in effect, a discount rate) also affect measured pension fund obligations. In the example of Ms. Landers's DB plan liability computation, the normal costs would have been much lower had a discount rate of, say, 8% been chosen, because this would have allowed the computed present value of future benefits to be much lower.

The discount rate should be related to existing capital market rates and should not be arbitrary.[13] The rates on either long-term government bonds or perhaps long-term government agency bonds are reasonable. The fact that aggregate pension obligations might stretch out for sixty years (the time at which the currently youngest worker or surviving spouse would be expected to die), whereas the customary maturity of long-term bonds is only twenty or thirty years, should not be a reason to adapt an arbitrary rather than a market-based number. Indeed, what happens after twenty years does not matter very much anyway, because big changes in discount rates more than twenty years out have very little effect on the computed value of the liability today. More to the point, a market rate should be used because this is a rate that investors believe will obtain over the foreseeable future. It is the rate investors use to value bonds. Because pension obligations are, in many ways, similar to bonds held by employees, they should be valued similarly. Should a sponsor wish to be more precise by applying different discount rates to different future periods, a reasonable approach to doing this is to compute forward interest rates.[14]

If a sponsor uses a market rate to discount future obligations, the value of the liability will vary as market interest rates vary. Given that interest rates have been volatile in recent years, this means that liability values will be highly variable, even though this may be untidy. A constant discount rate determined arbitrarily should generally not be used to value liabilities—or to project asset values, for that matter. Such an arbitrary discount rate would divorce estimates of the financial soundness of pension plans from reality. Of course, some pension plan sponsors have chosen assets that will vary in value with the estimates of their pension liabilities. This issue is explored in later chapters.

Liabilities, Contributions, and Investment Policy

Not only is the measurement of unfunded pension liabilities sensitive to the choice of future funding schemes and to the rate chosen to discount future obligations, it is also sensitive to the rate of return forecasted to be earned on plan assets. Further, as the estimated rate of return will be a function of how much risk the sponsor wants to bear, assumptions about the risk/return trade-off implicit in various asset allocations must be made and will, in turn, affect the measurement of the liability.

How much real cash has to be set aside in each period to meet obligated payments depends on the assumptions made about discount rates, forecasted rates of return, and other factors, such as the degree of risk aversion on the part of the decision maker. A formal data analysis can help in informing decisions about how to allocate assets and how to structure the contribution stream (an example is presented in Chapter 9). One thing is clear: there is a trade-off between the investment performance of pension assets and the contributions the company must make. The asset allocations that are most likely to reduce the sponsor's contributions in the long run, however, also have high investment risk. If there is adverse market action, there may be unexpected funding needs, and in especially severe market downturns, the financial health of the plan could be threatened.

A partial solution to the question of what degree of risk is appropriate is to use a hybrid approach that distinguishes between that part of the asset pool that matches relevant liabilities (as defined by the sponsor) and that part that exceeds liabilities. For instance, some employers may consider the relevant "serious" liabilities to be the present value of the actuarially expected amount that must be paid to the current population of retirees; this amount would rise or fall only as the retired population increases or decreases. Against these claims, the sponsor might determine that an appropriate policy is to set up a dedicated bond portfolio—that is, a bond portfolio, the value of which would rise or fall with the present value of liabilities and in essence match them in value.[15] For the nonretired group, the sponsor would hold assets such as stocks that would be most likely to increase in value as the size of the claim rose because of wage increases resulting from promotions, productivity gains, and inflation. Of course, the more the value of the assets rise, other things being equal, the smaller the contributions the equity holders or taxpayers of the sponsoring organization would have to make. This would be the risky portion of the portfolio. Sponsors who establish pension funds in this bifurcated way apparently consider the pension ownership issue to be different for retired and active employees, with the former being treated as owners and the latter being treated as if the equity holders or taxpayers are the owners of the asset pool.[16] This inconsistency can lead to suboptimal decision making as managers ignore important interactions that affect the financial well-being of the plan, its beneficiaries, and the sponsor.

Plan sponsors and those who manage pension asset pools must recognize that the questions of joint ownership, integration, and funding affect the pension plan's asset structure and, hence, its risk/return profile. Further, senior managers, board members, and others who are charged with the responsibility of setting or implementing investment policy must understand that the way the liability is measured will affect their perception of the adequacy of the plan's funding. Finally, managers must understand how the willingness of the sponsor to make contributions is entwined with the demands for investment returns (and risks) that will be placed on the plan's asset pool. These factors have a profound effect on the strategic side of pension investment policy.

CONCLUSION

Investment policy for DB pension plans originates in a philosophical choice: should the management of the plan be integrated with the management of the sponsoring organization? In general, the answer to this question is "yes," because the two are so closely entwined. However, this answer is conditional on doing what is in the best interests of plan beneficiaries. Sometimes employers and those who manage the pension plans they sponsor have an adversarial relationship. This certainly is not an optimal circumstance, but it may be unavoidable, especially in political environments. Even if this is the case, however, there is still much to be gained by using an integrated perspective to structure policies regarding factors such as diversification. Policy also requires that those who set policy understand the relationship between plan liabilities and assets as well as the effect of investment performance on the contributions the sponsor must make. Ultimately, the financial health of both the sponsor and the pension fund are at stake. This interdependence is rife with potential conflicts of interest. It presents numerous opportunities for mistakes to be made. Only through forward-looking policy—policy that anticipates conflicts (e.g., between aggressive investment strategies and contribution levels) and that specifies the parameters to be used in decision making (e.g., the liability to be managed is the economic liability)—can decision makers get the guidance they need.

Policy can be constraining; that is its nature. Policy writers should be careful not to take away the flexibility that decision makers need to do their jobs. However, the absence of sound policy leaves a void in accountability that is not consistent with prudent behavior. Those who are fiduciaries, therefore, must insist on good investment policy as a prerequisite to good investment management of plan assets.

9

Asset Allocation for Defined Benefit Plans

The strategic asset allocation decision is the most important decision a plan sponsor can make. This chapter starts by defining the strategic asset allocation decision and discussing in general terms how the strategic asset allocation should be set. Next, the chapter introduces the factors that should be considered in setting the DB strategic asset allocation. Theoretical arguments favoring allocations to stocks and bonds are considered, followed by empirical evidence that shows what pension funds actually do. The chapter also includes an example of how scenario analysis may be used to evaluate the trade-offs inherent in the strategic asset allocation decision. The final sections discuss how DB assets may be reallocated over time.

FUNDAMENTALS OF ALLOCATING ASSETS

How should pension fund managers, trustees, administrators, and other fiduciaries allocate the pension fund's assets? The starting point is determining the optimal asset mix—the strategic asset allocation. To simplify the basic concept somewhat, this is the mix of equities, bonds, and cash that will best meet the pension fund's return needs without taking on more risk than is prudent. A more complete approach would use a more comprehensive set of asset classes, including international stocks and bonds, real estate, and other alternative assets. It would also differentiate on the basis of attributes such as capitalization and maturity/quality.

The fund's strategic allocation across the three primary asset classes is the single most important investment decision that pension planners can make. A widely cited study indicates that as much as 93.6% of the variation in returns of pension portfolios may be attributed to their normal asset allocation weights and market index returns.[1] Unfortunately, the asset allocation decision sometimes gets shunted aside for more glamorous decisions: how much should be invested in emerging markets? How much should be invested in venture capital? The reality for most pensions is that very little will be placed in these exotic classes. However, whether to invest 70% or 30% of a fund's total assets in stocks is a decision that will have a considerable effect on long-term financial health.

Determining what proportion of a pension fund's assets should be invested in each type of asset class requires understanding the plan's return requirement and risk tolerance as well as expectations of the risk/return relationships offered by the capital markets. This blending of investor risk/return objectives with capital market expectations is an exercise in what is known as constrained portfolio optimization—selecting the optimal portfolio of assets subject to the joint constraints of tolerance for risk and the desire to achieve high returns.

Risk/Return-Efficient Portfolios

To select the right strategic asset allocation, the plan sponsor must quantify current expectations for asset class returns, the volatility of these returns, and the relationship (comovement) among asset classes over time. The obvious starting point is the historical record of the asset classes. A review of how the different classes have performed shows that the more volatile asset classes (e.g., stocks) have also provided the highest returns over long periods of time. However, the analyst should be careful to avoid naively projecting the historical record into the future. Knowing that stocks have provided higher returns than bonds over long periods of time tells us little about how stocks will do next year or over the next five years. Nonetheless, the historical record is a good starting point in forming long-term expectations that will help to make a sensible allocation of the pension plan's funds.

Ambachtsheer suggested that analysts can improve their expectations for future risks and returns by considering factors that may cause future performance to differ from past performance.[2] He suggested that the analyst consider replacing the historical yield curve with the actual yield curve at the time of the analysis. Further, the analyst should adjust for apparent biases and trends in history (e.g., artificially low interest rates in the 1940s and 1950s and the corresponding decline in stock dividend yields). Finally, the analyst should try to anticipate the effect of such factors as savings and trade disequilibrium, globalization, and recapitalization.

For assets that trade infrequently (such as real estate or private equity), analysts should be aware that because of infrequent trading, prices may appear to be more smooth than they really are. For international returns, analysts should take into account imperfections such as segmentation and illiquidity.[3]

Scenario analysis, correlation models, and other techniques are also available.[4] Each technique has strengths and weaknesses that should be considered when applying it. As in much that investment professionals do, subjective judgment plays an important role in deciding which factors are truly important or less so, and what they actually mean for future returns and risks.

Once a reasonable set of expectations has been determined, the analyst may compute (or estimate) an "efficient frontier." The efficient frontier is the collection of portfolios that have the highest expected returns for a given amount of risk. The actual computation requires some mathematical programming, but there are many software packages that help. It is important that the asset classes used to define the efficient frontier be as complete as possible. In addition, the efficient frontier derived will be only as good as the quality of the expectations used.

Suppose that the pension sponsor was concerned only with investment risk and return. In that case, asset allocation could be approached formally through a mean-variance optimizer.[5] Given expectations of capital market returns, variances, and correlations, a mean-variance optimizer solves for the asset-class weights that minimize risk at each level of return. The results of such an exercise are informative, but they should be approached cautiously. In particular, sensitivity analyses should be conducted to gauge the sensitivity of the solution to changes in inputs. Small changes in expected variances or correlations may lead to dramatic changes in suggested asset-class weights. Managers should be aware of this sensitivity and treat the optimizer as one input into the decision-making process.

The problem becomes more complicated when the manager considers issues beyond expected returns and standard deviations. For example, DB plans may include in their formal models the pension liability and the expected pension payments the fund will have to pay out. The idea is to model not just the asset side of the pension plan but also the liability side and the interaction between the two. Investments are viewed not as isolated but in terms of how they match the payments the fund is expected to make.[6] Here it is useful to use Monte Carlo analysis, in which the range of possible outcomes and their probabilities is considered.[7]

Allocation Targets

After a set of efficient portfolios has been identified, the analyst must choose from the many asset allocation portfolios represented in that set. In very general terms, sponsors or beneficiaries wishing to structure a plan with relatively little exposure to risk will favor allocations weighted toward bonds and other fixed-income assets. Where more risk is acceptable or more return is desirable, the allocation will tend to favor equities. The extreme choices range from a relatively low-risk portfolio (typically one in which asset and liability durations are matched in an effort to minimize the volatility of the pension surplus for DB plans) up to a much more aggressive portfolio that pursues high total return (and attempts either to maximize pension surplus or to minimize the present value of sponsor contributions or maximize future real values). Various factors affect the selection of the optimal portfolio mix at or between these two extremes. For example, DB plans must consider the financial strength of the sponsor, the plan benefit formulas, the sponsor's desire to reduce funding costs, and the demographic features of the workforce. The asset allocation that most closely corresponds to the desired expected risk and return profile is, of course, a fundamental element of policy.

Most pension plans set asset allocation policy targets as percentages of the whole, so the policy is formulated, for example, as 30% of plan assets in long-term bonds, 60% in stocks, and 10% in cash. The sponsor/beneficiary may also set acceptable ranges for deviation from this target allocation (e.g., 30% ± 5%). Money managers, whether internal or external, are then responsible for adhering to the policy limits. Individuals are less likely to hire external managers and, thus, tend to serve as their own internal managers. Where external managers are being used, the sponsor/beneficiary must be prepared to adjust contributions among managers as needed to maintain the desired mix.

SETTING THE STRATEGIC ASSET ALLOCATION IN DB PLANS

Conceptually, there is nothing difficult about how the strategic asset allocation should be set. It is simply the mix of stocks, bonds, and cash (more finely parsed to other asset classes as appropriate) that, in the long run, best meets the circumstances and constraints the pension plan faces and that provides an appropriate rate of return on plan assets without exceeding the plan's ability to bear risk. Translating this simple concept into a sensible asset mix that is an operational plan that can be justified to others and is economically sound is not so easy, however.

Readers should bear in mind that the strategic asset allocation (SAA) is the operational side of investment policy. It is the result or consequence of decisions that policy makers make. Although the SAA is the structure that positions the pension plan to obtain its long-term investment goals with an appropriate level of risk, the goals themselves reflect many competing interests and diverse philosophies about what the purpose of the asset pool really is. Of course, the actual allocation chosen (whether it is 80% stocks or 40% stocks, etc.) reflects beliefs about long-term capital market returns and risks and correlations.

The appropriate strategic asset allocation is determined in part by the preferences the sponsor has for funding the plan, in part by the interaction of plan assets with plan liabilities, and in part by a choice as to which of two philosophical views is taken with respect to whether to integrate the plan's assets with those of the sponsor. This section discusses these issues and shows how they affect the strategic asset allocation.

The Funding Decision

The pension plan sponsor faces several conflicting goals with respect to funding. First, the sponsor wants to minimize the present value of expected long-term contributions. This means that the portfolio should be heavily loaded with stocks, because they have a potentially higher return. Moreover, from the sole perspective of the plan, too heavy a reliance on contributions is too much like too heavy a concentration in the securities of one company or one industry; relying too heavily on the sponsor for contributions may undo the effect of portfolio diversification.

Second, sponsors generally do not want a highly variable contribution rate—that is, they do not want to face the uncertainty of unexpectedly having to put a lot of cash into the plan, particularly if the need for this high infusion of cash occurs at a time when they themselves are experiencing cash shortfalls and cannot make all the real investments they wish, either because of lack of access to capital markets or because of self-imposed capital rationing. This means the portfolio should be heavily loaded with bonds because bonds have less return volatility than do stocks.

Third, most private sponsors want to meet their obligations to employees without harming shareholders by unexpected shortfalls. Most public sponsors similarly may want to avoid the harm to taxpayers that may occur in the event of a pension shortfall. However, in both cases, the sponsor must also attempt to meet the needs of plan beneficiaries. Beneficiaries want to maximize the value of their expected benefits and reduce the likelihood the benefits will not materialize. The conflict this presents to a goal of minimizing contributions is obvious but not easily resolved. ERISA offers some balance to this conflict for private funds; no such arbiter exists in the public sector except for public employee unions that choose to represent their members' pension interests. Although this conflict has elements that may be addressed through contracting, the dynamics of the capital markets and the expertise required indicate that good faith is a significant issue.

The Effect of Plan Liabilities, Surplus, and Integration

DB plans have explicit and implicit liabilities, the value of which may be calculated. These liabilities are determined by the benefits promised (the pension deal), the nature of the workforce covered (e.g., average age, mortality, compensation structure), and current interest rates. Changes in any of these factors change the economic value of the liability. In turn, the potential for changes in the value of the liability can have a profound effect on the way the assets of a plan should be allocated among the asset classes. Consider the following examples of how these factors interact:

1. Sponsors who increase the amount of the promised benefit also increase the present value of the pension liability and, all else the same, reduce the funding status of the plan. This creates pressure to either increase contributions to the plan or improve investment performance. Pressure to improve investment performance affects the asset allocation by encouraging reallocation toward more risky assets (e.g., stocks).

2. Sponsors with young workforces and few current retirees ordinarily can tolerate high levels of risk (i.e., may invest heavily in stocks) in part because the present value of the plan liabilities is relatively low and in part because the immediate liquidity needs required for benefit payments are low. Further, they probably must tolerate risk because wages are likely to grow at least at the rate of inflation, and thus future benefits will grow accordingly. As the workforce ages, however, the liquidity needs of the plan increase, and the nearer-term pension payouts increase the size of the pension liability. At this point the allocation of plan's assets should reflect this different set of circumstances and financial claims.

3. Plan assets and plan liabilities are both exposed to changes in interest rates. When interest rates rise, option-free bond prices fall. Normally,

so do the values of other assets, although the relationship is not as direct. Pension liabilities are, for all practical purposes, bonds issued by the sponsor—promises to make certain payments in the future. Herein lies an important aspect of the relationship between the pension plan's asset allocation decision and the plan's liabilities. With changes in the level of interest rates affecting both assets and liabilities, asset allocation policy must anticipate the possibility of a change in interest rates disproportionately affecting one or the other, and hence affecting the financial health of the plan.

Surplus Volatility

The financial health of a pension plan typically is defined in terms of the surplus (deficit) of assets over liabilities. The surplus, and hence the financial health, of a pension plan is thus a function of whatever affects the values of plan assets, plan liabilities, or both. This had led an increasing number of authorities to argue that a pension plan's risk tolerance should be defined in terms of the volatility of the plan surplus.[8] Because a primary purpose of a plan's assets is to fund the plan's liabilities, and because the sponsor must conceptually make up any shortfall, this view suggests that the appropriate stocks/bonds/cash mix is the one that provides sufficient return subject to an acceptable level of surplus volatility.

Managing the volatility of the pension surplus indicates that a risk-minimizing pension fund should define the minimum-risk portfolio as that in which there is no volatility in the pension surplus. This may be accomplished by using cash flow-matched portfolios and immunized, duration-matched port-folios.[9] From this, it follows that a pension that can or that chooses to bear risk in pursuit of lower funding costs or higher benefits will define its efficient frontier of possible portfolios from this riskless portfolio.

In this framework, asset or portfolio volatility is replaced by surplus volatility in analyzing alternative strategic asset allocations. Similarly, asset or portfolio return is replaced by return on plan surplus.[10]

The Appropriate Liability

Finally, before the appropriate asset allocation mix can be chosen, the sponsor must decide what liability is to be funded. If the sponsor takes the view that the ABO must be funded, then an all-bond strategy will be fine because it has the potential of producing a portfolio that is a perfect hedge relative to the liability. Here, the objective of the all-bond portfolio is to compose a portfolio that will rise or fall in value as the ABO rises or falls because of interest rate changes. One side effect of this, however, is that it virtually ensures that contributions over time will have to be much higher than if stocks were held in the portfolio, assuming, of course, that stock returns will generally exceed bond returns over the long term.

Many practitioners and academics believe that the pension liability that should be funded is what might be termed the total pension obligation, at least for long-term strategic planning purposes. This is the best estimate as to the present value of just about all future obligations, including salary increases, a greater number of years worked, and a changing workforce perhaps resulting from the growth of the sponsoring organization. This number is certainly larger than the ABO. (Indeed, even the PBO, which accounts for future salary growth, generally underestimates a plan's true liability, because it does not account for expected future years of service.) Because the total pension obligation may grow much more rapidly than the ABO, the timing and magnitude of future pension contributions become significant factors in setting the right strategic asset allocation.

The Integrated Approach to Managing Plan Assets

Recall that there are two views concerning the relationship between plan assets and the sponsor. One approach regards the pension plan as separate from the sponsor, as an appendage rather than an integral part of the whole organization. The integration approach considers the operating aspects of the sponsor and the pension plan as two components of the same entity. The idea that the sponsor and the pension plan are virtually independent will lead to a very different approach to deciding on the appropriate asset mix, a mix that is usually substantially different from the mix arrived at by viewing the plan as part of a whole. Thus, one's philosophical approach will significantly affect the ultimate choice of asset weights in the plan's strategic allocation. However, the view that an optimal portfolio should be constructed without regard to the sponsor's other assets and liabilities is seriously flawed. This view ignores one of the most important assets the pension plan has: its claim on the sponsor's cash flows.

Legally, a private pension fund has a senior claim on the corporation's cash flows in the form of periodic contributions and on cash distributions from asset sales if the firm fails; thus, it has an important financial stake in the corporation. Failure to recognize that stake as a pension fund asset and to take account of it when deciding the asset mix of the pension plan is wrong from an economic perspective, because it can lead to misdirected diversification and hence too much risk for the return expected. For example, an auto company's pension plan has enough exposure to the economic cycles of the auto industry by virtue of its reliance on the company's ability to make timely contributions from its automobile business's operating income. It does not need more exposure by also owning shares in other automobile companies or in companies that correlate closely with the automotive industry.

Similarly, a public plan has an implicit economic claim on future taxes paid by residents and others who are part of the tax base. Tax capacity is thus a claim held by the plan—claim that will compete with infrastructure needs and other tax-funded services. The diversification issue is similar: how much should a plan invest in local businesses when it is already dependent on the local economy?

If the operating entity and the pension plan are considered to be an economically unified body, as is appropriate, then the plan should make asset allocation decisions that consider the plan's financial exposure to the sponsor. Investments that are highly correlated with the cash flows of the sponsor should be avoided.

Further, the asset allocation should not harm the sponsor's shareholders or tax-payers, as the financial health of the sponsor affects the financial health of the plan.

To underscore the notion that sponsors should integrate their DB plans with their organizations, consider this rendition of the facts surrounding many private pension plans. First, assume that pension liabilities are growing by 12% per year. Second, assume that the total expected return on pension assets is 9%. Finally, assume that the plan initially is adequately funded and that assets (including sponsor contributions) must grow at the same expected rate as liabilities. Because the sponsor must make up the difference between the growth in liabilities and the total return, the sponsor must annually contribute an amount equal to 3% of the size of the plan. (Incidentally, note also that a 1% increase in asset performance would allow a 33% reduction in contributions.) The fact that the sponsoring firm must contribute an amount equal to 3% of the fund each year is roughly equivalent to the plan having 3% of its assets in a single instrument— the sponsor. Very few plans allow that much concentration in individual assets, but here it cannot be avoided. What can be avoided is additional exposure to assets that have returns that are highly correlated with the sponsor's financial health.

Despite the seeming conflict of interest between beneficiaries and taxpayers/ shareholders, potential plan beneficiaries are not necessarily detrimentally affected by an integrated approach to plan asset management: presumably they will be cared for because of their superior security status relative to shareholders/ taxpayers. If private plan sponsors become financially distressed, corporations then must assign their pension liability to the PBGC. Of course, the employee's pension benefit could be less than promised. Along with this assignment, the pension plan has a preferred status in the distribution of cash flows; pension beneficiaries are provided for before all nontax claims, including the claims of bondholders and shareholders, when wringing cash from the distressed corporation. As such, the ERISA prescription that the pension fund be run for the benefit of the beneficiaries is met—just not in the conventional way.

Public plans, which have no counterpart to ERISA or the PBGC, face a more ambiguous situation. The financially distressed public plan must rely on the largess of the taxpayer or turn to the courts. Any given tax base is limited in its ability to cover unfunded pension liabilities.

Thus, the resolution of financial distress will depend on tax capacity and the willingness of one generation to support the former. This, in fact, is slowly becoming a matter of concern, as public plan beneficiaries and taxpayers become more aware of the significance of underfunding, sometimes exacerbated by asset allocation decisions that have political rather than economic motivations.

In summary, the diversification/funding interdependence that exists between pension plans and sponsors overwhelmingly favors as least partial integration of plan asset management with the management of the sponsor's assets. This does not mean that decisions that might harm the plan but that help the sponsor should be permitted. Nor does it mean that the costs of monitoring the likely areas of conflict between the sponsor's interests and the interests of plan beneficiaries should be ignored. In fact, these conflicts of interest and the difficulty of arranging agreements to minimize them are central to any effort to manage plan assets in an integrated manner. What integrated asset management does offer is the idea that complete separation of assets is not sensible; rather, it is less than optimal for both the plan beneficiaries and the plan sponsor because it ignores the implicit investment the plan has in the sponsor and the benefit the sponsor receives from good investment performance of the plan's assets.

LESSONS FROM ALL-STOCK AND ALL-BOND PORTFOLIOS

Two completely different asset allocation philosophies emerge directly from the axiom that the sponsor and its pension plan should be integrated and that the financial policies of both should complement rather than ignore each other. These competing views suggest that pension plan assets could be invested entirely in common stock or entirely in bonds, but not in a combination of the two.

The premises of each view, of course, represent extremes between which most analysts believe the optimal strategic asset allocation for a given plan actually lies. The strategic asset allocation is affected by far too many factors to be summarized as neatly as these two views suggest. Nonetheless, evaluating the merits of each helps demonstrate the trade-offs that the strategic asset allocation must somehow resolve.

In Favor of the All-Stock Portfolio

The arguments in favor of stocks are based on the high returns stocks have historically provided and the resultant lower contributions the sponsor must make if these high returns are realized. However, the structure of the argument differs somewhat for private and public plans.

Private Plans

Sharpe was the first to persuasively argue that the shareholders of a sponsoring corporation are better off when pension plan managers invest only in common stock.[11] A corollary is that the level of funding be kept as low as permissible under ERISA.

The argument assumes that the price of PBGC insurance is too low—that is, it is not fairly priced in terms of the underlying risks being insured—and that its claim on the firm and its shareholders is quite limited. Even with the advent of a risk-related premium schedule, which replaced the flat, universally applied premium that each firm had to pay for each worker, PBGC insurance premiums may still be too low given the insurance provided.

The PBGC insures pension benefits up to a specified level that is indexed to the Social Security wage base. In 2003, the maximum insured benefit was nearly $44,000 per year. The corporation, in essence, holds an "in-the-money" put option by means of which it can "put" its pension liability to the PBGC in return for the pension plan assets plus some portion of its own net worth. (Of course, the firm always holds a put, except that before the PBGC, it could put the liability to its workers by reneging on its pension promise.)

If a company has an underfunded pension plan, it has a much better chance of fully funding the plan with the same contribution dollar outlays by holding stocks instead of bonds because stocks have a higher expected return. However, stocks are risky. If stock prices fall and the unfunded pension liability rises so that it exceeds the set percentage of the company's net worth that must be given to the PBGC on exercise of the pension put, the put is in the money and may be exercised.

There is a favorable asymmetry to the payoff for private pension sponsors who allocate all pension assets to stocks given PBGC insurance. If stocks rise (because of factors other than a decrease in interest rates), the pension plan gets funded with smaller contributions from the company than would be required if the pension plan held both stocks and bonds. However, if stocks decline by enough, the company can exercise the pension put, and its liability and subsequent loss is limited.

The conclusion that the value of the pension put is maximized by holding all stock is compelling, as long as the pension put is underpriced because PBGC insurance premiums are set too low to compensate for the riskiness of the insured pension plan. The 1994 change in the premium schedule for PBGC insurance has somewhat altered the attractiveness of maintaining a portfolio that exploits the pension put, however.

Public Plans

The arguments in favor of stocks are somewhat different for public plans. First, many public plan sponsors find it politically simpler to increase employee compensation by increasing pension benefits rather than raising salaries.[12] Unless funding is increased in proportion to the increase in the liability this causes, the natural result is underfunding. This underfunding provides an incentive to take on the riskiness of stocks in pursuit of higher total returns.

Consider that, in the absence of insurance such as that provided by PBGC, the ability of a public pension plan to meet its obligations depends on increased funding through higher taxes, cuts in public services, or an asset allocation that pursues high total return. Because of the political unattractiveness of the first two, there may be an incentive to reduce the use of tax dollars by taking on greater investment risk. In the long run, many analysts believe this will work, but remember the fallacy of thinking that risk somehow disappears in the long-run. The higher expected returns with any asset arise from a corresponding increase in risk.

All-Stock Allocations: Summary

Although the logic behind an all-stock portfolio (or at least a heavy orientation toward stocks) is compelling for sponsors because of its potential to reduce long-term future contributions, it is hard to find sponsors that have completely embraced the prescription. In the private sector, the put option scheme really works only for financially weak firms. For financially sound firms, the value of the net worth that would have to be given over to the PBGC would exceed the unfunded pension liability. Some public funds have negotiated contractual minimums for funding and thus are able to resist the pressure to invest solely for high returns. Further, when people who are not familiar with or knowledgeable about financial markets and assets are involved in setting pension investment policy parameters, too large an allocation to stocks can be politically unacceptable, and there may even be limits on the exposure a fund can take to stocks. Most public funds, however, choose to gamble on risky assets, with the expectation that a higher return will lower the need for future taxes.

In Favor of the All-Bond Portfolio

There are arguments that support large allocations to bonds as well. These generally take the form of taking advantage of the tax arbitrage opportunity provided by bonds.

Private Plans

The persuasive view that pension plans should hold all bonds was first advanced by Black and Dewhurst and by Tepper.[13] The primary motivation is tax based. Whatever stock the company, taken as the combination of the operating corporation and the pension plan, wants to hold would be held by the sponsor outside of the plan. This would facilitate tax arbitrage by the operating arm of the company because dividends received by corporate shareholders are taxed relatively lightly. The pension plan itself would hold only bonds. Bonds must yield enough to compensate for taxes paid by marginal bond holders. Thus, the untaxed pension plan investor earns excess profits in the form of the premium required to entice taxable investors to hold bonds. In short, the taxable firm should take advantage of the fact that interest on its own bonds is tax deductible, whereas interest on the bonds it holds in its pension portfolio is not taxed.

To exploit this insight the firm should engage in these transactions:

1. Sell all equities currently held by the pension fund;
2. Take the money from this sale and buy bonds that are as risky as any bonds the firm itself might issue;
3. Sell bonds (i.e., borrow) for the firm's own account; and
4. Use the proceeds of the bond sale to buy stock for the firm's own account.

The corporation is protected against the growth in the pension obligation attributable to rising wage rates and so forth by holding stocks in its general portfolio, the value of which tends to rise with productivity growth and inflation. Recall that corporate holdings of stock are tax advantaged, because only a fraction of the dividend income generated by those holdings is taxed. By arranging its investments this way, a corporation can achieve slightly higher overall posttax investment returns without changing any of its fundamental business activities, because it pays less tax that it would otherwise pay.

A second way to think about tax arbitrage possibilities is to assume that the capital markets are in an after-tax equilibrium. That is, the expected after-tax returns are linearly related to risk, where the appropriate tax rate is that of the marginal investor.

The concept of after-tax equilibrium can be illustrated with an example. Assume the top marginal (corporate) tax rate on interest income is 35%. If corporate bonds with low default risk yield 6%, the after-tax equilibrium return is $0.06 \times (1 - 0.35) = 0.06 \times 0.65 = .039$, or 3.9%. Because all outstanding bonds must be owned, assume the last ones sold are owned by the marginal, or most heavily taxed, investors. That is, the last investor to buy these bonds will be the one who receives the lowest after-tax yield. Dividends on common stock are tax-advantaged for corporate holders, whereas dividends are taxed at regular rates for individuals.

Capital gains, let us assume, are taxed at nontrivial tax rates for corporate and individual holders. However, the holder of stock can decide when to sell stocks. Capital gains taxes can thus be deferred; taxes on capital gains do not have to be paid until the securities are sold. Thus, investors who hold such securities have a valuable "timing option." Assume, then, the appropriate effective tax rate on common stock investments, the rate that adjusts for full taxation of dividends and the deferral of capital gains until it is advantageous to realize them, is 20%. Let us also assume the expected return on stock is 9% with, say, a 5% dividend yield and a 4% expected capital gain; the expected after-tax equilibrium return on common stocks is $0.09 \times (1.00 - 0.20)$, or 7.2%. The corporation that holds the common stock receives 9% pretax, then pays a tax of 35% on only 30% of the dividend. Assuming no sales are made, so no capital gain taxes get paid, the after-tax return is

$$0.04 + 0.05 - [0.05(0.3)(0.35)] = 0.085, \text{ or } 8.5\%.$$

For after-tax equilibrium, bonds must yield 3.9% on an after-tax basis to compensate for risk, and stocks must offer total after-tax returns of 7.2%. In every case, the marginal investor is the most heavily taxed. By holding bonds in the tax-exempt pension fund, the tax-advantaged holder earns a "rent" of from 6.0% minus 3.9%, or 2.1%. The holder gets this much (2.1%) more than should be received in view of both the investment's risk and capital market equilibrium. This difference, the gap between what this inframarginal holder gets and what those investors who produce the equilibrium get, is termed a rent. The rent is the difference between what can actually be realized after tax for a particular investor less the amount the market requires on an after-tax basis. By holding stocks in the pension fund, the gross rent is only 9% minus 7.2%, or 1.8%— the difference between the pre- and posttax equilibrium expected returns. Holding bonds yields a higher rent: 2.1% versus 1.8%. Moreover, holding stock in the corporation still leaves a rent of from 8.5% minus 7.2%, or 1.3%. Thus, pursuing of a strategy of all bonds in the pension fund and funding the purchase of common stock through the borrowing via sale of bonds can generate earnings against the U.S. tax code, and it can all be done without increasing the risk of the combined entity. It is the tax collector that loses.

Stewart has been a recent proponent of the all-bond strategy.[14] In addition to the tax advantages, he notes that bond funds are much less expensive to operate than equity funds, because of both lower transaction costs and lower management fees. He also argues that bond funding stabilizes reported earnings and cash flow, which attributes are attractive to investors, especially in the current environment.

The all-bond strategy says nothing about how much stock should be held by a corporation. It indicates only that 100% of the pension fund's assets should be invested in bonds. Overall, the strategy implies that the pension plan should be as highly funded as the tax code allows because contributions to the plan are tax deductible. Thus, maximum contributions to the pension plan will minimize taxes paid.

Public Plans

Before the 1986 Tax Reform Act, public pension fund sponsors and plans could run a similar arbitrage operation. By issuing tax-exempt debt (sometimes called pension bonds) and investing the proceeds in higher yielding corporate bonds of the same level of risk, sponsors were able to capture the yield differential of perhaps 2% to 3%.

Since the 1986 reforms, public plans can no longer do this, although they may issue taxable pension bonds.[15] The temptation to issue taxable pension bonds is that when interest rates are low, issuing taxable debt and investing in a higher yielding portfolio of assets produces higher expected returns for the pension, thus lowering the unfunded liability. Unfortunately, this is not arbitrage, it is simply funding by borrowing—leveraging—and investing in a higher risk asset pool. Leverage can deliver the desired results if the performance of the asset pool exceeds the costs on the pension bonds. If investment returns are poor, however, the bet goes bad and the issuer—the sponsor—still must service the debt and the pension liability, a liability that could be much higher than before.

Although public entities cannot explicitly sell tax-exempt debt to fund their pensions, the commingling of proceeds from bond sales with tax collections and other revenues indicates that a partial arbitrage is possible. The steps in this process are to borrow to reduce the use of general revenues to fund road repairs or new buildings or whatever, so that general revenues are available to fund the pension plan.

Thus, public funds cannot benefit as private funds theoretically may from an all-bond portfolio. No complete tax arbitrage is possible for public funds. With either type of fund, public or private, it may, of course, be sensible to use bonds to immunize a portion of the pension liability, but this is another issue.

All-Bond Allocations: Summary

Similar to the all-stock strategy, the all-bond strategy offers only partial guidance to many sponsors. To make everything work, the pension plan sponsor must be able to sell debt and get tax deductions on interest payments or favorable tax treatment (i.e., tax-exempt interest) for investors. If the sponsor is in poor financial condition, it may not be able to sell enough debt at low enough interest rates to allow it to be able to meet its obligations. Further, private sponsors must have taxable income against which the tax shield on interest payments can be applied. Accordingly, the strategy is useful primarily to financially strong, taxable, pension-sponsoring companies and is useful only somewhat to strong public pension sponsors. Nonetheless, there are many of these financially strong organizations, and hence many sponsors should consider using the strategy of borrowing and buying bonds.

HOW PENSION PLANS ALLOCATE PLAN ASSETS (AND FUND PENSION PLANS)

Theory aside, when attempting to arrive at the correct strategic asset allocation, it is helpful to have a sense of what pension plans are actually doing. This section reviews the most comprehensive studies that have been performed on asset allocation of pension funds and offers some interpretive comments on factors, such as profitability, taxes, the nature of the workforce, and funding, that influence the strategic asset allocation.

The Empirical Perspective

Several large empirical studies have been conducted that explore the extent to which private sponsors behave in ways suggested by the broad hypothesis that firms manage their pension plans as integrated parts of the company. In general, the studies found that few of the firms studied pursued either all-bond or all-stock allocations—virtually all pension funds in the samples had a mixture of stocks and bonds. However, several studies found that the pension plan asset allocations were tilted in ways that showed the operating corporation and the pension plan were being jointly considered when asset allocation decisions were being made. There were enough systematic connections between the corporations' overall financial conditions and their pension funding and allocation decisions that it seems clear that the decisions are treated jointly.

Friedman performed the first relevant study in 1983. He used pension plan data that firms use to report to the IRS on Form 5500. His sample consists of 24,426 firms that filed these forms in 1977. His principal findings are that

1. Firms with volatile earnings hold relatively less equity and more reasonably safe debt in their pension plan portfolios.
2. Firms with a great deal of outstanding debt tend to hold more debt in their pension plan portfolios and correspondingly less equity than do firms with low financial leverage.
3. Firms that are highly profitable tend to hold relatively more equity in pension portfolios than do firms with comparatively low profitability, as measured by return on equity and return on assets.
4. Firms with comparatively young workforces tend to invest more heavily in debt securities than do firms with older workforces.

The second study, performed by Bodie and associates in 1987, also found relationships between the asset structure of the pension plan and the operating corporation, but once again these are only tilts: they do not perfectly match all-bond or all-stock prescriptions.[16] This study examined 939 corporate plans or subsamples thereof for the year 1980. They learned that

1. More profitable firms tend to use lower discount rates (interest rate assumptions) than less profitable firms in computing their pension liabilities. This allows them to achieve greater tax deductions for contributions and let them warehouse the funds, a sensible strategy given that excess funding could be recaptured in later years.
2. The greater the long-run profitability of the firm, the higher the degree of funding. Again, this is consistent with the idea that contributions are used to reduce taxes. It also is consistent with the idea that the pension plan is a reservoir for financial slack for the corporation.
3. The more highly funded a pension plan, the greater its investment in bonds; the less highly funded, the more stock it holds. Both are consistent with the theory of the pension put that supports the all-stock portfolio, but again very few firms conform exactly to the theoretical prescriptions of all of one kind of instrument or the other.

The third study, by Petersen in 1996, examined more than 47,000 observations drawn from the Form 5500 that firms file with the IRS.[17] The time frame of the study was from 1988 to 1990. His results indicate that

1. More profitable firms invest a greater portion of their assets in stocks.
2. Riskier firms allocate a smaller portion of their assets to stocks.
3. Overfunded plans invest a greater portion of their assets in stocks than do underfunded plans.
4. The less mature the plan—that is, the lower the ratio of current benefits to asset size—the more the plan's assets are invested in stocks.

Public pensions have not been studied as extensively as private plans. In large part, this is attributable to the lack of a unified body of regulation requiring that data be reported. What data there are suffer from the uneven investment rules imposed by various legislative bodies (e.g., legal lists and other restrictions) that may force public pensions to invest in ways they might not if they were following their economic instincts.

Although, traditionally, public funds were less oriented to equities than was the case for private funds, public fund equity allocation has increased substantially in recent years. In one study covering fiscal year 2000, 60% of public pension fund assets were held in either domestic stocks or international equities.[18] Why are public funds choosing equities? Perhaps it is because the plans are under pressure to produce higher returns and reduce contributions. Perhaps it is because plans and sponsors are working more closely together to determine the optimal mix of risk, return, and contributions for both.

Interpretations

One interpretation of these findings is that pension sponsors make marginal adjustments in pension plans to compensate for the sponsors' financial policies, conditions, and preferences regarding the trade-off between contributions and investment returns. These marginal adjustments tend to push pension plan allocation policies toward more bonds or more stocks, but very few sponsors go all the way.

An alternative interpretation is that the data show only that the theories are incomplete. Ippolito, for example, argued that when viewed as a multiperiod tax arbitrage problem, the tax system that existed before the Tax Reform Act of 1986 and the Pension Protection Act of 1987 encouraged private pension plan overfunding.[19] Taxable companies were allowed to reduce taxable income by the amount of the contribution they made to the pension plan. The allowed contribution was linked to the difference between the actuarially measured liability and a measure of asset value. Before the new laws, only a portion of the increase in asset value relative to liabilities needed to be considered when determining how large contributions can be. Thus significant pension overfunding was possible. Because investment returns are likely to be higher with equity than with debt, a firm could get to a highly overfunded position more quickly by using equity than by using debt. Once the level of funding relative to liabilities was sufficiently high to preclude future contributions, then it would be sensible to switch the portfolio to all (or more) bonds, as Black and Dewhurst and Tepper argue, to take advantage of the tax arbitrage, the gains from which would partially offset the tax shields lost because of the firm's inability to continue making contributions. If Ippolito is correct, then the reason all-bond portfolios are not observed is not because there is no conscious coordination between the operating company and the pension plan, but rather because the interaction is dynamic, not static, and is more complex than initially thought. It is also affected by the tax laws regarding the amount of funding that is legally permissible in any given year.

In Summary

Companies seem to manage their corporate financial policies more or less jointly with their pension plans. Although the connections are not as vivid as early theory suggested they might be, nonetheless they are present. Moreover, anyone designing a private plan to maximize tax benefits—that is, to minimize the present value of future tax payments, all other things being equal—would still have to develop an asset mix policy in which the pension fund would hold only bonds, and the corporation would hold equities. However, workforce demographics, volatility of operating cash flows, funding regulations, and other factors are also important. Simply maximizing tax benefits is not sufficient.

The connection between integration, funding, and asset allocation is not so clear with public sponsors and pension plans. The tax motive is much weaker. In addition, the relationship between public sponsors and plans can be adversarial. Some public pension plans feel they must sue their sponsors to force payment of contributions. Others, however, work closely with the sponsor and presumably work toward optimal asset allocations that are integrated with the financial policies of the sponsor.

The increase in funding from investment returns noted above suggests an increased attention to asset allocations that emphasizes a higher return and, hence, more risk. Public funds, of course, do not have the tax incentives or ERISA mandates that private funds have. This is consistent with the low levels of funding (in essence, the pay-as-you-go approach) taken by many public fund sponsors. The implied relationship between underfunded plans pursuing the risk premium associated with stocks seems especially appropriate for public plans, as does a reallocation to bonds for well-funded plans. Accordingly, there is still a need to develop a model that embodies the pension sponsor's risk tolerance and that selects an acceptable mix of stocks/bonds/cash for the combined plan/ sponsor, irrespective of where each category of investment happens to reside.

SETTING THE STRATEGIC ASSET ALLOCATION: AN ANALYTICAL APPROACH

In spite of the complexity of the decision, the strategic asset allocation must be set. The strategic asset allocation will not simply appear, nor should it be merely that which the "average" pension fund has. To make the appropriate allocation of funds to stocks, bonds, and cash, the analyst must bring together the inter-dependency of the fund's returns and the sponsor's contributions, the interaction between the value of the plans assets and liabilities, and all the relevant financial market information that will bear on the decision. This requires a fairly comprehensive analytical approach. One such approach is presented in this section.

The Approach

The approach suggested here is to use simulation analysis coupled with scenario analysis to generate reasonable data with which to examine the interplay between asset allocations, contribution rates, and likelihood of benefits. The sponsor can analyze the data produced and choose the asset mix that optimally trades off expected contributions, contribution variability, surplus volatility, and benefit assurance. Private sponsors should do this while considering the firm's share-holders as well as its pension beneficiaries. Public sponsors should do this while considering taxpayers as well as beneficiaries. Sponsors are, after all, in the unusual position of having a fiduciary responsibility to both shareholders/tax-payers and pension beneficiaries.

The first step in the process is to lay out plausible assumptions regarding the performance of various sectors of the capital markets and the other markets in which investments might be made. The decision maker may also wish to specify several different scenarios that might prevail over the relevant planning horizon (e.g., five years). Table 9.1 offers an example of a set of financial market expectations, which are used here to illustrate a sensitivity analysis. (To simplify the calculations and allow the reader to follow the logic of the analysis more easily, zero correlations are assumed among the asset classes. Note, too, that the

Table 9.1 Alternative Financial Market Scenarios

	Stocks	Bonds	Cash
Scenario A (unexpectedly high inflation, low growth)			
Expected return	0	2	6
Expected standard deviation	16	10	3
	Stocks with Bonds	Stocks with Cash	Bonds with Cash
Correlation coefficients	0	0	0
	Stocks	Bonds	Cash
Scenario B (normal growth and inflation)			
Expected return	12	5.5	3.5
Expected standard deviation	20	8.5	1
	Stocks with Bonds	Stocks with Cash	Bonds with Cash
Correlation coefficients	0	0	0

standard deviations differ depending on the scenario. This is consistent with the idea that different general economic conditions produce very different financial market behaviors.)

The second step is to identify the alternative asset allocations that the analyst wishes to examine. Table 9.2 considers three alternative allocations.

Now, the analyst must ask what one would expect to happen to the value of specific alternative portfolios and to the value of the pension surplus over the next five years under each of these scenarios. Although a constant 7% growth in liabilities is assumed here, alternative estimates of liability growth should be made under each scenario to pick up differences in salary growth and size of the labor force. Table 9.3 offers the results of the analysis. For simplicity, the analyst may wish to estimate these values first without allowing for any contributions over the period. However, the analyst will eventually have to evaluate the estimates of contributions to the plan that the sponsor must make. If full

Table 9.2 Alternative Asset Allocations

Asset Allocation	Stocks (%)	Bonds (%)	Cash (%)
1	85	10	5
2	60	30	10
3	20	70	10

Initial portfolio value = $100,000; initial liability value = $100,000; assumed rate of liability growth = 7%.

Table 9.3 Analysis of Alternative Asset Allocations under Different Financial Market Scenarios

Asset Allocation	Scenario A			Scenario B		
	1	2	3	1	2	3
Stocks	85%	60%	20%	85%	60%	20%
Bonds	10%	30%	70%	10%	30%	70%
Cash	5%	10%	10%	5%	10%	10%
Expected return	0.5%	1.2%	2.0%	10.93%	9.2%	6.6%
Expected standard deviation	13.64%	10.06%	7.70%	17.02%	12.27%	7.17%
Expected portfolio value	$100,500	$101,200	$102,000	$110,925	$109,200	$106,600
Expected liability value	$107,000	$107,000	$107,000	$107,000	$107,000	$107,000
Expected surplus (deficit)	$(6,500)	$(5,800)	$(5,000)	$3,925	$2,200	$(400)
Maximum surplus	$20,775	$14,325	$10,405	$37,968	$26,737	$13,941
Minimum surplus	$(33,775)	$(25,925)	$(20,405)	$(30,118)	$(22,337)	$(14,741)

Maximum and minimum surplus are before funding and are based on two standard deviations above and below expectation; 95% of the time, the actual surplus (deficit) will be between the maximum and minimum figures.

funding is assumed, the funding required is equal to the expected surplus (deficit), whereas a range of funding outcomes is provided by the minimum and maximum surplus (deficit) values given in table 9.3.

The analysis will require some other fine tuning. For example, a rebalancing rule will have to be assumed. Are asset categories rebalanced annually or quarterly, or will the plan follow a pure buy-and-hold strategy? Finally, a single period is shown for simplicity. Five- and even ten-year annual projections are typically more helpful.

Choosing the Right Asset Mix

With this type of data, there are several approaches the decision maker may use to choose an asset mix. The approach chosen should be consistent with the analyst's judgment about the relative importance of the competing claims made by taxpayers, shareholders, and employees. Well-written policy will serve as a guide when evaluating the alternative scenarios.

One approach is for the decision maker to choose the asset mix that requires the lowest contribution under the worst scenario—termed the min-max strategy. The logic for choosing this asset mix could be that, during good times, the sponsor could increase its contributions without really feeling the pinch of a cash shortage. It is only during bad economic times that the size of the contribution matters.

Another approach might focus on choosing a portfolio that would lead to the lowest average contribution or to the lowest present value of future contributions irrespective of which scenario actually comes about. Here the decision maker may need to be informed only that, should the worst occur, the asset mix chosen would not require Herculean funding efforts.

A third approach would be to choose the asset mix that, under all scenarios, results in the lowest volatility of the surplus (deficit) of asset values over expected liability values. This is appealing for pensions that want to protect an existing surplus but are not especially sensitive to funding concerns. This shift in attention to the surplus can be followed by a review of the likely funding consequences and further analysis (e.g., more asset class combinations tried) to see whether a superior joint surplus/contribution solution appears.

Obviously, there are many alternative approaches to choosing the appropriate mix. The rules for the decision are situational and depend on the circumstances of the plan and the ability of the various parties to work together.

Just as obviously, the preceding analysis lends itself to computerization. More realistic correlations can be assumed, probabilities of alternative scenarios can be incorporated, and the effects of changes in multiple factors can be included. Long time periods can be used and alternative asset allocations evaluated in the context of, for example, the last thirty years of capital market performance. In addition, the estimated contributions may be adjusted to present values to evaluate more readily the current effect of the contributions on the sponsor's economic value.

A word of caution: there are numerous simulation and optimization models available. Some are well designed, some are not. Larger plans can probably develop their own models in-house, perhaps with the help of a consultant. The very process of participating in model design can be immeasurably helpful to identifying the issues relevant to a particular plan and to understanding the consequences of various actions. For plans that leave the modeling to others, care should be taken to question the model's underlying assumptions and to understand the data being input.

Finally, there is an important side effect of this analysis. Although the analyst often starts with a presumably acceptable level of risk tolerance in mind, the process of making the decision will reveal the actual risk tolerance of the plan as those involved in the decision-making process see it. The numbers generated force the decision makers to explicitly confront the interrelations that exist between various factors and to decide what is really important; that is, what they really believe in the presence of many possible outcomes. Given the complexity of the decision and its dependence on knowing the plan's tolerance for risk, it is hard to overstate the value of decision-makers' elimination of some alternatives in favor of others. This process of elimination ultimately leads to an informed assessment of what the plan's tolerance for risk is.

Other Allocation Issues

Once the broad asset mix is chosen, the pension plan sponsor must decide how to allocate within each category; that is, how much of the total equity pool will go toward passive investing, how much toward active management, and so forth.

There is a caution here worth reiterating: the manager must remain alert to excessively high reliance on sponsor contributions, because too heavy a reliance could undo the effect of diversification.

Managers generally tend to rebalance portfolios on at least an annual basis, and many will rebalance on a quarterly basis or when a range limitation has been crossed (e.g., when the actual equity allocation exceeds the strategic allocation by 5% or more). As noted earlier, the choice of rebalancing strategies depends on the investor's risk tolerance and willingness to exploit beliefs about the capital markets. This is more or less subjective, so there is no one right answer. However, note two things. In the absence of increasing supplies of securities—for example, new issues of stock or bonds, and so forth—the only strategy that can be pursued simultaneously by all investors is the buy-and-hold strategy. If there are changing supplies (e.g., if corporations choose a policy of constant debt to equity, thus selling more debt when equity values rise), then investors will have to trade back toward a constant mix policy to ensure an equilibrium such that all securities that are available get held in some portfolio.

STRATEGIC ASSET ALLOCATION AND REALLOCATIONS OVER TIME

It is useful to consider more completely how fluctuations in valuation in the financial markets affect initial asset allocations, and also to consider ways to reallocate assets as time passes and things change. We use as our framework a structure William Sharpe has suggested in various works.[20] We begin by discussing alternative ways to maintain the strategic asset allocation once it has been established and then address, in turn, tactical asset allocation and insured asset allocation.

Once made, the strategic asset allocation is maintained in one of two ways. The first is a simple buy-and-hold strategy in which positions in various asset classes are established according to the risk/return preferences of the plan sponsor/beneficiary. In this strategy, no trades are made other than those necessary to meet plan liquidity needs (e.g., investing new contributions or selling securities to meet payment requirements). The effect of market action on plan assets and, hence, on allocations is ignored. This is an important issue as, over time, asset classes experience periods of underperformance and overperformance relative to other asset classes. These market actions translate into a change in the proportions of funds in each asset class. For example, if stocks do unusually well relative to bonds, actual bond weightings in a real portfolio go down and stock weightings increase as a percentage of the whole even though no trading has taken place. The buy-and-hold strategy presumes that these variations in actual asset weights are acceptable because, on average over long periods of time, the average mix of assets will meet policy targets as markets reverse direction and as new contributions or liquidations are made in ways that will rebalance the overall portfolio. So if the target allocation for stocks is 60% and the stock market has risen so that 70% of total assets are actually invested in equities, new contributions could be directed toward bonds until the actual stock allocation falls to the target. Alternatively, if new funding is not substantial, the pension plan may simply wait for markets to restore the initial asset mix by reverting to the mean. As should be apparent, the buy-and-hold strategy incurs little in the way of transaction costs. However, at any given point in time, the actual asset allocation and the strategic allocation may differ from each other, and the risk/return profile of the portfolio thus may not match the target profile.

The alternative approach to maintaining strategic asset allocation is to follow a disciplined rebalancing or constant mix strategy. Rather than the no-action approach that is characteristic of the buy-and-hold strategy, disciplined rebalancing is a dynamic strategy that requires the plan manager to rebalance the portfolio periodically—whenever actual asset allocations fall outside the targeted range or on a predetermined schedule. The general trading rule followed by disciplined rebalancing is to buy assets that perform poorly relative to other asset classes and to reduce holdings in asset classes that perform relatively well. In essence, this is a trading strategy that buys when prices fall and sells when prices rise. The objective of any set of trades is to return to the long-term strategic weights as defined by policy. That is, the disciplined rebalancing strategy attempts dynamically to restore a constant mix. Disciplined rebalancing should be done at the level of the overall pool of assets, not by individual managers. Thus, someone must be monitoring the overall asset allocation. Because disciplined rebalancing requires trading, it may incur greater transaction costs than the buy-and-hold strategy. These costs can be reduced by the use of derivatives. The advantage of this strategy over the buy-and-hold approach is that the actual portfolio weights, and hence its risk/return profile, will be more closely aligned with the targets specified in the policy statement.

The relative performance of these two strategies—disciplined rebalancing versus buy-and-hold—depends on the nature of the market action. To see this, consider a simple two-asset allocation among stocks and Treasury bills. If the absolute or relative performance of stocks relative to Treasury bills makes a sustained move either up or down (i.e., if it trends), the buy-and-hold strategy will produce performance that is superior to that of disciplined rebalancing. This is because disciplined rebalancing will sell stocks into a rising stock market in which stock prices continue to rise, and vice versa. In contrast, if an asset class such as stocks is mean reverting—that is, if reversals occur following upward or downward changes in valuation of market sectors—then the disciplined rebalancing approach will provide superior performance. This is because disciplined rebalancing will sell stocks into a rising stock market that subsequently falls, and vice versa. In either case, the sponsor should be aware that both of these strategies are primarily passive in nature, in that their intent is to maintain preselected policy target weights rather than to exploit insights or beliefs about market sectors.

In one study, a typical manager with a 60% stock/40% bond mix would gain sixteen basis points more per year using disciplined rebalancing every month, after allowing for transaction costs, versus allowing allocation drift (the buy-and-hold strategy) as market values of each sector moved apart.[21] Thus, there is some evidence that frequent rebalancing may pay, though the frequency must be traded off against the costs of frequent trading, and as noted above, it may not work well in all markets.

Tactical Asset Allocation

An increasing number of pensions are using or exploring tactical asset allocation (TAA) strategies. In TAA, the strategic asset allocation targets are still considered to be valid in the sense that they provide the broad framework for the long-term investment of pension assets. However, within that framework, the pension plan sponsor intends to adjust the asset mix to exploit what the sponsor believes to be incorrect relative valuations of asset classes, sectors, or individual assets.

For instance, suppose the strategic asset allocation is 60% equities, 30% bonds, and 10% cash. Further suppose that the stock market drops suddenly and sharply. Because the dollar value of stocks has decreased relative to the dollar value of the other asset classes, adhering to the strategic asset allocation plan would require that either bonds and cash equivalents be sold and stocks bought to return to the 60/30/10 policy mix (the disciplined rebalancing approach) or, simply, that nothing be done (the buy-and-hold approach). The tactical asset allocation plan would not necessarily pursue either of these trading strategies. It could, instead, elect to remain heavily in bonds until more information regarding the stock decline becomes available. Alternatively, a plan manager may develop a belief that equities now are underpriced. As a result of this belief, and the corollary expectation that stocks now are likely to perform unusually well, he or she may decide to do more than merely return to the initial allocation and purchase more than the target amount of stocks necessary to restore the strategic asset allocation, so that the mix becomes 80/15/5. The additional exposure to stocks (i.e., the 20% of the allocation that is above the strategic weight of 60%) is an active bet that stocks will do unusually well in the future.

This latter strategy is most typical of what normally is considered tactical asset allocation and is consistent with an effort to exploit the tendency of asset markets to experience reversals of movements. Implicit in any TAA program is a theory of relative asset valuation. Reversals are responsive countermoves that occur after sharp upward or downward changes in valuation of markets, sectors, or individual securities. A belief in reversals generally is supported by a belief that investors overreact to new information that the market may have received and that once this overreaction is recognized, the prices of securities that rose (or fell) sharply will move in the opposite direction nearly as sharply. Note that although this specific, reversal-based tactical asset allocation trading strategy is driven by an expected reversal, it looks fundamentally the same as disciplined rebalancing—buying when prices fall and selling when prices rise. The difference is that the motivation is to exploit a perceived mispricing rather than simply to return to target policy weights.

The results of the reversal-based TAA trading strategy described above relative to a buy-and-hold strategy are the same as for the disciplined rebalancing in that tactical asset allocation will outperform a buy-and-hold strategy when there are reversals, but it will underperform when there are sustained moves away from normal values. The greater flexibility to take on weights outside policy guidelines, of course, permits tactical asset allocation potentially to achieve greater returns (or incur greater opportunity costs) than disciplined re-balancing permits.

Tactical asset allocation can also be applied as sector-tilting, which is over-weighting and underweighting sectors of a market that are expected to do rel-atively well or relatively poorly, or as security selection, which is the identifi-cation of over- or undervalued stocks. There are numerous models for those who wish to allocate assets tactically either by timing asset class returns or shopping for undervalued assets. Many favor a contrarian approach like that described above. As one investment manager says, "Buy when there is blood in the streets." The essence of this approach is to buy when no one else seems to want the asset (or class of assets). When assets become oversold, their prices can fall below their true values and, if one simply waits long enough, their prices will recover. One must be careful in adapting this strategy—a bargain that remains a bargain is, of course, no bargain.

Note that underlying TAA is an attempt to earn excess returns by exploiting beliefs about expected returns and risks. Thus, the reversal-based (contrarian) model used for illustration is only one way of forming beliefs. Other examples of TAA approaches are

- momentum-based strategies (if stocks rise, buy more stocks, expecting upward momentum to continue), and
- dividend discount or cash flow discount-based strategies that use fun-damentals to determine a market's (or an asset's) intrinsic (or fair) value.

If a plan sponsor wants to implement a tactical asset allocation plan, there are three elements that must be very clearly specified. The first is the limitation on the percentage by which the investment and various categories can deviate from the strategic asset allocation targets. That is, the strategic asset allocation plan specifies the appropriate asset mix, but a specified range of tactical discre-tion is predetermined and permitted. The second element is the decision model that will be used explicitly to trigger actions to buy or sell on the basis of relative valuations. The third element is a commitment to doing the things the selected model says ought to be done.

The last point is worth further discussion. Failures to act on the predictions of tactical asset allocation models may lead to returns that are much worse than they should be. The advantage of any active trading strategy is that it brings to bear all the science and intuition that a decision maker can muster. The fallacy in changing one's mind about the usefulness of the output of a model and thus overriding its mechanical decision is that it effectively throws out one's best systematic thinking and substitutes an isolated component of intuition. Indeed, if an investment manager behaves differently than the manager has committed to behave, it could lead to a legal challenge on prudence grounds. The prospect of litigation alone should caution a manager against ad hoc intuitive behavior.

Does TAA work? There are studies[22] reporting that gains can be made if tactical asset allocation is correct as little as 51% of the time. Some experts[23] argue that because pension plans have very long time horizons, pension plan risk tolerance can be thought of as remaining constant regardless of changes in the average risk tolerance and, hence, changes in asset class valuations. If this is true, TAA may be a sensible way to pursue excess returns because, from time to time, the average expected risk premium may be much higher than the pension plan ordinarily would require. Other authorities[24] suggest that traditional measures of value such as dividend yield and the price/book ratio are related to stock market returns but not in a way that can be exploited by TAA strategies that rely on mean/variance analysis. Rather, they argue that successful TAA strategies must consider the skewness—the likelihood of a large number of outcomes skewed above or below the expected outcome—of the probability distribution of equity returns if the strategy is to work.

In summary, achieving success with tactical asset allocation requires a belief in actively managing portfolios by trading on expectations of values—expectations that tend to be contrary to popular wisdom. Hence it requires considerable discipline and a model of asset valuation. If the model being used needs adjustment, by all means, make the adjustment, but do it in a long-term, strategically aware way just as strategic allocations are determined. Do not ignore the serious risk of having the sponsor or manager chicken out, and not do something that should be done simply because prevailing folk wisdom is contrary to the model.

Insured Asset Allocation

In the mid-1980s, portfolio insurance became the darling of many in the institutional investor crowd. The equity market crash of October 1987 greatly reduced the attractiveness of portfolio insurance when it became apparent that the trading strategies on which it relied could not be executed in all types of markets or in a timely enough manner to provide the insurance promised. Nonetheless, portfolio insurance may, from time to time, be appropriate for pension funds, and it can be a useful, if only occasional, ingredient in successful asset allocation. In addition, insurance-like trading rules may be useful in markets that can be characterized as trending over time.

In its simplest form, insured asset allocation consists of reducing a plan's exposure to risky asset classes when those classes are performing poorly (i.e., when asset values are decreasing). As Sharpe and Perold (1988) have pointed out, the essence of portfolio insurance is to establish and then maintain a floor or minimal asset value beneath which no exposure to risky assets will be taken. Above the floor, the portfolio can invest in risky assets in proportion to the size of the cushion; that is, if a risky asset class, such as stocks, is doing well and values are going up, the portfolio will increase its exposure to stocks by purchasing more. If, however, stock prices begin to fall so that the cushion above the floor is eroding, the exposure to stocks will be reduced by selling stocks.

The trading dynamic of this strategy is just the opposite of that of the disciplined rebalancing and tactical asset allocation strategies. In fact, the performance of this strategy relative to a buy-and-hold strategy also is just the opposite. Insured portfolios will outperform buy-and-hold strategies (as well as tactical asset allocation and disciplined rebalancing strategies) when markets make sustained moves either up or down and when the trades can be executed at the proper "trigger" prices. When markets are relatively flat but volatile (e.g., when reversion to the mean is taking place), portfolio insurance strategies will underperform the buy-and-hold strategy (and also underperform the tactical asset allocation and disciplined rebalancing strategies) because of buying high and selling low. As with TAA, insured asset allocation may be implemented with derivatives (liquidity permitting).

When is portfolio insurance appropriate? One way to think about portfolio insurance is to consider it to be an occasional strategy. The primary motivation to insure should come from a sufficiently unique circumstance wherein the pension plan's risk tolerance is determined to be more sensitive to changes in market values at a specific time than is the risk tolerance of the market as a whole. When markets fall, one interpretation of the reason for the decline in market prices is that the societal or average risk premium has increased, driving asset values down. If a pension plan's sensitivity to changes in asset values is greater than the average change in risk tolerance implied by the change in asset prices, there is a case to be made for insuring the portfolio—reducing the plan's fundamental definition of an acceptable level of risk. For example, consider a sponsor who decides to terminate its DB plan and use its assets to purchase annuities to affect plan liabilities. The plan now has the unusually short time horizon of perhaps one year, or until the annuity contracts are arranged. In this situation, the plan might wish to insure its portfolio against loss of value.

CONCLUSION

Asset allocation is one of the most critical investment decisions that is made. Moreover, it is never settled. It is a process in which decisions regarding the appropriate strategic mix for the long term must constantly be reviewed and occasionally revised as plan or sponsor circumstances change or if fundamental beliefs about the capital markets change.

For sponsors of DB plans, the process of choosing the appropriate asset mix ultimately indicates a tremendous amount of introspection on the part of pension plan sponsors and on the part of all who are involved in the decision making or have a fiduciary relationship with the plan. It requires the sponsor to specify a risk-tolerance level in the face of competing ownership claims in recognition that, whatever level is chosen, risk taking has substantial financial implications for numerous parties as the pension plan goes forward.

There is little question that the financial health and the financial policies of the sponsor should be integrated into pension fund decisions. Equally as clear, the nature of the plan liabilities—the pension plan's financial commitment to employees—must be carefully analyzed in setting the plan's strategic asset allocation. When the allocation is set, the decision-making process should be capable of withstanding the scrutiny of all parties affected by the decision, and the trade-offs made should be both evident and acceptable to those involved.

Simulation analysis seems to be the most useful (though not necessarily the most scientific) quantitative tool for asset allocation decisions for both individuals and DB plans. Decision makers derive considerable insight and some comfort from having the array of possible outcomes over time laid before them. The process of specifying the data to be run and the assumptions to be made forces the analyst and those who will evaluate the results to answer some important questions before any decision is made. Experience reveals that simulation analysis is one of the most effective ways available to identify risk tolerance levels. This is well worth the effort in determining the best asset allocation for the pension plan.

No single one of the asset allocation techniques discussed in this chapter is exclusively the best. Rather, as Sharpe (1990) has proposed, the best approach is an integrated approach in which full attention initially is given to establishing the correct strategic asset weights. Once this is done, the sponsor then needs to make the fundamental choice of allocating money to be actively managed or passively managed. If the sponsor/beneficiary believes that active management may lead to above-average returns on a risk-adjusted basis, perhaps because one or more of the markets in which the fund intends to invest are not informationally efficient and may be subject to overreaction, then tactical asset allocation becomes a viable alternative. Presumably, there also will be times in the future, as there have been in the past, when market sectors are doing nothing special. During these times, it seems likely that the fund will benefit more if it pursues a simple buy-and-hold strategy or a disciplined rebalancing approach. From time to time there may be particular circumstances in which insuring plan assets makes sense. At these times, of course, a shift in asset allocation strategies again seems warranted.

Without question, the initial strategic asset allocation decision should get the bulk of the decision maker's attention. Tactical, insured, and disciplined rebalancing are all legitimate alternatives to a simple buy-and-hold strategy. A poor strategic allocation, however, will be difficult to overcome.

10

Accounting for Defined
Benefit Plans

Accounting for pension funds could possibly mislead pension fund decision makers. In part, this is because accounting uses an accrual procedure that relies on matching transactions with the time periods they presumably affect; in part, it is because some accounting rules are arbitrary and inconsistent; finally, in part, it is because those who apply the accounting rules have considerable leeway in selecting key variables that affect the numbers produced.

Most pension decisions should be based on sound economic data. Over the very long term, accounting measures and economic measures may tend to be reasonably close. However, over the shorter term—say, several years—such measures as the economic value of the pension liability, cash contributions to the plan, and cash payments to beneficiaries can be substantially different from accounting measures of the pension liability and pension costs.

This difference between measures in the short term creates a problem for decision makers and, indeed, for all parties interested in the financial strength of pension plans. Sound decisions generally require information. If accounting data are potentially misleading, what should a pension manager or other fiduciary use? What do they need to know about pension fund accounting?

This chapter provides the nonaccountant with sufficient background and insight to understand the accounting data typically provided in financial statements. The decision maker can then access additional information as needed to make sound decisions. The first section reviews the basics of pension fund accounting and illustrates the key components of pension fund accounting data. The second section examines some of the critical assumptions that are made in pension accounting and how those assumptions may differ from economic reality. Finally, the chapter examines the investment and pension fund management implications of pension fund accounting and shows how accounting-based decisions can be suboptimal for sponsors, plans, and beneficiaries.

ACCOUNTING BASICS

Accounting for DC plans is straightforward. In most cases, unless there is delayed funding, the pension plan assets and the pension plan liabilities equal each other by definition. The only problematic issue is whether the assets are valued properly. For publicly traded securities, this is not a serious issue, as valuation is comparatively simple. If, however, a DC plan has investments in real estate, company stores, venture capital funds, or other illiquid assets, valuation becomes more difficult. In general, organizations turn to appraisal firms for help in assessing the worth of these investments.

Accounting for DB plans is anything but straightforward. Accounting and financial disclosure requirements for private DB plans are governed by Financial Accounting Standards Board (FASB) Statements 87, 88, and 132. Accounting guidelines for state and local governments, government-owned enterprises, and public school teachers are set forth in Government Accounting Standards Board (GASB) Statements 25, 26, 27, and 34.[1] The two sets of accounting standards for DB pension plans are sufficiently similar that no further distinctions are necessary for current purposes. The two sets of standards do, however, differ in some ways, particularly in the way in which actuarial costs are amortized. These differences involve levels of detail that only certified public accountants need to understand, however. They are not highly relevant for pension plan managers because they deal with reports, not decisions.

Before exploring the key accounting rules, it is helpful to understand some philosophical issues. First, accounting as a discipline treats the pension fund as an entity that is separate from the sponsoring organization; that is, the balance sheets and income statements of the plan are not fully integrated with the company's financial statements. This, of course, implies that decisions affecting the plan do not have to consider the effect they may have on the sponsor, a position contrary to sound pension fund management. Second, changes in the market value of plan assets and the economic value of the pension liability are not given equal treatment in the accounting approach, thus distorting the true effect of various factors on the adequacy of pension funding. Because many decisions of importance rely on a reasonable estimate of the adequacy of funding—for example, determining the risk tolerance of the plan to set the strategic asset allocation—this creates problems for decision makers.

Those who play a role in managing pension plans must compensate for these problems when dealing with the numbers presented. To do so requires a basic understanding of how the accounting numbers come to be and how they deviate from the underlying economic reality.

THE ACCOUNTING RULES

Both private and public sector pension plan accounting requires estimates of the following values:

- ABO,
- PBO,
- fair market value of pension assets,
- annual pension expense,
- actuarial interest rate,
- benefit projection interest rate,
- estimated growth of employee's salaries,
- actual plan return, and
- expected plan return.

The sponsoring organization is also required to report its annual service cost, the growth in its pension liabilities through the passage of time, and its annual contribution to the pension fund. A pension fund's assets must be compared with its liabilities in the footnote to the main accounting statements. Private firms are also required to reconcile the unfunded portion of the plan with liability amounts reported elsewhere in the financial statements. Governments need not do this.

Definitions

Following are definitions of some terms common to private and public pension plan accounting.

Accumulated Benefit Obligation

The ABO is the actuarial present value of benefits, both vested and nonvested, accumulated by an employee as of a specific date. The ABO is based on employee service through the present and on compensation as it currently stands. It is the present value of the pension plan if a fully vested employee left the firm now and began collecting benefits later. This can be viewed as a "wind-up" measure of pension obligations; it does not allow for future work or future pay increases. If a pension plan is to be terminated, this is the best initial estimate of what must be set aside for workers. Of course, if the subsequent annuity provider can produce better returns than the terminating pension plan can produce, then the cost of the pension plan termination annuity will be less than the ABO. Note, however, that selecting an appropriate annuity provider can be a challenging task. Should the provider subsequently fail, as did Executive Life, the plan's liabilities may again become the responsibility of the sponsor.

Projected Benefit Obligation

The PBO is the present value of pension benefits under the assumption that the amount of employee compensation will rise between the reporting time and the employee's time of retirement. The PBO will exceed the ABO only as long as the expected final salary exceeds the present salary. The PBO measure does not, however, incorporate the additional years of service that will be acquired between now and retirement. For firms with a flat pension benefit system—for example, $1,000 for every year worked—the ABO and the PBO will be the same.

Fair Market Value of Pension Assets

The fair market value of pension assets is computed by determining the aggregate current amount that a pension plan reasonably could expect to receive by selling an investment to a willing buyer and by having itself behaving as a willing seller. That is, this assumes a price that is not a fire-sale price or any especially concessionary price. For actively traded stocks, government bonds, and high-grade corporate bonds, estimating this is reasonably easy. Valuing real estate, venture capital investments, junk bonds, and perhaps some other types of investments—rare coins, for instance—requires exceptional effort. Most companies have third-party appraisal experts perform this service for them periodically.

Annual Pension Expense

The annual pension expense is the net amount that is needed each year to keep the plan's assets abreast of its growing liabilities. This entails a complex calculation, an example of which is given later. Annual pension expense includes service cost (the growth in pension liability resulting from another year's work on the part of the employees), interest, any amortizations or deferrals owing to prior service, the difference between actual returns and expected investment returns, and the difference between actual mortality experience and expected mortality experience factors.

A word of caution: annual pension expense may not be the same as the cash actually contributed to the plan by the sponsor, nor is it necessarily equal to the cash needed to restore an underfunded plan. Cash contributions are calculated by using one of a number of actuarial cost methods and, for private plans, are subject to ERISA and IRS rules.

Actuarial Interest Rate

The actuarial interest rate is the interest rate the actuaries use to determine the present values required for the ABO and PBO computations. This is the discount rate that brings future payments into present value terms.

Benefit Projection Interest Rate

The benefit projection interest rate is the rate the actuaries use to project forward the current salaries of employees so that the PBO can be computed. It is the rate that converts current salaries into future salaries.

Estimated Salary Growth

The estimated salary growth is the expected nominal rate of growth of employees' salaries. This is the estimated salary growth and may be different than the benefit projection interest rate used in the actuarial calculations.

Expected Plan Return

The expected plan return is the return that is estimated on pension plan assets. Conceptually, it is set using the combined wisdom of the plan sponsor and the actuaries informed by historical investment performances and assumed future asset allocations. Although the explicit estimate is based on historical experience, it may be shaded down to reflect the inherent conservatism of actuaries.

Actual Plan Return

The actual plan return is the actual investment return on pension plan assets. It is comprised of both income and capital change components.

COMPUTING PENSION EXPENSE

The most complex component of the required disclosures is the pension expense calculation. It has four components: service cost, interest cost, return on plan assets, and net amortization and deferral. The last component itself has four parts: asset gain or loss deferral, amortization of cumulative unrecorded net gains or losses, amortization of transition assets or liabilities, and amortization of prior service cost.

Example

A much-simplified example can illustrate each of these components. Managers need to understand how the books are kept to make good management decisions. Thus, the intent here is to convey the essence of the rule, not to develop sophisticated pension accountants. Bear in mind that many of the possible issues are treated in a simplified way.[2]

Suppose there is only one employee, Harry, who expects to retire at the end of the year after the current one, which is just beginning. To this point, he has worked for the sponsor for twenty-three years and will have worked for the sponsor for a full twenty-five years at retirement in two years. His current salary is $60,000. There is no integration with Social Security benefits under the pension plan. The pension benefit formula of Harry's employer is

0.015 (or 1.5%) × final year's salary × number of years worked.

This formula yields the annual pension benefit that Harry anticipates receiving on retirement.

At present, the ABO on his behalf is the present value of the annual benefit, assuming no further work. He begins to collect in two years and will continue to collect for an expected twenty years after retirement. Here are the computations for the ABO:

$$0.015 \times \$60,000 \times 23 \text{ years} = \$20,700.$$

Assuming the actuarial interest rate applied to future benefits is 7%, the present value at time of retirement of annual retirement payments is

$$\text{benefit} = \Sigma(\$20,700/1.07^t) = \$219,296,$$

and the present value right now is:

$$\text{benefit} = \Sigma(\$219{,}926/1.07^2) = \$191{,}542.$$

The ABO is $191,542.

The PBO allows for salary increases. Let us suppose that Harry's salary will rise by the benefit projection interest rate of 6% per year between now and retirement. His final salary will thus be $67,416, or $60{,}000 \times 1.06^2$. His annual pension benefit will be $0.015 \times \$67{,}416 \times 23$ years, or $23,258.

The present value at time of retirement of annual retirement benefit is

$$\text{benefit} = \Sigma(\$23{,}258/1.07^1) = \$246{,}395.$$

The present value today is

$$\text{benefit} = \Sigma(\$246{,}395/1.07^2) = \$215{,}211.$$

Thus, the PBO is $215,193.

Service cost may be computed as the amount of increase resulting from the fact that the employee works an extra year. For the next-to-last year of Harry's employment, this would be the difference in the present value of the new ABO less the stepped-up-by-one-year present value of the old ABO. Service cost is thus the difference between $191,542 stepped up by one year to reflect the fact that Harry is a year closer to retirement, or $191{,}542 \times 1.07 = \$204{,}950$, and the new ABO. The new ABO, which takes account of the extra year and the pay increase, is computed as

$$\text{annual pension benefit} = 0.015 \times \$60{,}000(1.06) \times 24 \text{ years} = \$22{,}896.$$

Thus, the present value of benefits at time of retirement is:

$$\text{benefit} = \Sigma(\$22{,}896/1.07^1) = \$242{,}560,$$

and the present value is

$$\text{benefit} = \Sigma(\$242{,}560/1.07^2) = \$226{,}692.$$

The new ABO is $226,692, and the old ABO, merely stepped up to reflect the new proximity of Harry's retirement, is $204,950. The difference—service cost—is $21,742. It reflects a pay raise of 6% and an extra year of work.

The ABO-based pension cost will be more than this difference, however, as it includes the interest cost as well as the step up in the old ABO. Interest cost is $0.07 \times \$191{,}542$, or $13,408.

One way to view pension cost is the total difference between the old and the new ABO. To shortcut the calculations, just compare the new ABO, $226,692, with the old ABO, $191,542 not stepped up. However, accounting standards require this difference to be split into its two components. The first is service cost. In the example this is $21,742. The second is interest cost, which is $13,408 in the example. The total of the two is $35,150, which is the difference between the new ABO and the old ABO not stepped up.

So far our pension cost could be (taking some small liberties with the actual accounting rules) reported as:

ABO last year $191,542
Interest cost   ($13,408)
Service cost   (21,742)
Gross pension cost $35,150
(Excluding amortization for past service, or benefit enhancements, or prior deficiencies).

One could argue that using the ABO as the basis for pension cost computation and reporting is the correct way to do it. This approach is consistent with the idea that the pension plan could terminate at any time. All the employees get is the ABO, the "wind-up" measure.[3] Computing pension costs in this way would ratify the idea that pensions do not constitute implicit contracts. Rather, the ABO is consistent with the view that the labor market is a spot market, and there is no expectation that an employee is entitled to more than is explicitly promised. Indeed, this is what happens in pension plan terminations that are brought about to revert excess assets to the sponsoring organization.

As explained in Chapter 3, however, many analysts believe that the labor market is governed by implicit contracts. Accordingly, the true pension obligation of the organization is not merely the ABO, but much more. Indeed, it is even more than the PBO, because the PBO does not allow for using any more years of work in the computations. Employees may expect not only salary increases but also continued employment. Salary increases cannot occur without employment: to compute a PBO that assumes pay raises but no more years of work seems to mischaracterize the labor market. Accountants use PBO because they measure both assets and liabilities at the levels considered to have accrued at a point in time.

The computation of reported pension expense for all organizations begins by taking the difference in PBOs. Last year's PBO was $215,193. This year's PBO is $0.015 \times 67,416 \times 24$ years, adjusted for the twenty-year annuity factor and discounted back to the present. It is

$$(1/1.07)\Sigma(\$24,270/1.07^i) = \$240,296.$$

This computation yields a pension cost of $240,296 less $215,193, or $25,103. Of this total cost, $13,828 is interest cost and $11,275 is service cost. The reason that pension cost is lower using PBO than ABO is that both the early and late PBO measures use the same future salary, whereas the early and later ABO computations use different actual salary figures that depend on the true salary computation that enters the benefit formula.

To compute net expense (once again deferring discussion of all the specific nuances of the actual accounting rules), first compute the actual return on the pension fund assets after investment fees and expenses. This includes unrealized and realized capital gains, interest, and dividends. The actual return is then offset against the pension cost estimate.

Of course, actual pension fund payments to retirees also affect the net pension expense. Benefit payments alter PBOs: those already retired are still included in the estimate of the fund's liability, and with the passage of time will get less future benefit from the pension plan because they get nearer to death. Benefit payments also alter net pension fund returns because fewer of the fund's assets are available for investment after benefit payments.

Suppose that at the beginning of the year (the end of the prior year) the pension fund had a value of $300,000. Further, suppose that over the course of the year it experienced a gain of $20,000, so its value at the end of the current year was $320,000. The pension cost of $25,103 would be off-set against the portfolio gain. Net pension expense, again ignoring some complexities, would be $25,103 less $20,000, or $5,103.

To keep the pension plan whole from an accounting perspective, and assuming that nothing else (such as pressure from ERISA, the IRS, contracts, or legislation or strategic concerns) was affecting the firm's contribution requirements, and also assuming that the sponsor followed a policy of aiming for zero reported under-or overfunding of its pension plan, the sponsor would contribute $5,103. This would be its cash payment. Of course, if the organization had underfunded in the past, the cash payment would have to be larger to close the funding gap. Similarly, if the sponsor enhanced its retirement benefits, say by changing the 0.015 multiplier to a 0.016 multiplier in the benefit formula, it would also have to contribute more to pay for past service costs.

FURTHER DIFFERENCES BETWEEN ECONOMICS AND ACCOUNTING

It is clear by now that the accounting rules do not capture future pensionable employment, even though this may be economically relevant. There are other differences between the accounting approach and the economic approach.

Actual versus Expected Return

In addition to the actual gain or loss on the pension fund, the sponsor must incorporate prior unexpected portfolio gains and unexpected portfolio losses in its pension expense. To see how this works, suppose the sponsor projected that its annual return on the pension funds would equal 6%. Assuming that the $300,000 it had invested at the end of last year (the beginning of this year) equaled what it expected to have invested at the time, the actuarially determined expected value of the portfolio at the end of this year was $318,000, or $300,000 × 1.06. If the actual value was $320,000, the sponsor could defer this unanticipated portfolio gain of $2,000. If it did, its books would be as follows:

Service costs	$11,275
Interest cost	$13,828
Actual return on plan assets	($20,000)
Deferred gain on plan assets	$2,000
Pension expense	$7,103

The effect of backing out the $2,000 deferred gain is to make the sponsor's pension expense appear larger than it truly is. The sponsor may wish to contribute more money now to get a bigger tax deduction and "bank" the gain. Alternatively, it may only wish to bank the gain in an accounting sense, using it—that is, drawing on it—in some year when investment performance was not good but the company nonetheless wanted to report low pension expense. Note how this moves the "pension expense" away from the cash contribution that may be necessary to make the plan whole.

For companies, if the cumulative discrepancy between actual and expected returns begins to become large, it must be reported on the company's income statement and must be dealt with explicitly. Small cumulative discrepancies may remain hidden in the footnotes. Specifically, according to Revsine (1989),

> At the start of each reporting year, the cumulative unrecorded gain (or loss) is computed. This cumulative gain or loss will be amortized over future years if it exceeds 10% of the larger of (1) the present value of pension obligations based on assumed future compensation levels (termed projected benefit obligation), or (2) the market-related value of pension plan assets. If the 10% threshold is triggered, the cumulative gain or loss is amortized straight line over the estimated average remaining service life of active employees. (p. 65)

The total effect of these accounting practices is that it allows organizations to smooth their reported pension expense. However, it changes nothing fundamentally about the economics of the organization or its obligations.

Benefit Enhancement

Sometimes organizations change the formula for determining benefit amounts that affects all existing employees. Private firms may simply decide to increase the rewards for long-term employees. Many state and local governments enhance pension benefits instead of current salaries to avoid raising current taxes while still increasing total compensation.[4] In addition, organizations sometimes enhance their pension benefits in response to prior unanticipated inflation. Indeed, many state and local governmental entities contractually commit themselves to provide COLAs that are built into their pension liability estimates. Corporations will, in contrast, typically offer ad hoc periodic adjustments.

When the benefit formula is made more generous, a larger pension obligation results. Because the change in the formula applies to years already worked, it represents not only a service cost for this year but one for all past years as well. This is termed a "past service cost." For accounting purposes, the present value of future pension benefits attributable to the formula change is computed. This value is then amortized over the remaining working life of the employee (or the actuarially estimated lives for the current group of employees).

Transition Gains and Losses

There is also a transition asset or liability amortization. When FASB Statement 87 was introduced, some companies had pension plans in which the fair market value of assets exceeded the amount of the liabilities that had to be reported under the rule. Others had underfunded plans. The amortization component allows companies to report the closing of the gap between what they had in the pension plan and what they need to indicate their pension expenses are for financial accounting reporting purposes. That is, the overfunding or underfunding gaps are amortized.

RECONCILING ECONOMICS AND ACCOUNTING

Amortizations and deferrals complicate the reconciliation between the economic status of the pension plan and its status in accounting terms. Senior plan managers, administrators, and fiduciaries must look beyond the reported accounting numbers. They should seek additional information from internal sources. They must also understand how to adjust reported values. The most important adjustments are those in measuring plan surplus, in measuring pension expense against cash flow, and in the underlying actuarial assumptions.

Plan Surplus

The measure of pension plan surplus or deficit that FASB Statement 87 and GASB Statement 27 require is the difference between the fair market value of the pension plan assets and its PBO. As noted earlier, even the PBO generally is less than a true economic rendering of pension obligations because it ignores potential future years of work. Also, as noted, if a company terminates a pension plan, the amount it can recapture is the difference between the market value of its assets and its ABO, not its PBO, or what an annuity costs that has a present value equal to the ABO.

Decision makers must be aware that the accounting measure chosen to measure pension plan surplus or deficit lies between the alternative realities of long-term implicit contract types of labor markets and short-term spot labor markets. This is important because pension plans are fundamentally contracts between employees and employers. Managing pension plans, therefore, must reflect this reality if the strategic asset allocation is to reflect the actual risk tolerance of the parties affected by the pension plan (sponsors, employees, shareholders, and taxpayers) and to avoid "gaming" the numbers to obscure from one or more parties the economic realities of various decisions. In general, decision makers should be on the lookout for understated pension liabilities and a corresponding overstatement of the pension plan's financial health or funding status.

Pension Expense versus Cash Flow

As suggested earlier, the reported pension expense figure does not necessarily represent the cash flow to the plan from the sponsor nor the benefits paid out of the plan. Though possible, it is difficult to estimate the actual cash flow precisely by using standard financial statement analysis techniques.[5]

For corporations, ERISA imposes minimum standards on annual funding to enhance the safety of pension plans, whereas the IRS limits tax-deductible pension funding if a plan is economically overfunded. Even overfunded plans report pension expense; however, they are precluded by law from putting additional cash into the plan on a pretax basis. Governmental entities face no such externally imposed constraints. Many are pay-as-you-go plans; others, such as New Hampshire, impose their own minimum funding standards.

Decision makers need to consider the actual level of funding that is occurring and to determine whether it is adequate in view of the plan's tolerance for risk (keeping in mind that risk tolerance is really a joint tolerance involving the sponsor as well). Decision makers must be careful not to be misled about the funding status of the plan—funding requirements and the actual funding status of the plan are interdependent.

Interpreting Pension Accounting: An Example

Tables 10.1 and 10.2 are simplified sample financial statements. Footnotes explain each entry. Table 10.1 is the pension expense table. Table 10.2 tells us how much is in the plan and how much is owed, and reconciles the gap between plan assets and plan liabilities as measured by the PBO.

Assumptions, Measurements, and Games

From the prior discussion and the simple illustrations in Tables 10.1 and 10.2, one can see how an organization can affect its reported pension obligations.

Table 10.1 Pension Expense for a DB Plan

Item	Value
Expense for service during the year[a]	$300
Interest cost on projected benefit obligation[b]	$1,000
Actual return on plan assets[c]	$2,700
Amount deferred to future periods[d]	($1,500)
Amount reducing current year expense	$1,200
Amortization of excess of market value of plan assets over PBO on adoption of FASB Statement 87[e]	($100)
Net pension expense	$0

[a]Present value of benefits earned this year.

[b]Interest on the PBO at 7%.

[c]This is the total earnings on the pension assets.

[d]This indicates that true investment earnings have been exceeding expected investment earnings for some time, so some portion of the earnings are being deferred. In this illustration, actual earnings were $2,700 and expected earnings must have been $1,200. This leaves $1,500 of gain that can be deferred to future periods.

[e]This is transition year amortization. Before FASB Statement 87, this plan was overfunded. A portion of that historical overfunding is being used now to offset expense.

Table 10.2 Reconciliation of PBO with Net Pension Obligation

Item	Value
Accumulated benefit obligation[a]	
Vested benefits[b]	$11,000
Nonvested benefits[c]	$300
Total accumulated benefit obligation	$11,300
Projected benefit obligation[d]	$15,000
Less market value of plan assets[e]	($17,000)
Unrecognized transition gain (10 years remain)[f]	$1,000
Other unrecognized experience gains[g]	$2,500
Unrecorded pension obligation based on projected benefit obligations[h]	$1,500

[a]This is the present value of future benefits assuming no salary growth and no continued employment.

[b]These are benefits that are "owned" by employees.

[c]These are benefits that are not yet "owned" by employees.

[d]This is the present value of future pension benefits assuming salary growth.

[e]This is the fair market value of assets in the pension plan.

[f]At the time FASB Statement 87 was adopted, the value of its assets in the plan exceeded the PBO by some amount. This excess is amortized gradually and taken into income by applying it to future pension costs. The legend indicates it will be amortized over 10 years.

[g]Mortality experience and employee termination dates deviate from projections. The amount on this line, which could be negative, is the net of these experiences caused by actual investment income, mortality, and termination rates differing from expectations.

[h]This is the amount by which pension liabilities are understated relative to what is expected to be given to employees.

Superior investment returns will reduce pension expense. Further, to be able to produce a larger or smaller PBO, a sponsor can assume that salaries will grow by a higher or lower rate. Sponsors can use a higher or lower interest rate to discount future pension benefits, and this too will lower or raise the PBO. Finally, sponsors can use a higher or lower actuarial assumption regarding the expected return on pension plan assets. The use of a very high expected rate of return means that companies' actual rates of return may fall short of the expected value. Hence, prior deferred profits will have to be used or a loss will be accrued, but no matter what, the company can report a low pension expense. By using a high expected return rate, the organization will report lower pension expense and will probably have to infuse less cash into the pension plan on a year-to-year basis. That is, with high enough return assumptions, the plan can move closer to a pay-as-you-go plan.

Overall, then, accounting requires that judgments be made about a number of factors. Once these judgments have been rendered, the various measures—pension expense, PBO, and so on—are computed. Given the rules, these numbers are not likely to match up with reality. The nature of the process leaves the computation open to manipulation by those who may wish to understate or overstate a given factor. This "gaming" can erode the usefulness of accounting measures to those who must ultimately make important decisions about the pension and its asset pool.

INVESTMENT AND MANAGEMENT IMPLICATIONS

Despite the efforts of FASB Statement 87 and GASB Statement 27 to reduce the ambiguities surrounding pension fund reporting, there are still opportunities for organizations to manage their accounting reports. Worse, some can also structure their pension fund asset portfolios in particular ways to affect the pattern, though not necessarily the level, of reported pension expense.

There are two broad areas in which accounting results can be aggressively managed. The first is motivated by a desire to reduce the volatility of reported pension expense or reported plan surplus—to smooth the numbers. In general, smoothing is of little consequence until, as will be shown, it affects either the asset allocation decision or the rebalancing strategy that is followed. The second is motivated by the desire to manipulate or "game" the numbers or, more accurately, the assumptions that underlie the numbers, perhaps to achieve political ends such as disguising pay raises by burying them as increases in pension benefits, or to disguise deterioration in financial strength or to manage reported earnings.

Smoothing Activities

Some organizations are less worried about the magnitude of their reported investment expense or plan funding than about variability in these factors.[6] They prize forecastability. These sponsors think it is sensible to select asset allocations for the pension asset pool that will have a true rate of return equal to the assumed discount rate on the PBO because by doing so the pool can produce very predictable pension expense reports far into the future. Unfortunately, this sometimes comes at the expense of total return on the pension portfolio, thus putting an undue financial burden on the sponsor or imperiling the financial health of the plan.

To reduce the volatility of the reported pension expense figure even more than the amortizations allow, many companies have adopted specialized pension asset allocation schemes. With these schemes, as the present value of the PBO changes, the market value of the pension plan assets changes with it. The object is generating (reported) pension expense that is never larger than anticipated. The motivation behind this is to ensure that the company does not have to report a decline in the pension plan surplus. If the value of the pension assets is perfectly correlated with the PBO and initially exceeds it, the pension plan will always be in a surplus or overfunded situation, assuming, of course, continuing contributions at the required level.

There are two broad classes of schemes that have been developed to eliminate the unpleasant surprises and to sustain pension plan surpluses. These rely on dedicated bond portfolios and portfolio insurance.

Dedicated Bond Portfolios

One way to reduce the variability in reported pension expense is holding pension plan assets that move exactly as the present value of the PBO moves. Because the PBO's present value will rise or fall as interest rates decline or increase, an asset portfolio that moves in exactly the same way will insulate reported pension expense from the effect of changing asset and liability values. This goes beyond just holding an all-bond portfolio. Here the cash flow characteristics of the structured bond portfolio are important.

Immunization of the pension expense figure from changing values can be achieved in several ways. The sponsor could hold a portfolio of bonds such that the timing of the cash throw-off from the bonds (i.e., the interest payments plus maturities) matches the cash payments of the pension plan sponsor. Another way to immunize the pension expense figure is for the sponsor to use one of the various bond duration measures and structure a bond portfolio so that its duration matches the duration of the pension liabilities. The idea here is taking a measure of the weighted average maturity of a bond portfolio and matching it to a corresponding measure for obligations of the pension fund.[7] This approach offers no guarantee that the value of the liabilities will correlate perfectly with the value of the assets because duration measures generally work well only when the yield curve experiences small parallel shifts, upward or downward. (The term "parallel shift" refers to shifts in which short-term and long-term rates change by the same amount.) Nonetheless, duration matching tends to work tolerably well.

There are, however, two major drawbacks to adopting one of the dedicated bond portfolio approaches. First, equities have historically produced better investment returns than have bonds. For instance, from 1926 through 2002, long-term government bonds enjoyed an average annual return of 5.8%, whereas the average return on large-company common stocks over the same period was 12.2% per year.[8] Accordingly, using all-bond portfolios to reduce fluctuations in reported pension expense may lead to significantly larger average pension expense in the economic sense—higher cash contributions, in this case—than would an investment strategy that emphasized common stock.

The second drawback to adopting a dedicated bond portfolio approach is more subtle. The PBO can be separated into two components. One is the (fixed) liability to employees who have already retired. The pension plan sponsor is under no obligation to increase those payments as time passes. The present value of this annuity, the fixed liability to retirees, will fluctuate with interest rate changes only, ignoring mortality and other demographic factors. The other component of the PBO is the projected liability to active employees. The present value of this component changes with interest rate changes and, perhaps more important, also changes with unexpected changes in wage rates. Indeed, if unexpected wage changes are more significant than interest rate changes, then a dedicated bond portfolio cannot offset variations in this component of the PBO. The bond portfolio's value will rise or fall with interest rate changes, but it may not change at all in value with wage rate changes.

Arnott and Bernstein (1988) point out that the use of all-bond portfolios is the result of "an inappropriate restructuring of the pension fund in terms of the true as opposed to the accounting-defined risks of the pension plan. The oversimplification arises from too much attention to the interest sensitivity of the pension surplus, a result of [the FASB's] emphasis on defining the surplus in terms of the interest sensitivity of the fund's liabilities" (p. 95).

Arnott and Bernstein argue that the value of the active workers' component of the PBO is more likely to vary with dividends than with interest rates. Thus, the asset mix (the proportions of common stock and all of the other possible asset classes in the portfolio) of the pension plan should not be determined by the way pension expense or pension liabilities are reported. Rather, it should be determined by the demographics of the past and current workforce and the plan's tolerance for risk, as opposed to FASB Statement 87 reporting risk.

Arnott and Bernstein (1988) conclude,

> Many companies, however, are putting too much emphasis on the structures of FASB 87, and are looking to long-term bonds to save the day. Long bonds are appropriate for stabilizing the surplus in the short run where the net present value of the liabilities is the crucial consideration. Bonds are also appropriate where the liability estimation is highly certain, as in the case of retired lives or a pension fund for a mature work force. But there is danger in viewing all pension funds in these terms. . . . In reality, the size of pensions the corporation pays in future years will have little to do with today's level of long-term interest rates. (p. 102)

They correctly admonish pension plan administrators not to let the tail of accounting wag the dog of investing. Emphasizing bonds at the expense of equities to keep short-run reported volatility of pension expense low can be a very costly thing to do.

Portfolio Insurance

Portfolio insurance was widely hailed as an excellent way to insulate a company's financial reports from fluctuations in interest rates and the market value of assets[9] while not eliminating the opportunity to participate in positive movements in stock prices. Under FASB Statement 87, fluctuations in pension expense can significantly affect earnings. Under GASB Statement 27, the reported government surplus or deficit can be affected. Conceptually, portfolio insurance could dampen that variability.

Portfolio insurance schemes explicitly recognize the fact that equities have historically provided higher total returns than have bonds. Recognizing this, many companies decided to pursue a different investment strategy to hold the promise of significantly higher returns than (safer) fixed-income portfolios. Portfolio insurance strategies typically require choosing a floor for the portfolio value. This is the value below which the portfolio will not be allowed to fall. The difference between the portfolio's current value and the floor is called the cushion. As the actual portfolio value approaches the floor—that is, as the cushion shrinks—risky assets are sold to reduce exposure and safe assets are bought. As the portfolio increases in value, risky assets are bought to capture more of their potential future appreciation.

The principal flaw of portfolio insurance schemes and the reason that they have fallen out of favor with the investment community is liquidity: everyone cannot sell stocks at the same time; everyone cannot move funds from risky stocks to safe bonds simultaneously without affecting market prices. Indeed, if enough investors demand portfolio insurance, a small drop in stock prices could become an avalanche, as investors sell more and more of their stocks-and have to make large price concessions to do so. In doing so, the value of the plan's assets may fall far below the "floor" that had been established.

Gaming the Numbers

Gaming the numbers has two possible motivations. One motivation is simply to make the plan or some aspect of the plan's operation look better than it really is: window dressing. The other is to disguise the effect of economic decisions in accomplish a similar goal, but this time on a grander scale—typically the scale is that of the sponsoring organization.

Window Dressing

Unfortunately, those who decide what the inputs into the accounting process should be—the interest rates, expected returns, and so forth—too often fail to ask what is economically sensible from a decision maker's perspective. Instead, they ask what numbers are needed to make the financial reports look good.

Part of the problem stems from the previously mentioned desire to achieve low variability in reported numbers. Innocuous at times, this activity can obscure important trends such as a worsening of the pension's financial condition or an increased exposure to factors such as inflation. Worse still, it may mislead decision makers, employees, retirees, shareholders, or taxpayers into thinking that little risk is being taken—after all, the funding ratios appear stable, and pension expense does not vary greatly from one period to the next—when the reality is that there are significant exposures of which decision makers should be aware. In addition, it may result in an overstatement of earnings for public companies, misleading investors.

This problem can be especially severe for public funds when a state or local entity applies pressure to change one or more of the underlying assumptions for the sole purpose of making the pension plan appear to be better off. The motivation may be to balance a budget or to reduce funding payments. Whatever the motivation, fiduciaries should resist such pressures.

Disguised Decisions

Employer/sponsors have from time to time granted employees increased pension benefits to avoid a pay raise that they may feel shareholders or taxpayers might find unacceptable. In a world of economic accounting, this would be seen for what it is: a substitute of one form of compensation having real economic value for another. In a world in which accounting procedures allow considerable leeway in selecting fundamental inputs in the measurement process, the effect of these decisions can be hidden from view, at least in the short run, and accountability can be avoided.

Viewed from the perspective of the pension plan, however, an increase in benefits (future or retroactive) increases the present value of the plan's liability immediately. As a result, the surplus deteriorates and pressure increases for higher returns (and risk) or for increased contributions. These are the economic realities. They occur immediately on granting increased pension rights and should be incorporated into the decision-making process. However, the leeway organizations have in computing the liability can be used to mask the real effect of the change in benefits.

Note that there does not have to be an ulterior motive to hide a pay raise from those taxpayers or shareholders who ultimately must pay it. Benefit increases may be the product of fully informed negotiations in which the parties fully disclose to all affected parties what is going on. Even here, though, the consequences of the action must be correctly assessed. Unfortunately, accounting rules can get in the way.

CONCLUSION

If it does nothing else, this chapter should caution pension fund managers and other fiduciaries about the complexity of pension fund accounting and how it may pervert good decision making. Reporting organizations have a great deal of discretion in their choice of assumptions, and these assumptions can affect reported values rather significantly.

Trustees and others whose role is primarily that of oversight and long-run strategy must know enough about accounting for pensions to know how it can mislead and thus interfere with the decision-making process. This does not mean they need to be certified public accountants or even be able to do the calculations. It does mean they must know that funding adequacy (as measured by funding ratios), pension expense, and other decision inputs can be gamed. Even if the accounting is honest and devoid of an ulterior motivation to mask reality and make things seem better than they really are—and that is often the case—the rules sometimes lead to obscuring that which the decision maker needs to know.

What should pension fund decision makers do? Ask for interpretive commentary. Insist on estimates of the economic consequences of alternative courses of action or events that have already occurred. Do not accept the effect on the accounting numbers as adequate justification for a planned course of action. Make certain that the discussion, and ultimately the decisions made, turn on the economics of the matter rather than on appearances.

In closing, it is worth repeating something every finance text ever written has preached: do not make what are essentially uneconomic decisions just to try to get the books to look good. Never let the way accounts are presented prevent your organization from making wealth-maximizing choices that have the short-run effect of making an accounting statement look worse than it might otherwise look.

PART III

Defined Contribution and Hybrid Plans

11

Investment Policy and Asset Allocation for Defined Contribution Plans

This chapter begins by discussing the much-publicized trend toward DC plans over the last twenty-five to thirty years. Because of this trend, more and more sponsors are in a situation in which it is the employees themselves who are responsible for choosing the asset allocation that will determine their retirement pension income. The remainder of the chapter discusses employer responsibilities in this setting.

The second section discusses investment policy for DC plans. This includes the choice of investment alternatives and the approach to employee financial education. The third section discusses asset allocation for DC plans. It includes an analytical framework that demonstrates the effect of the asset allocation decision on expected risk and return. It also discusses some of the evidence of how employees do allocate their DC assets.

THE TREND TOWARD DC PLANS

Beginning in the late 1970s, DC plans have grown relative to DB plans. Public (state and local employee) plans have remained predominantly defined benefit,[1] but in private plans, DB participation has been falling and DC participation has been rising.[2]

At the end of 2001, DB plans accounted for 44% of total private pension assets. This percentage is down from 55%, which occurred as recently as 1990. DB plans have not, however, been declining in absolute terms. Between 1990 and 2001, private DB plan assets more than doubled, from $900 billion to over $1.8 trillion. DC assets were simply growing faster—more than tripling in the same time period.[3]

Several economists have documented and analyzed the shift in private plans.[4] Much of the shift is to the result of new firms adopting DC plans, rather than firms switching from DB to DC. There are several possible causes:

- Sectoral employment shifts have favored DC plans: DB plans have been prominent in large manufacturing and unionized jobs. Part of the decline in DB plans is the result of the shift in the economy away from such jobs.
- The government made DC plans more attractive. As noted above, 401(k) plans account for 75% of private DC assets, yet the government did not make them widely available and attractive until 1981.[5] Much of the growth in DC plans can be attributed to the availability of these plans.[6]
- The government made DB plans less attractive. In the late 1980s, Congress instituted "reversion taxes" on DB plans. Suppose a company terminates a DB plan and that at the time of termination, plan assets exceed the benefits the plan must pay. In the past, the company could receive the excess assets as income (paying income tax on the gain). Beginning in the late 1980s, however, Congress began to impose additional taxes on these excess assets. By 1990 the reversion tax reached 50% (on top of the income tax). Several authors have said that these taxes made DB plans much less attractive to companies.[7]
- There is less expectation that workers will stay many years with one employer. Many observers have tied the rise in DC plans to their portability. They hypothesize that in the modern economy there is less value to remaining many years with a single employer. If true, this change could explain a shift toward more portable DC plans.[8]
- DC plans have been buoyed by rising securities prices. The 1980s and 1990s were decades of strong economic growth and strong stock market returns. In the late 1990s many employees had come to believe they were wealthy—their 401(k) assets were huge! However, as the bear market of 2000 to 2002 made clear, financial returns and asset values are risky. It is likely employees did not appreciate the economic risk they were taking with DC plans. If a less naive view of risk is adopted, employees may come to prefer DB plans, in which the sponsor absorbs much of the investment risk.

INVESTMENT POLICY FOR DC PLANS

Because of these trends, more and more sponsors are faced with determining the investment policy for DC plans. With DC plans, sponsor responsibilities are conceptually similar to those that would arise with DB plans. The operational shape these responsibilities take, however, differs significantly. In part, this is because DC plans are structured as separate accounts for each beneficiary rather than as large asset pools jointly claimed by all beneficiaries. In part, this is because DC plans offer sponsors the opportunity to shift investment risk to employees. Sponsors who make the plan's investment decisions, however, or who fail to meet Department of Labor (DOL) guidelines for self-directed plans face substantial risk of litigation if employees decide they are not happy with the investment results on their DC asset pools.

Sponsors must first decide whether the assets of the DC plan will be invested by the sponsor or the employees. To the extent that plan assets are to be invested by the sponsor, the responsibilities are similar to DB plan responsibilities, recognizing that the sponsor retains significant responsibility for the consequences of the investment decisions it makes. If the decision is to provide an employee-directed plan, private sponsors should ensure that the plan is in compliance with various ERISA regulations. Public sponsors have no clear legal incentive to comply with 404(c)-like rules, but in general the guidelines are consistent with prudent management and should be carefully considered.

Advice versus Education

In 1992, the DOL issued regulation 29 CFR 2550.404c-1. This regulation described some requirements that a plan must satisfy to be 404(c) plans (plans in which the sponsor is not liable for losses resulting from employee decision-making.) There are two general requirements. First, a plan must provide employees the opportunity to take control of the decision making. For example, the employees must have reasonable opportunities to give investment instructions to an identified plan fiduciary. The participant must also have access to sufficient information to make informed decisions. For example, the participant should be provided an explanation of the fact that the plan fiduciaries may not be liable for losses resulting from the participant's decisions. The participant should also be provided a general description of the risk and return characteristics of the plan's investment alternatives.

The second general requirement is that the plan must offer a broad range of investment alternatives. The investment alternatives should allow the participant to materially affect his or her risk and potential return. The participant should be able to choose from at least three investment alternatives, each of which is diversified and each of which has materially different risk and reward characteristics. The participant should also be able to diversify his or her individual account to minimize the risk of large losses.

The 1992 regulation also said that a participant's exercise of control over his or her individual account must be independent. To be independent, the participant cannot be subjected to "improper influence" by the plan sponsor. Likewise, the participant is not acting independently if a plan fiduciary has concealed material nonpublic facts regarding the investment.

The 1992 regulations did not resolve the issue of whether sponsors should or could provide investment education to employees. On the one hand, it seems prudent to provide financial education to employees who are making their own investment decisions. On the other hand, under ERISA, if a person provides investment advice for a fee, that person is a fiduciary of the plan. Many sponsors wondered whether if they provided education, it might be interpreted as providing advice, and hence make them liable if an employee incurred losses after taking financial education.

In 1996, the DOL addressed these issues with interpretive bulletin 29 CFR 2509.96-1. This bulletin provided some safe harbors: categories of information and materials that plans could provide and that would be considered education and not "investment advice." The bulletin listed four categories of information. First, plans can provide plan information such as descriptions of the investment alternatives, the different philosophies behind them, and their risk and return characteristics. Second, plans can provide general financial and investment information. For example, they can provide information about tax-deferred investment, historic differences in return among asset classes, and the effects of inflation.

Third, plans can provide asset allocation models based on generally accepted theories. These models should include clear statements of their underlying assumptions. They should also include a statement that in applying a model to the employee's own situation, the employee should consider all of his or her assets, including home equity, individual retirement account (IRA) investments, and other investments, whether tax deferred or not.

Fourth, plans can provide interactive investment materials that allow an employee to estimate retirement income needs and the effect of different asset allocation models. These models can and should take into account historic differences in asset class returns. They should also allow the employee to provide inputs into the calculation (e.g., the employee's current age and expected retirement age). These materials should either take into account the person's other assets or should include a statement saying that the employee should take these assets into account in applying the models.

Of course, the financial services industry has lobbied and continues to lobby for safeguards that would enable them to provide investment advice to plan participants.[9] As this chapter is written, in 2003, there are active legislative efforts working toward this end. In December 2001, the DOL took a first step toward allowing plans to offer advice. This first step took the form of an advisory opinion[10] that approved a plan by SunAmerica. In that plan, an independent financial expert might recommend asset allocations for a participant. The retention of the expert and the payments to the expert would not be dependent on the expert's recommendation. The idea is that the use of the expert ensures that the investment advice is generated for the benefit of the participant or beneficiary.

At present, advice is not generally allowed, but education is. The question arises of how effective the education is. There are certainly case studies of effective education programs,[11] but it is often not clear whether the programs actually cause employees to make long-term changes in practice. Some recent studies tracked individuals who attended a financial education seminar.[12] These studies compared the individual's 401(k) savings behavior both before and after receiving the training. After attending the training, many employees reported that they intended to increase their savings, but up to six months later, relatively few had actually implemented those changes.

Education, however, remains important, and sponsors should use it to inform their employees of their options. The basics of investor education should start with information concerning the primary asset classes and their historical risks and returns. This foundation allows the sponsor or the sponsor's designee (e.g., a consultant hired to provide investment education programs for employees) to discuss the basics of modern portfolio theory (diversification, the nature of market risk, and so forth).

Alternative investment strategies should comprise the next part of an investor education program. Employees should be informed about the differences associated with various asset allocations, the actively and passively managed funds in which they might invest, and how different strategies might be expected to perform (or have performed) in various types of market conditions. Some sponsors also are now providing alternative portfolios, which are typically designed to be more conservative or more aggressive.

Other elements of investor education that sponsors should address include how to match investor circumstances and objectives to specific investment funds, how to form portfolios of funds rather than selecting individual funds, and how to integrate pension assets with other investments an employee may have. Throughout, to avoid future liability, the sponsor should be careful to avoid making—or giving the appearance of making—specific investment recommendations.

Performance Information

It is common for DC sponsors or their designees to provide woefully inadequate information on plan performance to employees. As a result, it is very difficult for employees to determine how the DC plan asset pools are doing. Prudent sponsors will develop policies that will provide the information that plan participants need to make informed decisions. The four elements of communicating investment results to employees are providing comprehensive performance figures, providing effective asset mix information, providing clear and understandable descriptions of the investment strategies followed by the funds made available to employees, and showing employees the basics of interpreting actual investment results.

Performance presentation should include total returns for one-, three-, five-, and ten-year periods as well as annual returns for at least five years, and preferably for ten years. In addition, one or more standard measures of fund volatility, such as its standard deviation (calculated on the three-to-five-year record using monthly numbers) comprise useful information and should be provided. An informative variation on the standard deviation is a volatility index on which an investment of average volatility would have an index number of 1 and higher (or lower) volatility investments would have index numbers of greater than (or less than) 1. Finally, DC participants need appropriate benchmarks. These should include broad market indexes and averages for fund or investment-style categories.

Participants also need information on the effective asset mix of each fund in which they may invest to maintain an asset allocation (including assets outside the pension plan) that is appropriate. Again, recent history indicates that the information typically provided is less than adequate. Specifically, funds should be described to employees in terms of asset class exposures, allocations within asset classes (e.g., large-cap versus small-cap stocks, or domestic versus international stocks differentiating emerging markets from developed markets), the interest rate sensitivity of bond funds, whether the funds are passive or index funds or actively managed funds, and so forth.

The third element of investment information is an understandable description of the investment strategy that a fund chooses to follow. Although the debate over the merits of passive versus active investing is far from over (and will probably never be settled to everyone's satisfaction), it is an important parameter in fund selection and portfolio construction. Therefore, the sponsor has a moral obligation to ensure that whatever strategy a fund pursues, it is adequately disclosed so that investors know what they are investing in.

Finally, in addition to providing reasonable numbers to employees, allowing them to assess the adequacy of their investment planning and the performance of the funds in which they are invested, the sponsor should educate plan participants about the effect of a variety of factors on the performance they will achieve. For example, participants need to understand that purchasing patterns (the timing of investments) will affect the returns that they realize. Similarly, investors should know they virtually never get the index or benchmark returns that are presented unless those returns are adjusted to mimic the cash flows associated with a specific investment, with trading costs, and with the effect of cash holdings. Performance evaluation, of course, is difficult to do. However, giving investors performance data without informing them of how to interpret the results provides them with only part of the information they need to make informed decisions about their retirement portfolios.

Investment Choice

How many investment alternatives should be offered? ERISA Section 404(c) regulations require at least three choices. The upside of having more rather than fewer alternatives is potentially happier employees and evidence of meeting fiduciary responsibilities. The downside of having more alternatives is also having higher administrative costs and an increased educational burden for the sponsor. Thus, the sponsor needs to think through the elements of how many choices is enough—or too many. (Note also that employees should be allowed to make changes in their allocations among funds at least quarterly—or more often if fund volatility is high.)

A comprehensive set of investment choices will provide participants with an opportunity to gain exposure to passively or actively managed funds, small company stocks as well as large company stocks, fixed-income investments of various interest-rate sensitivities, balanced funds containing both equities and fixed-income investments, asset allocation funds (that offer different asset mixes for different risk/return objectives), international equities, money market funds, and perhaps guaranteed investment contracts (GICs). For most DC plans, these exposures can be achieved by offering six to ten alternatives.

In choosing the fund alternatives, sponsors should recognize that some employees will not be financially sophisticated. For example, faced with five alternatives, some employees will choose to put 20% of their allocations in each alternative.[13] These employees may feel that they are "diversifying" by choosing equal amounts of each fund alternative. Thus the employees' asset allocations will be affected by the sponsor's choice of funds. For example, the more stock funds an employer chooses, the more the employees may allocate their investments to stocks. An education program should make employees aware that they may be tempted to divide allocations equally across the alternatives, but that this is not necessarily the appropriate diversification for them.

Another important choice for the plan sponsor is that of the fund provider. The basic issue is whether to go inside or outside. Only large sponsors have the resources to consider offering internally managed funds. Even in these cases, the sponsor may not feel it has the investment expertise available in-house to manage the funds internally. Of course, for smaller organizations, the only alternative is to turn to an insurance company, a bank, a mutual fund, or other outside fund manager. Regardless, fiduciary duty requires attention to due diligence in selection.

Management and Administrative Costs

The importance of the management and administrative costs of the investment vehicles chosen for DC plans and the returns on employee portfolios is quite simple and direct: cost affects return. If all else remains the same, the higher costs are, the lower the returns will be for plan participants. The lower that net returns of costs are, the less accumulation will occur and the less adequate employee investment accounts will be on retirement.

How will plan participants react when they reach retirement and find out that their asset accumulations are inadequate for the lifestyles they had envisioned? It is not unreasonable to suspect that suits will be brought and sponsors that cannot show appropriate due diligence with respect to pursuing the low-cost alternative or, alternatively, with respect to paying only for services that are essential, will be found liable in the courts.

Many sponsors of DC plans do not even know the total costs associated with the plans that they are offering. In one study, a hypothetical $10 million plan with 500 participants might range in cost from $61,000 to $260,000.[14] Because these costs are borne by the employees, the responsibilities with which a prudent fiduciary is charged seem to make it clear that plan cost is a due diligence issue in which fiduciary responsibility may be properly carried out or that, if it is not properly carried out, significant liability may result.

Many sponsors have turned to the mutual fund industry for investment selection services, record keeping, and the like. Observers of fees recognize, however, that mutual funds charge from twenty to one hundred fifty basis points for their core management and administrative activities. Compare this to the five to fifty basis point fees commonly charged by professional money managers in the wholesale marketplace.

The Investment Policy Statement for Employee-Directed Plans

The primary focus of an Investment Policy Statement is to explain[15]

- who is responsible for what—among the plan participants, fund managers, plan trustee, and any oversight committee;
- the investment alternatives that are to be available to participants;
- criteria for monitoring, evaluating, and potentially replacing investment managers and investment choices; and
- how the various parties can and should communicate with each other.

As far as who is responsible for what, the policy statement might indicate, for example, that the oversight committee is responsible for evaluating, monitoring, and replacing managers or investment choices. It might also provide that the same committee is responsible for providing investment education to participants. The participants for their part are explicitly responsible for their own asset allocation decisions. They would also be responsible for taking advantage of the investment education provided.

STRATEGIC ASSET ALLOCATION FOR EMPLOYEE-DIRECTED DC PLANS

Setting the strategic asset allocation for individuals who participate in employee-directed DC plans is primarily a matter of trading off investment risk against the prospective returns necessary to achieve the individual's retirement goals. This does not mean it is easy, nor does it mean the sponsor should be completely passive. Sponsors who do not want to bear responsibility for the performance of DC plan asset pools should give employees access to the tools necessary to the job themselves. This implies extensive education about the factors that should guide employees in making the strategic asset allocation decision. This section discusses these factors and offers sponsors insights into helping their employees make sensible decisions without giving investment advice.

Liabilities, Life Cycles, and Taxes

Several issues make individual investors different from DB plans when it comes to setting their strategic asset allocations. First, most liabilities are unique to each individual and, unlike those of many institutional investors, are not fixed or specific (other than liabilities such as mortgages); rather, many "liabilities" are goals or preferences that can be changed if circumstances change (e.g., if accumulations fail to meet certain targeted objectives). Second, individuals are very exposed to inflation, because they have few fixed liabilities to hedge the inflation risk of the assets they might accumulate. Third, individuals are mortal. Their expected life spans are finite and change with the passage of time and changes in health. Finally, individuals are subject to taxes. Although earnings on qualified pension asset pools such as those of DC plans are not taxed until they are withdrawn, the effect of taxes on investments held outside of pension plans affects the choice of the assets in pension plans.

Liabilities

Employees desire to a prosperous retirement in which they can maintain or even improve on current lifestyles. This is the fundamental nature of the DC plan liability: an adequate retirement. Employees must integrate their pension management and goals with the day-to-day business of living—putting the kids through school, purchasing a home, and so forth.

Unlike employees covered by DB plans, the beneficiaries of DC plans have no promise from the plan's sponsor to increase funding if the accumulation of pension assets is not sufficient because of poor financial market performance, poor investment decisions, inadequate funding, or some other reason. If the accumulation of assets is substantially less than anticipated, employees may sue employers, claiming the sponsor was not prudent in some way or another. Perhaps the suit will be successful, perhaps it will not—perhaps it will take a long time for the courts to decide. In the meantime, the individual unhappily changes his or her lifestyle.

Life Cycles

A common approach to framing the strategic asset allocation decision is to divide an individual's life into four phases.[16] Consider that the normal life cycle consists of a long time horizon of perhaps thirty to forty years to retirement and of twenty-five years or so in retirement. Over this fifty-plus-year period, an individual needs to accumulate an asset pool that will provide adequate retirement income. Thus, phase one is referred to as the accumulation phase. The primary objective is to accumulate sufficient assets to retire and live a lifestyle that is suitable. The length of this phase is long as is the lifetime of the investor. Inflation exposure is high as the ability to bear risk. Accumulation comes about through employer and employee contributions and through investment performance. Contributions are constrained by regulation; investment performance is constrained by the asset allocation decision. Adequate usually implies achieving a wage replacement rate that will allow the desired standard of living once the individual retires. Unfortunately, over this long a time, even modest inflation can seriously erode the purchasing power of the dollar, so the growth in assets must be sufficient to offset the effect of inflation. Most authorities agree that the general allocation during the accumulation phase should favor equities, with allocations of 70%–90%, or even as high as 100% for someone with a very high tolerance for risk. The rationale is that long time horizons provide sufficient time to recover from short-term adverse market actions, making the capacity to bear risk high. This high capacity for risk, coupled with the exposure to inflation that long time periods bring, makes equities appropriate for most individuals.

Toward the end of the accumulation phase, the consolidation phase begins. This is characterized by a much shorter time to retirement and by the likelihood of wages and possibly contributions to the DC plan being at a peak. The nearness of retirement brings a lower tolerance for risk—there is less time to recover from adverse market action—and increases the incentives to save even more. Hence, there is at least the possibility of a reallocation of assets from growth-oriented, high-volatility assets (e.g., stocks) to more conservative allocations encompassing bonds or cash (Treasury bills). Although there is some disagreement on this point, most authorities argue against allocations to long-term bonds because of the interest rate risk they pose. As noted earlier, individuals do not

have interest rate–sensitive liabilities, so they cannot offset exposures to liabilities that are sensitive to interest rates with long-term bonds. Rather, if interest
rates increase, bonds held by an individual will lose value but the liabilities—
the retirement income goals—do not change. As a consequence, individuals
probably should avoid bonds or bond funds with maturities longer than 3 to 5
years unless the bonds are indexed to changes in interest rates.[17]

The spending or retirement phase follows employment termination. In this
phase, the now former employee uses his or her retirement portfolio to provide
income. Some authorities assert that this means an orientation to bonds; others
assert that large equity allocations still are appropriate and that such income as
is needed should come from dividend-paying stocks and disciplined sales of
portfolio assets. Individuals with large portfolios may find this latter approach
palatable. Those who have not been so fortunate or wise may rightly worry
about the effect of a run of poor stock market performance on their portfolios.
In general, those who have just entered retirement and have perhaps twenty to
thirty years to live must pursue the equity risk premium to offset inflation. Those
who are about to die do not have to worry about inflation unless they are concerned for their heirs. One rule of thumb often used to determine the appropriate
allocation to equity in this phase is to use the equation $100 - \text{age} = \%$ in
equity. This is, however, simply a starting point. There are far too many variables
for such a simple rule to be applied without further analysis.

The final phase is the gifting phase. Here, the objective of the portfolio is to
provide for people (e.g., grandchildren) or organizations (e.g., charities) that
have investment horizons well beyond that of the current owner of the assets.
The bequest motive becomes the main factor at work, and there is a reorientation
toward growth and a return to asset allocations that may look like those appropriate to the accumulation phase.

Note that lump sum distributions to employees on retirement create a reinvestment problem for individuals. This problem is especially severe when the
sponsor has been directing the investment decisions of the plan and then simply
hands the responsibility over to the employee, who is not likely to be well versed
in investing. Of course, the distribution may be annuitized, but this may not be
the best use of the funds, and it may not relieve fiduciaries of their duties to
find creditworthy, cost-efficient providers.

Taxes

In many cases, DC asset pools will not be sufficient to allow employees to retire
when they wish or to live the retirement lifestyle they want. This may be the
result of low contributions, poor investment performance, job switching coupled
with vesting rules, or other factors. Social Security may help some, although its
current financial status raises serious questions. Regardless, those who want to
increase the probability of living as they wish later will save more now. Once
tax-exempt contribution limits to pension plans have been reached, the only
alternative is to form portfolios that are subject to taxes.

There is far too much to say on this matter to cover it in a book on pension
management. What must be said here, however, is that the individual must view

his or her pension assets and nonpension assets as parts of a greater whole to avoid making suboptimal asset allocations. The goal should be to maximize after-tax real returns subject to the risk tolerance of the individual across the individual's entire portfolio. For example, intermediate term tax-exempt bonds should never be held in a pension portfolio, but they may be sensible in a taxable environment. Individuals in an accumulation phase who hold stocks and intermediate-term corporate bonds may want to hold some or all of the stocks in the taxable environment, where capital gains are deferrable and dividends and capital gains may be taxed at lower rates than interest, and where taxable income yields are low. The bonds may be placed in the retirement portfolio, where the income produced will be sheltered. Of course, as the spending phase nears, some reallocations may be appropriate, especially if postretirement tax rates are expected to be lower than preretirement tax rates.

Approaches to Setting the Strategic Asset Allocation for Individuals

How can sponsors help employees learn to define the appropriate levels of risk that can be tolerated and how investment risk should be evaluated in light of the threat of the erosion of purchasing power that inflation brings? One approach to helping individuals evaluate the trade-off between their tolerance for risk and their accumulation goals (return objectives) is described in this section. One approach is used by the American Association of Individual Investors (AAII) in their investment seminars for individual investors.

Many individuals view risk in terms of adverse consequences. Thus, an analysis that demonstrates the effect of risk on a portfolio by examining how seriously adverse market actions can erode portfolio value in the event of a major bear market can give individuals an opportunity to assess their willingness to accept significant interim decreases in the value of their retirement assets. However, it is important not to stop here. The counterpoint to risk and adverse outcomes is the damage that even modest inflation can cause to real asset values and its resultantly adverse effect on future standards of living. For example, because the long-term returns on the least risky asset class (Treasury bills) have only matched the rate of inflation (providing no real growth before taxes and negative growth if taxed), the analysis illustrates the importance of pension accumulations in real terms and how risk becomes a necessary, if undesirable, factor.

The trade-off between risk and return requires presenting alternative model portfolios and their performances over various time periods. Consider two such portfolios: Portfolio A has 90% of its assets in aggressive equity mutual funds of one type or another and 10% in a money market fund. Portfolio B, a more conservative portfolio, has 70% of its assets invested in less aggressive equity mutual funds, 20% in fixed-income mutual funds, and 10% in money market funds. It is possible to evaluate how these portfolios would have performed historically by simply using past performance data. (Although no one believes the historical record can naively be projected as an expectation, it is nonetheless instructive to look at the past and see what could have happened given the risk exposure brought about by alternative asset allocations. The insights gained are quite helpful in forming reasonable expectations of future performance differences among different asset allocations.)

To help individuals get a sense of their tolerance for risk, the analyst computes returns for the model portfolios by assuming that the worst one-year performance of various market sectors from the post–World War II period occurs and by assuming that this adverse performance occurs in all market segments more or less simultaneously. Although this is admittedly a very low probability event, it has the usefulness of demonstrating that risky financial assets can and do from time to time suffer severe declines in value. During the post–World War II period, for instance, the worst that would have happened to these two portfolios is that portfolio A would have suffered a one-year loss of around 33% of its value, whereas the more conservative portfolio B would have lost only 22% of its value.

In counterpoint, however, the analyst then should examine the real rate of return (the actual historical return less the rate of inflation) that would have been earned on the model portfolios over a twenty- or thirty-year period. In the example, portfolio A would have provided an annual real rate of return of around 6.7% versus 5.2% for portfolio B. These percentages can be easily converted into dollar accumulations and retirement income. For example, if each portfolio had begun with $50,000, no additional contributions were made, and the historical record is a reasonable approximation of the expected annual returns to be earned over 20 years, then portfolio A would be worth $183,000 in real terms, and portfolio B would be worth only $138,000 in real terms—about 25% less than portfolio A.

With this information, individuals investing for retirement through self-directed DC plans can get some sense of their willingness to accept the low probability but nonetheless real possibility of losing a significant portion of their investment. At the same time, they can see how inflation affects portfolio values and, hence, retirement income. (For younger employees, it may be hoped the loss will be recouped over time as market performance improves and reversion brings markets back to some average or normal level of performance. This will not necessarily happen, however.) The strategic asset allocation decision still must be made, but the central parameters—the trade-offs of investment risk and inflation—should now be more apparent.

A second approach involves the use of Monte Carlo analysis. This more sophisticated and more informative approach allows questions such as, "Given $500,000 split equally between stocks and bonds, what is the probability that a 5% withdrawal (or spending) rate will last thirty years?" To perform a Monte Carlo simulation, estimates of expected returns, standard deviations, and correlations are required, and computer algorithms must be run. In addition, employees will need help interpreting the output. That said, the benefits of a richer understanding of the interaction between accumulation rates, amounts accumulated, spending rates, asset allocation, and time are immense, and Monte Carlo simulations are more widely available and more cost effective than ever before.

DC Plan Performance

As with DB plans, DC plan performance depends primarily on the asset allocation choices of the overall manager of the plan's assets—either the sponsor or the employee. For employee-directed plans, the asset allocation will be affected by the available alternatives, the employees' knowledge of investment fundamentals, the employees' circumstances and preferences, and the expenses and fees incurred by the investments made.

How are DC pension assets allocated? For 2001, the distribution was as follows[18]

Company stock	35%
Stable Value Fund (GICs, etc.)	13%
Equity (other than company stock)	32%
Balanced or hybrid	9%
Cash	5%
Bonds	3%
Other	3%

These data indicate that employees in self-directed plans may be allocating assets too conservatively to provide adequate wage replacement on retirement. In addition, the most striking feature of these results is the high percentage allocation to company stock. Chapter 12 discusses company stock in greater detail.

One way to judge DC asset allocation is to judge how well the participants themselves view their asset allocation choices. One study compared employee's asset allocations with professionally chosen allocations and median (typical) allocations.[19] Financial software was then used to predict the range of retirement income under the different allocations. The employees were then asked which range they preferred. The results indicated that the employees often preferred the median or professionally chosen allocation to their own choice. On the basis of their own preferences, employees in DC plans may not be making the best choices.

Ultimately, the correct way to look at DC plan performance is in terms of whether or not a given plan is likely to provide adequate retirement income; that is, a sufficient replacement rate. There is no way to measure this in a meaningful sense, but there are some factors that correlate highly with accumulating a DC plan asset pool that is sufficient for retirement.

First, employees must know enough about investing to make informed decisions. Second, the alternative investments available to employees need to provide a comprehensive enough set of risk and return possibilities that it is possible for an informed employee to achieve a reasonable accumulation of retirement assets without undue risk (e.g., excessive use of company stock). Third, contributions into the DC plan asset pool have to be large enough to make a reasonable wage replacement possible. Finally, return-inhibiting factors such as administrative costs and management fees have to be controlled so they do not erode the value of plan assets.

Regardless of the cause, poor DC plan performance may result in legal action that is potentially detrimental to sponsors and shareholders or taxpayers. Thus, plan fiduciaries should be concerned.

CONCLUSION

There has been a trend toward DC plans, but DB plans remain significant in the economy. Public policy can have a significant effect on which plan types will prosper in the future. Because of the increase in DC plans, more and more employers must address the issues of providing employee education, deciding the number of investment choices to which employees will have access, and ensuring that employees have adequate performance information. Investment alternatives must be provided at reasonable cost to employees, and these alternatives must in the aggregate represent a comprehensive set of investment alternatives. Sponsors must also take care to avoid crossing the line, murky as it may seem, between educating employees and offering investment advice. Overall, the more control participants have, the less liability the fiduciary or sponsor is likely to have.

For individuals managing DC plan asset pools, the consequences of good or bad decisions are direct, but unfortunately it may be several years before they are known or understood. Sponsors need to help employees gain the knowledge they need to make sensible decisions, and employees must be willing to take the time to become their own money managers—or to hire outside advisors. In particular, employees must be aware of how poor planning, inflation, and other factors can have truly catastrophic results.

12

Employee Stock Ownership Plans and Company Stock

The Enron 401(k) pension plan held a lot of Enron stock. Therefore, when the company failed, its employees lost their retirement savings—in addition to their jobs and their current incomes. In the public controversy that followed, many economists pointed out, rightly, that employees are extremely vulnerable when their retirement savings depend on their employer. The controversy led to much discussion about whether there should be restrictions on use of company stock in DC plans.[1]

The issue is not unique to Enron, of course—Global Crossing was in a similar situation. As noted in the last chapter, 35% of assets in profit sharing and 401(k) plans were invested in this company's own stock in 2001.[2] Many large, well-known companies—Proctor and Gamble, Dell Computer, Pfizer, Annheuser Busch, Coca-Cola, and McDonald's, for example—have large portions of their defined contribution pension plan assets invested in company stock.[3]

There is a special form of DC plan, the ESOP, which is designed to be primarily invested in company stock. Both 401(k) plans and ESOPs are subject to litigation if the value of company stock declines and decimates employee retirement savings. Such litigation has been filed against fiduciaries at Lucent and Xerox, among others.[4]

The first section in this chapter describes and discusses ESOPs. The second section is a general discussion of the advantages and disadvantages of using company stock in a DC plan. The costs associated with using company stock are greater than many people realize—for plan participants but also for shareholders generally.

ESOPS

ESOPs are a special form of defined contribution plan available to corporate sponsors. They are an example of DC plan in which the investments are not employee directed. In 2002 there were approximately 10,000 ESOP plans covering roughly 8 million employees in the United States, according to the ESOP Association. Employees sometimes use these plans to purchase employers in entirety—complete worker ownership. At least 51% of the assets of an ESOP must be invested in the sponsoring employer.

ESOPs and Taxes

Generally speaking, there are two types of ESOPs: ESOPs that borrow money to buy stock in the sponsoring employer, and ESOPs that do not borrow money. Although the former are referred to as leveraged ESOPs, the latter can be leveraged as well. Functionally, there is virtually no difference between the two types.

There are tremendous tax advantages for both types of ESOPs. Corporate contributions to the ESOP are tax deductible. Dividends that the sponsor pays on shares held by the ESOP that flow directly to employees (whose receipts are taxable) or that are used to pay down debt are also tax deductible, unlike ordinary dividends. Further, if the ESOP owns a majority of the shares outstanding, qualified lenders to the (leveraged) ESOP can exclude from their taxable income 50% of the interest received by the lender on the ESOP loan. Thus, lenders have an incentive to lend to ESOPs. Finally, shareholders in a closely held sponsor may obtain a tax-free rollover if they sell their shares to an ESOP that eventually acquires ownership of 30% of the sponsor and if the shareholders buy new qualifying securities, such as bonds.

USE OF COMPANY STOCK IN DC PLANS

Should sponsors use company stock in DC plans? Should employees be allowed to diversify out of company stock in their 401(k) plans? Management has obligations to plan participants, and management also has obligations to shareholders in general. Both sets of obligations come into play in choosing whether to include company stock as part of a pension plan.

The primary claimed advantage of using company stock in pension plans is that the increased stock ownership by employees will result in employees thinking like owners: they will work harder and work smarter. Thus, both nonemployee shareholders and employee shareholders could benefit. In addition to this motivation effect, the other issues to consider are the issues of corporate control, labor market competition, and employee financial education.

Employee Motivation

The first question is whether company stock does motivate employees to work harder and smarter for shareholder wealth. At first sight, it seems plausible: it is certainly in the employees' interest to have a high share price. Won't they therefore work harder and smarter? There are a number of problems with this simple view.

First of all, there is the "free rider problem." Any one employee is a small part of a large corporation. If John Smith has some company stock in his 401(k) plan, is he going to work especially hard in the hope of influencing the stock price? For John to work hard because of his 401(k) plan, he not only has to have stock in the plan, he has to plausibly believe that his actions can affect the stock price. If he is in a large corporation, he may feel he cannot affect stock price. He can hope that everyone else works hard, but it is not clear he will put in extra effort himself.

Second, even if a company does want to tie employees' compensation to share price, there are probably better ways to do it than using a retirement plan. For example, a company can tie bonus income to stock price performance adjusted for market movements. Companies can also offer employees company stock at a discount: this gives more choice to the employees. These alternatives have the advantage of not being labeled as "retirement" plans. Employees take their retirement assets seriously. When company stock is tied to people's retirement, it carries special weight for the employees. Indeed, it is not difficult to imagine a strong negative effect on employee morale if the value of a company's stock drops precipitously and retirement savings are greatly diminished or even lost. This can create an environment in which employee cynicism runs rampant and productivity suffers.

Third, there have been many empirical studies attempting to ascertain the motivational effects of tying retirement plans to employer securities. The results have been mixed. According to one recent study, the evidence indicates there is "at best, only a short-term boost to corporate performance."[5]

One study reported survey evidence obtained from 2,700 workers from thirty-seven employers. It was found that "the more stock employees owned in their sponsor, the more committed they were to the employer, the more satisfied with their work, the less likely they were to look for another job, and the more effort they said they made of the job."[6]

Another study generally supported the contention that ESOPs are employee motivators.[7] It found that the stock prices of publicly held companies generally rose around the time they announced the formation of ESOPs. Indeed, for those companies that adopted ESOPs as wage concessions, average stock prices rose by nearly 4.2% after adjusting for risk and market movements on the day before and the day of the announcement. For those employers announcing the establishment of ESOPs as pure employee benefit plans, the average two-day excess return was nearly 2.5%. Clearly, shareholders tend to respond positively to the creation of ESOPs. It is unlikely that their entire response is attributable to the impoundment of future tax savings into current share prices. Thus, it is reasonable to conclude that some of the benefit is attributable to shareholder anticipation of improved employee motivation.

Another study confirmed that ESOPs provide positive incentives, but find that this is true only for firms with large, independent outside shareholders.[8] One hypothesis is that these "blockholders" are good enough at monitoring their holdings that they will not permit management to expropriate the ESOP's voting rights for their own interest. Thus, in this circumstance, ESOPs tie together shareholder and employee interests without entrenching management.

Corporate Control

The second question that should be asked, by shareholders if not by managers, is whether the use of company stock is in fact really intended to help shareholders. Many employers adopted ESOPs either in anticipation of a control battle or in response to a contest for corporate control. ESOPs associated with publicly controlled employers are required to pass all their voting rights through to the employees owning claims against the ESOP. However, many issues—such as tender offers—do not have to lead to shareholder voting. Moreover, when asked to vote their ESOP interests, employees generally tend to vote with management because, in most corporate restructurings, the great fear of employees is the loss of jobs, and current management is perceived as more likely than outside raiders to do what can be done to preserve existing jobs. ESOPs associated with employers that are not publicly held do not have to pass voting rights through to beneficiaries. In these cases, ESOP trustees, generally managers and their appointees, control the votes.

Scholes and Wolfson contend that the major reason for ESOPs is found in their antitakeover characteristics.[9] They argue that the tax incentives of ESOPs are overstated; some of the same tax incentives can be obtained through other devices, and existing ESOPs seem not to exploit the incentives as fully as they might. However, with ESOPs, managements can generally count on more shares voting to sustain them than might occur otherwise.

When management is supported by ESOP votes, shareholders suffer. In one study of 32 employers, the average two-day abnormal return on the announcement of ESOPs for takeover defense purposes was roughly -2.3%.[10] Clearly, shareholders, presumably including ESOP holders, lose when ESOPs are used to protect entrenched, possibly inefficient managers. A second study confirmed this by demonstrating that, without monitoring by large, independent outside blockholders, performance losses and the proportion of ESOP ownership are positively related.[11]

From management's perspective, putting company stock in a pension plan puts stockholder voting in friendly hands. If there is a takeover battle, current management may correctly expect employees to preserve the status quo. Thus, funding pension plans with company stock may be used to entrench current management and to protect them from a takeover.

In so doing, it takes some pressure off of current management to act in a value-maximizing manner. It gives current management more latitude to pursue its own goals, rather than acting in the best interest of shareholders. The net result can be to reduce long-term shareholder returns by giving management a free hand to do as they chose rather than act in the best interest of shareholders.

Labor Market Considerations

In deciding whether to use company stock, employers should also ask how it fits as part of the company's overall compensation package. Employers who have to compete for good employees must offer what the labor market—or more precisely, the interaction between the buyers of labor and the sellers of labor—dictates. To attract and keep good talent, a company needs to offer competitive compensation. This means that if a company offers low compensation in one area, it has to offer higher compensation in another area. If it saves in one place, it needs to pay more in another place.

However, when company stock is a disproportionately large amount of a pension asset pool, these advantages may dissipate. Modern financial research indicates that when a company includes a lot of company stock in its pension plan, it is getting less bang for its pension buck. The reason is that undiversified portfolios are less valuable than diversified portfolios. With a diversified pension portfolio, employees get a fair expected return for the risk they take. When employees hold an undiversified portfolio heavily weighted with company stock, they are taking risk that could be diversified away.

However, because of competition in the financial markets, the expected returns on the company stock depend only on the systematic or "market" portion of the stock's risk. Thus, in an undiversified portfolio heavily laden with company stock, employees have to absorb the unsystematic, company-specific risk of the stock without compensation for that risk.[12]

Managers may believe that it is "inexpensive" to contribute company stock (as opposed to, say, cash) to a pension plan, but competition in the labor market and the financial markets implies that it is actually relatively expensive. The value of an undiversified portfolio is less than the value of a diversified one; that is, employees may view the value of a dollar of company stock as worth only $0.70 or so if they are forced to hold an undiversified portfolio heavily weighted with company stock. Thus, to keep total compensation competitive, if a company offers an undiversified pension portfolio, it has to offer additional compensation somewhere else. In other words,

If a company puts a lot of company stock in its pension plan, then to keep compensation competitive, it may have to pay higher salaries, or greater cash bonuses. This side-effect may not be easy to track or observe, but in a competitive labor market, the firm must be compensating somewhere if it is to be able to attract and retain the employees it wants.

One last lesson to consider from the labor markets is that of labor mobility. If a company has a lot of company stock in its 401(k) plan, it may actually be encouraging its better (and hence more mobile) employees to move to another company that does not include as much company stock in its pension plan. This may be the only way the employees can diversify out of the company's stock.

Employee Financial Education

Even when company stock is simply an alternative included in the company pension plan and there are few or no limitations on selling the stock, there is the risk that employees will hold too much company stock and thus will hold undiversified portfolios. How well do employees understand the importance of diversification to their retirement plans? Do they recognize the trade-offs associated with investing in company stock versus being diversified across a number of companies and asset classes? As discussed in Chapter 11, some recent applied research shows that in fact some 401(k) participants are surprisingly naive about portfolio allocation.

Regarding company stock in particular, there is evidence that the better a company performs over the past five- or ten-year period, the more its employees will choose to allocate discretionary 401(k) funds to company stock.[13] In other words, if a stock has done will in the past, employees will be more likely to choose company stock for their 401(k) accounts. However, these higher allocations were not correlated with future returns on the company stock. Employees thus seem to believe that past performance predicts future performance, when in fact it does not. The same study examined companies that match employees' 401(k) contributions. If the match was made in company stock, the employees were more likely to invest their own discretionary funds in company stock. This indicates that employees may interpret a company-stock match as implicit investment advice.

If a company's top decision makers believe the company's employees will be better workers if they feel they are fairly compensated, the company should recognize that it has obligations to educate employees regarding portfolio choice. Such education is particularly important when company stock has performed well in the past and a large percentage of the employees pension assets are allocated to company stock through a 401(k) plan or an ESOP.

CONCLUSION

The demise of Enron has reminded us all how an undiversified portfolio with an excessive concentration in a single stock can wreak havoc on people's lives. There are essentially two counter arguments used to justify funding pension plans with large amounts of company stock. The first is that it will align the incentives of employees with shareholders; the second is that it is an inexpensive way to compensate employees. Neither of these stand up to careful scrutiny. There are studies that question the validity of the incentives argument. Furthermore, using company stock may entrench bad management at shareholder expense. Finally, the excessive risk associated with a concentrated investment in company stock means that its value will be lower than will be other forms of compensation. Thus, the labor markets will force firms to raise compensation in other areas or risk losing skilled employees. Finally, when management restricts employees' abilities to diversify a pension plan, it may be breaching a trust, a fiduciary duty. In fact, it not only may be breaching its duty to employees but it may also be breaching its duties to shareholders.

When this chapter was being written, there was continued talk of legislative restrictions on the use of company stock in DC plans. Management will adjust to any legislative changes that occur, of course, but it should not stop there. It may be optimal—for shareholders as well as for employees—to go beyond whatever new limits emerge and think more carefully about the use of company stock when funding pension plans. For firms that do it right, employees, managers, and shareholders will all be better off.

13

Hybrid Plans

In addition to DB and DC plans, many companies are establishing "hybrid" plans—plans that have features of both DB and DC plans.[1] In addition, many companies have already converted or are attempting to convert their current DB plans into a hybrid plan form. Hybrid plans, and in particular conversions from DB plans, have been extremely controversial. Since 1998, there has been substantial negative press coverage of, and sometimes successful litigation against, companies converting to DB plans.

The first section of this chapter describes several types of hybrid plans, including combined plans, cash balance plans, pension equity plans, and target benefit plans. The second section discusses the controversies surrounding these plans. Sponsors who are considering a cash balance plan should consider both the facts about these plans and the public perception of them.

HYBRID PLANS: BASIC TYPES

Combined Plans

Following an in-depth analysis of DB and DC plans, Bodie, Marcus, and Merton do not find either to be clearly preferable.[2] They suggest that a hybrid floor plan could come to dominate either type in terms of employee/employer preference. This plan consists of a minimum guarantee of retirement income (the floor) based on a DB formula. The floor is then supplemented with a DC plan.

Many employers already have such plans, with the DC plan being a 401(k) type of plan. The DB portion offers the employer the opportunity to partially create desirable incentives (e.g., raise the cost of leaving through backloading) and offers employees the benefits of risk-sharing insurance. The supplement (the DC portion) offers reduced investment risk for the employer and has desirable customization and portability attributes for the employee. Both, of course, are attractive because of their tax-advantaged status.

Recall the importance of organization-specific knowledge discussed in Chapter 3. Most organizations are somewhere between the two extremes—those that favor DC plans (organizations requiring little organization-specific skill of their employees) or those that favor DB plans (organizations that do require employer-specific skills). Thus, a combined plan offering attributes of both will make sense for many sponsors. The issue to resolve will be the relative importance of organization-specific capital. The rule of thumb is that if organization-specific capital is important, make the DB plan relatively important. If an employer does not require much organization-specific capital in its employees, make the DC plan relatively important.

Cash Balance Plans

For private employers, cash balance plans are subject to ERISA funding regulations and are covered under PBGC insurance. Cash balance plans are technically DB plans, but they also have some of the features that make DC plans attractive. Benefits accrue in a manner consistent with DC plans, the plan payout is normally in the form of a lump sum, and benefit values are defined in terms of account balances. However, assets are pooled, and the employer bears some investment risk. In addition, similar to DB plans, cash balance plans can be structured to induce early retirement, and similar to DC plans, the risk of outliving plan assets is borne by the employee (unless the plan is annuitized by the employer on retirement or the employee uses the proceeds to purchase an annuity). The employee also bears the risk of inflation after retiring. Cash balance plans are portable, allowing vested employees to take accrued benefits with them on leaving the organization. They also are easier for employees to understand because plan accounts accumulate pay and interest credits that are tied directly to benefits to be paid.

To see how a cash balance plan works, consider an employee who has been with a sponsor for ten years and earns $100,000 a year. The sponsor credits participant accounts based on a percentage of a salary schedule, which may vary by number of years worked. In this example, assume that someone who has worked for ten years receives a credit of 5% of his or her salary each year. The account also may receive interest credits based on some observable market index or interest rate. Thus, if the index is a long Treasury bond rate, and Treasury bonds in the previous year provided a 4% return, the interest credit on the account balance would be 4%. In the example, further assume the employee has an account balance of $50,000 at the beginning of the eleventh year. At the end of this year, assuming the above Treasury bond rate and pay credit, the employee's account will increase by $7,000 ($5,000 because of the 5% pay credit [0.05 × $100,000] and $2,000 [0.04 × $50,000] because of the 4% interest credit). At the end of the eleventh year, the employee's account has a cash value of $57,000. Should the employee then leave the organization, this balance is paid out.

Cash balance plans cannot be easily backloaded (unlike traditional DB plans). It is possible, however, to tie credits to a final average pay/years of service formula, offering some of the advantages of backloading. In addition, there is investment risk because the assets invested in support of a plan may earn less than the value of the pay and interest credits. This risk, however, may be beneficial in that the sponsor can keep any excess above the total credit amount. Cash balance plans can be coupled with minimum-benefit levels, 401(k) plans, matching plans, and profit-sharing plans.

Cash balance plans affect other aspects of plan management as well. For example, the additional liquidity needs brought about by lump-sum payouts may result in holding larger percentages of plan funds in short-term money market investments and income-producing securities such as bonds. This increased emphasis toward lower total return asset classes could increase future contributions for any given implied replacement rate for wages. Cash balance plans can be less costly to administer than DC plans, as they do not have loans, self-directed investment options, and the like.

Pension Equity Plans

An alternative hybrid to the cash balance plan is the pension equity plan (PEP) described by Wyatt. First used by RJR Nabisco in 1993, PEPs are designed to factor in age and final average pay in determining benefits. In so doing, they address some of the benefit accrual disadvantages of cash balance plans.

To see how this works, consider the PEP adopted by IBM in 1995.[3] Benefits accrue on a point basis that varies by age. Employees who are twenty-nine years old or younger earn seven points a year, whereas those who are forty-five years old or older earn sixteen points a year. On retirement, the total number of points accumulated (there is a cap) is multiplied by the average of the final five years' pay and then converted to an annuity. The joint effect of the age and final salary weightings make the plan more attractive to midcareer hires and more effective than a cash balance plan in rewarding fast-track employees.

Target Benefit Plans

A target benefit plan (TBP) is a DC plan that is structured to replicate the payout structure of a DB plan.[4] The targeted benefit can be a specified dollar amount or a percentage of pay. Thus, in appearance, the TBP seems to be a DB plan, while legally, it is subject to DC rules. Sponsors gain some of the flexibility associated with DC plans and plan participants have a pension plan that conceptually mimics DB plans by directly targeting a specific payout to beneficiaries.

Contributions are not age related, and benefit accrual is similar to that of DB plans. Annual contributions are based on actuarial cost methods as well as interest and mortality actuarial assumptions. Plan participants have separate accounts to which contributions and investment earnings are credited. The actual benefit received will be determined by the actual amount of the plan participant's account on retirement. Because actual investment returns may be more or less than the interest assumptions used to calculate the annual contribution, the benefit actually received by plan participants may be higher or lower than the targeted benefit. In addition, as is the case for DC plans in general, beneficiaries bear the mortality risk of outliving their retirement assets unless they use the proceeds to purchase an annuity.

These plans may be especially attractive to small businesses that want to offer pension benefits that favor highly paid employees and yet keep the administrative costs of the pension plan low. TBPs also may be attractive to businesses in which the employees who are more valuable to the organization tend to be older on average than employees who add less value. Thus, TBPs are useful in attracting midcareer employees. A disadvantage of TBPs is that the nondiscrimination rules are complex. Therefore, although there are safe harbor rules available to sponsors, the design of a TBP's plan documents can be challenging.

THE CONTROVERSY AROUND CASH BALANCE PLANS

In the 1990s, many employers began to shift their traditional DB plans to cash balance plans. A commonly quoted figure is that 300 companies made such a conversion. However, the conversions met with substantial controversy and litigation. A primary focus of the controversy has been the question of whether cash balance plans discriminate on the basis of an employee's age. A second concern, which has received less public discussion, is the question of whether cash balance plans have treated fairly workers who leave the plan and who choose to receive a lump-sum distribution. The issues of age discrimination and lump-sum payouts are addressed here in turn.

Age Discrimination

There are three versions of the claim that cash balance plans discriminate against older employees. The first two versions say that older employees are treated unfairly during the conversion from a traditional DB plan to a cash balance plan. The third version is a broader claim that cash-balance plans may be per se illegal.

Treatment of Older Employees during a Conversion

As emphasized in Chapter 1, traditional DB plans are heavily backloaded: employees accrue benefits rapidly toward the end of their careers. Cash balance plans, in contrast, are typically not heavily backloaded. Thus, when DB plans were converted to cash balance plans, the sponsors stopped backloading pensions. New workers can simply accept the new pension regime as part of the employment relationship.

Some older employees, however, had come to expect that they would receive a rapid buildup in pension benefits at the end of their career. When sponsors switched from traditional DB plans to cash balance plans, the sponsors could have offered older employees either their pension under the old plan or their pension under the new plan, but many sponsors did not "grandfather" all their older employers in this way. As a result, during the conversion, many older employees found themselves in a cash balance plan under which they would receive far less in retirement than they had expected before the conversion.

In newspaper accounts, not only were employers lowering employees' expected benefits, but they also were not being up front about doing so. Cash balance plans were being sold to employees as being better suited for "today's more mobile work force,"[5] but older employees were not being clearly told that their benefits would be lower after the conversion.

There were even allegations that actuaries and the consultants who were pushing these plans were trying to keep older employees in the dark. For example, "a partner at the consulting firm that invented the plans in the 1980s told a client in a 1989 letter: 'One feature that might come in handy is that it is difficult for employees to compare prior pension benefit formulas to the account balance approach.' "[6] At an actuarial meeting in 1998, an actuary reported that "Converting to a cash-balance plan does have an advantage as it masks a lot of the changes. . . . There is very little comparison that can be done between the two plans."[7]

Thus, the first version of the age-discrimination claims is just that older workers often received less under the new plan than they would have received under the traditional DB plan. In many cases, such cuts were legal, although they may have violated implicit agreements among employers and employees. The public response of employees and some employers was that if employers do choose to cut benefits in this way, they should at least be up front about the cuts they are making and about the reasons for the cuts.

The second version of the age-discrimination claims also deals with the treatment of older workers after a conversion. This is the phenomenon referred to as "wear-away," and it occurs if the employee's initial account balance in the cash balance plan is less than the amount he or she would receive on leaving the plan at the time of the conversion. The plans cannot reduce a person's benefit after that benefit has accrued. So if an employee's initial cash balance is less than the accrued benefit under the old plan, the employee is entitled to the higher, old-plan benefit. In this situation, however, if the employee remains with the employer, his or her cash balance increases each year, but the amount he or she is entitled to remains at the set old-plan level. The benefit the employee is entitled to does not actually increase until the cash balance catches up with the original plan benefit. That is, there is a period after the conversion that the original plan benefit is "worn away" before the employees plan benefit increases.

Again, many employees were not informed up front about the wear-away possibility. They were then surprised to learn that they were not getting any apparent credit for additional years of service after the conversion. Some companies did clearly communicate the wear-away feature to employees. Indeed, at least one company offered early retirement at the same time as the cash balance conversion. The wear-away period effectively made the early retirement option more attractive.[8]

General Age Discrimination

The third variety of the claim that cash balance plans discriminate on the basis of age is the most sweeping. This is the claim that most or all cash balance plans—regardless of whether or not they are conversions from traditional DB plans—violate the federal laws against age discrimination.

The argument is quite simple. It says that cash balance plans are technically DB plans, and hence they must pass the age-discrimination laws that pertain to DB plans. Those laws say that the rate of benefit accrual can not decrease with age. Under one reading of the law, they also say that for a DB plan, accrued benefit should be thought of as the future value of the annuity payment that the employee will receive at normal retirement age, say sixty-five years.

Everyone can agree that, if the accrued benefit is measured as the future value of the annuity payment received at age sixty-five years, then under cash balance plans, the rate of accrual does decline with age. The reason is simply that older employees are closer to normal retirement. When a sixty-four-year-old employee receives a $5,000 addition to his or her cash balance account, that $5,000 will only receive one year of interest credits. Hence, it will translate into a lower age-sixty-five annuity payment than will a $5,000 contribution for a younger employee.

From an economic perspective, it is natural to think in terms of present values instead of future values. If the interest crediting rate is also the appropriate discount rate for the cash flows, then a $5,000 credit is worth $5,000 in present-value terms regardless of the age of the employee.[9]

Some courts, however, have admitted the argument from an economic point of view, but they have still found cash balance plans to be age discriminatory. That is, they have found that cash balance plans do not meet the DB age-discrimination laws as those laws were written.[10] Other courts have disagreed, saying that even for a DB plan, accrued benefit could be interpreted as the account balance, and that once this is done, cash balance plans pass the age-discrimination tests.[11] As for the Treasury Department, in 1999 it stopped formally approving of cash balance conversions. In December 2002, however, it proposed regulations under which eligible cash balance plans could measure benefit accrual as the additions to a participant's cash balance account (without including future interest credits on that contribution).[12]

The cases continue to make their way through the courts, and the Treasury Department's proposed regulations are not final. In the meantime, companies continue to convert DB plans to cash balance plans despite this basic legal challenge to them. Many companies may be assuming that the cash balance movement is just too big to be declared illegal per se. Indeed, even in 1998, at the time the controversy was coming to public attention, it had already been observed that too many conversions had already taken place, and even then, the cash balance movement was "too big to fail."[13]

Lump-Sum Payouts

A second area of controversy for cash balance plans is in the calculation of lump-sum payouts. Again, the controversy arises because cash balance plans may look like DC plans, but they are actually DB plans and they therefore must meet DB plan rules.

Consider someone who leaves an employer before age sixty-five years and who wants to take their pension as a lump sum at the time of their departure. That is, they want to take money out of the plan at the time they leave instead of waiting for age sixty-five. If the person is a participant in a DC plan, then the person is entitled to his or her cash balance in the plan. The rules for DB plans, however, are more complicated. The person is entitled to the actuarial equivalent of the amount they would receive if they waited to age sixty-five to receive the benefit. The actuarial equivalent is essentially the present value of the benefit the person could expect at age sixty-five. In taking the present value, the law specifies the discount rate that should be used.

What about cash balance plans? How are lump-sum payouts determined there? Some companies tried to treat the cash balance plan as a DC plan: they offered a lump-sum payout equivalent to the person's cash balance account value at the time of departure. Employees have challenged this procedure in the courts, however, and they have been winning.[14]

Courts have said that because cash balance plans are DB plans, lump-sum payouts should be determined by estimating the value of the account at age sixty-five and by then discounting that value back to present value. This process will produce the same value as person's cash balance only if the interest crediting rate exactly equals the discount rate used to derive the present value. If the crediting rate used by the plan exceeds the discount rate specified in the law, then employees will receive lump-sum payouts greater than their cash balance account levels.

All cash balance plans are "hybrid" plans, as the title of this chapter notes. One company tried to argue that its plan was not a prototypical cash balance plan; instead, its plan was allegedly a "hybrid cash balance plan." However, Judge Richard Posner said that the only thing that made the plan "hybrid" was that it calculated lump-sum payouts as though the plan were a DC plan. Judge Posner concluded, "so for 'hybrid' read 'unlawful.' "[15]

PART IV

Measuring, Evaluating, and Improving
Investment Performance

14

Evaluating Investment Performance

The fiduciary responsibilities of pension plan sponsors, administrators, managers, trustees, and others mandate that they periodically evaluate the investment performance of the fund's asset pool. If done properly, investment performance evaluation provides valuable information. First, it shows how well a fund is doing in meeting its investment objectives. Second, it helps those involved in policy see whether the current investment policy is helping meet the goals of the pension plan or whether it is hurting. Third, it helps establish whether or not the managers are following the investment policy and guidelines provided by the sponsor. Fourth, performance evaluation offers insights into the general competence of the investment managers used. Finally, performance evaluation offers information as to whether the managers' behavior is consistent with their espoused investment philosophy; that is, are the managers following the investment strategies they said they would follow?

The tools of performance measurement should be applied to each portfolio within a pension plan and to the plan's entire asset pool as a whole, as well. To see why, suppose a plan has two portfolios. Portfolio A has an unusually good historical performance relative to all benchmarks, whereas portfolio B has a mediocre historical performance. This does not necessarily mean that the total fund is performing well. To the senior managers of the pension plan's sponsoring organization, it matters a great deal whether it was portfolio A or B that began with $1 million or with $100 million. Only by evaluating the overall plan can a sponsor determine what the results from the components mean to the total plan. Likewise, only by evaluating the whole plan can top pension managers and administrators find out whether the entire set of investment strategies and managers selected are satisfactory.

Ultimately, those who have a fiduciary relationship to the pension plan need to be able to determine whether the investment policies and managers are doing well relative to alternative policies and peers and also relative to alternative, unmanaged, benchmark portfolios. This is equally important for DB and DC plans.

To make these comparisons, managers should understand that performance evaluation has several components:

- the alternative computations used in measuring returns,
- the correct ways to measure and adjust for risk,
- how benchmarks should be chosen or constructed, and
- attribution analysis—decomposing investment performance into the exposure of the fund to various market segments, the quality of the selection of assets, and the timing of movements of capital among asset classes.

None of the above is sufficient by itself to evaluate performance. Rather, each has its own stories to tell. The complete story requires using all of the available tools. This chapter describes how each of these issues should be handled and what each contributes to understanding performance and to decision making.

INVESTMENT RETURNS

Return is realized as income yield (i.e., dividends and interest), capital appreciation or depreciation (i.e., the change in the market value of the fund's assets), and currency appreciation or depreciation (e.g., if the dollar strengthens against the yen, the pension will suffer a currency loss on its Japanese investments). Income is a desirable attribute for pensions that have near-term liquidity needs such as payments to current retirees. Income not spent may be reinvested and can also thus contribute to long-term growth. The capital change component is desirable because, over long periods of time, it should help the fund grow in real (inflation-adjusted) terms. The currency component is considered by some to be a source of return if a manager is skilled in selecting undervalued currencies. Others consider currency simply a cost of investing outside the United States—a risk to be hedged.

The greater the investment return on a pension fund, the lower future contributions need to be to achieve a postretirement payment target or accumulation target. In 1998, contributions to private and public DB plans approximated $150 billion. If the investment performance on the DB asset pool of roughly $4 trillion was just 1% better, $40 billion more in investment returns would have been achieved, and contributions could have been cut by 27% without reducing the financial security of the plans.[1] The same general result applies to DC plans— the higher the return, the higher the future benefit payments, given a fixed contribution schedule.

Investment return calculations are sensitive to the various choices the analyst may make. One important factor is the time period chosen: annual returns may differ substantially if a calendar year return is compared to a twelve-month return using other starting and ending dates. Similarly, investment managers with poor annual results may present annualized five- or ten-year results to average in one or more good earlier years, whereas managers with good recent results may present only recent data. Year-by-year, multiyear annualized, and cumulative returns all have stories to tell—stories that are necessary if the full picture is to be seen. Another factor is the influence the timing of cash inflows and outflows to a portfolio or pool of assets has on actual performance. Significant cash flows (as in a sponsor's decision to allocate more funds to a specific manager) can lead to overstating or understating the returns the manager achieves, depending on subsequent market action. Finally, when investment managers present composites representing the returns on groups of portfolios they manage, whether the portfolios are equally weighted or weighted by size can matter greatly.

Measuring return correctly depends on what the analyst is trying to accomplish or evaluate. For example, time-weighted returns are useful in evaluating managers of individual portfolios that are components of the overall pension fund. Dollar-weighted returns are useful in evaluating the return on the overall asset pool and in evaluating managers who are trying to time asset allocations. The use of one when the other should be used can lead to poor decisions. For example, a poor money manager may be rewarded for the sponsor's fortuitous decision to give him or her more money just before the market went up if the dollar-weighted return is used. The time-weighted return would allow the manager's poor performance to be uncovered, however. These and some other return measures are discussed in Appendix D.

RISK-ADJUSTED RETURNS

Because expected return and anticipated risk are so intimately entwined, a careful balancing of the two is necessary when constructing a pension portfolio. For the same reason, when evaluating historical investment decisions, most investment professionals construct measures that allow risk to be considered along with return. Accordingly, when they speak of investment performance, they do not refer to realized returns, but to realized returns adjusted in some way for the risk borne by the portfolio.

To measure investment performance in economically sensible and managerially useful ways, therefore, estimates of return must be combined with estimates of risk. The metric must be compared with benchmark results that could readily be achieved by naive portfolio management techniques, say by buying and holding all the stocks in the S&P 500 index in proportion to their weight in the index (i.e., a passive index fund, which is discussed later).

Broadly speaking, there are two types of performance measures, depending on the way the sponsor views risk. The first focuses on the investment returns achieved by a fund relative to the fund's total or absolute risk. This type of measure is particularly useful when evaluating the pension plan's total asset pool rather than simply one or another of the portfolios that may be included in it. Measures of the second type consider only the systematic risk of a portfolio rather than its total risk, part of which will likely be offset whenever the portfolio being evaluated is a portion of a much larger pool of assets. The technical aspects of both of these measurement techniques are discussed in detail in Appendix E.

Risk of the Total Pension Portfolio

William F. Sharpe developed and tested what has come to be known as the Sharpe measure. It compares the average portfolio "excess return"—the rate of return in excess of what could have been earned by investing in comparatively risk-free assets, such as Treasury bills—to the variability of portfolio return measured over the return period. The result is a "reward-to-variability" ratio. It captures in a single measure the excess returns earned per unit of total risk (volatility) borne. The formula is

$$Sh_p = (R_{ap} - R_{af})/SD_{R(p)},$$

where R_{ap} and R_{af} are, respectively, the arithmetic averages of the portfolio return and the risk-free rate over the period, and SD_R is the standard deviation of the portfolio's returns over, perhaps, five years. By using total risk, the Sharpe ratio explicitly considers diversification. A fund with poor diversification should have a higher standard deviation, which has the effect of penalizing the fund for being poorly diversified. In other words, it requires higher excess return.

Over the period from 1926 to 2002, the average annual return on S&P 500 index stocks (i.e., relatively large company stocks) was, with dividends reinvested, 12.2%, and the standard deviation of annual equity portfolio returns was 20.5%. The average return on one-month Treasury bills over the period was 3.8%.[2] (Interestingly, Treasury bills had a positive standard deviation because the strategy of rolling over one-month Treasury bills did not produce a perfectly risk-free constant return. However, this small standard deviation is customarily ignored in practice.) Using these data, the Sharpe measure for large company stocks was

$$(12.2 - 3.8)/20.5 = 0.410.$$

Over the same period, the average annual return and standard deviation of annual returns for corporate bonds were 6.2% and 8.7%, respectively.[3] The Sharpe measure here is

$$(6.2 - 3.8)/8.7 = 0.276.$$

One inference that may be drawn from this result is that corporate stocks performed substantially better than bonds on a risk-adjusted basis. The former achieved an excess return of forty-one basis points for every unit of risk borne, whereas the latter had a reward of only twenty-eight basis points per unit of risk borne. With the advantage of hindsight, an investor interested solely in high risk–adjusted returns would have been better off in stocks than in bonds. However, this does not automatically mean that stock investments alone should be the future strategy. Going forward, it is the ex ante risks—those yet to be faced—not the realized risks of the past that ought to guide decision making. That is, ex post Sharpe ratios might be used as unbiased forecasts of future

Sharpe ratios. Looking backward, however, it is the realized returns and risks that distinguish ex post what strategies worked well and which did not.

The Sharpe measure generally is used to compare the results of one investment strategy (or total portfolio) against those of another. For instance, the historical performance of a portfolio consisting of 60% stocks and 40% corporate bonds might be compared with one containing, say, 70% stocks and 30% cash equivalents (i.e., very short term securities). The Sharpe measure will identify which strategy historically produced higher rewards for each unit of variability, thus providing insight into its likelihood of doing so in the future.

There is no absolute number against which an aggregate pension portfolio might be compared. An absolute value of 0.4 or 0.9 or 2.0 is meaningless except in that it may indicate poor absolute performance when it is negative or good absolute performance when it is positive. Rather, an absolute value is a ranking measure that has real meaning when it is compared with its benchmark portfolio counterpart or with other, similar funds. Users should recognize that the Sharpe ratio does not address correlations between different strategies or asset allocations. Thus, its use in analyzing strategies that are not highly correlated requires further effort to incorporate the effect of correlations. Finally, note that, relative to other commonly used measures, the Sharpe measure has very few purely statistical problems. Specifically, there are no serious difficulties arising from violation of the economic and statistical assumptions necessary to compute the numbers. Of course, standard deviation is only a measure of dispersion, not a perfect representation of risk.

An extension of the basic Sharpe ratio is the differential return Sharpe ratio. In place of the risk-free rate, the differential Sharpe ratio uses a benchmark return that can be achieved passively. A positive differential return implies that the portfolio produced an active (or selection) return that exceeds the return that is obtainable without active management. Thus, the differential return Sharpe ratio offers insight into the value added by active management relative to a comparably risky passive strategy. (Measuring the success of active strategies and benchmarking are both discussed later in this chapter.)

In summary, the Sharpe measure is an appropriate way to adjust a total pension fund's return for the risk taken. In general, it is not as useful in evaluating component portfolios.

Risk of Component Portfolios

A pension plan may employ many different managers, each bringing a very different investment focus and asset valuation theory to portfolio management. Frequently, these investment strategies result in component portfolios that are not well diversified. Therefore, the component funds or subportfolios of a pension plan's asset pool should be evaluated using only the systematic risk of a portfolio to avoid penalizing specialty managers for taking undiversified exposures that the plan sponsor wants. Systematic risk is risk that cannot be reduced by diversification. Investors may choose to take less systematic risk, but if so, theory suggests they must accept lower expected returns as well.

A measure that adjusts returns for only the systematic portion of total risk is the Treynor measure.[4] The Treynor measure does not penalize a portfolio manager for investing in a narrow segment of the overall market. Rather, it considers the incremental systematic risk a manager adds to the total portfolio. Of course, use of the Treynor measure does not create any incentive for a money manager to diversify the portfolio's holdings, nor, for that matter, should it, as diversification presumably is being implemented by the plan sponsor.

Similar to the Sharpe measure, the Treynor measure is a ratio that allows interpretation as a relative reward-to-risk ratio. In addition, a negative value reveals that the portfolio did poorly on an absolute basis. Again, however, similar to the Sharpe measure, the performance metric can be interpreted only in the context of a group of similar observations, a universe of other managed portfolios, or some other benchmark. Apart from wanting the number to be greater than zero, at the close of any period knowing that the measure is X or Y does not alone reveal whether the portfolio manager did a good or poor job. Only when the performance is compared with that of other managers or with a benchmark portfolio can it be determined whether a satisfactory investment performance was produced relative to the risk taken.

The Treynor measure is

$$TR_p = (R_{ap} - R_{af})/\beta_p,$$

where R_{ap} and R_{af} are, respectively, the arithmetic averages of the subportfolio return and the average risk-free rate over the period, and β_p is the beta of the portfolio's returns over, perhaps, five years. To demonstrate, suppose R_{ap} was 12% over the year, R_{ap} was 2.4% over the same period, and β_p was 0.9. Then,

$$TR_p = (12.0 - 2.4)/0.9 = 0.1067.$$

This equation says that for every incremental whole unit of risk, the portfolio achieved a 10.7% return. If this measure is high when compared with the Treynor measures for other portfolios, this money manager may have achieved abnormally good investment results. (Unfortunately, the Treynor measure does not say whether the cause is skill or merely luck.)

Market Risk and Active Management

Many portfolio managers pursue what are called active management strategies in an attempt to earn returns above those that might be obtained through passive exposures to an asset class (e.g., stocks). Measuring the success of these managers in generating excess returns requires first adjusting for the risk characteristic of their strategies and then seeing whether the returns produced are higher than can be explained simply by pursuing an equally risky strategy.

Jensen (1969) developed a measure of investment performance that, similar to the Treynor measure, recognizes that a single portfolio may not be as fully diversified as the overall pension plan and, thus, focuses on the relationship between systematic or market risk and a portfolio's return. On an intuitive level, the Jensen measure is the difference between the actual return on a portfolio minus the return on a broad-based market portfolio, such as the Wilshire 5000, adjusted for the relative riskiness of the portfolio being evaluated.

Specifically, the Jensen measure (α_p) is

$$\alpha_p = R_{ap} - [R_{af} + \beta_p (R_{am} - R_{af})],$$

where α_p is the measure of performance and β_p is the estimate of the systematic (market) risk of the portfolio. If α_p is greater than zero, the portfolio "beat the market" on a risk-adjusted basis. If it is less than zero, the portfolio underperformed the market on a risk-adjusted basis.

To illustrate the calculation, suppose a portfolio had an average monthly return of 1.0% and the estimated β_p was 0.8 while the monthly average return on short-term Treasury bills was 0.2%. Further, suppose the average monthly return on a broad-based market portfolio was also 1.0%. Then,

$$\alpha_p = 1.0 - [(0.2) + 0.8(1.0 - 0.2)] = 0.16\%.$$

This means that this portfolio did better than might have been expected, given its systematic (market) risk: the portfolio produced excess risk-adjusted returns of 0.16% per month or 1.92% per year. In other words, after allowing for risk, the portfolio did well—it beat the market—because the risk-adjusted monthly returns on the market were only 0.64% above the Treasury bill rate, whereas the risk-adjusted monthly returns for the portfolio were 0.8% above the Treasury bill rate. In general, the higher the α_p the better the portfolio performance.

Users should be aware there are statistical problems with estimating β_p reliably. These include correctly choosing a market benchmark and assuming that its estimation is not contaminated by much alteration in the composition of the subject portfolio. In addition, the measure may be misleading about how well the portfolio did absolutely. That is, following a market that dropped sharply, the α_p could be 2.0%, which would merely mean that on a risk-adjusted basis this portfolio beat the market. The absolute loss, however, could be horrendous. It is cold comfort to know one beat the market by 2% while the market itself experienced a decline of 30%. Regardless, computing a portfolio's α_p is most useful when comparing the performance of pension plan segments (portfolios) or managers of these segments to one another.

Another useful approach to evaluating risk relative to active management is the appraisal ratio (also known as the information ratio) developed by Treynor and Black. It adjusts excess market-adjusted portfolio return for the amount of unsystematic or nonmarket risk—risk that can be reduced by diversification—that is borne. Conceptually, this excess return is the gain received from taking an exposure to diversifiable risk. Presumably, managers would take this exposure only if they believed they possessed useful special information or insight. Mathematically, the appraisal ratio is

$$A_p = \alpha_p/SD(\varepsilon_p),$$

where α_p is the measure of performance (the same α_p in the Jensen measure) and $SD(\epsilon_p)$ is the standard deviation of the error term in the market model discussed in Appendix D—the variability in the portfolio return that is not explained by the variation in the chosen market portfolio or benchmark. The more closely related the movements in the portfolio in question are to movements in the market portfolio, the smaller $SD(\epsilon_p)$ will be, other things being equal, because it measures risk that could be diversified away by holding a broad-based portfolio.

To illustrate the appraisal ratio, if α_p were 1.92% for the year and if $SD(\epsilon_p)$ were 15% over the same period, then

$$A_p = 1.92/15.0 = 0.128.$$

This equation says that for every unit of risk that could be avoided with proper diversification, the manager achieved a 0.128% excess market and risk-adjusted return. Successful active managers should be able to generate consistently positive appraisal ratios. (Furthermore, positive appraisal ratios should be statistically significant.) Poor active managers will produce negative appraisal ratios. Thus, this measure is most helpful when compared with corresponding measures for other actively managed portfolios and the managers who run them, as well as on an absolute basis.

BENCHMARKS

Woven throughout the preceding discussion is an unstated assumption that the evaluator has an appropriate benchmark or standard of comparison to answer the following two questions:

- How has the overall fund done?
- How has manager A or portfolio A done?

Too frequently, those attempting to measure performance oversimplify this issue, resorting to the use of an index such as the S&P 500 or turning to a simple manager universe. Neither of these standards is necessarily the best. Thus, in spite of some fairly sophisticated statistics, one can still reach the wrong conclusions—for example, that a manager is bad when he or she is good, or vice versa—if the appropriate standard is not used. A viable alternative to these oversimplified approaches is the normal or benchmark portfolio: a theoretical portfolio that is structurally identical to the investment strategy without whatever active management takes place. Benchmark portfolios are constructed specifically to serve as the standard against which an actual portfolio is judged. This section examines the strengths and weaknesses of using indexes and manager universes and then looks at how benchmark portfolios can improve performance measurement.

Comparisons Using Indexes

Sometimes a pension analyst, rather than making any technical adjustments for risk, may simply compare the return on a portfolio against the return on a broad-based index of security returns. For this purpose, many analysts have used the S&P 500 Stock Index. This index is a market-value-weighted index of the 500 common stocks that the Standard & Poor's Company believes are representative of the broad market. Of course, although the pension plan sponsor would compare only the return on the equity portion of the pension portfolio with the S&P 500 return, even here the analyst is likely to be making a sizable mistake because using market indexes can create serious problems that may lead to incorrect conclusions.

A major problem with using an index for comparison is that the index may not be appropriate for the portfolio for which it is being used as a standard. There are several issues here. First is the matter of choosing an index that has a comparable level of risk to the portfolio being evaluated. For example, using the S&P 500 as the standard when evaluating a portfolio of small capitalization stocks may provide misleading results because standard risk adjustments (e.g., beta) may not completely capture the difference in risk between the index and the actual portfolio. Thus, a sponsor could conclude that a manager is successful because he or she has been beating the market when the reality is that the manager has been taking excessive risk. Alternatively, the sponsor might conclude that a manager has been unsuccessful when the reality is that the manager has been very successful in generating returns with very little risk.

Roll and Ross point out a related problem.[5] Using an index as the standard presumes that the index represents a portfolio that is efficient (i.e., it offers the highest possible return for its level of risk). They demonstrate that if the index is not efficient, the results of the evaluation may be completely different from the results of an evaluation that uses an efficient index. It is extremely unlikely that the S&P 500 is efficient. Thus, using it as a benchmark introduces two possible benchmark errors. First, the beta of a portfolio may be underestimated, leading the analyst to conclude that a portfolio or manager is taking less systematic risk than is really the case. This can corrupt any attempt to use measures like the Treynor ratio. Second, it may underestimate the true trade-off between risk and return (i.e., the true trade-off may require higher incremental return for incremental risk). This can corrupt measures like Jensen's alpha. The basic issue for either is that portfolios may be ranked inappropriately. Typically, they will look better than they really are.

Indexes differ in the way they are constructed. For example, the S&P 500 is value weighted: its performance is affected more by what happens to the stocks of the larger market capitalization companies than by what happens to the smaller ones. The stocks in the Value Line index are equally weighted, however, making it an appropriate index for portfolios that hold equal dollar amounts of each security; and the Dow Jones Industrial Average is weighted by price, making it an appropriate index for portfolios that hold equal numbers of shares of each security. Further, bond indexes differ according to how bonds are priced (a very important issue, as many bonds do not trade frequently) and how maturing bonds are replaced. They differ as well by credit risk and maturity. There is a point to this delineation of index differences: a portfolio that does not share the construction attributes of a given index will, of course, perform differently from the index, even though it may hold roughly the same assets. Yet this difference should be attributed to differing construction. It is not attributable to investment strategy per se unless the difference in construction is a strategic decision.

Another problem with using an index is that, in computing the total return, dividends must be collected and reinvested. Many consultants and money management firms compute the rate of return on the S&P 500. However, because each of these organizations makes different assumptions regarding the reinvestment of dividends, some ambiguity arises. Specifically, organizations can assume that dividends get reinvested in the same stock that paid them at the closing price on the payment day or at the next day's opening price. They can also assume reinvestment in the index rather than the dividend-paying stock at the closing or at the next day's opening.

One study that looked at this found that S&P 500 returns as computed by different organizations can differ by about twenty basis points.[6] This is a small difference, but what is important here is that there is measurable difference in something most observers would view as unambiguous. Different portfolio performance–measuring organizations compute the same benchmark differently. Given the competitiveness of the money management industry and the generally very narrow dispersion of realized returns across different money managers, both among themselves and relative to benchmark portfolios, it is clear that many who might be classed as beat-the-market managers using one index measurement could move to the beat-by-the-market category using another organization's version of the index return.

Are these issues important? One study found that the rankings of portfolio managers are very sensitive to the choice of proxies for the market—to using the S&P 500 instead of the NYSE index, for example.[7] In concluding that a manager has done well or poorly, the cumulative effect of the kinds of errors as described here may be quite large, and a sponsor who makes important decisions based on faulty data may be making poor decisions indeed.

The lessons for plan sponsors are these: be cautious regarding the choice of index. Do not mistake a popular index for the market. Recognize that indexes are at best subsets of the market and that they frequently are subsets of the asset classes that correctly make up the market. When using an index for a specific comparison, choose one that is an appropriate representation of the risk to which the portfolio being evaluated is exposed. Use an index that represents the right market segment (e.g., large capitalization stocks) and that is constructed in a manner consistent with the way the actual portfolio is formed (e.g., value weighted). Understand what assumptions are built into the index data computations that could make this proxy tougher or easier to beat. Use one organization's index consistently to make reasonably robust, long-term evaluations of money managers over time and among themselves.

Comparisons Using Manager Universes

Another common approach to comparative analysis is to select a set of performance numbers (return and risk measures) compiled from a sample of performance numbers from presumably comparable money managers. This method has the naive appeal of a horse race in which manager A does better (or worse) than manager B. In addition, it is easy to get information because numerous pension consultants make manager universe data accessible so that a sponsor does not have to develop its own base of comparison. However, this type of data has three serious flaws.

The first is that a manager universe is useful only if the managers represented follow similar investment styles, such as small capitalization growth stock investing and so forth. Because managers may follow more than one stylistic discipline over time, the accurate, appropriate grouping of managers becomes problematic. In addition, large numbers of managers are necessary to achieve reasonable statistical significance; however, the larger the universe, the more dissimilar the styles of the included managers are likely to be.

A more serious problem is that of survivorship bias. Any manager universe with a number of managers with reasonably long records presents the performance of managers who have been good enough to survive in a competitive business. Looked at another way, poor managers having poor performance are not likely to be proportionately included in the data presented as representative of performance standards.

Finally, the results of manager universe comparisons are difficult to interpret in a useful fashion because the rankings change from period to period. Furthermore, the return rankings that are generated frequently conflict with the risk rankings. It is worth noting, however, that the risk rankings do offer some insight into whether an investment manager is complying with policy.[8]

Collectively, these problems make manager universes of only limited value for a sponsor evaluating performance to decide who to employ in the future—a decision of considerable importance.

Normal (Benchmark) Portfolios

In recent years, many analysts and researchers have criticized the risk-adjusted measures described earlier because they either assume that total risk is the relevant risk for a portfolio, which it is not when the portfolio is part of a much larger plan, or because the statistical measures α_p and β_p are specific to (dependent on) the proxy chosen for the return on the market portfolio.[9]

Consider a portfolio manager who is constrained to a narrowly defined strategy—for instance, purchasing stocks with high book-to-market (B/M) multiples. This manager is not likely to hold a well-diversified portfolio; hence, the Sharpe measure will not be an appropriate way to measure this manager's performance. Similarly, if the index portfolio or market portfolio proxy is only imperfectly and variably correlated with the universe of high-B/M stocks, then the statistical parameter estimates (the alphas and betas) will not mean very much. Thus, the Treynor-Jensen or Treynor-Black measures would not be helpful in evaluating this manager. To circumvent this problem and the problems posed by published indexes and manager universes, many analysts have suggested the use of normal or benchmark portfolios.

A benchmark portfolio constitutes the universe of all the stocks that the portfolio manager may consider. In essence this is the neutral or passive portfolio that represents the manager's style without any active decision making; that is, the benchmark portfolio should represent an available level of performance that can be achieved by randomly selecting securities from the style universe. In general, each portfolio manager in a group of managers who are collectively responsible for the pension plan should have a well-defined, very specific investment strategy. For example, one manager may be responsible for evaluating and selecting growth stocks, whereas another may be searching for value stocks. With benchmark portfolios, the portfolio manager's actual investment returns may be compared with the returns on the specially constructed securities universe, allowing a meaningful comparison of an actively managed portfolio to a stylistically comparable benchmark portfolio.

For example, consider a portfolio manager who has agreed to manage a high-B/M portfolio. This manager's return should be compared with a portfolio containing all the stocks that have B/Ms above a specified level and that otherwise qualify for inclusion, perhaps because they are listed on an organized exchange or are traded on the National Association of Securities Dealers Automated Quotation (NASDAQ) system; that is, they are investable. If the manager beats the customized benchmark on a pure return basis without changing styles, that would be considered superior performance attributable to the manager's skill.

Of course, this approach requires that portfolio managers and pension plan sponsors agree beforehand on what constitutes an appropriate benchmark portfolio. They must also agree on the conventions applied to dividend reinvestment; otherwise, the same problem noted above could arise here.

The benchmark portfolio approach to performance measurement is gaining popularity not only because it avoids some troublesome theoretical issues (such as how many risk factors are relevant) and some thorny statistical issues (such as the optimal measurement period) but also because large computerized databases accessible by personal computers can be used to construct these customized, normal portfolios. Generally speaking, the construction of benchmark portfolios is not an easy process. It requires a very sophisticated understanding of the investment strategy that the money manager and the sponsor agree to use. The benchmark portfolio must represent the manager's style (defining and replicating this may be difficult), it must be investable, and it must be useful in differentiating between active and passive management.[10] In spite of the difficulties, construction of benchmark portfolios is not impossible. Importantly, from the analyst's perspective, separating a manager's ability to select securities (or to time the market) from the plan sponsor's ability to select investment strategies to be implemented by managers is critical to evaluating how managers are doing.

Using benchmark portfolios allows plan sponsors to see how well a manager does within the parameters of the strategy that he or she was contracted to pursue by the plan sponsor. It has the added advantages of defining expectations before the fact—as such, it is a useful communication tool—and of encouraging managers to stay with the style they were hired to deliver. Finally, although the Sharpe, Jensen, or Treynor measures may be satisfactory combined measures of the quality of security selection and strategy selection, they will not do for managers who are constrained to narrowly defined security markets: there are just too many nuances in markets and management behavior that these measures might miss.

Finally, a word of caution is appropriate. Benchmarks can easily be misused. This commonly occurs when an index naively is chosen as a benchmark without proper attention to what the sponsor and investment manager are really trying to accomplish. Sometimes an index may not be investable, or factors such as crossholdings (a big problem in Japan) are not taken into account. Other times, the wrong benchmark is selected; for example, the S&P 500 index is selected for a small company stock manager or as a proxy for the entire U.S. equity market. Those who help select benchmarks should bear in mind that investment managers have incentives first to mimic the chosen benchmark and second not to stray too far from the benchmark. This is fine for passive strategies; in fact, it is exactly what is wanted. However, for actively managed portfolios, it can force the manager away from her area of expertise and into portfolio strategies that are different than the one for which he or she was hired. In other words, naive benchmarks can be harmful because they introduce a bias against actions that otherwise may be desirable.

COMPONENTS OF INVESTMENT PERFORMANCE

To understand whether the decisions made have been good or poor, it is necessary to understand why actual returns are what they are. The various measures of investment performance discussed so far may indicate whether Fund A beat Fund B or beat the market, but they do not reveal why, nor do they reveal how much of the actual performance is attributable to passive exposures to various asset classes or to active management. Generally speaking, superior or inferior returns can be attributed to one of two active management strategies. The first is security selection: unusual selections of specific stocks or bonds relative to all of those that could be bought or sold, and perhaps buying those that are thought to be underpriced. The second is market timing: being heavily invested in the stock market when it is expected to perform unusually well, or more heavily invested in bonds when they are expected to do comparatively well.

Performance Attribution

Several authors[11] have offered schemes designed to help analysts detect whether total plan performance is attributable to exposure to a benchmark, to market timing, or to security selection. The benchmark portfolio, in essence, represents the return attributable to passive exposures to asset classes or market segments. The purpose of performance attribution, then, is to explain why actual portfolio returns differ from a given benchmark by identifying the effect active decisions have had. Table 14.1 shows a possible framework for the components of investment performance.

To illustrate, suppose that a pension plan (perhaps comprising many portfolios) experienced a total return of 25% over the evaluation period. Further, sup-

Table 14.1 Schema for Determining the Components of Investment Performance

	Selectivity	
Timing	Active Security Selection	Passive Security Selection
Active Market Timing	IV Actual return	II Policy and timing return
Passive Market Timing	III Policy and security selection return	I Policy return (passive benchmark)

Cause of Active Returns	
Action	Squares
Timing	II − I
Selectivity	III − I
Other	IV − III − I + I
Total	IV − I

Source: Adapted from Brinson et al. (1986).

pose that the overall portfolio was allocated so that 70% of the money was invested in stocks and 30% of the money was invested in bonds. Finally, assume that the stock portion of the total portfolio rose by 30% and the bond portion of the total portfolio rose by 13.3%.

To determine what portion of the total return was attributable to market timing and what portion was attributable to security selection, data regarding the investment policy and the investment experience of unmanaged funds must be used. In this instance, suppose that the long-term strategic asset allocation policy (the stock–bond mix) was 60% stocks and 40% bonds. Further, assume that an appropriate benchmark portfolio for stocks rose by 25% over the period and that an appropriate benchmark portfolio for bonds rose by 15% over the same period.

This information can be used to determine the components or sources of the portfolio's actual returns. This is done by filling in the matrix of Table 14.1. This can be seen in Table 14.2. Quadrant IV contains the actual total return experience of the fund: 25%. Quadrant I contains the performance the fund would have had if it both invested exactly according to policy guidelines for the strategic asset allocation and bought the index portfolios. Quadrant III contains the results that would have been obtained had the fund followed the strategic investment policy allocation of 60% stock and 40% bonds but selected the securities it actually held; that is, portfolio sector weights are changed from policy to actual. In doing so, Quadrant III isolates the effect of management's efforts to identify securities offering unusually high returns. Quadrant II contains the investment results that would have been achieved if the fund was allocated as it actually was, that is, 70% stocks and 30% bonds, but the fund simply invested

Table 14.2 Components of Investment Performance

	Selectivity	
Timing	Active Security Selection	Passive Security Selection
Active Market Timing	IV	II
	25%	22%
	(0.3) (0.7) + (0.1333) (0.3)	(0.7) (0.25) + (0.3) (0.15)
Passive Market Timing	III	I
	23.3%	21%
	(0.3) (0.6) + (0.1333) (0.4)	(0.25) (0.6) + (0.15) (0.4)

	Cause of Active Returns	
Action	Squares	Percentage
Timing	II − I	1%
Selectivity	III − I	2.3%
Other	IV − III − I + I	0.7%
Total	IV − I	0.4%

in the benchmark portfolios of stocks and bonds (index funds) instead of making the specific security selections it actually made. This isolates the effect of the market-timing decisions.

In this illustration, the gain from timing is 1%, and the gain from selectivity is 2.3%. The latter comprises very good stock selectivity and poor bond selectivity. The overall gain attributable to active management—the collective value added by active timing and active security selection decisions—is 4.0%. Note that the actual return of 25% exceeds the benchmark return (quadrant I) of 21% by 4%. Note also that further analysis would reveal that active bond selection appears to be poor because the actively managed bond portfolio underperformed its benchmark. However, underweighting bonds (holding 30% instead of 40%) reduced the effect of poor bond selection and magnified the effect of good stock selection.

Why Separate Performance Components?

There are several reasons why evaluating the components of performance can be worthwhile. If the pension plan sponsor is the one who makes the timing decisions by deciding whether the bond manager or the equity manager gets the next capital contribution to invest, this approach may help distinguish what portion of total performance is the result of the sponsor's decisions and what is the result of the decisions of money managers. Furthermore, for money managers who have latitude with respect both to selection and timing, the component approach is useful in distinguishing whether the manager is unusually good or bad at selection or timing. The plan sponsor could then write investment instructions that exploit the real skill of the manager and preclude him or her from exercising much discretion in the area of weakness. For instance, a good market timer but bad security selector may be given instructions that allow him or her to deviate from policy stock/bond allocations but that require such deviations to be implemented using only passive stock and bond portfolios.

Style Analysis

Many practitioners argue that style is an essential component of performance evaluation; that is, serious mistakes may be made if the analyst fails to consider style. Style refers to clusters of portfolios with similar risk and performance patterns, and groups of managers sharing certain ideas about the best approach to investing or philosophical views about key determinants of stock price movements.[12] For style to exist, style portfolio and style index returns must be significantly different from the market. This means that style portfolios and style indexes should have, on average, different factor exposure patterns from the market as a whole and from each other.

The benefits of defining and using style in performance evaluation are that using style indexes allows separation of style effects from larger benchmarks such as manager universes or a broad index. This can be important in evaluating manager results: when a manager's performance is compared to an appropriate benchmark, the conclusions may be different from when performance is compared to a broad market index.

In particular, when using short time periods, style analysis becomes important to avoid hiring a manager at a peak that may be solely caused by a style cycle, or firing a manager solely because the manager's style category has been doing poorly.

There are problems with overreliance on style analysis, however. First, it is difficult to distinguish among styles because many overlap in the securities they hold and in their exposure to other risk factors. More important, over long time periods, managers should be able to beat the market regardless of style. Otherwise, they are not earning their fees. So even though style cycles can last for long periods of time, it is essential to ask whether a manager is beating the market (e.g., the broad stock market, when evaluating an equity manager) as the time period under consideration lengthens.

ADVANCES IN PERFORMANCE EVALUATION

In an attempt to improve the performance measurement and evaluation process, scholars and practitioners alike are exploring new methodologies, and they are having some success. The most promising area of advancement is the use of multiindex or multifactor models for portfolios.

Multiindex Models

There is much to recommend the development of Jensen-type measures using multiindex models instead of the single-index model typically referred to as the market model.[13] The primary advantage of a multifactor model with respect to assessing performance is that it allows or offers multiple factors to explain a portfolio's performance when a single market factor seems to be inadequate. In addition, it does not rely on or require the identification of a single broad market index as the basis for comparison; instead, it allows for computing multiple risk sensitivities to multiple factors. For instance, the relationship between unanticipated real growth, inflation, and various measures of interest rate change might be thought to be the systematic factors to which a portfolio is exposed. If so, the risk premiums characteristic of these factors and the sensitivity of a portfolio to these factors may be computed and used in Jensen-type performance measures.

Multifactor models and the performance assessment results they yield still are very sensitive to the assumptions regarding construction of the underlying benchmarks. The choices of variables used to construct the multifactor models can also affect the usefulness of the model's results. Nonetheless, these models are adding to our understanding of the issues involved in defining style, constructing benchmarks, and understanding the sources of performance.

Returns-Based Style Analysis

One especially promising area is the multifactor work done by Sharpe.[14] He proposes that a portfolio's style can be identified by constructing an asset class-based (returns-based) factor model of the form

$$R_i = \beta_{i1}F_1 + \beta_{i2}F_2 + \ldots + \beta_{in}F_n + \varepsilon,$$

where β_{in} is the exposure of a portfolio (and hence its sensitivity) to asset class F_n (where n may be large company stocks, small company stocks, Treasury bonds, and so forth). The primary insight this approach offers is that a portfolio's or a manager's historical performance can be analyzed and a descriptive style defined in terms of asset classes and exposures. As long as the asset classes used in the model are mutually exclusive, collectively represent the "market," and have differing return profiles, this model offers an analytical approach to determining combination of weights (betas) and asset classes that will generate returns similar to that of the portfolio being analyzed. In other words, a real portfolio's "style" may be translated into a "comparable" portfolio of major asset classes—an effective asset mix. This has important implications for, among other things, understanding what style a manager offers (or has followed in the past) and for monitoring adherence to policy.

Benchmark Construction

Benchmarks are difficult to construct properly. Sharpe's multifactor (returns-based) model offers a relatively straightforward way to construct meaningful benchmark portfolios with which to compare a manager's performance. Ideally, actual returns over sixty time periods (five years) can be analyzed by factor analysis to identify the combination of asset classes and exposures a portfolio represents. This effective asset mix then may be used as the passive benchmark with which future performance will be compared.

Some cautions are necessary. Unconstrained factor analysis can lead to some incorrect (or highly suspect) conclusions. For example, if factor beta exposures (the percentage invested in an asset class) are not constrained to realistic values, the model may come back with the conclusion that the manager is taking large selling positions when this is not the case. Thus the analyst must use some judgment and evaluate what the model is saying in terms of the manager's articulated style. If the result does not conform to what seems reasonable, the factors must be constrained (e.g., if short-selling is not permitted, factor sensitivities must be greater than or equal to zero). In addition, the manager's current style may differ from the style implied by the last few years. Thus, the analyst must be careful to consider the possibility of "style drift" when interpreting results.

Performance Attribution

Sharpe's multifactor model is also useful in examining the sources of the returns a portfolio earns. Specifically, it indicates that the difference between the returns on an actual portfolio and the returns on the style benchmark may be attributed to selection decisions made by the manager. Thus, a manager who conforms to predetermined asset class exposures and yet beats the style benchmark can be presumed to have made good selection decisions.

Another multiindex approach with potential for return attribution insights was proposed by Fama and French in 1996.[15] The model is based on their now-famous 1992 article on the cross-sectional returns of stocks.[16] In that study, they concluded that B/M and firm size seemed to explain much more of the variation in equity returns than other models, such as the capital asset pricing model (the basis for the Treynor and Jensen measures). Fama and French's current work extends their findings into a three-factor model that attempts to explain the expected return on a portfolio above the risk-free rate as attributable to the sensitivity of return to a broad-based market-risk premium, a size premium (larger for smaller stocks), and a B/M premium (larger for high-B/M stocks).

This model seems to be useful in explaining the returns on portfolios that are formed according to size and B/M criteria. In addition, it appears to explain other portfolio return patterns such as earnings-to-price and price/return reversals. Critics argue that problems such as survivorship bias, data mining, and irrational behavior may be creating the results the model is trying to explain. The model is promising, however, as a tool for plan sponsors to use in evaluating the plan and components' portfolios, identifying the style of the manager, and monitoring the manager's conformance to that style.

CONCLUSION

Measuring investment performance is no simple task. There are many subtleties and pitfalls, and still much art to what looks like a science. Despite this, the prudent fiduciary must make every effort to measure performance correctly so that it can be evaluated properly.

The starting point for useful evaluation is to use the correct measure of return to answer the various questions that should be asked. Dollar weighting (for the total asset pool) and time weighting (for the multiple managers managing portions of the asset pool) are more than mathematical niceties—they can lead to profoundly different conclusions. Returns must also be adjusted for risk. The techniques for risk adjustment are not perfect, but they are much better than ignoring the relationship between risk and return. The sources of the returns produced must also be identified. It matters whether a manager is successful at selection but not at timing. It matters whether the active decisions add value to or subtract value from the asset pool. It matters whether performance comes simply from exposure to the market, but active management fees are being paid.

Finally, pension funds should benchmark their performance and the performance of their investment managers—and do so correctly. A major market index should not be naively selected unless this is the specific exposure that you have deemed appropriate. The benchmark should be customized to better match the portfolio being measured. The desirability and consequences of departing from the benchmark with the investment manager should be discussed before the management begins.

Sometimes, managers and consultants resist providing the data necessary to measure performance correctly. It can be costly and time consuming to do it correctly, but it is still important and must be done: do not forget who employs whom.

The real benefit of performance measurement is that, done correctly, it provides the data necessary to understand why performance was good or bad, and thus serves as a springboard to evaluate performance. Performance evaluation, in turn, helps fiduciaries make the difficult decisions of who to hire, who to continue, and who to eliminate. As discussed in the next chapter, performance evaluation does improve decision making, even though it does not foretell the future. It does let others know that monitoring is occurring, and it does provide an incentive for all parties to communicate about an important subject—and to look at where performance may be insufficient. In doing these things—in tying historical performance and forward-looking policy together—performance evaluation opens a pathway to better future performance, a pathway that begins with the performance measurement techniques described here.

15

Improving Pension Fund Investment Performance

The investment performance of pension fund asset pools is central for virtually all beneficiary and sponsor objectives. Improving the performance of a pension fund's asset pool can increase the likelihood that the promised or expected benefits will materialize. Furthermore, if the plan is a DB plan, better performance can reduce the financial burden carried by the sponsor or can allow the sponsor to increase promised benefits. If the plan is a DC plan, it can improve the financial well-being of the beneficiary.

Improving plan performance begins with a careful evaluation of the performance the plan has been getting. Depending on what is found, various actions may be undertaken to improve future performance.

The obvious prerequisites to evaluation are the measurement techniques discussed in the previous chapter. This chapter first discusses how these techniques may be used to evaluate pension fund performance; some important limitations of performance measurement are also discussed. Next, the chapter reviews the evidence on money managers' abilities to perform and looks at the issue of using historical performance to select managers.

USING PERFORMANCE MEASURES

Performance measurement systems that can be applied easily rely on historical data. These data are used, correctly or incorrectly, for many purposes: predicting future results, selecting managers, and evaluating the effectiveness of policy. Experience indicates that plan sponsors ought to take care to avoid reading more into performance data than is really there. What many sponsors really should want to know is whether current policy is being followed, whether current policy is likely to allow the pension fund to meet its goals, and whether measured good or bad performance is the result of luck or skill. Sponsors can and should answer the first two questions and should use historical data to help them. No one can really answer the last question, but it is important to make the attempt in a systematic manner that will provide some useful insights. These insights should not be mistaken for facts, however. Otherwise, the sponsor may take inappropriate action, perhaps based on the appearance of poor or outstanding measured performance over a few quarters. Such actions could have far worse consequences than doing nothing.

Historical and Future Performance

Does past performance predict future performance? Do active portfolio managers consistently beat passively managed portfolios or indexes on a risk-adjusted basis; that is, does superior performance exist? If it exists, does superior performance persist over time?

Although there is not a lot of comprehensive information drawn directly from the pension universe that bears on these questions, there is a considerable body of information that has been compiled on mutual fund performance. For current purposes, it is not unreasonable to use mutual funds as a proxy for pension portfolios because the issue here is the possibility of superior performance and the predictability of future returns as they pertain to managers of subportfolios.

At best, the evidence on managers beating fair benchmarks is mixed. Virtually all of the early studies of mutual funds concluded that there are very few managers who can consistently beat the market and that, across all funds studied, their returns are inferior on a risk-adjusted basis—they have negative alphas—after expenses.[1]

In any given period, some managers will beat their benchmarks. After all, there are many managers. An important question is whether superior performance in one period means that performance in future periods also will be superior. Does performance persist? Early studies found that successful managers in a base period are no more likely to be successful in later periods than are managers who are categorized as poor in the base period.[2] Some other studies have found hints of performance persistence,[3] but other researchers find that this persistence does not appear to be either statistically significant or strong enough to be useful in forming investment strategies.[4]

Some more recent studies argue that the historical returns of mutual funds are predictive of future returns.[5] One study found no evidence of persistence of equity fund performance but did find persistence for fixed-income funds.[6] However, the study concluded that using past performance to find fixed income funds that could beat the median performers was not an attractive strategy because the medians had negative selection return; that is, the median manager underperformed the benchmark.

What do these contradictory conclusions mean? How should fund sponsors interpret this mixed evidence?

One way to interpret the various studies is to recall that measurement results are very sensitive to the benchmark chosen to represent the "market." For example, one study found that using a different, presumably more appropriate, index for the benchmark changed the results from an alpha (excess return) of +0.4 to one of −1.59%.[7]

Another factor to consider is that the appearance of performance persistence may be attributable to the potential survivorship bias that is problematic for all performance studies. Simply put, survivorship bias enters a data set because poor mutual funds (or poor managers) do not survive to be included in the data samples. Thus, historical statistics tend to indicate that performance was better on average than it would have been if the disappearing losers were included in the sample. Because only funds (managers) that are good enough to survive remain, an appearance of persistently good performance may arise.

The importance of this issue can be demonstrated by examining two money managers, A and B. Both may make large bets on different investment strategies. If A's bet pays off, and B's does not, A survives but B disappears. The bet may not be based on an informed judgment (which presumably would be consistent with expertise), but all it has to do is pay off. Extend this simple example over several time periods and numerous managers, and it is easy to end up with a set of managers who beat the market or persistently beat their peers when in fact they are merely the beneficiaries of a run of good luck—they survived.

Two studies analyzed different data sets in a slightly different way and concluded that survivorship bias is real—and important.[8] Malkiel demonstrated that persistence findings are influenced by survivorship bias.[9] He found that the average return of all equity funds in existence in a given initial year is less than the average of all surviving funds by about 150 basis points. Performance data that fail to adjust for the bias is likely to significantly overstate the performance of the set.

Brown and Goetzmann's study found that relative performance seems to persist even after survivorship bias is controlled for.[10] The effect they found is stronger for poorly performing funds than for good funds. They note, however, that a strategy of chasing winning mutual funds has a high level of total risk and that this risk may be attributable to "loading up" on a common factor.

Traditional performance measurement studies have used unconditional returns—returns net of a benchmark—to look at issues like performance persistence. Some more recent work on performance persistence has used conditional performance evaluation of returns. The main idea of a conditional approach is that expected returns and betas vary over time; that is, they are not stationary as assumed by most measurement techniques. Consider, for example, that money managers may be motivated to trade on the basis of publicly available information such as dividend yields. If the trading activity affects expected returns and risks—that is, if the portfolios held by the managers change—an analyst's conclusions from average performance data should take into consideration the effect of what motivated the trade.

Using this methodology, one study found economically significant persistence in a population of 273 institutional equity pension fund managers.[11] Specifically, the study found that

- Poor conditional performance is followed by more poor performance.
- Unconditional alphas (excess returns) are not good predictors of future returns for the managers studied.

• Conditional measures seem to be more powerful in predicting future performance.

Historical Performance and Manager Selection

Few money managers would be hired if their historical records were poor. Sponsors would fear that they themselves would not be perceived as prudent. However, as already observed, there is no compelling evidence that the historical track record helps predict future manager performance.

Further, it is extremely difficult to differentiate between luck and skill. If 10,000 money managers are flipping coins, some of them will get long runs of heads and others will get long runs of tails. Few would argue there is skill in flipping a coin, however. For each new flip of the coin, of course, the odds of getting a head or getting a tail remain the same regardless of how many flips have been made. Similarly, few would look at a run of heads and conclude that the future result will be a similar run of heads. Statistically, however, this is the problem for sponsors who select managers based on their historical performance: is the manager's record luck, or is it skill?

What about the manager who already works for a fund? The same luck or skill conundrum exists. If the manager is generally close to a benchmark, say, within 10% of the target on the downside over a portion of market cycle—for example, the manager's return was 8.1% when the benchmark return was 9%, then there is only a weak case for termination. Even index funds experience as much as 10% tracking error during some periods. However, if an active manager falls below a benchmark over an entire market cycle by an average of, say, fifty basis points, then it may be time to place the funds with another firm. The reason is not that historical performance predicts the future particularly well, and performance this poor may be attributable to any of a number of factors that are not desirable. Perhaps there has been a dramatic deviation from the fund's investment guidelines or policies. Perhaps the manager has lost his or her touch or the inefficiency that existed in the past is no longer exploitable. Perhaps there is excessive trading or expenses. Of course, if the plan sponsor concludes that none of these reasons explains the excessively poor performance, then the plan sponsor must carefully consider whether it was merely bad luck or an investment strategy that is out of—or even gross incompetence—that led to the disappointing investment performance. These evaluations, of course, are subjective and require careful consideration.

Olsen suggests several qualitative factors to use in appraising a manager's historical performance.[12] The manager's employees can be examined to see whether the same individuals who made the decisions that created the performance are still there. If not, the past performance does not indicate anything about the current decision makers. In addition, it matters how stable the support staff (e.g., research) have been. High turnover could reduce the usefulness of past performance.

Other factors that matter are whether the investment process, especially if it is quantitative, is still the same. Have the assets under management grown so that it calls into question the manager's ability to manage? This is especially important for managers who built records on small stocks, because managers with more assets to manage may have to increase the number of stocks they own or increase the proportion of a stock's outstanding shares held. Managers who have made large numbers of decisions may have statistically more valid performance than those who have made a small number of decisions. Olsen argues that this is especially true in market timing and international management because a few decisions can have led to the observed performance.

Olsen also suggests that the more consistent performance is relative to a valid benchmark, the stronger the predictive value, and he suggests being careful with simulated results, as they may simply indicate data mining.

Finally, there are theoretical approaches that allow quite useful distinctions between luck and skill.[13] Such estimates are generally unavailable, however, for prior time periods or for many managed portfolios, but some fund managers are beginning to collect sufficient data to allow for the application of some of the more advanced evaluation methods.

In summary, most of the evidence shows that historical data have very little useful predictive content. There is some evidence that poor managers remain poor, but very little evidence to support a contention that a seemingly good manager is skillful and will remain good in the future.

Correct Uses of Performance Evaluation

Even though historical performance data are of limited value in forecasting future performance and hence in identifying those money managers who will outperform their benchmarks consistently, using historical performance data is prudent. In particular, performance evaluation based on such data may

- Provide the information necessary to compensate managers if they are being paid on an incentive-fee basis: performance evaluation, for example, can assure that incentive compensation is paid for returns that beat a fair benchmark rather than a "straw man" that may be easily beaten.
- Reveal whether actions that helped or hurt the pension plan were taken by the sponsor (e.g., the strategic asset allocation decision) or by the manager (e.g., security selection decisions).
- Provide information that may be helpful in altering or preventing harmful behavior in the future: for instance, a plan sponsor may discover that its method of allocating new contributions effectively got its pension plan into playing a tactical asset allocation game by unbalancing the asset mix relative to the policy mix; performance measurement could pinpoint this as a cause for poor investment performance and suggest remedies.
- Reveal whether a manager is following or violating the agreed-on investment instructions and policy parameters: individual managers do not have the complete picture. Thus, it is the sponsor's responsibility to ensure that managers conform to the fund's investment policies so that

the plan may accomplish what is in the best interests of the sponsor and the employees. Sensible policy only works if the managers of the fund do what they should.

- Advise pension plan sponsors whether or not managers remained true to the policies they said they would follow: when plan sponsors hire managers on the basis of style preferences or specialties, they generally want them to remain with their specialty and not switch investment strategies to chase investment fads or to invest in areas in which they may not be competent (e.g., exotic derivatives). Managers who rotate among styles most likely buy yesterday's winners and sell yesterday's losers in pursuit of the last period's performance. Unfortunately, there is evidence that this is just the opposite of what they should be doing.[14]
- Demonstrate due diligence and care: performance evaluation, if well documented, may help to show that fiduciaries are exercising care. This, in turn, may immunize them to some extent from legal actions by either reducing the likelihood of such actions or providing the basis for defense if such actions are brought.

Generally speaking, the quantitative analysis of historical data should be given equal or even less weight than some important qualitative aspects of a prospective investment management relationship. Does the manager have a clearly articulated investment philosophy? Does the philosophy make sense? Has the manager stuck with the philosophy even when it was unrewarded by the market? Has the philosophy produced excess returns over an entire market cycle or two for, say seven to ten years, even though any one- or two-year period could be dismal? Are the people honest and competent? Do they provide complete performance data? Will they explain what they do and why they do it when a plan sponsor wants to know?

In summary, even though measures of historical performance do not help very much in predicting future investment performance, they are useful in understanding the results of the decisions in which the fiduciary participated, either explicitly or by delegation to others. This is a prerequisite to making better decisions in the future. Without question, future decisions based on the measures described in this chapter will be more informed decisions and will, on average, be better, more prudent decisions.

Performance Evaluation in Practice

There is a huge performance evaluation industry designed to help the sponsor in evaluating performance. Brokerage firms, actuarial firms, banks that serve as master trustees for pension plans, and pension fund consultants provide a variety of services. Each of these services has special features. Some will even track the performance of securities that have been sold for a month or more after the sale to see what effect those decisions had on portfolio performance so that plan sponsors can second-guess everything their portfolio managers have done.

A common practice of money managers is presenting historical performance data in the hope of attracting (or keeping) business—more assets to manage.

This is commonly done by combining the portfolios of numerous clients at an investment firm into a single measure called a composite. Composites presumably represent a manager's ability to manage according to a specific strategy (e.g., growth or value), asset class (e.g., stocks or bonds), or some other factor.

The problem with composites, like other historical data, is that they are subject to manipulation, such as the selection of time periods, portfolios to include, and weighting schemes. Those who wish to look at the data provided by managers must understand that the data are not likely to be either uniform or comparable. Furthermore, the analyst may not have information about the way the performance composites were formed.

Of some help in this matter are the Global Investment Performance Standards (GIPS®) developed by the Association for Investment Management and Research (AIMR®). AIMR represents over 50,000 investment professionals throughout the world and grants the Chartered Financial Analyst® (CFA®) designation. (Before GIPS, AIMR promulgated the Performance Presentation Standards® [PPS®]. The AIMR PPS have been revised to be in compliance with GIPS. In fact, the AIMR-PPS are generally referenced as the U.S. and Canadian version of the GIPS.) In accordance with AIMR's mission of providing guiding investment principles for investment analysts and money managers, the GIPS provide guidelines for the computation of returns, asset valuation, composite construction, and numerous other elements that affect performance presentations. Central to the GIPS is the concept of presenting performance through the use of composites constructed from portfolios of similar investment objectives or strategies. GIPS require that all actual, fee-paying portfolios of a discretionary nature be included in the appropriate composite. At least five years of data must be shown (or data since inception, if the firm or composite has not been in existence for five years). Importantly, calculation methods are specified, as are certain mandatory disclosures.

The GIPS requirements substantially reduce the ability of a manager to present only attractive performance. They promote full disclosure and fair representation, increase uniformity in reporting, and encourage comparability among investment performance reports.

Plan sponsors and fiduciaries should require managers to comply with the AIMR GIPS. Plan staff members should be conversant with the standards, so that the strengths of the standards can be applied in analyzing manager performance and the weaknesses of the standards (and there are some) can be recognized. One caution: any set of rules can be "gamed," and the GIPS are no exception. If one remembers that a goal of performance evaluation is not necessarily to answer every possible question but, rather, to raise the important questions, this should not be an insurmountable problem.

ACTUAL PENSION PERFORMANCE

Any discussion of performance evaluation should consider how pension funds as a group have actually done. For DC plans, investment performance often depends on the investment choices of individual participants, as discussed in

Chapter 14. For DB plans, the empirical evidence on investment performance is not flattering.

The data indicate that actively managed pension funds have not performed as well as unmanaged, passive portfolios or as well as actively managed mutual funds. Note that when available, data on the component portfolios of pension asset pools may not show inferior performance. When one looks at total pension plan assets or all assets of a given class such as equities, thus effectively dollar-weighting the returns on all of the individual portfolios, the poor investment performance of the total asset pools of pension plans is uncovered. Only by analyzing total assets, which include all of a sponsor's pension portfolios of a given asset class or across all asset classes, can one draw serious conclusions about collective pension plan investment performance.

One of the early substantive analyses of total pension plan performance was performed by Berkowitz, Finney, and Logue in 1988.[15] Their study looked at the investment performance of a group of 119 ERISA (private pension) plans from 1976 to 1983 and compared this group with endowment funds, public pension plans, and a variety of mutual funds and market benchmarks over the same time period. Using raw (that is, non-risk-adjusted) returns as well as the Sharpe and Jensen performance measures, private pension plans did not compare favorably with either mutual funds or endowment plans. Public retirement plans showed especially poor investment performance relative to benchmarks, endowment funds, and mutual funds. Some examples from the study are set out in Table 15.1 with other funds' performance.

The results of the Berkowitz, Finney, and Logue study were consistent with those of Ippolito and Turner.[16] They analyzed pension plans using a database derived from information provided by firms on the Form 5500s they filed with the IRS, and they also concluded that pension performance was poor.

A later study examined the performance of the equity portfolios of pension plans.[17] The database included 769 all-equity portfolios managed by 341 managers. The study compared the performance of the funds from 1983 to 1989 with the S&P 500 Index for the same years, reasoning that the betas of the funds clustered around 1.0 and that the stated objective of most of the funds was to

Table 15.1 Private Retirement Plan Performance Compared with Other Funds' Performance

	Arithmetic Average Return (%)	Geometric Average Return (%)	Mean Sharpe Measure	Mean Jensen's Alpha
ERISA Plans (n = 119)	12.05	11.67	0.132	−0.1
Public Pension Plans (n = 31)	10.25	9.9	0.056	−0.38
Endowments (n = 33)	12.96	12.5	0.16	0.05
Mutual Funds (n = 325)	16.85	15.58	0.207	0.68

Note: The mutual fund group included various equity funds, bond funds, balanced funds, and so forth.

beat the index. The study also adjusted for the effects of holding cash. The results were interesting:

- Using equal weighting and annual returns, the group of pension funds underperformed the index by 1.3% before management fees of around fifty basis points.
- Using value weighting and annual returns, the group of funds underperformed the index by 2.6% before management fees of around fifty basis points.
- The net result of the funds' choices of strategy were that relative performance was poor across diverse styles.
- Using overlapping periods of three years, the index did even better relative to the funds.

The study also looked at performance persistence and whether a manager's historical performance suggested strategies for picking winning managers. The following conclusions were reached:

- Using the simple strategy of picking from the previous year's quartile winners, there was an expected deterioration in performance of 8%, whereas picking from losing quartiles had an expected improvement of 13% per year.
- Using a strategy of picking from triennial quartile winners, a fund can expect to beat the average manager by 100 basis points—a gain that does not cover the 130 basis points of underperformance exhibited by the average manager (nor the management fees incurred by using a manager).

The authors conclude (in their own words):

- Pension fund managers seem to subtract rather than add value relative to the performance of the S&P 500 Index.
- There is some consistency of performance, but . . . it is not clear that [the chosen manager] would be able to beat the market.
- [The relationship between pension funds and the money management industry appears] . . . to be driven by its need to provide sponsors with good excuses for poor performance, clear stories about portfolio strategies and other services that are only vaguely related to performance.

These findings have been challenged by more recent studies,[18] but they raise enduring concerns for pension fund sponsors' decision makers. Sponsors are "on the hook" for contributions, and fiduciaries may be held accountable if investment returns are poor.

Factors Affecting Actual Fund Performance

Avoiding factors that are likely to lead to poor performance is a sensible first step in improving performance. There are a number of factors that may contribute to underperformance; among the more important are attempting to market time, excessive portfolio turnover, agency problems, and regulation.

Market Timing

Can pension funds move into equities and out of bonds and vice versa at propitious times? Unfortunately, data limitations have kept this question from being asked of pension funds. However, several researchers have considered the effect of market timing on mutual fund performance, which can act as a proxy for pension fund performance. Specifically, researchers have asked whether mutual funds have successfully adjusted their portfolios in anticipation of declining or rising stock markets. The answer these researchers found was a resounding "No," despite some reasonably sophisticated tests.

Differences between mutual funds and pension plans hamper generalizing such results, however. Pension plans may consist of many portfolios; this is analogous to collections of mutual funds, not a single mutual fund. No single fund may time the market well, but investors who own more than one fund may astutely be switching back and forth between optimal market segments. Considering individual mutual funds thus may not reveal whether the markets were being timed successfully.

One 1988 study has looked directly at pension fund timing: Berkowitz, Finney, and Logue constructed a metric—the variability of portfolio allocation over time—that was designed to capture market-timing attempts by pension plans.[19] The basic idea is that a pension plan would attempt to maintain a constant mix of stocks and bonds if it did not follow a market-timing strategy. Allowing the actual mix to get well above or well below the target mix suggests betting on one sector or another (i.e., tactical asset allocation). The study found that the greater the variability in asset mix, the worse the investment performance of the pension plan. Accordingly, they concluded that attempts to time the market lead to higher costs and greater risks than are rewarded.

Portfolio Turnover and Trading Costs

Many scholars feel that high portfolio turnover (i.e., many purchases and sales) is one reason that pension investment performance has been so poor. Every time there is a purchase and sale of securities, the brokers executing these transactions charge commissions; in addition, there are market impact costs (the difference between the price paid or received and the equilibrium price that would prevail in the absence of a large transaction).

Although intuitively appealing, inferior performance has not been definitively tied to asset turnover by researchers. In other words, there is no hard evidence that turnover has a systematic, negative effect on investment performance. Some studies have even found a positive relationship.[20] It is clear however, that at the margin, the benefits of turnover, motivated by the desire to employ the most current information available regarding the relative and absolute worth of a security, must equal or exceed its cost to be acceptable.

Agency Problems

Lakonishok, Schleifer, and Vishny suggest that the poor performance of pension funds may be attributable to principal-agent problems that arise whenever a principal (e.g., the sponsor) delegates authority to an agent (e.g., a treasurer or a money manager) to act in the principal's interest. These problems arise in part because the incentives of the two parties are not the same and in part because it is costly for principals to monitor what agents are doing.

One fertile area for agency problems is the delegation of pension authority from the sponsor to the treasurer or another officer/employee. The treasurer-agent, for example, may want to build an empire and, hence, may be biased against economically appealing strategies that are passive in nature. Likewise, the treasurer-agent may enjoy using the services—the prestige, the free trips, the dinners, and so forth—provided by money managers, consultants, and others. The treasurer-agent may also be reluctant to take full responsibility for the pension plan, so he or she may want to have plenty of partners to blame if things go wrong.

If a treasurer-agent has decided to use external money managers, another agency problem arises: the difficulty of measuring and evaluating what these managers are doing. This problem occurs in part because the external manager has better information than does the treasurer and in part because the measurement process is costly and complex.

The money management community contributes to this problem by offering a vast array of differentiated products, products that are "story-driven" and difficult to analyze and understand. In addition, managers have incentives to "dress-up" their portfolios at the end of standard measurement periods. They do this by selling their poor investments and, if they have had some success, by shifting to index portfolios to lock in their relative performance. Managers who are doing poorly may increase the riskiness of their strategies (e.g., by using unauthorized derivatives to leverage the portfolio) in an attempt to obtain better performance.

One other potential agency problem should be recognized: once the pension scheme has been determined, the sponsor becomes an agent for the collective employees. Thus, there is the potential for a conflict between the employee/principals and the sponsor/agent. For DB plans, the higher cost of contributions to make up for poor performance seems to be incentive enough for the sponsor to pursue good investment performance. It may not be sufficient incentive, however, to encourage funding beyond what is required. For DC plans, the contribution level is independent of investment performance, at least in the short run. The costs of unresolved agency problems are therefore potentially very high for plan beneficiaries. These costs may take the form of inadequate attention to selecting good managers (or mutual funds), failing to control the fees charged by managers, and offering a poor selection of investment alternatives.

At their most benign level, agency problems such as these may contribute to poor performance. They may also, however, lead to catastrophic events such as the Orange County, California, municipal investment pool bankruptcy that occurred in 1994.

Sponsor fiduciary obligations, explicit and implicit, would seem to compel senior management to address the potential for agency conflicts at all levels. The cost of not doing so—possible significant underperformance leading to higher contributions for DB plans, or inadequate accumulations for DC plans and the possibility of legal action—would seem to warrant more monitoring and control.

Regulatory Incentives

Does regulation affect investment performance? For example, do some investors choose stocks that are likely to appear prudent even if they may not be correctly priced according to their risk?

Del Guercio offers evidence that supports the contention that the constraints imposed by prudent investor laws bias pension funds toward investing in what courts have found to be prudent investments because of fear of litigation.[21] (She defines prudent stocks as those that have high S&P safety rankings and that are issued by large firms.)

It seems that some portfolio managers and pension sponsors make choices that reflect their perception of how others will react. These "others" may be regulators, the courts, or the newspapers, for example. The problem this causes is that, when imprudent stocks (stocks with poor earnings histories or high B/M ratios or what have you) outperform prudent stocks (stocks that have strong earnings reports, stocks that are in every pension portfolio, stocks that have recent histories that make them "look good"), pension funds are likely to underperform benchmarks that contain "imprudent" stocks.

Worse, if pension funds are avoiding imprudent stocks, they may be missing a significant source of risk-adjusted returns. Several studies have suggested that the stocks of smaller firms with high B/M ratios may provide superior performance because the market may have overreacted to factors such as bad news (forcing prices too low) or good news (forcing prices too high).[22] If these studies are correct, regulations may be discouraging pension funds from investing in potentially attractive investments. In addition, incentives to hold "good-looking" stocks rather than stocks that may be good investments could be encouraging a strategy of buying last period's winners and avoiding last period's losers, which may be about to turn around. Del Guercio speculates that this effect may be more pronounced for public funds than for private funds, as public funds as a group have no safe harbor regulations that recognize the portfolio effects of securities. Of course, if pension funds are assumed to be managed by rational investors who correctly evaluate the economic consequences of the regulatory environment, their performances may not be inferior when compared with a benchmark portfolio that accounts for regulatory influences on investors.

Overall, then, the portfolio manager/pension sponsor may be able to escape serious criticism because the portfolio holds prudent, or "good-looking," stocks: the same stocks that other pension funds hold and that regulators consider prudent. Unfortunately, although criticism may be avoided, poor performance may be the all-too-costly result of this herdlike mentality.

Other Performance Factors

It seems reasonable to expect that other factors may also affect pension fund performance. A study by McCarthy and Turner offers some insights[23]: using data derived from Form 5500, they computed annual raw returns and geometric mean returns over the period (not adjusted for risk). Though little can be done with the results analytically because of missing observations, the data do, however, reveal that no highly visible characteristics of the pension plans themselves—collective bargaining status, DB versus DC type, or activity level of management—seem to influence rates of return in any profound way.

CONCLUSION

Better investment performance is achievable for most pension plans. Although the specific path to improvement may differ, the following are important elements to consider:

- Start by using the performance measures described in Chapter 14 to evaluate whether or not the plan's strategic asset allocation is likely to allow the plan to meet its goals. Over the long term, the strategic asset allocation will drive the plan's performance more than any other single factor.
- As a general rule, be cautious about market timing. There is no persuasive evidence that it can be done successfully.
- Be aware of transaction costs. Avoid trades unless the benefits of the trade are thought to outweigh the costs.
- Give very careful attention to agency costs. It is here that prudent behavior often meets its greatest challenge. Plan policy makers must anticipate the potential for conflicts of interest between boards, senior management, and employees; between the plan and external managers; and between the plan's beneficiaries and its sponsor. Failing to monitor these relationships can be detrimental to plan performance when individuals fail to act in the best interests of the plan.
- Ask whether decisions are being made in an environment that supports sensible risk taking and the application of sound investment theory or, instead, focuses on avoiding responsibility and liability. If the latter is the case, change the environment by restructuring the decision-making process to be conducive to responsible decision making. Address regulatory concerns by fully documenting the decision-making process.

Note that in discussing how to improve performance, nothing has been said about allocating assets to emerging markets or leveraged private equity or other secondary asset classes. There is nothing wrong with these as investments per se. However, consider that if 5% of assets are allocated to a secondary asset class that is expected to return 2% annually (200 basis points) more than a diversified portfolio of large company stocks, the potential increase in return—before the probably high management fees and trading costs of this asset class—may add 0.1% (ten basis points) to the pension plan's overall return. How much top management attention is this worth? Alternatively, consider the effect of reallocating from a stocks/bonds mix of, say, 40/60 to one of 60/40. Using the historical perspective, one might expect stocks to return 5% annually more than bonds over several years. The potential increase in returns is 1% annually (100 basis points). This is a decision that has a real effect on performance.

Finally, a key to better performance is to run the pension plan like a business. This means that those at the top must first be able to answer the question, How are we doing, given our current asset allocation, investment strategies, and organizational structures? Once this question has been asked, the answers will suggest numerous opportunities to improve.

16

Managing Pension Fund Risk

Risk is pervasive and is a fact of life for pension funds. Not only do the funds face investment and other risks on the asset side of their balance sheet, they also face numerous risks on the liability side. As if that is not enough, there are risks that arise from the unique relationships between pension plans and the plan sponsor.

This chapter outlines the basics of risk management, defines the major risks a pension fund faces, and discusses how these risks may be managed. The principles of hedging and return enhancement (called view implementation by some) are explained, and the conditions under which they are sensible are examined. Throughout, the chapter presents effective techniques for managing the three major types of risks that pension funds face: investment risks, surplus risk, and sponsor/plan risk.

Some of these techniques are prescriptive: plan wisely and avoid unintended risks with no special favorable payoffs. Other techniques require choices: in general, the choice is how much risk to take and how much return to expect. The chapter concludes with a discussion of how pension funds can structure a comprehensive risk management program.

THE BASICS OF RISK MANAGEMENT

Risk management encompasses all financial and management strategies that are designed either to reduce a certain type of risk or to increase a return of one type or another through increasing the fund's exposure to a given risk factor (to enhance return, typically by implementing a view on asset prices or capital market conditions). One way to think of risk management is to view it as a continuum of points along a line that represents all possible combinations of risk and return. The decision to move from one combination to another is a risk-management decision; the process by which the change is achieved is a risk management strategy. Figure 16.1 offers a graphic representation of how risk management might be conceived within the framework of investment risk.

Notice that at the hedging end of the continuum, risk is very low and, at least conceptually, may be eliminated. The return that one can reasonably expect is similarly low—conceptually, the return of a risk-free strategy can be no more than the risk-free rate. Frequently, a Treasury bill or bond rate is used to represent this return. At the other end of the continuum, expected returns may be very high, but the risk associated with these returns also is very high. This, of course, simply describes the fundamental relationship between risk and return and a basic tenet of investing: there are no free lunches. Every decision has consequences. Strategies that pursue higher returns almost invariably are associated with higher levels of risk, and therefore, the possibility of significant adverse outcome is greater. The reverse also is true: strategies that are designed to reduce risk also reduce expected return, perhaps by paying a kind of an insurance premium or by foregoing a possibly profitable investment opportunity.

Thus, the true risk-management continuum itself stretches from strategies that are designed to eliminate risk of one type or another (strategies consistent with being fully hedged with respect to that risk) to strategies that involve taking on extremely high levels of risk in the pursuit of extremely high returns (strategies that might be termed aggressive or speculative). In between these two extremes are partial hedging strategies and return-enhancement strategies: these strategies represent incremental reductions in risk or increases in return.

Note that the strategic asset allocation decision selects a specific risk/return combination—a point on the risk/return continuum—as the appropriate long-term exposure for a pension fund given its return objectives, risk tolerance, and constraints. Similarly, when market action changes a portfolio's weights, this change can be thought of as a movement from one point to another created by an external influence. Thus, a strategy such as maintaining a constant mix is designed to restore the original asset allocations by moving back to the original point on the risk/return continuum.

Sensible risk management begins with an understanding of the motivations

Figure 16.1 Risk Management and Investment Risk

that underlie the choice of a given strategy and the possible consequences of that strategy. Is a hedge being constructed because adverse outcomes are feared? Is an investment view being implemented—a view that may be right or wrong—on the basis of a perception that an unusual opportunity for return is present? As long as pension fund fiduciaries, administrators, and managers who are hedging know that they are hedging, know why they are hedging, and are willing to incur the costs of hedging, there is nothing necessarily wrong with that hedging. Similarly, as long as those who are involved in decision making know that return-enhancement strategies must by definition be designed to implement a particular view and that there is an increased risk of adverse consequences, there is nothing wrong with any specific return-enhancement strategy per se. Where pension funds get into trouble is in not understanding the objectives of the strategy, the motivation behind it, or its possible consequences.

The stakes of risk management—of choosing among the many alternative positions along the risk/return continuum—are significant. For DB pension funds, the low-risk solutions are likely to lead to unacceptably high sponsor contributions. The high-return solutions may pay off handsomely, but then again, they also may bankrupt the fund or force the sponsor to increase its contributions unexpectedly.

The Big Picture

Pension fund fiduciaries, administrators, and managers must have a systematic way to think about risk and risk management. When evaluating the merits of hedging or return enhancement strategies, several kinds of questions should be asked

General Questions

- What are the risks currently faced by the fund?
- Are these risks understood by those who manage them?
- Are these risks being managed and monitored correctly?

Strategic Questions

- What is the motivation of the pension fund with respect to any given strategy?
- Is the fund trying to reduce risk? Why, and at what cost of opportunities foregone?
- Is the plan trying to enhance return? How, and what will the effect of such enhancement activities be on the plan's overall risk?
- Are these strategies consistent with the plan's investment policy?
- How will any specific strategy affect the total risk faced by the plan?
- What is the time horizon over which the strategy will be in effect?

Management Questions

- What types of risk management strategies and tools are available?
- What are the advantages and disadvantages of each type of strategy or tool?
- How will each strategy or tool behave in a variety of market conditions?

Organizational Questions

- What expertise do the pension fund's administrators have in choosing the extent to which various risks should be hedged or exposures increased?
- How knowledgeable are the fund's money managers in the use of the available risk management strategies or tools?
- What policies exist to guide the selection and monitoring of new risk-management strategies and the managers who will implement them?

These questions must not go unasked. They must be answered carefully and as accurately as possible if the pension fund is to be successful in managing its risks. In addition, they should be asked regularly enough so that changes in the answers can be evaluated within the context of the overall objectives of the fund.

The Risk–Risk Trade-Off

Frequently, changing the plan's exposure to one type of risk may increase the plan's exposure to some other risk factor. Consider a pension liability fully immunized by a 100% bond portfolio. Surplus risk is virtually zero. However, what about inflation exposure? Is this risk greater than it would be if the portfolio had a significant exposure to stocks? Or consider an investment strategy that focuses on low investment risk by maintaining a very conservative asset allocation structured to keep return volatility low. Does this affect the risk the sponsor bears in providing future contributions?

Defining Risk

The way to start managing risk is by analyzing the risks faced by the fund. To do this, it is necessary to develop some definitions of various types of risk. After these risks have been defined, the basic parameters of risk management can be explored for each type of risk.

Investment Risk

Investment risk has to do with how a given market, sector, asset, or investment strategy will perform over time. Investment risk is typically defined in terms of volatility of asset values or volatility of returns. Stocks, for example, have a higher investment risk than bonds in that the returns on stocks are more widely dispersed around their likely outcome. The value of stocks at any given point in time has also historically been less certain than the value of bonds.

For a DB pension fund, investment risk is important but, as a risk-management concept, it is incomplete and thus can be misleading. It does not fully capture the interaction of plan assets with liabilities, nor does it directly address the risk-bearing capacity of the plan as constrained by the riskiness of the sponsor.

For a DC plan, however, the concept of investment risk is normally sufficient as a risk-management paradigm from the employees' perspective. The employer's risk is not related to investment risk per se. Rather, DC plan risk for employers arises from fiduciary responsibilities. In particular, sponsors must provide participants with reasonable investment alternatives and should monitor and evaluate the performance of the managers/funds provided, terminating and replacing those that prove to be inept at delivering good performance.

Surplus Risk

The financial health of a DB pension fund is sensitive to the interaction between the fund's assets and its liabilities: if liabilities increase faster than assets, the surplus will get smaller (or the deficit will get larger). The risk of changes in the surplus caused by changes in the relative values of assets and liabilities is termed surplus risk. It is influenced by two factors: the relative interest-rate sensitivities of the assets and liabilities, and the market risk of the assets. Consider, for example, that in spite of the strong financial performance of the U.S. equity and bond markets in 1995, pension surpluses actually decreased for many U.S. pension funds because liabilities rose more than asset values rose because of the decrease in interest rates; in 1994, however, a poor year for U.S. investments, many pension funds saw their surpluses increase because of the decrease in liabilities brought about by rising interest rates.[1] The financial markets of 2000–2002 experienced the "perfect storm" of both a declining stock market and declining interest rates. The result was substantial underfunding as the declining stock market lowered asset values and the declining interest rates raised liability values.

Managing surplus volatility and the projected surplus pose a significant challenge to decision makers. Pensions with large surpluses can afford to take more risk in pursuit of higher returns (and thus they can pursue a higher assurance of benefits or lower sponsor contributions). Paradoxically, plans with deficits may find risky, high-return strategies appealing for their promise in reducing their deficits; however, these plans may not be able to bear the risk of short-term adverse consequences that could make their deficits worse. This possibility can be especially unappealing when the sponsor is facing financial difficulty and may not be able to make up any shortfalls.

Sponsor/Plan Joint Risk

Pension plans have a sizable stake in the fortunes of their sponsors. The sponsor is instrumental in determining the payouts to future beneficiaries and in other plan features that have a financial effect on the health of the plan. In addition, the sponsor contributes to the pension asset pool. The performance of the investment pool in turn affects the need for contributions. The risk to which such interaction exposes a pension plan is sponsor/plan joint risk.

Because of this interaction, the correlation between the cash flows of the sponsor and the asset pool of the pension plan matters greatly. Consider, for example, a pension asset pool that is sensitive to the same economic factors that affect the sponsor's profitability. When these factors result in good investment performance for the plan, the sponsor need not make large contributions, although it has the financial ability to. However, when the plan needs the sponsor to increase contributions to offset poor investment performance, the sponsor is also beset by poor performance and may be unable to deliver.

Interest Rate Risk

From our discussion of surplus risk, it is apparent that changes in interest rates affect the adequacy of a plan's funding. Interest rates also pose two very different forms of investment risk. One form of interest rate risk is the volatility in price associated solely with changes in interest rates. For example, when interest rates go up, the prices of assets such as "plain vanilla" bonds go down. The second form of interest rate risk is reinvestment risk. Consider an asset that provides, as part of its total return, a series of cash payments. If these cash flows must be reinvested as they are received, the return earned on the reinvested cash flows contributes to the overall return realized from the asset. When interest rates rise, the cash flows that this asset provides can be reinvested at a higher return, thus offsetting a portion of the decline in the asset's price.

Interest rate risk is a function of maturity (the longer the maturity, the greater the sensitivity to interest rates), cash flows (the lower the cash flows, the greater the sensitivity to interest rates), and the current level of interest rates (the higher the overall level of interest rates, the less sensitive assets are to changes in interest rates). Because these factors vary from one fixed-income investment to another and from one liability to another, it is helpful to aggregate them into a single measure. Duration, the weighted average of the time to each cash flow (using current interest rates), is a commonly used measure of overall interest rate sensitivity. We can use duration to estimate the sensitivity of a pension's asset pool to interest rate changes and to estimate the relative sensitivity of plan assets and liabilities to interest rates.

Duration, as useful as it is, is incomplete as a measure of interest rate risk because it ignores the rate of change in price sensitivity to interest rates as interest rates change. The rate of change in price sensitivity is called convexity. Adjusting for convexity, a somewhat complex task, corrects for the tendency for the price change estimated by duration to be different from the actual price change as interest rates change. For small changes in interest rates, this is not a problem. For large changes, it is.

Convexity can be positive (as for an option-free bond) or negative (as for most mortgage-backed securities subject to prepayment risk). In terms of measuring interest rate risk, it is important because it improves our understanding of interest rate effects on assets and liabilities (and hence on pension surplus). With convexity, we form a much more robust description of how the pension fund's financial health will be affected by changes in interest rates.

Currency Risk

International investing is increasingly popular among pension funds. However, if an investor is holding securities denominated in a foreign currency, changes in the value of that currency relative to the investor's domestic currency will affect the domestic return on the investment. This is called currency risk.

Currency risk is first of all a function of the allocation made to assets denominated in non-U.S. currencies, although this may overstate the risk if a sponsor has employees in numerous countries. Once the initial allocation is established, currency values relative to U.S. currency may fluctuate because of interest rate and inflation differentials, economic growth and productivity, monetary policy, and the market for foreign exchange.[2]

Concentration Risk

Concentration risk arises from excessive exposures to any one asset, sector, asset class, or macroeconomic factor (e.g., interest rates). The tenets of modern investment theory ordinarily would suggest that this should not be an issue—that proper attention to diversification should eliminate any such exposure. However, for pension funds this may not always be the case. Possible problems may arise from

1. Excessive exposure to the sponsor through overreliance on contributions from the sponsor rather than on investment performance (i.e., returns generated from the plan's investments);
2. Excessive exposure to the sponsor through an ESOP or a sponsor-directed DC plan that invests in the sponsor's stock or in assets used by the sponsor to conduct business; and
3. Excessive exposure to the local economy through economically targeted investments.

Concentration risk may also arise when no one is monitoring the effective asset mix of the total portfolio or when unintended exposures to economic factors (e.g., interest rates) occur because sophisticated or complex investment vehicles or strategies employed are not understood well. Concentration risk can be catastrophic and can ruin even the best and the brightest. Look only to the events surrounding the hedge fund Long Term Capital Management in 1998 for proof.

Inflation Risk

Inflation poses two major problems for DB pension funds. One is the unanticipated changes that may occur in nominal interest rates because of changes in expectations for inflation. If, for example, the financial market changes its collective assessment of future inflation by increasing the inflation premium agreed to among buyers and sellers of financial assets, nominal interest rates will increase and the values of most financial assets (and some real assets) and pension liabilities will decline. This effect is simply the same interest rate effect discussed in the surplus risk and interest rate risk sections. There is more to inflation risk, however. As wages rise in response to inflation, the size of pension liabilities based on final salary also increase. This in turn creates pressure for higher contributions or better investment performance, or both.

For DC plans, the effect of inflation is primarily felt through the potential erosion of purchasing power of the beneficiary's assets. As is the case for DB plans, this indicates that either higher contributions or stronger investment performance may be necessary to offset the effects of inflation.

Strategies for Managing Risk

Managing risk successfully depends in part on what risk is being managed and in part on the strategies and tools that are available. Strategic decisions, of course, require a goal or objective; for example, moving to a new point on the risk/reward continuum. This section describes the basic strategies of managing risk exposures by category. A common theme throughout is that it is better to anticipate risks and select appropriate exposures than to react to unanticipated events.

Investment Risk

The foundation of managing investment risk is to have clear, unambiguous policy guidelines that require diversification across and within asset classes. Further, these guidelines should quantify an acceptable level of exposure to market risk (risk that cannot be diversified away). Establishing what precisely is an acceptable level of market risk for a particular plan requires extensive analysis. The level will be unique to each plan and will depend on the numerous factors that affect the plan's tolerance for risk. Ultimately it will be operationalized through the plan's asset allocation and through such fundamental policy parameters as whether plan assets should be actively or passively managed.

Diversification, however, is easy to accomplish, and it is inexpensive—if there is a free lunch, this is it. With good policy and a commitment to diversification, the management of investment risk becomes a matter of occasional hedging if the plan's asset value needs to be temporarily protected or a matter of occasional return enhancement if the plan is willing to take on the additional risk.

Surplus Risk

Managing surplus risk begins on the asset side (assuming that plan liabilities are more or less fixed for any reasonable planning horizon) and involves a careful analysis of relative interest rate sensitivities. In general, surplus risk can be minimized by holding a portfolio of long-duration bonds. This probably is not desirable, however, if the plan has any exposure whatsoever to inflation through a wage-based benefit formula or through benefits that adjust to inflation. Nor is it desirable to hold a portfolio of long-duration bonds if the sponsor believes that higher investment returns are appropriate because those higher returns reduce the present value of long-term contributions. ·

Managing surplus risk is also a function of the size of the surplus itself. Leibowitz, Kogleman, and Bader suggest that plans with large surpluses (i.e., with healthy funding ratios) are able to take a fair amount of risk, at least in the short run, and therefore, that such plans should invest heavily in equities and other assets with high levels of investment risk.[3] For these plans, the duration of plan assets relative to liabilities is not especially important. As a plan's funding ratio declines, however—that is, as its surplus erodes and perhaps changes to a deficit—it becomes less tolerant of exposure to any factor that may erode the surplus further. Thus, the asset allocation strategy for plans at this stage should focus more on duration matching and possibly lower exposures to equities. This suggests floor-based strategies, such as portfolio insurance or contingent immunization. Contingent immunization means pursuing high total returns as long as the surplus is high and shifting into a progressively more immunized portfolio if the surplus decreases.

Another way of thinking about managing surplus risk is to redefine the efficient frontier of acceptable portfolios by replacing the risk-free asset with a portfolio consisting of 100% bonds that immunizes the pension liability.[4] Other higher-risk (in terms of surplus risk), higher-return portfolios of varying amounts of stocks and bonds can then be evaluated against this risk-free portfolio in terms of the incremental risks and returns offered by each. A simulation Haugen performed indicates that this set of portfolios is conceptually superior to the traditional investment risk-and-return-efficient frontier in that it will provide portfolios that are more efficient in terms of the surplus risk/return trade-off.[5]

Some funds have gained a measure of comfort by performing a scenario analysis that allows the sponsor/investor to ask whether there is, say, a 90% or 95% probability that its plan will still be fully funded X years from now. This type of analysis can be helpful in examining the interactions of interest rates, asset allocation, liability structures (especially at the time when the sponsor is considering changes to the benefit scheme), and funding. Scenario analysis is also consistent with value-at-risk (VAR) analysis and stress testing and with the analytical approach to strategic asset allocation. Larger pension funds will find it worthwhile to construct comprehensive and integrated analytical systems to help examine these issues both prior to plan changes and on an ongoing basis.

In conclusion, the focus for managing surplus risk should not be to minimize it; rather, the focus should be to receive adequate return on surplus for the surplus risk to which the plan is exposed. Because the volatility of the surplus is important, exposure to this risk should be compensated for. The traditional set of investment risk-efficient portfolios does not adequately address the interaction of plan assets and liabilities. Thus, pension plan decision makers should think in terms of portfolio risk defined in terms of surplus volatility, as well as investment risk. Further, decision makers must explicitly consider the link between the plan's funding status and the financial strength of the sponsor: sponsors that are financially healthy are capable of smoothing the effects of high surplus volatility, if need be, by increased funding; financially troubled sponsors can offer no such support.

Sponsor/Plan Joint Risk

Managing the joint risks faced by the sponsor and the pension plan is closely tied to managing surplus risk. When a plan has a large economic surplus, the joint risk is likely to be unimportant. For plans with small surpluses or sizable deficits, however, the joint risk can become very important.

Because the sponsor's ability to fund is a function of the magnitude, timing, and variability of the sponsor's cash flows, it is the correlation of these cash flows with those of the pension plan's asset pool that must be managed. One sensible step is limiting or eliminating investments that are highly correlated with the sponsor's financial strength (e.g., pension funds that are already exposed to the automobile industry because the sponsor manufactures automobiles should not invest pension fund assets in companies that are highly correlated with automobile company securities). Another step is gaining exposure to sectors with low correlations with the sponsor's cash flows. Direct investment in the sponsor generally is not a good idea. For private plans this should discourage holding any of the firm's stock, even in an ESOP. For public plans, this discourages ETIs if the ETI's returns are highly correlated with the sponsor's cash flows.

Interest Rate Risk

Interest rate risk is an element of both investment and surplus risk. As such, it may initially be addressed by choosing an appropriate level of exposure to interest rates. This requires evaluating the overall sensitivity of a portfolio of assets or liabilities to interest rate changes. Managing interest rate risk is similar to the process of choosing an acceptable level of market risk.

A simple approach to managing interest rate risk is the cash-flow-matching strategy presented in Chapter 9. The appeal of this strategy is that the matching of cash flows significantly reduces the risk of having to liquidate assets at possibly disadvantageous times solely to meet benefit payments. A somewhat more comprehensive approach is to immunize the pension liability (partially or completely) by managing the duration of the assets relative to the duration of the plan's liabilities. As explained in the section on managing surplus risk, full immunization (i.e., no surplus volatility) probably is not an acceptable goal. It is, however, situational. Traditional approaches to calculating duration (such as assuming a flat yield curve) make duration only an approximation of actual sensitivity to interest rates. This is fairly simple to correct. Not as simple are the matters of convexity and nonparallel shifts in the yield curve. However, these more complex factors can be managed with some fairly sophisticated mathematical techniques.

Currency Risk

Currency risk can be partially diversified away by holding investments denominated in numerous currencies: because currencies are not perfectly correlated, decreases in the value of one currency relative to the pension fund's domestic currency may be offset by increases in the value of another currency. In addition, the pension funds of multinational firms domiciled in the United States may be able to significantly reduce currency exposures brought about by benefits denominated in currencies other than the U.S. dollar simply by holding securities denominated in those same currencies.

Overall, it is not obvious that hedging currency risk is desirable.[6] Some authorities argue that currency is simply a source of risk and should be hedged; others, however, assert that currency is an asset class offering returns as well as risk. Some proponents of unhedged currency exposures argue that foreign currency offers pensions an opportunity to hedge domestic inflation and domestic monetary policy, over which they otherwise have no control. Froot suggests that the need to hedge currency may be related to the investment horizon of the investor.[7] In the short run, mean reversion is likely to reduce the need to hedge, and in the long run, purchasing power parity seems to hold and is more suggestive of the inflation/monetary policy hedging attributes of currency.

As Siegel observes, the near-term attractiveness of hedging depends on whether U.S. interest rates are higher than or lower than foreign rates.[8] Currency hedges are equivalent to borrowing the currency to hedge (the non-U.S. currency) and buying or investing in the domestic (United States) currency. Thus, if U.S. interest rates are high relative to the currency hedged, the hedge will increase the dollar-denominated return on the portfolio as the borrowed foreign currency falls in value relative to the long position in U.S. dollars.

In general, currency risk is relatively high for foreign cash and bonds but much lower for foreign stocks. Thus, given the long-term nature of investing in stocks and the ability of stocks to compensate investors for local price increases over long time periods, if hedging is desired, more attention should be given to non-U.S. cash and bond positions than to non-U.S. stock positions.

Concentration Risk

If all parties are committed to the rights of the plan participants to a reasonably secure retirement and are aware of the adverse consequences of concentration—the excessive investment risk for which the capital markets will not provide any offsetting return and the risk of liquidity problems—this problem should not arise. If it does, administrators and managers must recognize the potential breach of fiduciary duty implied.

However, with the vast array of complex financial products available today, and with our better understanding of the component or factor exposures that even simple investments such as callable bonds have, concentration risk may be incurred unintentionally. Thus, a fundamental part of managing concentration risk is to understand the investments being made, fully and completely, and to understand their role in the overall portfolio. The most powerful risk management tools that exist for managing concentration risk are both policy statements that set reasonable guidelines and position limits on exposures to asset classes and factor risks, and a monitoring or feedback system that immediately informs senior management and others if these guidelines are being violated.

Inflation Risk

The inflation risk that manifests itself through increases or decreases in interest rates can be addressed as described in the preceding sections on surplus and interest rate risk. What about the effect of inflation on wage-based benefits? Note that some DC plans are partially indexed to inflation through a contribution scheme that is a percentage of wages. As wages rise, so do the dollar amounts of the contributions. For DB plans, unanticipated inflation can be offset by higher contributions, better investment performance, or a combination of the two (assuming lower real benefits are not acceptable). Further, inflation risk can be managed somewhat directly by paying attention to the inflationary affects of compensation and retirement benefit schemes.

Some sponsors may mistakenly believe that wage increases disguised as higher pension benefits have little effect on pension plan financial health. The reality is that, with even modest wage inflation over 20 or 30 years, such schemes can dramatically affect funding ratios by increasing the size of the liability without providing more assets as an offset. The right way to think about this form of inflation risk is to directly incorporate it into the analysis of compensation and retirement planning by considering the effect on the pension liability and, hence, the implications for future funding and investment performance requirements.

DB plans have a built-in partial inflation offset, in that inflation-induced changes in interest rates affect both assets and liabilities (although not necessarily equally). Individuals, however, do not have liabilities as such. Thus, DC plans have no built-in protection. If inflation harms an individual's retirement asset pool, either by reducing the nominal value of the asset pool or by reducing the purchasing power of the retirement income that the assets will someday produce, the individual may have to accept a lower standard of living in retirement or make other similar adjustments.

Over long periods, both DB and DC asset pools can attempt to offset inflation by having relatively large exposures to common stocks. Historically, the risk premium earned on stocks has more than offset actual inflation, providing real returns of 6% to 9% annually. However, stocks are also risky, so there is a trade-off between the investment risk of stocks and the risk that inflation will inhibit real growth in asset values.

Nonfinancial Risks

There are more risks to consider than solely financial ones. Pension funds are exposed to the risks that come from not understanding investment technology and theory—those black boxes, the derivative contracts and securities and the investment strategies that the money management and banking professions may bring forth. For lack of a better term, this may be thought of as ignorance risk: the risk that comes from lack of knowledge. Other examples of ignorance-driven risks include the naive perception that increased exposure to international investments increases risk (a common mistake if one reads the financial press), thinking that hedging is costless and fail-safe, or believing that the recently top-performing investment strategies are riskless. Ignorance risk is best managed through trustee, administrator, manager, and staff education. The costs of not managing this risk can be high—witness the catastrophic events in Orange County, California, and elsewhere.

Most pension fund staff are well aware of what might be called political risk. This risk arises from the agency/principal problems and conflicts of interest that arise in any complex organization. Political risk takes many forms. It can come through pressure to undertake economically targeted investments. It may come in the form of "off–balance sheet" pay raises for public employees that increase the burden on plan assets, or it may come in the form of "gaming" the accounting numbers. It may come as undue influence in the manager selection process, possibly to repay campaign contributors, or it may come in the form of not being permitted to participate in corporate governance activities that are likely to increase share values. It may come in the form of unwarranted investment restrictions (such as legal lists of stocks in which the plan is allowed to invest) with unintended consequences. It may come in the form of excessive pressure to increase investment returns to reduce the sponsor's contributions. It may arise when managers do not do what they promised to do and someone must be held accountable. There is no easy way to manage political risk. Education is part of the answer; some of the politics may be well intended but naive. Accountability and wide dissemination of information may be helpful; some political pressures will not stand up well to public inspection. Careful monitoring and occasionally legal remedies may be necessary to protect the rights of beneficiaries from being abused.

Finally, pension plans should be aware of operating risk. This is the risk that no one is looking at the entire picture. It also is the risk that requisite monitoring is not being done or that various parties—plan employees, trustees, or managers—are not doing their jobs correctly. Operating risk should be eliminated. To do so requires applying the principles needed to manage any organization effectively.

HEDGING AND RETURN ENHANCEMENT

Many risk management strategies are intended either to hedge a given risk or to enhance returns by taking an exposure to a given return-generating factor. Hedging has the side effect of reducing expected returns that may accompany the risk being hedged; return enhancement has the side effect of increasing the exposure taken to the risk of the return factor being pursued.

Hedging is a strategy designed to reduce or eliminate the risk of future fluctuations of an asset or portfolio's value, of an exchange rate, of the asset-liability surplus, or, at least conceptually, of any other risk. A basic hedge might attempt to eliminate the price volatility of an asset (or a portfolio) by taking a position in another asset—the hedge asset—that offsets any change in value the asset that is hedged experiences. For example, in a well-designed price hedge, if the price of the hedged asset declines, the asset used to hedge should increase in value by a like amount.

Why hedge? The answer may be found in determining whether hedging will make the pension fund, the sponsor, or the employees for which the pension exists better off. In general, pensions may not want to hedge the majority of their risks. Hedging sounds very attractive to risk-averse pension trustees, administrators, managers, and employees. However, the very best return a fully hedged position may earn is the risk-free rate. If the hedge is not costless—and it is not—the return to the hedged position is likely to be less than what could be obtained by simply investing in risk-free securities. So hedging may increase the sponsor's funding costs, and it may reduce the future financial health of the plan because of the low returns it provides.

Why, then, is hedging done? There are several wrong reasons. Managers and investment officers may hedge to avoid being penalized for taking certain types of risk—risk that a prudent investor should take. These penalties may take the form of loss of job, loss of bonus, public pressure, or the like. Administrators may encourage hedging because they fear legal liability. Employees may encourage hedging because they sleep better at night, not realizing that the low investment returns characteristic of hedging may adversely affect their future retirement benefits.

There are economically sound reasons to hedge, in part or in full. Pension funds require liquidity to meet current benefit obligations. Thus, a liquidity hedge that locks in the value of securities to be sold to meet near-term payments to beneficiaries may be occasionally appropriate. There are risks that should not be carried because they do not offer a reasonable amount of offsetting return. For example, concentrated investments in illiquid assets may have adverse funding, plan liquidity, and other consequences if there is unexpected market action. Thus, a hedge-like strategy designed to reduce the exposure to these assets may be appropriate.

There may be a special circumstance that, for a brief period of time, makes hedging sensible. Consider, for example, a DB plan converting to a DC plan. A short-term hedge may protect the value of plan assets from the consequences of adverse short-term market action.

Finally, some hedging activity may be justifiable to reduce the volatility of the combined cash flows of the sponsor and the pension fund. For example, the pension fund may wish to hedge a specific risk, such as currency risk, to ensure that the sponsor does not have to forego profitable investment opportunities simply because the plan was affected by adverse currency movements.

Note that investment risk, surplus volatility, and interest rate risk normally should be addressed through the strategic asset allocation decision. From time to time it may be tempting to "hedge" these risks because the market appears to be overpriced, interest rates appear to be ready to spike up, and so forth. The problem with this strategy is that it begins to cross the line into active view-based strategies that are predicated on unusual capital market expectations. Thus, the apparent hedge is really an active decision to time a market or segment.

Return enhancement strategies cover numerous strategies that, although they may appear to be different, all share the common feature of being designed to pursue higher return. With this comes higher risk. If pension funds choose to pursue higher returns through greater exposure to risk, they should recognize that higher expected returns are an "on average and over long periods of time" concept. Risky bets that go bad early are often so costly that the gambler loses his stake and is unable to continue playing the game to achieve these on-average higher returns. For a pension fund, this could mean that an existing surplus may be eroded to an unacceptable level or that the sponsor must increase its contributions to meet ERISA or contractual obligations or otherwise ensure the financial viability of the plan.

Are view-based return enhancement strategies appropriate for pensions? Only if the fund's decision-makers believe the financial markets are at least partially inefficient. The caveat is to recognize the incremental risk that comes with the strategy chosen and to avoid any illusion of something for nothing. As an example of an appropriate use of return enhancement, consider a pension fund that has a belief that stocks are underpriced relative to their historical norms. If the pension fund is well funded, has a financially strong sponsor, and has policy-level authority to pursue active management, a return enhancement strategy may be a reasonable risk to take. If the fund's belief is correct, the subsequent higher-than-normal returns will increase the fund's surplus, increase the security of benefits, and reduce the sponsor's need to contribute.

Implicit in both hedging and return enhancement strategies is a sense that these are temporary or occasional strategies. If a pension fund were to hedge its investment risk fully and permanently, it would be simpler and more economically productive to buy Treasury securities. Similarly, a continual program of return enhancement strategies indicates that the fund should rethink its strategic asset allocation. Perhaps the plan should bear more long-term investment risk in pursuit of higher long-term return.

ASSESSING RISK EXPOSURES

For risk management to work, risk exposures must be identified, quantified, and, if necessary, modified.[9] The nature of risk and its complexity makes this a challenging task. The assessment tools available are risk audits, value at risk, stress testing, and risk budgeting.

Risk Audits

One useful tool for assessing risk exposure is a risk audit. This should, among other things, focus on the strengths of the internal control system and on the compliance of managers with investment policy and guidelines. The audit also should periodically evaluate the risk exposures of the fund on a systematic and comprehensive basis.

A complete risk audit will assess recent and prospective surplus volatility and assess the likely effect of various scenarios on funding and contribution patterns. The audit also will assess the sponsor's financial strength as it relates to funding plan shortfalls. Specific attention should be given to concentrations of exposures that may be unreasonable and to identifying those that are unintended. Further, compensation and reward structures should be reviewed to see whether they are correctly adjusting for capital at risk.[10] Throughout, the emphasis should be on net exposures—assets should not be judged in isolation, and portfolios should not be judged without reference to the overall asset pool, to plan liabilities, and to the sponsor. The results of the audit should be conveyed to senior management and the board of directors/trustees.

Value at Risk

Another approach to assessing risk exposure is to periodically measure the fund's VAR. This evaluations is commonly accomplished by asking the following questions:

- At a given level of statistical confidence, how large would the loss be if the financial markets repeat their worst performance from some previous historical period of time?
- How would this adverse performance affect the ability of the sponsor to pay current retirement beneficiaries?
- How would this performance affect the funding status of the plan?
- How would this performance affect the contributions the sponsor might have to make?

Value at risk may be calculated numerous ways and for various time periods. In 1996, Smithson described three methods: using historical data, using a Monte Carlo simulation, and using a variance/covariance analytic method that decomposes financial instruments into component cash equivalent positions.[11] Each method has adherents, and each has its own set of advantages and disadvantages. For example, the historical method is easy to program, but it does not permit sensitivity analysis. The simulation method is hard to program, but it does permit sensitivity analysis. The analytic approach requires application of a fairly difficult "mapping" process but requires no pricing models to be applied.

Beder has shown that the outcomes of VAR analysis are sensitive to numerous factors. The most important of these factors is the length of the time horizon chosen (e.g., a one-day loss or a one-week loss) and the data set selected (e.g., Does it use intraday or end-of-day values, and are outlying events indicators of structural change?).[12] In addition, if the analyst is asking, "How much might I lose 99% of the time?" the corollary question, "How much might I lose the other 1% of the time?" goes unanswered.

Value at risk measurement is a promising methodology for quantifying the totality of the risks an investor faces on a net basis. Its strength is that it aggregates virtually all factor risks—in option parlance, the price (delta), rate of change in price (gamma), volatility (vega), time (theta), and interest rates (rho) risk factors—as well as the correlations among factors. For pension funds to use VAR, however, the focus must be extended to how these factors affect both plan assets and plan liabilities; that is, the VAR query must be, "With a confidence level of 99%, how much might the fund's surplus decrease in one day (or however long)?"

An Example of VAR for a Pension Fund that Manages Surplus

Consider a pension fund asset pool that consists of a single bond. Table 16.1 uses historical data to illustrate the asset-based VAR analysis. From Table 16.1, the analyst could conclude that we are 99% confident the one-day loss on the pension portfolio will not be worse than a 2.1% loss. Now, consider the same information in light of the surplus of assets over liabilities (Table 16.2). The analyst would now view VAR as "the worst change in surplus that will be experienced in a single day is a decrease of 2.77% with 99% confidence that it will not be worse."

In viewing the above examples, remember that daily changes may not be the

Table 16.1 VAR Analysis for a Pension Asset Pool, Using the Last 100 Days of Asset Values

Day	Percentage Change in Asset Pool Value	Change in Asset Pool Value Sorted from Largest Decline to Largest Increase	
		Rank	Percentage Change
−101	1.1	100	−3.2
−100	−0.2	99	−2.1
			(99% confidence level)
−99	0.3	98	−0.5
−2	−0.5	2	2.3
−1	0.4	1	3.1

relevant time frame. More often than not, longer time periods will be of more use to pension fund investors, unless there are unusually large concentrated exposures that must be analyzed. In normal circumstances, VAR may be of more use in assessing outcomes weekly (requiring 100 weeks of data) or even quarterly. In addition, when using historical data (as opposed to data provided by simulations or statistical analysis), it is important to recognize that the past frequently does not predict the future.

Stress Testing

The third approach to assessing risk exposure is to conduct stress testing.[13] This approach is similar to VAR, but rather than choosing a statistical confidence

Table 16.2 VAR Analysis for a Pension Fund Surplus (assets less liabilities) Using the Most Recent 100 Days of Asset Pool and Liability Values to Compute the Daily Change in Surplus Assuming No Funding

Day	Asset Value ($)	Liability Value	Surplus	Percentage Change in Surplus	Change in Surplus Value Sorted from Largest Decline to Largest Increase	
					Rank	Percentage Change
−102	1,000	1,200	−200	—	—	
−101	1,011	1,205	−194	3	100	−2.8
−100	1,008.98	1,202	−193	0.5	99	−2.77
						(99% confidence level)
−2	990	1,170	−180	−0.7	2	3.00
−1	993.96	1,175	−181.04	−0.58	1	3.32

level, the focus of stress testing is on the consequences that a catastrophic event might cause. Stress testing assumes that the worst possible scenario occurs and then, even though it is an event with an admittedly low probability, asks how a portfolio—or a surplus—would be affected. Stress testing can be based on a single event (e.g., a currency crisis or a 200–basis point shift in yields) or on multiple events (e.g., a nonparallel yield curve shift coupled with a stock market crash). Stress testing lends itself to simulation and, thus, offers the analyst the ability to observe numerous, albeit improbable, outcomes as the effects of isolated events or combinations of different events are evaluated.

As with VAR, stress testing makes the most sense when it jointly considers assets and liabilities and when it incorporates the effect of a stress event on the plan sponsor. Like any model, stress tests will be as good as the analyst's ability to select appropriate events and to assess their consequences. Stress testing could have been helpful in weathering the "perfect storm" of 2000–2002, when interest rates dove (raising the present value of pension liabilities) and stocks tanked.

Risk Budgeting

Risk budgeting starts with the idea that the appropriate amount of risk for a pension fund can be separated into component risk elements. The overall level of risk is the risk budget. The risk budget in turn comprises component risk exposures that are a combination of a manager's proportion of the fund's total assets, the manager's correlation with the fund's overall portfolio, and the variance of the fund's total portfolio.

Sharpe proposes three phases for pension fund risk budgeting.[14] The first phase involves choosing an asset allocation and then allocating funds to investment managers to meet the chosen allocation. The second phase is establishing the fund's risk budget. In this phase, the expected excess returns for the various portfolio components (e.g., the stock component) are determined, and risk budgets are inferred for each investment manager. The risk budgets are the benchmarks that will be used in the third phase of monitoring and revision. In this later stage, more recent data are used to determine the amount of risk attributable to each investment manager. These data are compared to the original risk budgets, leading to analysis and possibly changes in allocations or investment managers.

Sharpe identifies several issues that limit the usefulness of the technique. For example, the monitoring phase may use different statistical inputs than the risk-budgeting phase, and it may be difficult to determine the cause if actual risk differs from risk budget. Of course, the exercise would still be useful in that event.

CONCLUSION

Risk management is an important part of pension fund management. The multitude of risks faced by pension funds, the dynamic nature of the financial markets, and the complex nature of pension fund interactions with sponsors, beneficiaries, and regulators make risk management seem daunting. Nonetheless, risk must be managed, and the activities that make up risk management must be woven into the fabric of the pension's overall management paradigm.

A comprehensive risk management system will identify, measure, monitor, and control the risk factors to which the pension is exposed. Measurement approaches begin with the risk-adjusted performance measures discussed in Chapter 14. Beyond this, VAR and stress testing should be used to help decision makers understand the net downside exposure that exists. Audit procedures designed to review the pension fund's exposures periodically and to identify significant or unintended changes in the fund's risk profile should become a part of the fund's information system. The findings of all the measurements and assessments should be communicated to senior management and trustees and the board of directors on a timely basis, with conformance to and appropriateness of policy foremost in the analysis.

Much of risk management is simply good investment or management practice. Diversify, consider the consequences before acting, and limit exposures through written policy. Make certain the fiduciaries, the administrators, and the managers know what they need to know to make sensible decisions and to evaluate the information provided. This, of course, implies—strongly—education about what the risks are, how they interact, how they can be managed, and what the costs of the alternatives are.

Finally, carefully evaluate all policies and strategies with respect to their motivations and goals. Understanding when and what to hedge and when and what not to hedge is important before you do decide whether to hedge. With hindsight, it is easy to see what should have been hedged, but of course this knowledge is of little help. Understanding the downside of a view implementation/return enhancement strategy before you undertake it is important. Making certain before acting on a decision that the decision is theoretically sound, that it is economically rational, that it has a realistic chance of working—these guidelines will take most investors far in managing their exposures, but do not forget: risk generates return. Without risk, there will be no return. Manage risk, but do not think you can or should eliminate it.

17

Risk Management Strategies Using Derivative Securities

Derivative securities, such as options, forwards, futures, and swaps, have become immensely popular in recent years as tools for implementing risk management strategies. At the same time as this increase in popularity, widely publicized disasters have given many managers and analysts reason to pause and ask whether derivatives are prudent and to what extent they should be used—if at all. Derivatives are complex and are often are not well understood by those who use them. Nonetheless, derivatives are here to stay and, in fact, are quite useful for controlling a variety of risks and lowering trading costs.

This chapter describes the primary types of derivatives used by pension funds to manage risk. It begins by discussing the advantages and disadvantages of using derivatives to carry out various risk management strategies. The chapter then discusses some hedging and return enhancement strategies that use derivatives and concludes with an explanation of how plan sponsors, administrators, trustees, managers, and other decision makers can decide when to use derivatives, how to choose from among the many alternatives available, and how to control their use.

THE USE OF DERIVATIVES BY INSTITUTIONAL INVESTORS

In a 1999 survey, 44.7% of respondent pension plan sponsors said that they use derivatives.[1] Of those who used derivatives, the vast majority reported that their stake was small: 7% or less of total assets. Half of those who used derivatives were aiming to hedge returns, and a quarter were using derivatives to enhance returns.

There are numerous derivative products available, both exchange listed and over the counter (OTC). The most popular derivatives according to the survey mentioned above were exchange-listed interest rate and equity futures and options.

It is clear that derivatives are being used by many investors for many different purposes. Simply knowing that other investors use derivatives, however, should not be sufficient reason to use, or to authorize the use of, derivatives. There is much more one should know to make informed and prudent choices in this area.

BASIC TYPES OF DERIVATIVES

Derivatives derive their value from an underlying asset such as a stock, a bond, a commodity, an index (such as the S&P 500 Stock Index), an interest rate, or a formula, such as 6% (the London interbank offered rate). The following discussion uses the term the "underlying" to represent the asset, index, interest rate, or formula from which a derivative contract derives its value. The discussion refers to the "payoff structure" of a derivative contract when discussing the possible values a contract can take, given a change in the value of the underlying asset ("the underlying"). That is, the payoff structure represents the range of values a particular contract can take over a range of values taken by the underlying.

Derivatives come in many forms, but they may be categorized as either contracts or securities. Contracts include options (puts and calls), futures, forward contracts, and swaps. Securities include collateralized mortgage obligations (securities issued on pools of mortgages), strips (coupon-only or principal-only securities constructed by "stripping" Treasury bonds), and inverse floaters (bonds structured to pay coupons that float inversely with changes in interest rates). Although all derivatives derive their value from changes in the value of their respective underlying, the payoff structures of different contracts on the same underlying can be considerably different. Collectively, these contracts offer a variety of ways in which pension funds can increase or decrease the risk of their portfolios; in other words, they represent ways in which pensions may achieve alternate positions on the risk/return continuum.

The most common derivative contracts are options, forwards, and futures. Descriptions of these contracts follow, and swaps are discussed later in this chapter.

Options

Options are the building blocks of the financial world. They allow investors synthetically to replicate the payoff structures of stocks, bonds, and even various combinations of asset classes. As such, they offer a foundation for understanding forwards and futures as well as other derivatives.

Options give the owner the right but not the obligation either to purchase an underlying (a call option) or to sell an underlying (a put option) at a predetermined price (the exercise, or strike, price) for a specific period. Users of options may go long by purchasing an option or go short by writing an option. Though owners have the right to decide whether to exercise the option or not, the writer has a defined obligation to sell the underlying at the exercise price (for a written call) or to buy the underlying at the exercise price (for a written put) if the option is exercised. That is, the option owner can tear up an option, but its writer must fulfill the contract if asked.

Users of call options first must understand what will happen to the value of the option if the underlying goes up or down in value. Second, users must also understand how the change in option value affects the long (purchase) or short (written) position taken by the user. Consider a call option on a stock market index such as the S&P 500. If the index goes up, the call option will increase in value. The percentage change in the value of the option, however, will typically be much greater than the percentage change in the value of the index. This leverage is an important attribute of derivatives.

Now consider the position taken in the option. A long position in the call option effectively establishes a long position in the index and hence in the stocks that make up the index. If the underlying index increases, pension funds that bought the call option (that took a long position) will see the value of their position in the option increase in value. However, pensions that wrote the option (that took a short position) will see the value of their position in the option decrease in value.

Long call positions and short put positions will increase in value when the price of the underlying increases; conversely, these positions lose value if the price of the underlying goes down. Short call positions and long put positions will increase in value if the price of the underlying falls; they will lose value if the price rises.

The payoff to an option is truncated rather than symmetrical; for example, the long position in a call can make a theoretically infinite profit but is at risk only for the premium paid for the option. Conversely, the writer of a call may lose an infinitely large amount but will profit only to the amount of the premium. (All profits, of course, are less broker fees and margin costs.)

Note that regardless of whether the value of the option position increases or decreases, this change in value should not be evaluated as an isolated event. Instead, it should be evaluated in the context of a more comprehensive picture that encompasses the total pension fund or the subportfolio using the option position. In addition, the payoff value should be interpreted with respect to the strategic motivation for taking a position in the option in the first place.

For example, suppose a pension fund manager anticipates funding from the sponsor in three months and intends to use the payment to buy large capitalization stocks. If the manager is concerned that the prices of these stocks will go up, he or she can hedge that risk by purchasing a call option such as the one described. If stocks do subsequently increase, there is a timing loss on the purchase of the stocks three months hence, but that loss is offset (completely or in part) by the gains on the call option. The joint effect is neither a gain nor a loss in total. Similarly, had the index gone down in value, the option position may have become worthless. However, the loss of the premium paid to purchase the option would be offset by the gain associated with purchasing stocks later at a lower price. Again, the result is neither a gain nor loss in total; the joint effect is approximately zero.

Options may be exchange traded, in which case they will be defined as a series characterized by the underlying (the stock, bond, index, or other asset), a variety of exercise prices, and a sequence of terms to expiration. Exchange-traded options are normally quite liquid, but a pension fund may not be able to find a contract that meets its specific needs. OTC options may be able to meet this need. These contracts have the advantage of allowing a customized structure, such as an unusual size or maturity or and underlying asset or exercise feature. They are not as liquid as exchange options, however, and holders of OTC options may have to hold them until expiration. OTC contracts are available from banks and other dealers.

Futures and Forwards

Forward contracts are agreements that commit two parties to transact at a future point in time. A forward contract includes an agreed-on price, an agreed-on deferred delivery date, and either an agreed-on underlying to be exchanged or a cash settlement formula to be applied at the future date and price. Forward contracts are available OTC and are extremely flexible because they are custom contracts between two parties; for example, between a pension fund and a bank.

Futures contracts are similar to forward contracts in that they are arrangements providing for either delivery of an underlying or cash settlement at a future date at an agreed-on price at maturity. Futures contracts, however, are traded on exchanges and, therefore, are standardized with respect to the underlying and the amount of the contract. In return for this standardization, users gain greater liquidity, but they give up some of the flexibility associated with customized forward contracts. Futures are guaranteed by clearing firms on exchanges; forward contracts are subject to credit risk. Futures positions are marked-to-market daily with daily cash settlement; forwards may not be marked-to-market frequently or at all (marking-to-market is the process of calculating or estimating the current value of a financial position and then posting gains or losses on the position to the account of the user). Futures positions may be closed by taking offsetting positions (e.g., a short position is offset by purchasing the same contract, resulting in a net exposure of zero); forwards are not as easy to close out. The discussion in this chapter focuses primarily on futures contracts, although most of what is said, with the exceptions just noted, holds for forward contracts also.

A pension fund that buys a futures contract (goes long) will see the position in the futures contract profit if the value of the underlying goes up. Conversely, a pension fund that sells a futures contract (goes short) will lose on the futures position if the price of the underlying increases. Thus, pension funds that wish to increase their exposure to an asset class in the hope of benefiting from an increase in the price of the underlying may do so by taking a long position in futures. Alternatively, pension funds that wish to reduce their exposure to a potential decrease in the price of some underlying asset in which they are long may do so by selling futures contracts. As for options, the correct way to evaluate the gains or losses on futures/forward positions is within the broader context of the portfolio and the strategy being pursued.

ADVANTAGES OF DERIVATIVES

The most obvious advantage of derivatives for pension funds is that they reduce transaction costs. For example, a study by Goldman Sachs estimated the costs of a round trip for U.S. stocks (this example used a $25 million trade, including commissions, market impact, and taxes, and excluding settlement and custody fees) at 0.69% versus a cost of 0.06% for a comparable futures contract.[2]

Another advantage of derivatives is that they allow risk to be separated into its component parts. Consider bonds: investors that purchase bonds are exposed to both interest rate risk and credit risk. Through interest rate and credit derivatives, portions or all of either risk may be transferred to other parties, or if desired, exposures to either may be increased.

A third attribute of derivatives is the versatility they offer investors in developing and implementing investment and risk management strategies. For example:

- Investors can use derivatives to create risk/return profiles that may not be ordinarily achievable. Customized portfolios can be created that would be impossible using only underlying assets.
- Derivatives permit currency risk to be managed without changing country exposures. Country considerations can be separated from currency considerations.
- Derivatives offer the possibility of exploiting mispricing between cash and derivatives markets if arbitrage opportunities arise.
- Derivatives offer a means of trading on a specific view regarding markets, assets, interest rates, and currencies. Derivatives allow the investor to make bets on very specific market aspects.
- Derivatives offer a means of hedging numerous risks, including market risk, interest rate risk, surplus volatility, credit risk, concentration risk, and currency risk. Derivatives allow for narrowing the range of possible outcomes.
- Pension funds wishing to establish (or terminate) an exposure to a broad market segment that is indexed may do so in a single transaction by purchasing (selling) an index derivative rather than by purchasing (selling) all the securities in the index. Derivatives are low-cost ways to do large changes.
- Pension funds that are constrained from direct investment in an asset (or asset class) by regulation or other factors may be able to increase diversification by investing in these assets through derivatives. (This, of course, should be done in conformance with policy and authority limits.)
- Derivatives permit strategies to be implemented quickly. Investing (or divesting) large positions in financial assets may require a relatively long time and may result in adverse market impact results. The desired position may be achievable in a shorter time through derivatives.
- Derivatives also are well suited to specific positions that have holding

periods (investment horizons) shorter than the overall time horizons of many pension funds.

Finally, there is a school of thought that argues that the widespread acceptance that derivatives have gained in the investment community means not only that the use of derivatives is prudent but that not using derivatives in some instances may be imprudent. Given the relatively low cost of modifying portfolio exposures with derivatives, this "prudence" argument would seem to be especially compelling for pension plans that hedge and regularly rebalance portfolios.

DISADVANTAGES OF DERIVATIVES

The use of derivatives is not without its problems, however. To develop sensible policy governing the use of derivatives, these disadvantages should be understood and carefully weighed against the advantages offered.

- Derivative positions generally have to be rolled over when the contract expires. Thus, over long time periods, the cost advantage can disappear. Furthermore, there is no guarantee the desired position can be established in the future.
- Derivatives are subject to investment risk; thus, the value of the derivatives position may decline. (In a hedge, this is not a problem because the position being hedged is increasing in value.) This problem is compounded (literally) by leverage. Relative to the investment risk of the underlying (say, a stock or an interest rate), derivatives may exhibit much greater price and return volatility than the underlying itself exhibits. Thus, poor performance in the derivative may be much worse than a naive investor might anticipate, even though the possibility of poor performance in the underlying may have been assessed correctly.
- In many cases, hedging and return enhancement strategies that use derivatives fail to live up to their promises because of tracking or correlation error. This occurs when the volatility of derivative instrument does not perfectly match the volatility of the assets being hedged or in which a position is desired. For example, if a fund attempts to hedge a position in small capitalization U.S. stocks with a contract deriving its value from an index consisting of large U.S. stocks, the tracking error could be large and the hedge, therefore, not very effective. This may also occur with futures when the basis—the difference between the spot or cash price and the futures price—changes and the futures position is terminated before contract expiration.
- Another disadvantage is that, although many derivatives are traded on the major exchanges and are thus normally quite liquid, this liquidity can dry up in unusually turbulent markets. Witness the failure of portfolio insurance programs during the market crash of October 1987: when investors tried to hedge positions by selling futures contracts, they were not able to find speculators (or portfolio rebalancers or tactical asset allocators) to buy the contracts.

- Further, many new derivative products that may seem attractive for a specific hedge today may not generate enough trading volume to warrant continuing to make a market in them. Thus, products are often taken off the market.
- For products that are not traded on exchanges, there is credit risk. This is the risk that the counterparty to the contract will default.

Finally, users of derivatives should be aware that there is the potential for misrepresentation and, consequently, for introducing unintended risks into a portfolio. This may occur when persons selling financial products become too aggressive or greedy. Related to this is whether those purchasing the products fully understand what they are buying. Many users of derivatives rely on brokers and bankers for information about the derivative products they are selling—information such as the attributes of the specific contract being used and its performance under various market conditions. This reliance provides an opportunity for a salesperson to sell something that is not needed and that may do great harm under some circumstances.

For sellers, the temptation may be too great. Instruments such as collateralized mortgage obligations (CMOs), for example, create exposures to principal repayments that very sophisticated users can only crudely estimate, let alone foretell with great accuracy. CMOs are perfectly acceptable for some investors who want the risk/return exposures they offer. However, an investor that does not understand the prepayment risk and the factors that affect the prices of CMOs when interest rates fall ends up exposed to risk that may not have been envisioned. The resulting losses can be nontrivial. (Note that a knowledgeable user of derivatives is not likely to be easily misled. Further, it is not uncommon for an investor to presume he understands the contract when it is profitable and to sue the dealer when there are losses, claiming he never really understood the contract.)

DERIVATIVES AND LEVERAGE

There are numerous strategies that use derivatives. Virtually all these strategies exploit the leverage that derivatives offer to increase or decrease exposure to one or more risk factors.

Consider investing $10,000 in the stock of company A or investing the $10,000 in at-the-money call options (an at-the-money option is an option with an exercise price equal to the stock's current price) on stock A. The stock is currently selling at a price of $50 a share, and the options may be purchased at $3 per option. Thus, one can invest $10,000 in stock A either by purchasing 200 shares of stock or by buying 3,333 call options. For the sake of analysis, assume that the price of the stock may be either $55 or $45 a share on the option's expiration date. Given these outcomes, the payoff to the stock position will be either +10% ([$11,000 − $10,000]/$10,000) or −10% ([$9,000 − $10,000]/$10,000), ignoring trading costs. However, the payoff to the option position will be either +200% ([$5 − $3] × 10,000/$10,000) or −100% ([$0

− $3) × \$10,000/\$10,000). The large difference between the possible payoffs to the stock position and payoffs to the option position is caused by the leverage the options provide.

The preceding example really describes two extreme positions: investing \$10,000 in stocks or \$10,000 in options. There are numerous combinations of stock A and call options falling between these positions. For example, if one merely wanted exposure to \$10,000 worth of stock A, this could be accomplished by purchasing 200 call options for \$600, thus limiting the potential loss to \$600 (−100%) while providing a potential gain of \$400 (+67%).

Leverage should not frighten users. However, it should be recognized that, as other forms of derivatives are essentially combinations of options, leverage is endemic in all derivative products. Every derivative creates a relatively wider band of plausible outcomes.

MANAGING RISK WITH DERIVATIVES

As explained in Chapter 19, risk management includes activities designed to reduce risk temporarily (hedging) and activities designed to increase return temporarily (return enhancement). This section introduces some common strategies and provides several examples of these strategies that may be implemented with derivatives.

Hedging with Derivatives

There are two types of hedges. A short hedge occurs when a pension fund has a long position (e.g., it owns stock) it wishes to protect by going short a derivative contract. A long hedge occurs when a pension fund intends to take a position at a future date (e.g., it intends to buy stock when the next contribution from the sponsor arrives) and to hedge the position will take a long position in a derivative contract.

To understand hedging, one must understand the concept of a hedge ratio and a delta-neutral hedge. The hedge ratio is the amount of the hedge asset needed to hedge a specific amount of an existing position to achieve a desired risk exposure. A delta-neutral hedge is a continuous hedge in which the effect of a price change on the underlying asset (such as a stock or a portfolio of stocks) is eliminated through an offsetting position in a hedge asset (such as a put option or a stock index futures contract). The delta hedge ratio changes as the value of the underlying asset changes; therefore, the amount of the asset held for the purpose of hedging must change also—hence the "continuous" nature of the hedge.

Note that the values and thus the hedging attributes of options and other derivatives are affected by many factors: the passage of time, the rate of change in delta, changes in the volatility of the underlying, and changes in interest rates. These factors are referred to as theta, gamma, vega, and rho factors, respectively. Complete hedges may require attention to the influences these factors exert.[3]

Option Contracts in Risk Management

Options are frequently used in constructing hedging and return enhancement strategies. The following examples illustrate some basic option strategies.

Option Hedges for a Long Asset Position

Consider a pension fund with a substantial exposure to common stocks. Theoretically, if there are options on these stocks (or on an index that is very similar to the portfolio of stocks held), the fund can hedge its long stock position by either writing covered call options or buying protective put options.

Writing covered calls entitles the fund to the premium (or price) of the call option and thus generates income that cushions the impact of any decline in the price of the stocks held. The cost of this cushion, however, is that it limits the upside price potential: if the stocks go up in price, they will be "called away"—the pension fund will not participate in return beyond the exercise price of the call option because the fund will have to sell stock to the owners of the call options. Conceptually, covered call writing locks in the current risk-free rate of return as long as the number of calls written is continually adjusted as the price of the underlying changes and as long as trading costs are trivial. The continual adjustments required and the actual trading costs incurred make this strategy only partially effective as a hedge.

An alternative to writing covered calls is purchasing protective puts. In the combined position of the long stock, long put option, if the price of the stock held declines, the value of the put rises. Thus, properly constructed, a protective put hedge can offset all of the loss on the long stock position. Again, this is not costless. A premium must be paid to purchase the put. This premium can be viewed as the cost of insurance. Thus, although the downside risk of holding the stock is effectively truncated, the expected return on the stock portfolio is reduced by the cost of the puts. Many investors view puts as too expensive and, thus, turn to other derivatives.

Pension funds may hedge the portfolio by using exchange-traded options—although there may be substantial tracking or correlation risk involved with using these options and it may be difficult to match time horizons—or by entering into an OTC market transaction. In the case of the OTC transaction, there is the advantage of avoiding or reducing tracking risk through a customized hedge asset that correlates well with the portfolio, and there is also the advantage of being able to negotiate an appropriate time horizon. As noted earlier, potential disadvantages of an OTC transaction are the lack of liquidity relative to exchange-traded contracts and the credit risk of the counterparty.

Return Enhancement through Options

Recall that hedging is fundamentally a risk-reducing strategy. From time to time, the pension fund manager may want to increase the fund's exposure to a risk in pursuit of higher total returns. The motivation for increasing the fund's exposure may be that the manager has a belief or view that an asset or sector is underpriced and, thus, offers unusually good expected returns. Or the fund itself may be temporarily more tolerant of risk than it usually is, and thus the manager wishes to try for higher short-term returns.

Regardless of the motivation, there are four paths to return enhancement through options. The first two are to purchase calls or sell puts if the view or expectation is that the underlying (e.g., stocks) will rise. If calls are purchased, the potential downside is the loss of the premium paid (a maximum loss of 100%) plus trading costs. The upside potential theoretically is limitless, although most exchange-traded options have times to expiration of only a few months and will expire at a finite time. If puts are sold, the worst that may happen is that the fund will lose an amount equal to the exercise price of the option less the net premium received. The maximum gain is the premium less trading costs. Either strategy has the potential to enhance returns; the success of both depends on an increase in value in the underlying.

The third and fourth strategies are to write calls or buy puts if the underlying is expected to decline. If the view is proved correct, the call writer pockets the premium and the put purchaser can profit by up to the strike price less the premium paid. However, if the underlying falls, the call writer can lose—a lot— and the purchaser of the put can lose up to the entire premium.

Futures in Risk Management

Like options, futures contracts (and, of course, forward contracts as well) may be used for hedging and return enhancement. However, with futures there is no premium to pay or receive and the payoff structure is not truncated; a long futures position, roughly analogous to a long call position, increases in value when the underlying increases (as does the long call). Similarly, if the underlying decreases, the long futures position declines in value, as does the long call position. However, the maximum loss on the long call is limited to the loss of the premium paid, whereas the loss on the long future may be much greater. The following examples illustrate some uses of futures in risk management.

Changing Equity Exposures through Futures

Consider a portfolio holding $100 million in stocks. Further assume that the beta of the portfolio—its market risk—is equal to 1.0. If the pension fund manager is fearful that the stock market is ready for a precipitous drop, he or she may want to reduce the portfolio's level of market risk substantially by reducing the portfolio's beta to zero. The fund can hedge the risk of a price decrease by selling futures contracts on an index such as the S&P 500, resulting in a portfolio that is long the underlying stocks and short the futures contracts. Suppose that the S&P 500 contract has a current futures price of $850. The contract's face amount is 500 times the futures price. Assuming that the stocks in the equity portfolio are large capitalization U.S. stocks and that they are held more or less in quantities proportionate to their market capitalization (i.e., the portfolio and the futures contracts are highly correlated in that they both have betas of 1.0), the number of contracts the manager must sell to hedge the position is

$$N = \$100,000,000/(500)(850) = 235.3.$$

The fund manager should sell 235 futures contracts. If the initial beta of the portfolio differs from that of the contract, the preceding equation is adjusted by multiplying N by the relative volatility (beta) of the portfolio. For example, if the stock portfolio has a beta of 1.2 (i.e., if it is estimated that the portfolio has 20% more market risk than the S&P 500), the hedge requires selling

$$235.5 \times 1.2 = 282 \text{ contracts.}$$

There are costs to this strategy. First, there are the broker fees charged to implement the transaction. These fees are small relative to those incurred selling or buying the underlying stocks instead of the futures contract, however. There is also the margin cost associated with taking a futures position. For an S&P 500 contract used for hedging, this may run in the neighborhood of 2% to 5% of the contract's total value. This requirement may be met by posting Treasury bills with the broker, who in turn, promises them to the clearinghouse. Because the interest earned on the Treasury bills goes to the party taking the position and, in this case, the purpose of the transaction is to hedge, this part of the cost is generally negligible. Finally, there is the opportunity cost of not being able to participate in a market that does unexpectedly well; that is, if the stock market goes up rather than down, the pension fund will gain in the long stock position but lose in the futures position. Again, because the motivation is to hedge, this is not a matter for concern, though it does serve as a reminder that there are no free lunches. Note that a protective put position allows participation in an up market; however, purchasing the put requires that a premium be paid by the pension fund.

Hedging is not a matter of all or none. Consider a decision to hedge 50% of the portfolio's market risk. Using beta, the volatility of the portfolio relative to the overall market, as the basic measure, a portfolio's target risk level—its target beta—could be described as

$$(\text{target beta})(\text{assets}) = (\text{actual beta})(\text{assets}) + N(\text{futures price})(500).$$

Using the preceding data, one can calculate the number of futures contracts needed to hedge 50% of the portfolio's market risk:

$$0.5(\$100,000,000) = 1.0(100,000,000) + N(850)(500);$$
$$N = -117.6.$$

The fund should sell 118 contracts. Note that this is half the number of futures contracts needed to construct a full hedge. The methodologies are, of course, consistent.

From the preceding example, it can be seen that a pension fund also may increase its beta (its market risk and, hence, its exposure to stocks) by purchasing futures contracts. The margin and broker costs are fundamentally the same as they are for hedging, although margin is generally higher for strategies that are not hedging strategies. The potential cost is that, if stocks fall in value, the loss on the long stock position will be magnified by the loss on the long futures position. As noted earlier, users should carefully compare the potentially large loss of a futures position to the loss of premium on a long call option on the same index. If, for example, the stock market plummeted, the loss on the long futures position could be high, greatly magnifying the loss on the stocks also held. The loss incurred by being long call options, however, is limited to the cost of acquiring the options. Thus, the combined call options plus stock loss could be large but could be much smaller than the combined futures plus stock loss. With an option, the loss is limited to its price; with a futures position, the loss can far exceed the price of an option.

Fixed-Income (Interest Rate) Strategies Using Futures

Consider a pension fund with substantial holdings in bonds. A hedge similar to the one constructed in the preceding example can be constructed if one fears an increase in interest rates and a corresponding loss in the bond portfolio.

One of several ways to approach this type of hedge is to compute the change in value of a bond portfolio associated with a change in interest rates of one basis point. This can be done as follows:

$$\text{price change} = \{\text{portfolio duration}/[1 + (\text{interest rate})/2]\} \times \text{value of portfolio} \times 0.0001.$$

The next step is to compute the price change for the desired futures contract. The choice of contract is affected by factors such as the liquidity of the contract and its correlation error relative to the portfolio. The third step is to select a target duration for the portfolio and to calculate the price change that will occur by using the equation above. In the case of a hedge, of course, the target duration will be well below the portfolio's current duration. Finally, the number of futures contracts needed is determined by

$$N = (\text{target price change} - \text{portfolio price change})/ \text{price change of futures contract.}$$

The hedge can be achieved by selling futures contracts using as an underlying either a bond index (e.g., Treasury bonds) or interest rates (in which the payoff to the contract is determined by an interest rate formula). This hedge creates a position in which, should interest rates increase, the damage done to the bond portfolio will be offset by a gain on the short futures contracts.

Of course, real portfolios are not likely to have bonds that are all the same, nor ones that correlate in all respects with the bonds in the futures contract. Further, there are other factors to consider, such as differences in the time to expiration of the contract versus the desired hedge period, relative volatility, and nonparallel shifts in interest rates.

Fixed-income return enhancement strategies simply increase the target portfolio duration by purchasing interest rate futures. These strategies are based on the belief or expectation that interest rates are likely to fall. The resulting position is one of long bonds and long futures. If interest rates subsequently fall, the value of the position will increase much more than if only bonds are held; whatever interest rate change occurs, the returns will be magnified relative to the straight long bond position.

Asset/Liability Interest Rate Risk Management Using Futures

Recall that, for a pension fund with a duration mismatch between its assets and liabilities, if interest rates change, the present value of the pension liability may change more than or less than the change in value of the assets. A mismatch in duration may lead to unacceptable surplus volatility.

Duration-Based Strategies. Derivatives can be useful for managing asset–liability mismatches. The preceding example demonstrated that the duration of a portfolio can be changed with futures. Consider a pension fund with an asset duration that is not equal to the duration of its liabilities. By purchasing futures contracts on bonds or using an appropriate interest rate formula, the duration of the portfolio that the pension is holding may be increased. If, however, the duration of plan assets needs to be lowered, the pension fund will sell futures. Thus, it is possible to construct a position in which a change in interest rates has no effect on the pension fund surplus because it affects liabilities and assets equally. If this is the desired position, the fund manager would conduct an analysis similar to that already described, with a duration target for the asset side of

duration of assets = duration of liabilities × (total liabilities/total assets).

Problems with Duration-Based Strategies. As in the case of delta hedging, duration and duration-based hedging strategies are sensitive to a variety of factors. Interest rate sensitivity is a function of the magnitude of the cash flows (higher interim cash flows reduce interest rate sensitivity), maturity (shorter maturities reduce interest rate exposure), and current interest rates (in general, higher interest rates are associated with lower sensitivity to changes in interest rates, although this is not always true for liabilities and assets with embedded options).

Further, duration as usually estimated assumes a linear relationship between price and yield. This ignores the fact that an asset's sensitivity to changes in interest rates is different at different levels of interest rates because of the convexity or the curvilinear nature of the actual relationship. Convexity indicates how rapidly a price changes in response to an interest rate change and is especially important for large changes in interest rates. Finally, assets and liabilities with embedded options, such as a bond with a call option, may have areas of negative convexity. This is where the normally inverse relationship between price and yield is eliminated (in the case of a callable bond that is "in-the-money") or reversed (in the case of a CMO during a period of falling interest rates and rapid prepayments of mortgages).

Collectively, this means that duration-based hedging strategies, like delta hedging strategies, are dynamic in nature and require continual monitoring and fine-tuning if they are to stay effective. Because duration-based strategies rely on imperfect estimates, further analysis designed to capture the true price/yield relationship better may be necessary.

SWAPS AS ALTERNATIVES TO OPTIONS, FORWARDS, AND FUTURES

A swap contract is an agreement between two parties to exchange prespecified cash flows at specified intervals for an agreed-on period of time. Like options and futures, swaps are useful in hedging exposures to specific asset classes, in achieving low-cost exposures to specific asset classes, in taking active positions consistent with one's beliefs about the performance of an asset class, interest rate, or currency, and in asset/liability management. Swaps can be especially useful for pension fund managers who wish to manage a specific risk for longer time periods than most option or futures contracts permit. When a futures or option contract expires, if the investor wishes to continue the strategy that was in place, new contracts must be arranged. This results in a rollover or stacking risk—the risk that the contracts may not be available or that the price required to reestablish the position may be prohibitive.

An Interest Rate Swap

Consider, for example, a plain vanilla interest rate swap from the perspective of an investor such as a pension fund. Financial institution A may currently have $50 million in fixed-rate bonds, but A wishes to hold bonds that pay a variable rate of interest. The motivation may be to hedge a variable component of its liability stream, perhaps where payments to third parties are indexed to some short-term interest rate. Pension fund B, however, owns $50 million in bonds that pay a variable rate of interest but that would prefer to receive a fixed rate of interest to more closely match the cash flows produced by its assets with the near-term cash flows necessary to pay its current retirees. The pension fund and the financial institution may, of course, sell the bonds that they are holding and purchase new bonds that have the characteristics they desire. Alternatively, and in part to avoid the transaction costs associated with the sale and purchase of the securities, they may arrange an interest rate swap in which they essentially agree to "swap" cash flows. Thus, A agrees to pay a fixed rate of interest on a notional principal of $50 million to B in return for receiving a variable interest rate from B. The actual payments are net amounts, with the party owing the larger amount paying the difference to the other party. The net result for B is that the variable rate it receives from the bonds it owns is "passed through" to A, whereas a fixed payment stream that matches all or a portion of its payments to retirees remains.

This type of interest rate swap typically is intermediated by a dealer such as a large commercial bank or an investment bank. Thus, the two investors just described probably are not transacting with one another directly but rather are transacting with a dealer that serves as counterparty to both. The interest rate swap itself will be structured in terms of the fixed rate that A is to pay (and B receives), the variable rate that B is to pay (and A receives), the notional amount (in this case, $50 million) on which the two payment streams are calculated, and the tenor or length of time for which the swap will be in effect. The variable rate is likely to be defined in terms of an observable short-term interest rate index such as the London Interbank Offer Rate (LIBOR). The dealer who intermediates the swap hopes to make a profit by matching swaps with other parties at a swap price spread (interest rate differential).

On the Risks of Swaps

Similar to other derivatives, swaps are subject to investment risk, correlation risk, currency risk, and so forth. Interest rate risk is an especially important risk for a pension fund that participates in the interest rate swap market. To understand this risk, it is necessary to understand the motivation behind a particular swap position.

Interest rate risk for swaps can be defined as changes in the market value of the swap resulting from unanticipated changes in interest rates. When a swap is entered into, the swap is priced off the forward rates embedded in the current yield curve. Thus, the fixed-rate pay leg and the variable-rate pay leg are set to yield present values where both legs are equal in value. If, then, interest rates follow the pattern implied by the yield curve over the life of the swap (swap contracts run from two to five years as a general rule), the net result of the swap is pretty much as all parties anticipate: given an upward sloping yield curve, the variable-pay party receives positive cash flows in the early years of the swap but makes cash payments in the later years of the swap. Similarly, the fixed-pay leg pays net to the variable-pay leg early in the swap, but then receives net payments in the later years of the swap. (In the preceding example of an interest rate swap, A and B still receive income from their bond portfolios. If B makes net payments to A in the later years of the swap, this simply reduces the proceeds B receives from its variable-rate bond portfolio, which is probably paying a higher rate than it was when the swap was initiated.)

What happens, however, if interest rates suddenly and unexpectedly shift? For example, consider an interest rate shift in which there is an upward parallel shift of an upward sloping yield curve. It may appear that pension fund B (paying the variable rate and receiving the fixed rate) is worse off and the fixed-pay party is better off. Is this true, however? There are two issues to consider. The first is that the floating- or variable-pay leg (pension fund B) now has the greatest incentive to default. Hence, there has been a shift in the counterparty risk of the swap. (Counterparty risk is the risk that the other party—or the dealer for an intermediated swap—will default.) The more important question concerns the original motivation behind the swap. If the swap was entered into to obtain a specific exposure to interest rates in order to hedge a portion of the liability structure of the pension fund, and if the swap is an appropriate hedge, any gain or a loss on the swap is being offset by a loss or a gain on the liability side of the balance sheet. Thus, the surplus of the pension is more or less unchanged and there really is no winner or loser; instead, what pension fund B is trying to accomplish with asset liability management is actually being accomplished.

An Example of an Asset-Liability Swap

Consider a pension fund that has one bond and one retiree.[4] The bond has a 9% coupon and is selling at its face value of $50,000. The one retiree has an expected lifespan of five years. The appropriate yield for valuing the retirement annuity of $10,000 a year is 8%.

Bond	Retirement Liability
$50,000	$10,000/year for
5-year maturity, coupon of	5 years
9%, annual pay, option free	yield = 8%

The initial asset/liability position is

	Asset	Liability
Present value	$50,000	$39,972
Duration	4.24	2.85

The surplus is $10,073 and the duration of the surplus is

$$\text{surplus duration} = [50{,}000(4.24) - 39{,}927(2.85)]/10{,}073 = 9.75 = D_S.$$

If the pension fund wants to remove this duration mismatch and reduce the sensitivity of the surplus to changes in interest rates—to lower its duration—the fund can enter a swap in which it agrees to pay a fixed interest rate on the notional or face amount of the swap, in exchange for which it will receive an amount determined by applying a variable interest rate to that notional amount. The actual payment will be a net of the two payments—that is, if the variable amount is greater than the fixed amount, the fund will receive the difference, and vice versa. Receiving a cash flow that varies with short-term interest rates reduces the duration of the fund's assets, whereas committing to fixed payments increases the duration of the fund's liabilities. The dollar duration of the swap is

$$S_D = D_{FRB} - D_{FI},$$

where D_{FRB} is the duration of a fixed rate bond and D_{FI} is the duration of a floating-rate bond.

For simplicity, assume the duration of the floating-pay leg is zero (it is actually something less than the time to the next payment) and the duration of the fixed-pay leg is 4.0.

To eliminate the volatility of the surplus, the swap needs a notional amount of

$$9.75(101073) + (-4.0)(N) = 0;$$
$$N = \$24,553.$$

The duration of the surplus is now

$$10,073(9.75) + 24,553(-4.0) = 0.$$

Thus, the volatility of the pension surplus in this simple example has been eliminated for small changes in interest rates.

Other Swaps

A pension fund manager may also find currency swaps and equity swaps appealing at times. Currency swaps involve an initial exchange of principal, an exchange of cash flows denominated in different currencies, and a final exchange (a re-exchange) of principal. Consider, for example, a pension fund that determines it is appropriate to make investments outside of the United States but has employees only in the United States. This pension fund manager may be able to eliminate all or a portion of its currency risk in its investments by arranging currency swaps in which a pension fund that receives, for example, Swiss francs from its investments in Swiss securities can swap Swiss francs to a dealer in return for U.S. dollars. (Currency risk also may be managed through currency options, futures contracts, and forward contracts.)

Equity swaps, however, can create long (or short) exposures to both U.S. and non-U.S. stock indexes. Consider, for example, a U.S. pension fund desiring long exposure to a non-U.S. stock market. The pension fund manager may arrange a swap through a bank wherein the bank commits to pay the quarterly percentage change in an index such as the French CAC in return for payments equal to those of six-month LIBOR.

In an equity swap, the payment from the bank may be negative—that is, the pension fund may have to pay the bank if the index goes down. In addition, equity swaps differ according to whether the notional amount on which the payments are calculated varies with changes in the index (whether gains and losses will be capitalized) or remains the same regardless of market movements. At issue here is the risk tolerance of the investor: does the risk tolerance change as markets change? An example of an equity swap is presented in Appendix F.

SPECIALIZED USES OF DERIVATIVES

As mentioned earlier, derivatives may be used for numerous purposes other than general hedging and return enhancement strategies. For example, derivatives are also popular for rebalancing portfolios, meeting liquidity needs, and alpha separation.

Rebalancing portfolios through futures contracts is commonplace. Disciplined rebalancing and tactical asset allocation strategies, for example, commonly are carried out by purchasing equity futures contracts when stocks fall in value and selling futures when stock prices rise. Similarly, insured asset allocation strategies sell equity futures when stock prices fall and buy equity futures when stock prices rise (liquidity permitting).

Pension fund managers occasionally find themselves presented with short-term liquidity issues. As noted earlier, if a contribution is due from the sponsor in a few months and the manager fears that stock prices may increase rapidly before the contribution is available, entering a long futures position (as a hedge) until the contribution is received can establish the desired position in spite of the liquidity problem.

Finally, some pension funds that pursue active management are finding alpha separation strategies via derivatives attractive. Consider a pension fund that believes the U.S. stock market will underperform non-U.S. stock markets and that thus intends to reallocate to non-U.S. stocks.[5] The fund uses a manager it believes is a good stock picker, but the manager invests only in U.S. stocks. Derivatives allow the fund to

1. Leave the current allocation of funds with the U.S. manager.
2. Sell stock index futures (or enter a swap) to reduce exposure to U.S. stocks.
3. Go long a non-U.S. stock index via a swap or futures swap contract to increase exposure to non-U.S. stocks.

In steps (1) and (2), the market risk of U.S. stocks is neutralized but the manager's selection skills—his or her alpha—remains. Step (3) gives the immediate exposure to non-U.S. stocks desired.

SECOND-GENERATION DERIVATIVES

As if the world of derivatives were not complex enough, a whole new wave of derivative products has emerged, and more will come. These derivative contracts are referred to as second-generation derivatives. A few of these are discussed in this section.

Barrier Options

Barrier options are options that come alive or are extinguished when a barrier on the underlying asset or index is crossed. For example, an up-and-out call option may be in-the-money until a barrier price is reached, at which time the call becomes worthless. This type of call has a lower premium than an ordinary call, which has no barrier; thus it may be attractive to a pension fund manager who wants to take a very short-term long hedge with calls but considers standard calls too expensive. For a pension fund manager writing calls to generate fee income, the up-and-out may be attractive because it caps the writer's potential loss.

Compound Options

Compound options are options that give the holder the right to purchase standard options. On exercise, the combined premium will be relatively high, but if the compound option expires out-of-the-money, the loss is much smaller. Consider using a call option on a put option to protect a portfolio or asset. If the under-lying falls in value and stays down, the put can be called and exercised to offset the loss. If the underlying falls but then rises again (or if the underlying stays the same or goes up in value), the call on the put is worthless but the premium lost is small.

Swaptions

A swaption is an option to enter into a swap—to take one leg or another—and it gives the holder the flexibility that a swap takes away. If subsequent events warrant it, the holder may exercise the option and enter the swap. If not, the holder lets the option expire.

There are many more derivatives; for example, exchange-traded FLEX options, which give writers and holders the right to negotiate various terms; structured notes, which allow investors to take specific interest rate views; and credit derivatives, which allow investors to increase or decrease credit exposure and thus effectively separate interest rate risk and credit risk. This "product differentiation" is driven by the demand for better or more specific risk management tools. As such, it generally is an economically productive activity; however, any specific contract may have no value whatsoever for a specific pension fund.

CHOOSING AMONG THE ALTERNATIVES

Options, forwards, futures, swaps-diversification, market risk, immunization—lions, and tigers and bears, oh my! How do you choose from among the number of tools and strategies available to manage risk? The starting point is good policy: what is the pension fund trying to accomplish, and how much investment and surplus risk can the fund tolerate? The next step is to apply sound investment fundamentals—to diversify—and to carefully analyze all the risks that the fund must address to avoid a knee-jerk reaction to perceived risk rather than a thoughtful assessment of the real risks that are actually present.

Pension fund sponsors and managers should view derivatives as tools that may from time to time be cost-efficient alternatives to trading primary assets to achieve desirable exposures. As a general rule, the longer the time period for which a given exposure is desired, the less attractive derivatives should be. Derivatives are a sensible means of rebalancing portfolios to restore target weights and constructing temporary hedges. For pension funds that pursue active management strategies with all or a portion of their assets, derivatives are useful in a number of ways (for tactical asset allocation, alpha separation, etc.).

When it is appropriate to use derivatives, pension fund managers, administrators, and other decision makers should ask the following questions:

- What is the nature of the underlying asset or liability? Does a matching contract exist? If not, what correlation risk exists?
- How liquid is the contract? How easy will it be to reverse the initial position?
- What are the broker costs and other fees?

- How desirable would it be to enter a customized contract and give up some liquidity?
- What is the most desirable payoff structure? For example, if a pension fund wants to reduce investment risk, a partial list of alternative strategies and payoffs includes

  - buy puts: pay a premium but keep the upside potential
  - sell futures: pay no premium but get no upside potential; face the possibility of margin calls as the contract is marked-to-market
  - buy puts on a futures contract: pay a smaller premium and keep the upside potential

- What length of time are you concerned with? For long time periods, investing in and rebalancing directly with the underlying is probably the best route. For shorter time periods, or in the face of restrictions that discourage direct positions, derivatives may be the best route. Be aware that the mismatch between a strategic time horizon and the shorter maturities of many derivative contracts introduces the risk that the derivative position may not be achievable when rolling over into a new set of contracts. Consider that

  - swaps commonly have maturities of five years or more and may go to twenty years
  - futures commonly have maturities up to two years
  - options have maturities of up to several months, although special option products such as long-term equity participations (LEAPs) and FLEX options have considerably longer maturities

- How available are quotes for accurate pricing?
- How is credit risk controlled? Are the contracts marked-to-market? How often?
- What denominations are normally available?
- What is the nature of the contractual obligation? For example, option writers must perform; option buyers have the right but not the obligation to perform.

CONCLUSION

Pension fund managers and decision makers should be cautious of new financial technologies and derivative products. First, the risk characteristics of the product may not be relevant given the pension fund's exposures. Second, it can be very difficult to understand fully the price and risk/return profiles of new products. An overpriced derivative is no bargain; nor is a derivative with unanticipated payoffs.

Derivatives should be used when appropriate, but their use should, as with all other important variables in pension management, be governed by policy and be subject to the appropriate controls and oversights. Acceptable hedging activities, instruments, goals, and times should be clearly defined in writing. Return enhancement and view-based strategies should be permitted only if the fund permits active management, and then they should be constrained to the type of strategies acceptable to the fund. Carte blanche authority should not be granted except within the confines of a leveraged vehicle such as a hedge fund or a managed futures program limited in exposure to the assets committed. Moreover, it is critical that the top management of a pension fund advise, in writing, all the brokers and money managers with which it does business what derivative contracts and strategies are acceptable—and under what circumstances—and which are not. These parties should be required to report when these written guidelines are violated.

The presence of derivatives in a portfolio does not necessarily increase or decrease the risk of that portfolio. Remember, derivatives offer leverage, a two-edge sword. This leverage can increase risk or decrease risk. Thus, derivatives must be carefully evaluated so that an unintended shift in the fund's risk/return profile does not occur: hedges that are not monitored can quickly become speculative adventures.

Derivatives are here to stay. They are versatile, they are cost-efficient, and they offer temporal advantages that may be valuable from time to time. The proper use of derivatives is commonly accepted as sound practice and arguably is evidence of prudent behavior. The potential for misuse of derivatives, however, should not be ignored. Catastrophes have happened; more will come. All in all, derivatives can add value to pension management and should be used—wisely, prudently, and as part of the overall pension management strategy.

PART V

Management Issues: Decisions, Strategies, and People

18

Selecting and Managing
Asset Managers

The effective management of a pension plan requires managing the people who manage the plan's assets. This involves selecting, monitoring, compensating, and if necessary, replacing money managers. These choices have a significant effect on the investment performance of the plan's assets. Thus, they significantly affect the funding status and future contributions required for DB plans and the accumulations for DC plans. For all pension plans they are an important aspect of due diligence and the fulfillment of other fiduciary responsibilities.

The decisions discussed in this chapter are typically made by pension plan boards or senior management. The decisions are sufficiently similar for DB plans and DC plans, so no distinction between plan types is made here.

Of central importance is whether the sponsoring organization should manage the pension plan internally or seek external managers. Once this is decided in the abstract, the pension sponsor must implement the decision by finding the most suitable money managers, must establish appropriate control procedures to ensure that the job is being done in accordance with policy, and must develop policies for such matters as manager compensation and, if need be, the termination of money managers.

INTERNAL VERSUS EXTERNAL MANAGEMENT

Some authorities argue that nonfinancial organizations should stay with the nonfinancial strategies in which they have expertise rather than trying to manage investment assets directly.[1] Anecdotal evidence from organizations that were designed for one purpose but that are actually investing as a sideline—such as in the case of Orange County, California—supports this position. However, there are consequences of going outside for expertise. For example, the costs of monitoring and control will be higher.

Most pension plans employ outside money managers. (Note that sponsors that hire external managers must still have competent investment personnel in-house to help formulate and implement policy and to manage the outside managers.) It also is common to manage some assets in-house and contract other assets out. One reason for hiring external managers is that money management enjoys substantial scale economies—$1 billion in assets can be managed at little more expense than $100 million—so sponsors may often find they can buy outside management for less than it would cost to develop and use inside management. In addition, the most skillful money managers will want to work where the pay is highest. Because a lot of money can be managed with little more effort than managing a small amount of money, the very best money managers can make significantly higher incomes working in dedicated money management firms managing large pools of assets rather than working for sponsors directly. Corporate, public, or union internal salary scales also can create constraints under which plan sponsors may be unable to pay competitive salaries to skilled money managers. Although some very large pension plan sponsors have circumvented this issue by establishing an internal money management company that is treated as an independent entity, most pension funds would generally find it more politically expedient to hire external money managers and pay them fees based on the amount of money managed (and, sometimes, on investment performance).

Note also that some plan sponsors may view the use of outside money managers as a form of legal insurance, as these managers, particularly those who manage the money of many other clients as well, would be difficult to question on grounds of fiduciary prudence. Thus, many pension plan sponsors believe they are less likely to be sued either by employees or by the Department of Labor over the investment choices a well-regarded outside manager might make than they would be to be sued over choices made by an internal manager.

One disadvantage of using external management is the question of control: it is easier to monitor and control internal managers. Similarly, it is easier to be certain that internal managers who promise to pursue a specific investment discipline or style do not end up doing something that is altogether different. Of course, even internal managers may pursue unjust enrichment or career advancement at the expense of the pension plan.[2] This profiteering may be as simple as empire building or as involved as collusion with outside providers of pension services through kick-backs or other schemes. Therefore, internal managers must be monitored as well. This is easier to do, however, as the sponsor should have access to better and more readily available information than is the case with external managers.

The issue, then, boils down to three matters. Does the plan sponsor have the resources and inclination to manage pension assets internally? Is the sponsor willing to bear the costs of maintaining and evaluating external managers? Is the sponsor willing to bear the responsibilities of internal management, or does it prefer to shift the responsibility to outside agents?

Hiring Internal Managers

The profile of a competent senior internal manager must include extensive knowledge of and background in the money management industry as well as strong people and communication skills. The investment profession has become very quantitative in recent years and has benefited greatly from numerous scientific advances in theory, empirical studies, and computer support systems. Thus, an appropriate educational background (specialization in finance and economics) is essential. Similarly, evidence of broad-based, relevant knowledge is desirable. One way for a manager to demonstrate this is by gaining the CFA designation—the current professional certification in the investment industry. Holders of the CFA designation have completed a self-study program; have passed three day-long examinations, each six months to one year apart; and have demonstrated work experience in investment decision making. The examination process is rigorous (in recent years, around 50% of candidates fail to pass the Level I and Level II exams) and comprehensive (it includes ethical and professional standards, economics, analytical methods, portfolio management, derivative instruments, and so forth). Note that competency as an investment manager per se is not assured by the CFA designation; rather, mastery of a broad-based body of relevant knowledge is demonstrated. Beyond such quality signals, sponsors should look closely at relevant work experience (management of similar-sized portfolios and similar types of assets) and familiarity with the current research in investments.

The other skills required by internal investment managers have to do with the ability to manage the people who make up the investment management team (analysts, accountants, clerical staff, and so forth) and to communicate effectively with staff and with senior management and trustees. The senior investment manager must understand the importance of hiring competent people and training them as necessary. Pension sponsors should want a management team that is not dependent solely on one or two individuals for successful investment management. Rather, the team should be a unit with several skilled people involved in decision making so that the team survives the departure of any one person. In addition, the senior manager should appreciate the importance of complying with policy and effectively communicating with his or her superiors on an ongoing basis about the implementation of policy and results of various decisions.

Selecting External Managers

Selecting an external manager differs considerably from selecting an internal manager because the "manager" is typically a firm, and because firms frequently specialize by asset class and whether they are active or passive managers. The fundamental task of the pension plan sponsor is to choose those money managers who are best suited to manage within the framework of asset allocation considered optimal for the plan. This can be done only after the plan sponsor has determined exactly how much risk is appropriate for the plan to bear and what the allocation of assets will be among actively managed strategies and passive or index strategies.

A related challenge is to choose managers who will actually stay within the boundaries that the sponsor sets, and who, perhaps as important, continue to use the same style or analytical methods that they used when they were hired. Many sponsors choose managers because they are convinced of a specific investment philosophy's usefulness and of the quality of the techniques applied to achieve that investment approach. Thus, sponsors do not want money managers to change the investment techniques without notification and approval.

After a sponsor is satisfied that a particular style or strategy is a good one, the sponsor must next be confident that the money manager can provide continuity of implementation. That is, the sponsor must be assured that the money management firm can survive the loss of one or two key employees and remain faithful to its espoused analytical principles.

A host of other factors that sponsors should consider are listed in Appendix G. All potential managers should answer the general questions listed in the first part of the appendix; the second part provides specific questions for fixed-income and equity managers. Once the answers are collected, they must be analyzed. Unfortunately, as they can be weighed only subjectively, they are subject to all the biases of those doing the selection.

A common practice in virtually every investment manager search is to require potential managers to provide at least one and possibly more historical measures of investment performance for many years in the past. Olsen points out that the correlation between a manager's past and future absolute performance is extremely low.[3] He suggests several factors that should be considered when analyzing past performance. For example, have the assets under management grown so much that the manager's ability to manage is called into question? This is especially important for managers who built records on small stocks because managers with more assets to manage may have to increase the number of stocks they own or increase the proportion of a stock's outstanding shares held.

An alternative to using the historical record in the selection of a manager is to evaluate what a manager *will* do rather than what he or she *has* done. Consider, for example, using an untested but appealing investment model. According to some commentators this may result in hiring managers that produce better investment results.[4] The basic argument for this method is that markets are efficient enough that whatever worked in the past is unlikely to work in the future. Thus, what may work must necessarily be unproven by a prior track record.

Those who hire external managers should be careful to avoid the "common wisdom" that may be circulating. For example, a popular misconception is that small money management firms achieve better investment results than large investment firms. There is no substantive evidence to support this notion, however, and it is likely to be a consequence of survivorship bias. Some startup investment management firms do well; others do poorly. Those that do poorly lose accounts and leave the business very quickly, sometimes even before they have enough years of operating results to leave a measurable investment performance footprint. Accordingly, when one compares the investment records of small investment management firms with large ones, one is really comparing the historical investment results of successful startups to those of large firms.

Further, some surviving smaller firms may have benefited from taking risky bets that fortunately paid off. Larger firms, by virtue of their size and prior reputation, may be better able to survive a period of poor performance than a small firm. Thus, although it may seem as if small firms do better, no findings substantiate the claim that small firms will be better investment managers in the future.

Note that investment management firms may become so large that diseconomies of scale may set in. Service may worsen. One-size-fits-all reporting may be the norm. Worse still, the desired investment strategy or style (such as investing in small company stocks or emerging market stocks) may not be implemented with the same results if the assets under management are too large.

The final step of the external manager decision is determining how many managers (firms) should be hired. The more managers, the higher will be the costs of monitoring what they do. Further, more managers means that unusually good or unusually poor performance by any one manager will be diluted and will thus will not have much effect on the total asset pool. Pension funds aiming for unusually good performance may be well advised to concentrate their efforts in a very few firms (taking care to achieve adequate diversification, of course), and those seeking "normal" performance may also choose a very few firms in forming passive, index portfolios. Overall, the trend is toward hiring fewer firms and hiring firms with multiple investment products (e.g., bond managers as well as stock managers). Given the difficulty and cost of monitoring, as well as the importance of monitoring the total portfolio, having fewer managers is a sound approach.

Often sponsors will hire consultants to help conduct manager searches. As with hiring outside managers in general, turning to consultants is perceived by some sponsors as a form of liability insurance: a way to demonstrate to others that they made a reasonable effort in due diligence. Overall, consultants provide a useful source of benchmarking information on what other, similar pension funds are doing (e.g., the number of managers that are being used) and how the various money management firms have done historically.

MONITORING AND CONTROLLING MANAGERS

Once investment managers are chosen, the senior managers, trustees, and others who represent the sponsor and plan beneficiaries must remain active in the management of the asset managers. Because it is the performance of the total portfolio that matters, their activities must be coordinated. Also, as managers, internal or external, may or may not do what they are supposed to do, or do it as well as they are expected to, their investments and actions must be monitored. Thus, plan sponsors must develop control systems to ensure conformance to policy and to provide timely feedback for performance evaluation.

Written Controls

The first lines of control are the pension plan's investment policy statement and investment guidelines. The policy statement indicates what level of risk is acceptable for the overall plan, and operationally, it defines which asset classes the plan will hold, what the target policy asset allocations are, and the extent of deviation from the targets that is tolerable. It also explains how the relationship between money managers and the sponsor will be managed.

When using multiple managers, the sponsor needs to develop explicit guidelines for each money manager. These guidelines should spell out very clearly what investment strategy the sponsor expects each to follow, what analytical or investment techniques are to be used in implementing that strategy, and what derivative instruments (such as options or swaps) are acceptable. The guidelines should also indicate how much discretion the investment manager has to shift back and forth among asset classes and should give specific attention to allocations in cash and other short-term money market instruments. For example, if the sponsor wants to be fully invested in a specific sector at all times, that requirement should be indicated. If some percentage of cash holdings is tolerable, the maximum percentage of assets that can be held in cash should be specified. The guidelines should specify how the manager's performance will be assessed and how management and incentive fees will be computed. The frequency of communications from the manager should be defined as well as the content of those communications. The guidelines might also indicate what actions would prompt the sponsor to fire a particular investment manager.

Finally, the sponsor may want to play a role in the investment managers' trading activities. For example, the sponsor may find it advantageous to require money managers to "advertise" both offers to sell and what they wish to buy to all the other money managers working for the sponsor. This could allow savings on brokerage commissions and could economize on market impact costs. Payment for order flow and its related issues have become increasingly important and should be addressed so that there are no hidden costs of trading (this is discussed in detail later in this chapter).

Monitoring Managers

Once the investment policy and investment guidelines are written and investment managers have been chosen, the sponsor must remain active by monitoring the managers' behavior. Monitoring should have as its goal ascertaining compliance with policy, evaluating performance, and ensuring that managers are not misappropriating the pension's assets through poor decision making or even unethical behavior.

Getting the right information at the right time is essential to any control system. For pension fund sponsors and managers, this implies regular communication between manager and sponsor. The sponsor must be concerned not only with the absolute performance (i.e., the risk-adjusted rate of return net of costs) of each money manager but also with his or her relative performance. Many pension plans hire consultants to help evaluate managers using techniques like those described in Chapter 14. These consultants have databases of managers and can construct customized benchmarks against which a single money manager may be compared. It may be some comfort to know that, although a particular manager working for a pension plan sponsor lost money last year, the rate at which he or she lost money was either lower than the rates of most of the other managers who were identified as pursuing a similar investment policy or lower than that of the appropriate benchmark.

The primary concern for the sponsor is what one does with the data being generated. If an investment firm produces a poor record of investment performance, for example, what does that imply for the future? Perhaps the poor record was produced by a manager who failed to conform to investment policy. Perhaps the manager demonstrated gross incompetence. Perhaps also the poor performance could have been avoided if the sponsor had not committed funds to a poor or out-of-favor strategy. Perhaps the data show that the manager did not follow the fund's investment policies and guidelines.

It is compliance with policy that is at the heart of accountability. On a quarterly basis, the sponsor should require the manager to demonstrate that the investment portfolio conforms to previously specified policy parameters, including allowable assets and proportions, investment strategy and style, appropriate use of derivatives, trading costs, proxy voting, and the other major elements of policy. Annually, the manager should be prepared to review policy and investment decision making with the sponsor.

As with the management of assets, the responsibility for monitoring should not be delegated away completely. Consultants can help, but the ultimate responsibility rests with the sponsor.

Audit Committee

A useful monitoring tool is a pension audit committee. This committee can ensure that the overall pension investment process follows a systematic, rational approach by participating in both policy formulation and monitoring of compliance and of the results of various decisions. An additional advantage to having an audit committee formally involved in both the planning and monitoring process is that it encourages establishing performance goals ex ante and provides for a formal review against this prior standard. Obviously, success in market forecasting or security selection is not the goal; developing sound investment policy and adherence to that policy is. The audit committee can oversee the sponsor–anager relationship and participate in developing standards both for what needs to be communicated and for the timing of that communication.

COMPENSATION OF EXTERNAL INVESTMENT MANAGERS

External managers' compensation is subject to negotiation. There are, generally speaking, three ways to structure compensation: a fixed-dollar payment, an asset-based fee (a percentage of the assets under management), and incentive fees (compensation that varies with investment performance). Fixed-dollar fees are virtually unused in the United States. Prior to November 1985, before the Securities and Exchange Commission allowed incentive fees, most investment managers of large portfolios were compensated with asset-based fees. Asset-based fees remain the norm. These fees range from two to ten basis points for the major market equity index funds available to DB plans, to perhaps 100 basis points or more for actively managed foreign equity portfolios, and to perhaps

200 basis points for private equity such as leveraged buyout funds and venture capital funds (in addition to performance bonuses or carried interests of up to 20% of the profit above a benchmark return).

Incentive fees have become more popular: more than 20% of all plan sponsors seek incentive fee arrangements with their money managers. Incentive fees are quite complex and, hence, are tough to implement. First, the sponsor and the investment manager must agree on what constitutes a suitable investment performance benchmark, and the trigger that activates the incentive fee must be determined. Second, the incentive fee formula must be specified. Specifically, it must be determined what the base fee, the bonus formula, and the fee limits are. Third, the time period over which performance will be measured to determine the fee must be established—the Securities and Exchange Commission has set a one-year minimum. Finally, all parties must realize that firms having incentive arrangements with some clients and not with others may find their loyalties divided. This can create serious problems.

Incentive Fees and Risk

The have been studies of how managers behave when their compensation is tied to relative performance. One study looked at 334 mutual fund managers from 1976 through 1991.[5] It found that managers who are midyear "losers" tend to increase the volatility of their portfolios during the second half of the year. This increase in risk is greater than the increase seen in a comparable group of midyear "winners." A more recent study also found that managers with incentive fees increase risk after periods of poor performance. It also found that funds with incentive fees take on more risk than funds without incentive fees, and it found evidence that incentive fees encourage good stock selection ability.[6]

This evidence of possibly excessive risk-taking is important. With incentive fees, when investment performance has been poor, managers have an incentive to improve overall performance by betting heavily on a few very risky assets; the gamble is worth the risk to the manager, who otherwise stands to lose the race—and have the assets taken away by angry clients—at year end. The implications of this for pension funds is that managers who are doing poorly may attempt to maximize their compensation by taking on riskier investments—a strategy that may not be in the best interests of the pension plan. If the risk pays off, the manager gets paid the incentive fee; if the risk does not pay off, the manager may be in no worse shape than would have been the case had the risk not been taken. Thus, the plan sponsor must develop methodologies to monitor investment managers to ensure that they do not alter (generally, increase) portfolio risk beyond that permitted by the pension plan to enhance the likelihood of receiving a performance-based fee.

MANAGING THE TOTAL ASSET POOL

All too frequently, pension funds fail to manage the overall set of managers they use—no one manages the managers or the total portfolio.[7] This can lead to paying too much for the net result obtained, inadvertent indexing, and unintended exposures to market sectors or styles.

What a pension plan pays to investment managers as compensation should be justified by the value the plan receives in investment performance. Thus, the after-fee performance of an active manager should exceed the performance of a portfolio that can be attained passively. However, it is not uncommon for a plan to pay relatively high fees to active managers but receive after-fee performance on the subportfolios managed that is substantially inferior to what could be achieved with an index fund. When these subportfolios are added together, of course, the performance of the total asset pool is poor as well. This mistake is a costly one, to be sure. The only way to avoid it is to monitor performance carefully and to switch to better managers or to indexed portfolios if the after-all-costs performance fails to match or exceed a reasonable passive benchmark.

A related mistake frequently occurs when pension funds use so many different managers and styles that the total pool of actively managed assets has simply become "the market." Closet indexing, as this is known, is an easy trap that catches many an unwary investor. The result of getting caught in this trap is poor net of fee performance under nearly all conditions, a result that is simply unacceptable. The trap may be avoided by taking care to evaluate the total pool of pension fund assets as one portfolio from time to time rather than always focusing solely on the component portfolios run by individual managers.

Finally, pensions that use active external managers but forget to examine the overall portfolio periodically end up taking unintended style exposures so that they inadvertently become under- or overweighted in a sector or asset class because of their choice of managers or their managers' choices of investments. Not surprisingly, a new money management product has appeared to remedy this problem: the completeness fund.[8] Providers of completeness funds analyze pension benchmarks and identify areas in which the actual portfolio is underweighted. The manager then acquires assets in these sectors, presumably to return the overall portfolio to its intended exposure. Critics argue that these funds simply contribute to expensive closet indexing and unusual holdings in the completeness subportfolio. Advocates argue that completeness funds focus the attention of the fund on the total asset mix and take appropriate action when it gets out of line.

REPLACING MANAGERS

Greenwich Associates estimates that 25% of U.S. pensions replace one manager every year.[9] What justifies this relatively high turnover? How do pension boards and senior managers make sensible decisions about terminating managers? What special problems should be anticipated in asset custody?

There are several reasons that a pension fund should terminate and possibly replace a current manager. First, the objectives and thus the needs of the fund may change. This change may lead to a change in the types of managers needed. Second, a manager may fail to conform to plan policy and investment policies provided. For example, the manager may change his or her investment style, fail to vote proxies in the interests of the plan beneficiaries, or maybe use soft dollars in ways that do not benefit the plan. Or the manager may not provide timely information on performance or other matters as required.

Third, the manager's investment performance may not be good enough on a risk-adjusted basis. Care should be taken to use appropriate benchmarks and reasonable evaluation periods, of course. Note that the better the design of the benchmark, the less time is needed to make a judgment. Note also that passive managers should track their benchmarks closely, and short-term deviations should be questioned. Active managers, however, are less likely to track their benchmarks in the short term, so some judgment and patience may be appropriate.

Fourth, the manager may be too costly. Management fees may be excessive, or trading costs may be too high. In general, performance figures reflect trading costs, but they may not reflect management fees, so the sponsor must be vigilant. Finally, the pension board or senior management may change its view on the merits of active versus passive investing or on the management of the risks the fund faces. Such a change will be likely to require a new set of managers, who will deliver the new strategy.

A fundamental problem in deciding whether to terminate a manager is that there is no good way to distinguish in the short run (say, within any period of less than three years, or twelve quarters) whether poor investment performance is the result of bad luck, whether an investment style or strategy was for a time being unrewarded, or whether the managers really are implementing the strategy well. Accordingly, most pension plan sponsors establish rules of thumb. One rule is to stick with a money manager over a market cycle—from a bear market through a bull market to the next bear market. If over the entire cycle the investment performance remains absolutely and relatively poor, the manager gets replaced. If over the cycle the investment performance is satisfactory, the manager will probably be retained. This, of course, presumes that the relative performance is tolerable. Significant underperformance relative to a fair benchmark can destroy value rapidly: if the manager is significantly underperforming a fair benchmark, it is a good bet that the manager is making poor decisions.

Termination and the Reinvestment Problem

When a manager is terminated, some special problems arise. If the investments of the fund are held by a trustee or custodian in the fund's name, there may be some book entry transactions, but no liquidation and reinvestment problem necessarily arises. Securities purchased by the terminated manager that are to be sold may be presented to other managers to see whether they are appropriate for their portfolios. Those that are not typically will be liquidated. The terminated manager should not conduct the liquidation. If there are large blocks of securities to sell, an orderly liquidation should be planned to reduce market impact costs (see the next chapter). If large blocks of securities will be liquidated, options or other derivatives may be useful in "locking in" a price for the securities. In addition, the fund should maintain its strategic asset allocation throughout the transition by using futures or other derivative contracts to avoid the drag on returns created by excess cash balances. Brokers can be offered commissions that allow them a share of gains realized on an orderly sale to reduce market impact and commissions.

CONCLUSION

Pension plan management requires real management. Indeed, for many sponsors, pension assets are the largest pool of assets the sponsor manages. Thus, managing these asset pools properly is imperative. Paying too little attention can be disastrous. Good management, however, can result in effective investment decision making, efficient management of resources, and better value for the resources consumed by pension funds and the pension industry.

Selecting and monitoring investment managers is a central issue. Pension plans are recognizing how costly it is to control thirty or forty external managers and are appropriately cutting the number of managers they use, often dramatically. Similarly, funds are becoming more responsible in taking the lead, supported by pension consultants, in demanding accountability and conformance with policy. These are steps in the right direction.

Monitoring investment managers is not easy. Control activities take time and consume resources. There are significant measurement and information problems. Further, as noted earlier, it is very often difficult to disentangle luck from competence. This makes it especially difficult to decide when to change money managers.

Regardless of the difficulties, control is an issue for which top pension plan managers should have well-articulated, preferably written policies in place before they are needed. Only through control can sponsors ensure that the policy they have decided on is being followed. A good investment policy out of control is, of course, no policy at all. The costs of lack of control may be high: increased liability for pension fiduciaries and higher contributions for the sponsor are the likely result.

19

Managing Costs

The effective management of a pension plan requires managing the costs of asset management. This involves understanding and ultimately controlling the costs of investing: the costs of trading, custody, and so forth.

In a recent survey, a significant fraction of institutional investors admitted that they did not monitor trading costs,[1] yet the potential benefits are enormous. According to the 2001 New York Stock Exchange Fact Book, member firms realized $26.8 billion in revenues from commissions and nearly $25.2 billion from trading in 2001. The fact that the market makers make so much shows that trading carries a large cost to regular investors.

Costs matter to both DB and DC plans. Transaction costs erode portfolio value. Thus, a trade must be motivated by an investment idea that adds more value than is destroyed or by a constraint such as liquidity that overrides the cost of the trade. To ensure that more value is added than is destroyed, pension boards and senior management must understand the costs incurred in trading and how they may be controlled.

THE COSTS OF TRADING

The cost of buying or selling exchange-listed securities consists of the commission that must be paid plus an execution or market impact cost. In general, over-the-counter securities are traded net of commissions, but dealers, nonetheless, make a profit from their markups or markdowns—the bid–ask spread. The magnitude of the spread compensates dealers just as commissions take care of brokers. Both of these costs are more or less observable and, hence, measurable at the time of the trade. Market impact costs, however, are not so easily measured. Some authorities have termed these costs the "invisible" costs of trading.

Impact Costs

At this time, serious attempts to measure market impact costs have been made only for equity markets. This is largely because of data limitations. For bonds or real estate, data pertaining to the transaction prices obtained by other investors buying or selling nearly identical assets throughout a particular time frame, or even the transaction prices that occurred just before the transaction in which we are interested, are simply not available. For common stocks, however, there are plenty of data. This is fortunate because common stock trading represents most trading for most pension portfolios.

In a perfectly frictionless market, equally patient buyers and sellers would get together and trade without cost. Communication would be instantaneous and trading would take place continuously. Market impact costs for traders would be zero. If either the buyer or the seller of a security became impatient to do the transaction, however, the other party could take advantage of this and negotiate a price concession.

Impatience can be motivated by an intense need to raise or invest cash (a liquidity motivation) or by what one believes is special but decaying knowledge about the value of the asset (an information motivation). The less patient transactor (let us say the seller) would have to make a price concession as a consequence of impatience, whereas the more patient transactor (the buyer) would earn a slight benefit. The seller's market impact cost would equal the buyer's market impact benefit. Trading would be a zero-sum game between the key transactors.

In the real world, buyers and sellers frequently meet through a third party— generally a broker. Moreover, it may also be true that one side of a transaction is not around when the other side wants to act. Thus, the party that has come to do business will have to offer a concession big enough to induce a prospective trader to do the trade. Frequently it will be a securities dealer who is so induced. The dealer will take the other side in anticipation of being able to square the inventory positions (long or short) when the other party to the transaction finally does arrive. For providing liquidity to a seller or stock to a buyer, the dealer must be compensated.

With dealers included in the market, trading is still a zero-sum game for the entire community. However, dealers make money while investors pay. For buyers and sellers who are not dealers, trading is not a zero-sum game. Nondealers pay dealers for providing immediacy of exchange. Thus, dealers capture the benefits of traders' impatience, but only when they are either as well informed about the asset's value as the impatient trader or when any special information possessed by one or the other party is not really special. The charge for the immediate execution of a trade is going to depend on the inherent riskiness of the stock that is sold or bought and the time that the dealer expects to have to wait before the matching side of a transaction arrives.

Measuring Impact Costs

There is some controversy regarding how the available data might be used to estimate the market impact cost of a transaction. Although there is no consensus as to how market impact costs should be measured, there are several proposed measures of this cost for a particular transaction. Conceptually, the market impact cost is the difference between the price at which the transaction is done and the price that would have been obtained in a perfectly frictionless market—a theoretical but never-observed ideal. One approach to estimating market impact cost is to assume that total transaction costs are equal to the commission plus the difference between the price of the security at the time the decision to buy or sell was made and the price actually realized in the transaction.[2] Unfortunately, although this is conceptually an objective standard—it includes the cost of delay along with the market impact cost—it could be subject to much self-serving manipulation. Beating this benchmark requires buying stocks that go down between decision and transactions. Moreover, its use would require substantial record keeping of a sort that is not currently used in most money management institutions.

Another conceptual approach to estimating market impact cost is to view total transaction costs as the difference in return between the real portfolio and an identical paper portfolio.[3] This approach is appealing for its simplicity and it focus on the reason investors care about costs: their impact on performance.

Finally, there is an approach used in some institutions that considers the market impact cost to be the difference between a traded block's price and the price that prevailed just before the trade, adjusted for market movements. In a sample of transactions, Wilshire estimated the market impact cost at 7.5 cents per share for buys and sells combined. To use this approach, the investor must know which blocks, as reported on the relevant databases, are those of a given investor. That is, the transaction record must be time-stamped so that it can be matched to an explicit transaction in each stock's computerized trading record. It is often impossible, however, to obtain the information regarding time-stamped transactions for any one pension fund. Other problems exist, too. Many money managers manage more than one portfolio. For instance, a money manager may manage a portion of the pension funds for sponsors X, Y, and Z. The manager may decide to sell all of each fund's holdings of a given stock. Assume total holdings are 50,000 shares, with X and Y each holding 10,000 shares and with Z holding 30,000 shares. The manager could trade one entire block of 50,000 shares. Each pension fund would then be told the price, and if time records are kept, each pension fund could compare the price it received in, say, a 1:32 PM trade of 50,000 shares with the trade that occurred immediately before it. Of course, if the prior trade was a big block of stock, then the use of the prior trade as a "frictionless market benchmark" would not be very sensible, for it, too, could reflect large market impact costs. If the prior trade was not itself a large block of stock, however, then the measure—the difference between the block transaction price and the prior price—might at least indicate the true market impact cost, or what the cost of disturbing the true equilibrium is.

Many, and perhaps most, money managers would not sell all the shares at one time unless a 50,000-share order was small relative to the total trading in the stock or the money manager had special, timely information about the stock (more specifically, a reason for being impatient). If neither of these two conditions existed, many money managers would break the 50,000-share order into several smaller ones. Suppose that in this case the manager's trader, with the manager's permission, split the large order into three smaller orders: two of

15,000 shares each and one of 20,000 shares. Suppose the first 15,000-share order sold at $50, the second 15,000-share order sold at $49.88, and the 20,000-share order sold at $49.75.[4] The price that each pension fund would be told it received for the sale would be the weighted average price of the transactions, or $49.86. This makes it impossible for the pension fund to link the price back to a specific transaction that appeared on the computerized trading record tape.

The weighted average price obtained by this money manager and the brokers chosen to do the transactions could be higher or lower than the price other managers or other brokers might have obtained, but the simple methodologies by which market impact costs are assessed do not permit such direct comparisons. Different-size trades could have affected the transaction price relative to the prior trade's price differentially. Further, different rates of trading could also have had an effect on the price at which the transaction was done.

To overcome these problems, there is a measure of execution or market impact costs that compares the actual price achieved on a trade to the weighted average price of the security over the entire course of the trading day.[5] The logic behind the use of the weighted average as a benchmark is this: the weighted average price is the price one would expect if one just fed orders into the system over the course of a trading day. As such, it is analogous to a passive benchmark for measuring stock performance that presumes that the trader has no special knowledge regarding when or how much to trade. Using the weighted average price, the estimated market impact cost on New York Stock Exchange stocks is about $0.02 per share, averaged over buys and sells. Sells were more costly than buys, in part because sell transactions were of larger average size than buy transactions; this also indicates that sellers may be a bit less patient than buyers.

Other approaches to the measurement of market impact costs are commercially available. The SEI Corporation compares the trade price with the stock's closing price on the trade day and for several days thereafter, adjusting, of course, for market movements. Callan Associates computes the market impact cost as the difference in the trade price relative to the average of the high and low prices for the day. Neither of these measures really captures the theoretically ideal notion of using as a benchmark the prices that would occur in a frictionless market. The closing price, SEI's benchmark price, does not seem to be representative of other daily prices, as much trading takes place at the end of the day, with the intent of influencing the price. The high and low prices are themselves likely to be contaminated by large block transactions, for they are likely to occur as a result of large block trades. There is no reason to believe that these two market impact costs (the buys affecting the measured high price and the sells affecting the measured low price) will cancel each other.

Commissions and Total Costs

Another important question is whether there is a trade-off between commissions and market impact costs. In other words, does paying higher commissions obtain better trade execution, resulting in lower impact costs and thus lower total costs?

The Berkowitz, Logue, and Noser study found that commission charges were around $0.07 per share. For the Wilshire sample, commissions were $0.028 per share. Using the method of Berkowitz and associates, total costs were around $0.09, whereas using the Wilshire method, total costs were about $0.103 cents.

Though the specific measures differ, it would not be surprising if traders who generated high total transaction costs under the Berkowitz method also incurred high measured total costs under the Wilshire measurement system, for there seems to be at least a mild, partial trade-off between commission charges and market impact costs. Most studies that asked the question discovered a trade-off between commission charges and market impact costs. Higher commission charges tended to be associated with lower market impact costs, and vice versa. Perhaps the brokers do a better job of finding the other side of a transaction when commissions are higher. Perhaps some brokers will themselves take the opposite side of a transaction for their customers by committing their own capital to a trade, thus lowering market impact costs but requiring higher commission charges to compensate for the risks they bear.

Though a trade-off exists, its quantitative significance is not firmly established. If a $0.01 increase in commission will induce broker behavior—either in the form of a more efficient search or in the form of the broker becoming a principal in the transaction—that leads to a market impact cost reduction of more than $0.01, it should encourage the use of the more expensive brokers. However, if the market impact cost of a transaction is reduced by less than $0.01 for every $0.01 increase in commission charges, then pension plan sponsors should be pressing their money managers to search for the lowest commissions.

The Berkowitz, Logue, and Noser study found that for every $0.01 increase in commission charges, there is less than a $0.01 drop in market impact charges. Thus, fund managers should seek low commissions; paying higher commissions to brokers, even those who commit their own capital to trading, seems not to produce commensurably low market impact costs.

REDUCING TRANSACTION COSTS

To the extent that all measurement systems yield roughly similar results regarding which money managers or which brokerage firms are consistently high or low cost, there should be sufficient information to draw at least moderately strong inferences about the quality and cost of trading. Hence, insight can be gained into how money managers can improve performance, which brokers ought not be used at all, and what sorts of transactions should be avoided.

The lower total transaction costs are, the better the investment performance of the funds being managed, other things being equal. Consider Berkowitz and associates' measure of total transaction costs at roughly a quarter of 1% of the value of each one-way transaction, or half of 1% for a round trip. If a portfolio has a beginning and ending asset value of $100 million and has executed on its behalf trades that are worth $200 million over the year, transaction costs can easily degrade total portfolio investment performance by fifty basis points. If the money manager could figure out how to cut transaction costs in half, investment performance would improve greatly. Indeed, control of transaction costs (e.g., by dealing with less expensive brokers) could contribute much to investment

performance without affecting security selection, allocation, or overall investment strategy.

Beyond selecting low-cost brokers, the obvious way to reduce transaction
costs is to trade less. Trading volume and frequency are functions of liquidity
(because of factors such as receipt of funding, reinvestment of income, and
payments to beneficiaries) and investment strategies (passive strategies have minimal trading and active strategies may have moderate or high levels of trading).
Liquidity is not amenable to much reduction in cost beyond what we have
already discussed. The choice of investment strategy, however, poses some interesting issues.

There is evidence that some active investment strategies may be more cost
efficient than others because, in the ordinary course of implementing the strategy,
they provide liquidity to the market.[6] Liquidity is a service; those who provide
it may charge for it. Other trading strategies, however, may ordinarily be liquidity demanding. These strategies will be, on average, higher in cost, as they
have to pay to acquire the liquidity to carry out their trades. For example,
consider a market in which prices are falling. Contrarian tactical asset allocation
and value investing are likely to be net buyers in a market that needs liquidity
on the sell side. Those who wish to sell in the face of falling prices (e.g.,
portfolio insurers and growth or momentum investors) may have to lower their
offer price to complete their desired trades. The party who buys (the contrarian
tactical asset allocator or the value manager) receives the benefit of this concession.

There are a number of other ways to reduce costs. These include using
crossing networks and limit orders. Trades motivated by information should try
to disguise their intentions to avoid high market impact costs and may be routed
through multiple brokers in an attempt to do so. A pension fund that is trading
simply because of a liquidity need without immediacy, however, may want to
make this known and to trade patiently by advertising for the best price trade.
Finally, derivatives offer a method of reallocating assets and changing portfolio
weights without incurring the costs of the cash markets.

THE IMPACT OF SOFT DOLLARS

In keeping with standards of fiduciary prudence, money spent by a pension plan
should be for the benefit of the pension plan. Nonetheless, many pension professionals feel that much of what gets bought with pension fund money is really
not necessary or does not directly benefit the plan, the sponsor, or the participants. This is because of the issue of soft dollars and directed commissions.
Soft dollars arise when trades are directed to a specific broker for execution. In
return, the broker gives the firm that decides where the trade is executed credits
that may be used to purchase research or other services.

According to Greenwich Associates, 45% of public funds and 32% of private
funds direct commissions in return for soft dollars. They estimate that total soft
dollars are around $0.8 billion of the $2.4 billion in annual commissions paid
by money managers.[7] Thus, this is not a trivial issue. In the best of all worlds,

the buyer of the product or service would have implemented transactions that would have generated this many commission dollars anyway. Soft-dollar arrangements, however, raise two very important issues.

First, does the buyer really need what is being bought? The directed commission approach makes buying a lot of possibly useless analysis very nearly painless, because the true value of the service is masked. Indeed, it is not difficult to imagine instances in which the product or service does not pass a cost-benefit standard on its own; often, what gets purchased merely serves as "fiduciary insurance"—that is, something that would make it less likely for a plan sponsor or money manager to lose a lawsuit brought under the ERISA or other statutes.

Second, soft dollars can obscure the true magnitude of the transaction cost. A buyer engaging in a soft-dollar deal may receive assurances that the commissions charged by the ABC Brokerage Firm are no higher than those charged by any other firm. Thus, the buyer sees the research analysis or other service as virtually free. However, as noted earlier, market impact costs are also an important part of transaction costs. The costs of extremely poor trade executions can far exceed the cash value of the research service. Thus, in many instances it is likely to be true that paying cash for what is truly needed and systematically selecting the broker likely to produce the lowest total transaction cost may be far less costly than the soft-dollar arrangements that may push a sponsor to deal with a brokerage firm that has very high market impact costs.

CONCLUSION

Many erroneously believe that transaction costs and soft dollars are mere "nickels and dimes." Accordingly, very few pension managers or money managers, let alone top managers, worry about them. Moreover, soft dollars generated by commission expenditures have been used like loose change to buy tempting little odds and ends that could come in handy while managing the pension fund, in much the same way that people buy the little things that clutter the areas around supermarket checkout counters because they never know when another disposable flashlight might come in handy.

But huge piles of nickels and dimes are big money. In 2001, there were 308 billion shares traded on the New York Stock Exchange. If it cost only one dime to trade each share, that is a total cost of $30.8 billion. Add to that the cost of trading on NASDAQ (471 billion shares) and the American Stock Exchange (16 billion shares), and it is easy to see how aggregate trading costs can be important. If pension staffs or the firms they hire have to pay cash for pension-related goods and services, these expenditures should not be hidden from top management or top management's auditors. Pension fund managers will be more accountable for using the plan sponsor's funds than they are when they can hide the purchase of some services by purchasing them with directed commissions.

Maybe it was the sight of 25-year-old stock traders for the ABC Brokerage Firm buying $90,000 automobiles that got the (now-jealous) pension managers and money managers to begin to worry about transaction costs as they do now. Or maybe it was the recent attention the SEC has given to the matter. Regardless of the reasons, this is going to be an increasingly important issue for managers. Better measurement systems for the market impact cost of trading U.S. stocks will emerge, and economically meaningful measurement systems for foreign stocks and fixed-income securities may also become available.

Top management, now aware that the magnitude of pension assets exceeds the net worth of many organizations, will begin to realize that the annual transaction costs on a billion-dollar pension fund might be as much as $10 million— 1% of the value of the assets; for many firms or governments with billion-dollar funds this is a very large number relative to such benchmarks as corporate profits and infrastructure needs. Moreover, top management will begin to look more closely at what all their soft dollars are buying. They will begin to monitor directed-commission business much more closely, asking all the while whether paying cash for a service and shopping on Wall Street for the best execution of a transaction might not be cheaper and more effective than continuing to do business as it is done now.

20

People and the Psychology of Pension Fund Decisions

Much of this book is based on principles of traditional economics and finance. Traditional finance has given us some powerful tools and concepts, like arbitrage, efficient portfolio construction through diversification, asset pricing models, and option pricing models. These concepts have served financial decision makers well, leading to more efficient allocation of resources, more informed decisions, and better decisions.

Traditional finance rests in part on assumptions of rational behavior. Rational behavior, to simplify somewhat, presumes that people will behave in a manner that is consistent with maximizing utility. For example, mean-variance utility theory, the basis of modern portfolio theory, says that rational investors are consistently adverse to risk and will choose the portfolio that offers the highest possible return, given the investor's risk tolerance.

Rational behavior also presumes people have unbiased expectations (beliefs) about the possible outcomes that may result from an action. When, for example, people are assessing risk and related factors such as the underlying distribution of stock returns, they will have all the information they need, and they will process it correctly. Further, they will update their beliefs when they obtain new information. They will not be overconfident, nor will they neglect information that fails to confirm their current beliefs.

Over the last 30 years, a small but growing and increasingly vocal group of researchers has begun to challenge many of the principles of modern finance. Why? Simply put, the traditional or "standard" finance models, although they have proven of great value, have left many anomalies that are unexplained.

These "behavioralists" draw heavily from the disciplines of psychology and make extensive use of experimental approaches to answer important questions. For example, they are asking whether people really do try to maximize utility as commonly defined, or if there are other factors or preferences that are not considered in the standard models. The behavioralists have found that many individuals use rules of thumb to make decisions in the face of uncertainty. Unfortunately, these rules are far from perfect and frequently result in systematic, predictable mistakes that are inconsistent with utility maximization.

There also are studies indicating that people act on the basis of biased expectations. For example, there is evidence that people are much more confident in their ability to predict the future than their past record indicates they should be. There are yet other studies indicating that people neglect information that disagrees with their beliefs, or that they pay far too much attention to recent events or small sample results. If people do have biased expectations, they will not understand the true nature of the risks they are facing (that is, they will misspecify the underlying probability distribution) and thus are likely to make poor decisions.[1]

Why should pension managers care about this? It's really quite simple—people make decisions, and people may not be rational in the sense traditional models assume. For example, people may make mistakes in forecasting. If so, it may be possible to improve results by consciously improving expectation formation. Alternatively, people may not conform to the models of utility that economists use to build their theories of "right behavior." People may have preferences other than those that are used to define utility maximization. If so, the models used to construct portfolios or to value assets may be flawed.

The study of whether the models common to modern finance may be based on flawed assumptions is in its infancy. However, there are many useful insights that have emerged that can help people make better decisions. Pension fund decision makers must deal with many complex decisions; these decisions should be made rationally—that is, they should be made in a way that maximizes a sound objective function (such as maximizing the probability that promised benefits will materialize), and they should be based on information that is as complete as possible and that is processed correctly. If not, the consequences can be dire.

This chapter discusses what the field of behavioral finance says about the decision-making process and about the potential pitfalls in that process and also discusses potential systematic mistakes and possible methods for avoiding them. The chapter begins by looking at some of the theoretical issues and then discusses how people involved in pension fund management might make use of this line of thought.

AN OVERVIEW OF BEHAVIORAL FINANCE

Behavioral finance distinguishes between "normal" behavior and "rational" behavior. Normal behavior is what people really do as opposed to what they should do according to the economic definition of a rational person.

Tversky argues that rational decision makers make decisions according to three principles.[2] The first is asset integration—when making decisions, people look at the total portfolio rather than at the parts. The second is risk aversion—people require higher return for higher risk. The third is rational expectations—

people are coherent, accurate, and unbiased forecasters who properly assess all information. On the basis of these principles, traditional finance tells us that rational investors will

- make decisions based on expected returns and variances, focusing on final outcomes;
- consider covariances (evaluating the portfolio as a whole);
- have consistent attitudes toward risk (and be averse to risk); and
- not make cognitive errors.

Observed investor behavior, however, suggests that things may not be so ideal.

Recent research indicates that there are several potential flaws in the way people actually make decisions. In particular, people frequently use rules of thumb that do not work very well, ignoring important aspects of a decision when evaluating what to do. In addition, there is evidence that people may not set goals as economic theory postulates they do—they may have concerns other than simply maximizing utility, and these concerns may affect how they set goals, evaluate alternatives, and ultimately, behave. And, there is evidence that people make numerous cognitive errors and frame decisions in ways that bias their expectations. Finally, there is evidence that principal/agent relationships and cultural influences may affect decision making adversely.

A Mistake: Asset Segregation and Mental Accounting

Rather than making decisions based on the effect of those decisions on the portfolios they manage, people tend to evaluate alternatives one at a time—that is they evaluate investments on an asset-by-asset basis. This segregation of a decision such as, for example, whether to buy high-yield "junk" bonds results in ignoring the covariance among junk bonds and the investor's portfolio. People ask: "Is this investment risky?" and frequently conclude that "Yes, junk bonds are very risky—too risky to be purchased." Instead, the better question is: "How will this investment affect the risk of my portfolio?" If the correlation of junk bonds with the existing portfolio is low and the expected returns are high enough, the addition of junk bonds to the portfolio could actual lower overall risk without reducing overall return.

A variation on this theme is mental accounting. Mental accounting is useful to investors who are subject to temptation because it seems to offer a way to improve control. People who use mental accounting establish separate accounts, with each account dedicated to only one purpose. For example, investors who have problems with self-control may segregate their money into different mental accounts—a capital account for growth and a dividend account for income. At some pension funds, trustees might argue that one pool of money is for the active-lives portion of a plan. For that pool, they agree that they can and even must take some risk to offset inflation. These same trustees, however, define another pool of funds as that for the retired-lives portion of the plan. For this pool, they agree that they should not take any risk at all. Or, a participant in a

DC plan might decide that 401(k) funds are for retirement and therefore no risk should be taken—retirement is much too important!

People who rely on mental accounting frequently have trouble moving money from one account to another—they save for college while borrowing to buy a car. They differentiate between dividends, which may be spent, and capital, which may not be spent.

As with asset segregation, the basic problem mental accounting creates is ignoring covariances among accounts. This substantially increases the likelihood of mistakes in decision making. If the total portfolio is never examined because managers are focusing on the parts, the result could easily be an overall portfolio with too little return or too much risk. There could also be a problem with putting excessive reliance on the plan sponsor to fund the plan because it is important that the retirement assets be "low risk." There could be a host of other problems.

Rational investors in the best sense of the term do not differentiate between dividends and capital; they simply create homemade dividends when they need cash. They evaluate assets in terms of the assets' expected risks and returns, including their correlations with the overall portfolio. They understand that portfolios must be well diversified, or the overall portfolio will be below the efficient frontier.

The result of asset segregation and mental accounting, no matter how well intentioned, is that overall decision making may be poor even though the individual decisions have seemed sensible.

Problems Setting Goals: Loss Aversion and Reference Points

Contrary to standard theory, people appear to be more averse to losses than they are pleased by gains of the same magnitude. This "loss aversion," in which the unhappiness of a loss is greater than the happiness of the same size gain, can impede good decision making.

First, people seem to be unwilling to realize losses even though taking a loss may be the most rational act to take. Consider stocks that have fallen. Investors frequently are unwilling to sell such stocks (taking the loss) even though there may be evidence that the stocks are likely to fall further. Or consider that although taxable investors have an incentive to realize losses—realized losses can be used to reduce taxes paid—many do not do so. (Interestingly, there is also evidence that people sell too soon, apparently satisfied with modest gains even though there may be considerable upside remaining. Further, most "sells" tend to be prior winners; losers are sold less frequently.[3])

There is also evidence that, rather than being consistently risk averse, people prefer risk when they are evaluating losses. That is, they may be more willing to take a risk when facing expected losses than when facing expected gains.

There are several implications of loss aversion for investment policy. First, if people really are loss averse, they may dislike investments with symmetric payoffs (e.g., people may dislike stocks because stocks have a distribution of returns that have equally positive and negative returns). This is consistent with work by

Benartzi and Thaler indicating that investors are unwilling to take the risks of holding equities.[4] According to this line of thought, pension funds that have the ability to bear the risk of equities should invest more in equities than they do, because the sponsor is the residual claimant.

Another implication is that loss aversion may encourage people to define gains and losses relative to a reference point rather than in terms of final outcomes. For example, pension trustees may not focus on long-term strategies. They may prefer instead to evaluate outcomes in terms of short-term gains or losses in terms of the funding status of a plan: will investing in stocks increase the probability of a decline in the plan's funding status over the next twelve months? Or, a person with a 401(k) plan may ignore terminal wealth goals and focus instead on gains or losses relative to the current level of wealth: will investing in stocks mean that the investor might "lose money"? Note that in both of these examples, there is a time dimension. There is nothing obviously wrong with being averse to losses per se. The perversion with respect to decision making is that of fearing losses over short time horizons when the investor should be thinking long term. Decision makers for the DB plan should be evaluating alternatives based, in part, on implications for long-term financial health—not on short term concerns—and 401(k) participants should be evaluating alternatives based on long-term goals such as offsetting the erosion of purchasing power and reducing the risk of outliving their assets. Loss aversion coupled with using inappropriate time horizons can be harmful.

Illusions or Facts? Cognitive Errors and Decision Framing

Effective decision making requires quality inputs and sound decision models to process the inputs. That is, when choosing among various alternatives, one must have reasonable expectations about the range of possible outcomes, and one must also have good models to process that information. Cognitive errors interfere with this process by leading to either biased expectations or an inappropriate model.

Considerable evidence has come to light that people are subject to cognitive illusions and are overconfident in the predictions they make. People seem to have considerable difficulty seeing that they are just like everyone else—that what they see is what others see as well.

Cognitive errors affect investment decision making along a number of dimensions. These errors include

- seeing patterns in data where no cause and effect relationships exist;
- remembering good forecasts while conveniently (and systematically) forgetting poor forecasts;
- overweighting the recent past, leading to a belief that extremely good or bad performance will persist in the future;
- preferring the stocks of good companies, confusing a good company for a good investment (a good investment is one that is available at a good price); and

• concluding that evidence on the past performance of an individual manager is sufficient to decide whether a manager can beat the market (the
willingness to base expectations on a very small sample size can lead
an investor to infer that a manager can beat the market based on his or
her five-year track record, which ignores evidence from numerous studies using larger samples that indicate that the vast majority of managers
cannot beat the market).

Statman provides a nice example of how cognitive errors can lead to poor
decisions.[5] In an efficient market, stocks of good companies and stocks of bad
companies are fairly priced. When a "quality" rating such as that done by *For-
tune Magazine* comes out, there should be no correlation between the rating on
the quality of management and the value of the company as a long-term investment—management quality should already be reflected in stock prices.
However, investors seem to favor companies that are perceived as having high-
quality management and buy these stocks even though these companies also
tend to be large and have low B/M ratios. These attributes are identical to those
found by Fama and French (1992) as characteristics of stocks that provide low
returns.

Statman suggests this is the result of what he calls the "representativeness
heuristic." When presented with two events where one is a compound event, the
compound event must, by definition, be less likely to occur than the single event.
People, however, may judge the probability of the compound event as more
likely than that of the single event—the compound event is being judged based
on the characteristics that are similar to or representative of the single event.
Thus, people may conclude that good companies equal good investments because they are similar. Thus, these "good" companies become overbought and
the share price becomes too high to be justified by any reasonable expectation
of cash flows and earnings. Eventually, the market recognizes and corrects the
mistake, resulting in low (and even negative) returns. Further, this dichotomy of
behavioral versus standard investors might explain why the high B/M companies
ultimately have had high returns—bad companies are mistaken for bad investments and are oversold, and eventually the market recognizes and corrects the
mistake, resulting in high returns.

Decision framing is another source of cognitive errors. Framing refers to how
the frame or context in which investors see a situation influences their investment
decisions. Decision frames can be illustrated by comparing two positions: a long
position in treasury bills and a short position in call options on the S&P 500
index.[6] Investors who use frames will tend to view the option position as the
most risky because they will segregate it from their existing portfolio. However,
the U.S. Treasury bill portfolio is the more risky of the two if an investor who
is trying to reduce risk has a portfolio that is positively correlated with the S&P
500. This is because the options position has a negative correlation with the
investor's actual portfolio. Thus, a short call position reduces risk more substantially than the Treasury bill position does. Rational people who desire to
reduce risk would always choose the option position because they would see

the combined portfolio/option position. Normal people are more likely to frame the decision and see the written calls as riskier than the Treasury bills.

Woods has suggested another way in which decision framing can adversely affect investment decision making. He postulates that the threat of losing assets causes money managers and plan trustees to ignore long-term potential because of concern over the risk of immediate loss.[7] For example, managers who want to keep an account may be unreasonably conservative in attempting to avoid losing money so they will not lose the account. In other words, framing may lead to such excessive loss aversion that good long-term potential gets swamped in concern over the risk of loss. Again, note the time dimension—it is short-term losses that are feared and that drive the decision when longer-term potential is as or more important. Of course, excessive conservatism has a cost—excessively low returns (and possibly too high risk).

In summary, cognitive errors and decision framing may lead to irrational behavior and biased expectations. Biased judgment and overconfidence, in turn, may lead decision makers to neglect evidence that disagrees with conclusions they have reached. In addition, cognitive errors may lead to mistakes such as excess trading and failing to diversify adequately. Cognitive errors may also affect the efficiency of the financial markets and explain why value stocks have outperformed growth stocks over long periods of time.

Dealing with People: The Principal/Agent Conflict and Culture

When agents (managers) work for principals (investors or clients), a principal/agent relationship exists. In any principal/agent relationship there is a control problem that is typically addressed via monitoring. If the monitoring is not effective, the differing incentives of principals and agents may lead to dysfunctional behavior.

One agency issue in investment management is that principals frequently insist on too frequent a review of accounts. The justification is that frequent reviews are necessary for effective monitoring. However, too-frequent reviews may create a short-term mentality that leads to evaluating a manager's performance on short-term results when the manager is (or should be) trying to attain sensible long-term goals. Note that frequent reviews are not in and of themselves inappropriate. The problem is one of what gets reviewed and what is done with the review. Consider an equity manager who has a mandate to beat the market by 200 basis points. It is perfectly appropriate to frequently ask whether the manager is complying with policy, for example, or to examine the manager's performance relative to a carefully selected style benchmark. It is foolish to ask whether the manager is beating the market on the basis of quarterly (or even annual) performance. To do so invites the manager to be the market, rather than to beat the market, as beat-the-market strategies may take time to pay off.

Another agency issue is that many agents, for example, internal money managers at public funds, frequently have much shorter time horizons ("careers") than the investors for whom they work: the managers expect to move on to other jobs at some time. The consequence is that managers make decisions that are likely to have attractive short-term payoffs (e.g., avoiding out-of-favor stocks or underinvesting in stocks) even though pension plan portfolios have much longer time horizons. This problem is exacerbated by too-frequent performance reviews that focus on the wrong metrics. (Many plan trustees share this same problem of having a shorter time horizon than the fund they run.)

Related to the principal/agent problem is work by O'Barr and Conley. What O'Barr and Conley found by applying anthropological research techniques to pension fund decision making is that culture—the shared beliefs and practices that guide individual members of a society in making decisions—affects decision making in pension funds as much as do economics and finance.[8]

One of their findings is associated with what they term "creation myths." These are stories that members of a society use to explain the current state of the world. They are "self-evident," and thus they discourage looking for alternatives. The result is that various structures and strategies are likely to be accepted without being questioned. One possible result is that modestly paid staffs of public pension funds may value security over achievement; this can, in turn, affect the decisions that are made.

O'Barr and Conley also suggest that some pension funds seem to desire to avoid responsibility for making decisions. One way to do this is to develop complex decision-making processes that cannot be identified with individuals. Another way to duck responsibility is to hire large numbers of external managers. This allows blame to be shifted to ERISA and the prudent person standards. Funds that are willing to bear responsibility for their decisions would tend to make small numbers of individuals within the fund responsible for the success or failure of the fund strategies. O'Barr and Conley hypothesize that a fund that clearly identifies who is responsible for investment decisions might have better decision making.

A third cultural influence O'Barr and Conley identify is associated with language and thought. The type of information that is released typically tends to be short term—this crowds out more important long-term "language." Note the similarity of this to the time horizon issues raised above.

Finally, the authors examine the importance of personal relationships (particularly in regard to decisions to fire or retain money managers). From what they were able to discern, these decisions are not quantitative, but are qualitative in nature. Firing managers seems to be rare. Managers may be hired because they will not make those who hire them look bad. The relationship between fund executives and managers is that both have the illusion of control, and both patronize the other.

BEHAVIORAL FINANCE AND DC PLANS

Behavioral research can also help sponsors with DC plans. This research can help sponsors understand how plan participants are likely to respond to alternative plan features and options. Some of this research was discussed in Chapters 11 and 12. For example, those chapters discussed "naive diversification" among plan participants as well as employees' perception of their own company stock. Three additional insights are highlighted here.

First, DC plan sponsors should understand that many participants will follow the "path of least resistance."[9] For example, many 401(k) plans require an employee to fill out a form or otherwise actively initiate participation in the plan. If the employee does nothing, the employee is not enrolled in the plan. Some plans have tried the opposite: these plans automatically enroll employees in the plan. To be excluded from the plan, the employee would have to actively opt out. If the employee does nothing, the employee is enrolled.

It turns out that many employees take the path of least resistance in that they stick with whatever alternative is automatic under the plan. Thus, if a plan automatically enrolls people, few people will actually choose to opt out, and enrollment rates will be higher. If a plan does not automatically enroll people, few people will actively enroll, and plan participation will be lower.

Likewise, if a plan uses automatic enrollment, it has to choose a default contribution rate (what percentage of salary is deferred), and it also chooses a default asset mix. Again, the evidence indicates that many employees will take the path of least resistance. They will stick with the default contribution rate, and they will stick with the default asset mix. The bottom line is that there are no "neutral" plan design choices. For better or for worse, the very design of the plan will influence participation levels and the savings rates of employees.

A second behavioral insight for DC plans is relevant for a 401(k) plan sponsor who wants employees to defer more of their salary to the plan. The employer might first educate employees about the importance of savings—but educated employees may not make optimal decisions. The employer may choose to help the employees increase savings rates by providing some structure to the problem. For example, in a program called Save More Tomorrow,[10] employees choose to increase savings, but the increased deferrals are scheduled to occur in the future. In addition, the increased deferrals occur as the employee's salary increases in the future. Thus, the employee does not sacrifice at the time of the commitment, and it is future pay increases that are committed, not their current salary level. The evidence to date indicates that such a program can increase deferrals to a 401(k) substantially.

A final insight is relevant for a sponsor that wants its employee participants to diversify their 401(k) holdings—for example, a sponsor may want employees to diversify out of company stock. Behavioral insights indicate, again, that the sponsor may help the employees by structuring the problem. An example is Sell More Tomorrow.[11] Under this program, participants would be educated about the advantages of diversification. They would then set a goal for the percentage of company stock they would like to have in their 401(k). A participant with a current 80% allocation to company stock would probably not choose a 0% allocation, but he or she might choose, say, 15%. Then, under the program, the company holdings would be sold off gradually month by month until the individual reached the target percentage. Such a gradual change is expected to be much more palatable to employees compared with a sudden dramatic shift in allocations.

BEHAVIORAL FINANCE AND ACTIVE MANAGEMENT

Several people have suggested that behavioral finance is building a strong case for active management and "beating the market" by taking advantage of the mistakes made by other investors. Is this a reasonable conclusion to draw? If investors are making mistakes, for these mistakes to be exploitable, they must be systematic and predictable. Further, they must be tradable—that is, investors must be able to execute strategies to take advantage of them.

Efficient market theory is based on rational behavior and an absence of frictions to impede trading and information flows. In an efficient market, there are no abnormal risk-adjusted returns available to those who gather and process information because all information is already reflected in a security's current price. If stock prices get out of line with fundamental values, rational investors will buy the underpriced stocks and sell the overpriced stocks, locking in an arbitrage profit and driving prices to their correct values.

Behavioralists point to a large body of anomalies indicating that some groups of stocks earn higher average returns than other groups of stocks after adjusting for risk. These studies indicate to some strategists that the markets may be inefficient. In an efficient market, the observed anomalies should not exist or persist, but they seem to have both existed and persisted over time.

One school of thought is that the anomalies are simply statistical illusions. After all, there are numerous investors looking for abnormal returns, so it seems unlikely to many observers that the competition for profits would allow an anomaly to persist once it has been discovered.

In fact, there may be reasons why prices are not always driven to their fundamental values. As Barberis and Thaler[12] observe, efficient pricing may be impeded by limits to arbitrage. For example, arbitrage may not always be riskless, possibly because of liquidity problems or costs.[13] Thus, although most observers would agree that if prices are clearly wrong, investors would move quickly to exploit the mispricing, limits on arbitrage may interfere and result in prices that differ from values for prolonged periods—that is, even rational traders may not be able to exploit obvious mispricings caused by irrational investors if short-run investment results of an arbitrage are poor and liquidity disappears.

It is important to remember that numerous studies have demonstrated that most professional money managers do not beat the market. Although an analyst may conclude that the market is, in fact, inefficient and that prices regularly stray from their true values, there is considerable evidence that the market is difficult to beat. Thus, take care not to get caught up in the story side of behavioral finance and forget that just because prices may be wrong does not mean that there are $100 bills lying around to be picked up.

CONCLUSION: IMPLICATIONS OF BEHAVIORAL FINANCE FOR PENSION DECISION MAKING

As of the writing of this chapter, behavioral finance offers a lot of interesting stories and anecdotes; theories and operational strategies are somewhat harder to extract. However, there are several useful thoughts behavioral finance can contribute to pension decision making.

A fundamental principal in sports such as golf and tennis is that, to win, you must not make mistakes (or at least not many)—that is, you must get the ball over the net or keep it on the course, or you lose virtually as you begin. One of the clear lessons from behavioral finance is that humans make mistakes. Because we are human, it seems reasonable to conclude that we may be subject to mistakes, and can improve our decision making simply by not making mistakes.

What mistakes might we wish to avoid? What affirmative actions might improve pension decision making? First, in spite of all the interesting stories told by behavioralists and money managers, although it may be possible to beat the market, it will not be easy.

Second, agents may exhibit excessive loss aversion. Thus, if pension funds want agents to act appropriately, they should structure policies that will encourage agents to behave appropriately. If, for example, potential regret may motivate trustees to underinvest in equities, policy should address this. If there are groups of stocks such as low Price/Earnings (P/E), out-of-favor stocks that you may believe are good long-run investments, policy should address this as well. If you believe it is sensible to try to beat the market (see the first point), allow enough time for the strategies you select (or for the managers you hire to implement the strategies) to work.

Third, framing decisions correctly should improve decision making. Framing the decision correctly means avoiding the short-term focus that is so common in evaluating returns. Instead, in the short term, the focus should be on conforming to policy and on returns relative to style benchmarks. Longer term, of course, an active money manager should be able to beat the market if he or she is earning his or her fees. Extending this to DC plans, helping employees and other beneficiaries frame decisions correctly will result in better asset allocations and better performance.

Fourth, decision makers should always look at the entire picture rather than looking at assets on an investment-by-investment basis. Do not ignore diversification—focus on the incremental contribution an asset or asset class makes to a portfolio, not simply the total risk of the asset or asset class.

Finally, decision makers should take care not to underweight "risky" asset classes (e.g., stocks). Back to framing: keep the long-term perspective in mind for DB plans and help employees with DC plans understand the problems that can occur if time horizons are not evaluated correctly.

In summary, the implications of the growing body of behavioral finance research are fairly straightforward—people make mistakes they should not make. This leads to poor decisions that translate into excessive risk and inferior return. Those who are aware of the psychology of investing should be able to improve performance by avoiding mistakes and may be able to improve performance by exploiting the mistakes of others.

21

The Pension Plan as Shareholder

The American Federation of State, County and Municipal Employees (AFSCME) Pension Plan has been active in attempting to get companies to make it easier for shareholders to get their own nominees elected to company boards. For example, it has submitted shareholder proposals, and it has challenged the SEC on these matters.[1] TIAA-CREF (Teachers Insurance and Annuity Association–College Retirement Equities Fund) has been active on the issue of stock-option plans. For example, it successfully sponsored a resolution at Mentor Graphics Corp that asked that any stock-option plans be approved by shareholders. Several pension funds—including the AFL-CIO and the General Board of Pensions and Benefits of the United Methodist Church—successfully backed a resolution at EMC Corporation that required a majority of independent directors.[2]

Pension funds such as TIAA-CREF and the California Public Employees' Retirement System (CalPERS) have been longtime shareholder activists. Other plans are taking their shareholder roles more and more seriously. Should other pension plans follow suit? Should pension plans be more active in monitoring and even working with the managements of the firms in which they own stock? Will such intervention lead to higher risk-adjusted returns after the costs of intervention are weighed?

A fundamental investment problem is that poor corporate performance leads to poor relative or absolute stock performance. This, in turn, can contribute to poor performance for pension funds that own stock in these corporations. Pension fund money managers of pension plans that hold shares in corporations that are not providing acceptable investment returns must decide what to do.

According to Hirschman (1970), there are three alternative strategies that may be followed by pension fund shareholders. These can be summed up in three words: Exit, Voice, or Loyalty. Loyalty occurs when the owner or shareholder takes no actions to monitor or control management behavior but, rather, trusts company management to do what is right. Exit is defined as the purchase and subsequent sale of stock. Thus, trading is a form of shareholder activism. Shareholders demonstrate approval of company management by buying the stock, and show disapproval by selling. In contrast, Voice is the use of ownership power, including voting rights, to affect the direction of the firm in which an investor holds a stake. Rather than selling, the pension plan keeps the stock and attempts to influence the direction of the firm in any of several ways.

Historically, private pension plans primarily have chosen to follow the strategies of Loyalty or Exit. There are a number of reasons why this type of behavior has been so predominant. A growing number of public plans and some private plans, however, are choosing Voice in an effort to boost returns and avoid the potentially high costs of Exit or Loyalty. In part, they feel they must exert their influence to be responsible fiduciaries—to protect the plan's beneficiaries and even the sponsor from poor performance that is correctable—and in part, they feel they must because the costs of Exit are far too high. Today, pension funds own such a large proportion of outstanding shares that many have begun to fear that a precipitous sale would lead to exceptionally large transaction costs, principally the result of the market impact on price of a large block trade. For many pension funds, these transaction costs could be far greater than the cost of trying to correct the wealth-reducing behavior of the corporation.

Even pension funds that are committed to passive investment strategies using index funds face this problem because these index funds must, in turn, hold stocks. If some of the companies in the index can be persuaded to perform better from a financial standpoint, the index portfolio will perform better, too. Of course, larger companies have more of an effect on the value-weighted indexes that are most commonly used, so focusing attention on smaller companies offers less potential benefit.

This chapter begins by providing an overview of how U.S. corporations are governed. The chapter then reviews the empirical work that has tried to determine whether active shareholding actually makes a difference or not. Next, the chapter outlines the alternative strategies that are available to pension fund managers who wish to be more active in the affairs of the companies in which they are invested. The chapter also discusses reasons why some pension funds are not active shareholders and concludes by discussing some practical issues that should be considered by funds that choose to be more active shareholders.

CORPORATE GOVERNANCE

Corporate governance is the process by which decisions are made that determine the direction and performance of corporations. The participants in this decision making are the stakeholders of the company, including the customers, the suppliers, the creditors, the shareholders, the managers, and the board of directors. When discussing issues of corporate governance, particularly in the United States, the primary three participants are the board of directors, the shareholders, and the management.

Effective corporate governance requires "a necessary tension between the freedom of managers to make decisions and take risks yet be held accountable to shareholders, and the freedom of shareholders to buy and sell their interests in the corporation at will, yet hold managers accountable so long as the investment relationship exists."[3] The board of directors has long been considered the intermediary between managers and shareholders. Boards and managers jointly are responsible for designing and implementing the corporate strategy. The board is responsible for representing the interests of shareholders and ensuring that management is effective.

The first regulations passed by Congress that were instrumental in defining these roles were the 1933 Securities Act and 1934 Securities and Exchange Act. The initial model of governance was intended to provide shareholders with the ability to protect their financial interests. The system was designed to operate in a way similar to the American political system, where the shareholders were each voters with one equal vote, the board members were the elected officials, and the corporate charters and by-laws were the governing constitutions.[4]

In practice, the American equity market consists of a broad-based group of investors that are primarily decentralized and not able to monitor their holdings actively and effectively. The cost of a minority shareholder actively monitoring management often outweighs the benefits that are then shared by all shareholders. John Pound of Harvard University describes historical corporate governance in this country in this way:

> [The] American system of governance has never relied on a stable set of close relationships between large financial institutions and major corporations. Rather, it has relied upon no one and everyone—upon the actions of uncounted numbers of individual, corporate, and institutional investors, operating within a deep, liquid, and anonymous securities market.[5]

In contrast, the German, French, Japanese, and to some extent, British systems have relied much more heavily on the close relationships between corporations and financial institutions. This has encouraged some to speculate that, as the amount of assets managed by institutional investors, including pension plans, becomes a larger and larger percentage of the capital markets, the United States system of governance may begin to look more and more like that of other countries.

Central to effective corporate governance is the mechanism for changing the behavior of poorly performing firms: to push corporations to behave economically and to be organizations that are keenly focused on the creation of shareholder value. Until the late 1980s, poor corporate performance was often rewarded with a hostile takeover bid. Indeed, the ease with which hostile bids could be mounted and financed probably served as a deterrent to keep corporations from squandering shareholder money. This is corporate governance in its most extreme form—a contest for control.

This approach has become less common, however, for three reasons:

1. Many corporations have developed new methods of defense from takeovers. Companies and their lawyers have become well skilled at designing amendments to corporate charters that would make hostile takeover bids extremely costly and risky.

2. The raiders of the 1980s provoked considerable political backlash, resulting in significant state regulation inhibiting takeover activity. By
1991, 40 states had enacted laws that militated against hostile takeovers
of companies incorporated in their states.
3. Finally, state and federal laws limiting the amount of non-investment-
grade debt that banks, savings and loans, and insurance companies can
hold made financing hostile takeovers much more difficult and costly.

As a consequence, the market for corporate control no longer plays the same
role that it did in pushing companies to run efficiently and invest wisely.

To compensate for the decline in the efficacy of the market for corporate
control, many legal and financial scholars have urged large institutional investors
to exert their muscle in monitoring corporate behavior and promoting shareholder privacy.[6] Natural players in this game are public and private pension
plans.

ACTIVE SHAREHOLDING

How might pension plans try to influence corporate behavior? There are a number of tactics that can be pursued. These range from those that are relatively
benign to those that are aggressive and even confrontational.

First, pension funds may exert influence on the direction of a firm through
their votes on corporate proxies. They can vote against specific management
proposals. Even if they cast votes for the losing side, they will still have sent
the message to managers that a large shareholder is unhappy with one action or
another. Note that under ERISA, the DOL interprets fiduciary responsibility to
include proxy voting. The responsibility for this voting may be delegated to
investment managers, but plan fiduciaries must periodically review voting procedures and keep adequate records.[7]

Second, pension funds can press to get their own proposals on the proxy
ballot. For instance, they can press for eliminating provisions in the corporate
charter that make takeovers more difficult, or they can push for divestitures that
seem sensible.

Third, pension funds can encourage firms to structure boards in ways that
maintain independence and better align board member interests with shareholder
interests rather than with manager interests. For example, they can encourage
companies to pay board members in stock, as recommended by the National
Association of Corporate Boards,[8] or lobby to get some independent directors
of their choice elected to corporate boards. (Note that independence can be a
subtle concept. Chief executive officers of other firms are frequently touted as
independent when, in reality, their firms may have a business relationship that
can be imperiled by taking a stand against the management they are supposedly
monitoring. Similarly, consultants may be sought for their expertise. The reality
may be that they also do business with the firm and thus have a vested interest
in the status quo.)

Fourth, pension funds can lobby and cajole from the outside. Because this form of active shareholding can be quite adversarial at times, some authorities advocate less adversarial relationship investing.[9] The argument is that large owners should develop a relationship with companies' top managements and boards, perhaps even taking a board seat, to influence corporate decisions quietly without the embarrassment of public shareholder proposals. The result, it is hoped, is better accountability by managers and better communication between managers and shareholders than is currently the case. Relationship investing is similar to the model successfully employed by a number of private equity funds. It may or may not, however, be a productive model for large public corporations.

Examples of Shareholder Activism

Perhaps the most visible proponent of shareholder activism is CalPERS. In the early days of its activism, CalPERS identified companies that paid "green mail" (a form of bribery intended to make a hostile bidder disappear), adopted antitakeover provisions without shareholder approval, or did not use secret shareholder voting mechanisms (thereby opening the way for reprisals by companies against those institutions that voted against the wishes of management). Later, CalPERS switched to a system of simply identifying poor market performers and linking them to a single governance proposal, such as changing management compensation systems or altering the board's composition. Before pressing to get shareholder votes on its proposals, CalPERS tried to meet with the target companies to negotiate an agreement. If no compromise could be reached, CalPERS put the shareholder resolution, even if nonbinding, on the proxy ballot—an action facilitated by the SEC's shareholder proposal Rule 14a-8.

Another example of shareholder activism is provided by the Council of Institutional Investors (CII), a Washington, D.C.–based group of public and private pension plans. The council includes large state retirement funds such as CalPERS and other noncorporate plans such as CREF. CII provides a mechanism by which a practical barrier to activism may be circumvented. It is hard for single institutional investors to own more than 5% to 10% of a company's stock because of SEC registration requirements. However, the SEC's 1992 reforms have made it easier to communicate with other holders of large blocks of stock. This indicates that pension funds can pool their financial stakes by working with other institutional investors to encourage management to behave in desirable ways and to select minority representation on the boards of directors of companies in which they have investments.[10] This pooling, facilitated by CII, helps plans that wish to be active in corporate governance gain a louder voice.

Does Shareholder Activism Matter?

By now institutional shareholder activism has been going on long enough that some empirical work has been possible. Unfortunately, however, because shareholder activism is a recent phenomenon, the empirical studies are concerned with only relatively brief periods of time. What happens over longer periods is simply not known. For example, if a firm's share price does not respond immediately to one or more activist interventions, does this mean there will not be a long-term positive effect? Or, where a positive price reaction is observed, will the effect persist over a longer time period—that is, are changes that are induced by active intervention enduring changes? For now, these questions cannot be answered, but other questions have been addressed.

Two studies suggest that the early stages of pension intervention through the proxy process do not have much effect:[11] there are no short-run price jumps at the time of announcement. Wahal does find a short-run price increase at the announcement of negotiations between firms and large shareholders, however.

Michael Smith studied the most active and vocal pension plan activist, CalPERS.[12] From 1987 to 1993, 51 firms were identified by CalPERS as being unusually poor stock market performers and were targeted for action. For those companies that agreed to change their governance structures in response to CalPERS pressure, there was an increase in share price. For those that refused, the stock price declined at the time of the refusal's announcement. However, despite the stock market's reaction to announcements, Smith was not able to detect a significant change in the operating performance of the affected companies.

Another insightful study has been performed by Stuart Gillan and Laura Starks.[13] They studied the shareholder proposals put forward by a variety of investors—public pension funds, CREF, shareholder groups, union funds, individuals, and churches. In their sample period, the main proposals fell into several categories: elimination of takeover defenses, voting issues, board matters, compensation, and other issues such as divestitures.

Gillan and Starks's results show that in their early sample period, from 1986 to 1989, the announcement of shareholder proposals seemed not to have much effect on stock prices, possibly because the securities markets felt they would not affect corporate behavior very much. From 1990 to 1991, however, the authors find a significant positive stock price reaction to the announcement of public pension funds' proposals. A recent study found evidence that public pension plan shareholder proposals are a negative signal to the market and that they are especially negative for companies that are the targeted more than once.[14] These shareholder proposals may signal to the market that nonconfrontational negotiation is not working with these companies.

Another study evaluated the effect of a shareholders association, the United Shareholders Association (USA), on corporate governance.[15] The evidence shows that when this group targeted a company, its stock price rose after adjusting for risk and the market. More important for current purposes, the rise was more pronounced for companies with large institutional ownership.

Opler and Sokobin showed that companies targeted by the CII have responded to their urgings to change strategies, divest, and alter the composition of boards.[16] In the year after targeting, the earlier poor performers experienced a rate of return on their stocks of 11.6% above the return on the S&P 500 Index. A follow-up study took the group of companies targeted by the CII and divided it into two subgroups: those that were underperforming because of poor decision making (those with "performance slack"), and those that were underperforming for other reasons.[17] The study reported evidence of improvement in stock prices for the subgroup of companies with performance slack.

Finally, Admati, Pfleiderer, and Zechner model large shareholder activism and monitoring technology.[18] They conclude that monitoring by large institutional investors can have good results even though other investors may be getting a free ride.

If these results are indicative of sustained improved performance in the future, then the current shift in corporate governance toward activism could result in more efficient, better-performing companies that will, in turn, produce better stock market returns. This, in turn, should lead to better pension fund performance. Although some risks of institutional abuse may exist, these risks are probably outweighed by the potential gains from the elimination of the current management abuses that already exist as a result of passive investor governance. It is really too early to say for certain, however, given the limited history of activism and data available for analysis. In general, solid evidence on long-term results is not yet available. It is one thing to observe a positive abnormal return resulting from a price increase attributable to shareholder activism. It is another altogether to be able to say that firms will restructure, will allocate resources more efficiently, and will develop more sensible business strategies over the long term because of shareholder activism. As the current changes in governance evolve, there is the hope that the management/shareholder tension that Ira Millstein suggested is "the heart of corporate governance" will find its optimal level.

The Downside to Active Shareholding

Those pursuing or contemplating active shareholding should be aware there may be a downside to active intervention. There are two areas of concern: one concerns the judgments that may be exercised: is the pension plan right or wrong? The second is specific to the structure of the organizational, legal, and regulatory environment in which pension funds operate.

Errors in Judgment

First, and most obviously, the activist shareholder may be wrong regarding what optimal corporate behavior ought to be. Running a large pension fund does not necessarily mean that the management of the fund has the knowledge or background to judge the quality of every firm's strategic vision or the wisdom behind every proposal made. Business decisions are complex and the environment in which businesses must operate can change rapidly. There are numerous stories of CEOs who, through hubris, made disastrous decisions. Pension funds should take care to avoid the same mistake.

Second, the pension fund investor may step over the line that separates fiduciary judgment and business judgment. That is, if the activist investor pushes the corporation to do certain things, and the corporation does them, the investor may begin to bear the same sort of legal responsibility that regular board members and senior managers bear. Thus, once a pension fund decides to become active in corporate governance, this activity invites lawsuits for mistakes made.[19] Ordinarily, the protections offered pension funds under the prudent investor standard provide some protection. However, the more active a pension plan becomes, the more likely it is the business judgment standard applied to business decision making in the boardroom will be used to decide whether liability for mistakes exists.

Structural Inhibitions

There are three factors that arise from the structure of the pension fund environment that inhibit pension plans from being active in corporate governance. The first is the nature of the managerial control structure. Corporate pension plan managers have two groups to whom they are accountable: the executives of the sponsoring corporation to whom they report and the plan beneficiaries. Many corporate executives have an unspoken golden rule that pension managers should do unto other companies as they would have those companies do unto them. The result is that pension plan managers' superiors discourage them from participating actively in corporate governance. This means that the "meaningful exercise of ownership rights of private pension assets is thankless. No investment manager, in-house or outside, ever got paid extra for voting proxies well, because that would mean a number of votes against management recommendations."[20] Public pension plan managers do not have the same broad mandate to avoid ruffling the feathers of corporate managers. From time to time, however, political pressure is applied to stop plans from pressuring managers of firms having substantial local economic effect.

Diversification requirements are the second reason that some pension plans have avoided corporate governance issues. ERISA has promoted diversification in private pension plan assets, and ERISA-like requirements are increasingly common for public pensions. Once a fund holds equity stakes in hundreds of organizations, it becomes too expensive to monitor or be active in all of them. In addition, large portions of pension plan assets have recently been invested in index funds specifically to receive the benefits of diversification without the substantial costs of active stock selection. Index funds, narrowly construed, do not encourage shareholder activism. However, as pointed out in the earlier discussion of fiduciary responsibility in Chapter 4, index fund managers probably ought to consider some form of shareholder activism as a way to improve the performance of some of the companies held in an indexed portfolio.

The third reason is the prudent investor rules and related regulations and guidelines. These rules, particularly in the context of ERISA, have encouraged fiduciaries to imitate other fiduciaries in their investing behavior. Because pension plans have historically been passive in their corporate governance, they continue to stay passive. In addition, the prudent investor rules as generally interpreted may discourage active involvement in corporate governance because of the liability issues that could arise in the event that the actions favored by the activist shareholder unintentionally harm shareholder value.

PRACTICAL ISSUES FOR ACTIVE PENSION FUNDS

Private pension plans will find activism sensible only if they believe that it will lead to better performance and if they can be assured that their actions will not elicit retaliatory moves by the managements or pension plans of targeted companies against the activist pension plan's sponsor. Even if this could be accomplished in principle, it may be difficult to get top managers to believe this—and they must if they are to let their pension plans publicly attack or privately challenge the performance of other firms. The potential costs of lost business or reverse intervention as firms that are attacked retaliate may be perceived as too high.

So far, it is public pension plans that have led the way as far as shareholder influence on corporate governance is concerned. They have been very active in getting takeover-impeding features of corporate charters repealed. Public pension plans—indeed, most investors—clearly feel that market forces are important factors in getting managers to behave as economically as possible. Unlike other institutional investors (including corporate pension plans), public pension plans are relatively free from the conflicts of interest other investors may have.[21] "Perhaps the public pension funds' most significant contribution has been to make the world an uncomfortable place for a director of an underperforming company," wrote Monks and Minow.[22]

Whether public pension funds can continue to play this role is a major issue. Some public pension plans may eventually be throttled by political concerns that override the interests of the plan and its beneficiaries. Politicians are no less immune to threats than anyone else. Accordingly, if a state's pension plan targets a company, and that company threatens to close a plant in that state, the state's top politicians could put pressure on the pension plan to back away from its accusations and proposals.

TOWARD A MORE ACTIVE ROLE FOR PENSION FUNDS

There are a number of reasons why pension funds may need to become more active than they have been in encouraging management to do economically sensible things. Without takeovers as a threat, the market is searching for new mechanisms to effect change in corporations that are deemed inefficient. "Poison pills," cumulative voting for directors, a preponderance of inside directors, and directors who are not independent of management or whose compensation aligns them with the status quo simply entrench management, insulating it from the forces of efficiency and good performance. As the potential of pension funds to contribute to efficient control is recognized, and the harm of simply trusting current managers or voting with their feet becomes more apparent, the pressures to influence corporate behavior may increase. Lawrence Perlman (1993), the chairman and chief executive officer of Ceridian Corporation, wrote

> The power of the shareholder activism movement is the simple elegance of its underlying proposition that boards and managements of public companies must be held accountable for improving performance to those who own the companies. Governance issues that support this fundamental proposition strengthen companies. (p. 38)

As more and more corporate managers come to appreciate the benefits of shareholder activism, pension funds may be forced to respond.

Another reason pension funds may not have to become more active arises from the joint effect of both the rapid increase in pension plan assets under management and the incentives many funds face to invest in the larger, more "prudent" stocks. At some point, it becomes less expensive to monitor and promote change within a poorly performing company than to exit or wait patiently for change that may never come. Sametz goes so far as to argue that any pension fund choosing to follow active investment management strategies must implicitly accept responsibility for monitoring the performance of the companies whose stocks they own.[23] In the face of the high cost of exit, to do otherwise is philosophically inconsistent with the search for superior risk-adjusted returns via active money management.

Finally, the emergence of DC plans is having an effect on the acceptance of activist roles for pension plans. As the assets in DC plans continue to grow, the natural management resistance to corporate governance has been eroded. The fund managers that individual employees select to manage their DC pension plans are not subject to quite the pressures faced by the corporate and public pension plan managers. These more (although not completely) independent money managers may well start taking a more active part in getting corporate managers to work for shareholders, because they will be working directly for beneficiaries, not corporate managers or politicians; that is, they are not subject to the same conflicts of interest to which DB plans are subject. (Of course, if XYZ Mutual Fund has been hired by ABC Corporation to manage ABC's DC assets, they are not likely to vote against ABC management or for that matter, against the management of other potential clients.)

These factors being as they are, however, Longstreth suggests that pension funds proceed cautiously regarding the "new orthodoxies" in corporate governance.[24] He rightly suggests that pension funds should be careful of unproven claims and should support the right of corporations to experiment with various business strategies.

Longstreth provides two examples of good intentions gone awry that are of special relevance here. The first is how the cry for "independent" directors has led to a proliferation of CEOs on boards. These CEOs seemingly have no difficulty approving possibly excessive pay increases for the CEOs they presumably monitor, possibly because the ripple effect on CEO salaries may be good for them as well. The second is a reminder that emerging wisdom may be wrong. In the early 1990s, some experts called for U.S. businesses to be more like their Japanese and German counterparts to improve competitiveness. Recent history indicates that this move was certainly ill-advised. So, too, might excessive zeal for interventionist tactics have unintended consequences.

CONCLUSION

Shareholder activism should increase beyond its current level because the pension plan, be it private or public, has a fiduciary responsibility to make its portfolio perform as well as possible within the parameters of its risk tolerance. This should not be done in an irresponsible manner, however. Corporate governance and shareholder intervention represent a continuum of possible strategies and activities. Not all should be or need to be used in every case. It is possible to go too far or to too quickly adopt a common wisdom that may not be proven true in future years.[25]

Being an active shareholder carries a risk that the relationship between the pension fund and the management of a corporation can become too adversarial, to the detriment of the corporation and ultimately the corporation's shareholders. Further, although pension funds should be encouraged to be at least somewhat active in the affairs of the companies in which they own stock, a clarification is now in order: the motivation to become involved with the activities of a company must be solely to influence the decision-making process as it relates to long-term shareholder returns. It is a serious and imprudent mistake to use pension fund market power for social or political goals that are not directly tied to maximizing shareholder wealth. The ultimate purpose of the pension fund should not be put aside to serve some other agenda. To use pension assets to advance noneconomic goals could put the pension beneficiaries at risk and adversely affect the sponsor's need to fund the plan.

In general, active involvement in corporate governance to ensure that the interests of the beneficiaries are being considered indicates a shift toward a more balanced sharing of power between management and shareholders rather than simply implying a shift toward investor control. If this shift occurs, management will have to be more accountable to their shareholders. Activist shareholders should not forget, however, that the relationship between these two entities should be the result of a dynamic process that allows managers to manage and experiment to stay competitive and to adapt to an ever-changing business landscape.

With this shift will also come a new focus on corporate boards. In particular, there will be an increase in focus on the relationship between the board, the shareholders, and the managers. Increasingly, boards will be held accountable by shareholders for management behavior. Boards will be examined to see what their incentives are and to whom their members are accountable. There do seem to be benefits to corporate governance. Specifically, better returns with possibly lower risks are at least conceptually achievable. However, these benefits are not costless. Information and solicitation have costs, and legal liability for mistakes in business judgments may prove to be nontrivial. It is not sensible to expend a lot of effort on a small investment. Corporate governance activity also invites politicians and others to become active in the pension's or sponsor's affairs. Thus, pension plan decision makers should proceed cautiously and, as for any other strategic decision, know their goals and motivations and watch out for hubris.

22

The Path to Better Pension Plan Management

Pension plans and the asset pools they manage play a major role in the allocation of resources within our economy. Their active investment management helps to keep markets efficient and funds flowing to the worthiest enterprises. They even possibly lead to higher aggregate domestic savings and thus to a stronger, more rapidly growing economy.

More important for our purposes, they are useful to employers in accomplishing a variety of goals, not the least of which is motivating employees. They are important to employees for the role they play in providing retirement income and security, and they support a veritable army of investment managers, consultants, accountants, actuaries, and other service providers.

Pension plans are too important to be managed as an afterthought or to be delegated to lower-level executives—or those who cannot cut it as managers elsewhere in the organization. The stakes are too high. The employers who sponsor pension plans should worry about the effect of plan decisions on future funding requirements and, ultimately, on their own long-term financial health. They should worry about whether the plan is attracting desirable types of workers and motivating proper behavior. Employees should worry about plan solvency and whether or not the promised benefit or the DC asset pool will be sufficient to provide the type of retirement they desire. Politicians should worry about the adverse consequences, frequently unintended, that regulations or political actions may have on a system that, most agree, works pretty well. Plan managers, corporate board members, plan trustees, and investment managers should worry about all of these factors. Mostly, everyone involved should be concerned about how the plan can be better managed.

Pension plans will face tremendous challenges in coming years as the size of the retired population swells through retirement and increased longevity. What returns will the capital markets provide? What risks will dominate the landscape? Will federal policy change in a manner that will affect the relative desirability of one form of plan or another?

No one can answer these questions with any degree of certainty. However, those who are responsible for pension plans can ensure that their plans are prepared for whatever the future brings by thinking about their pension plans as businesses that must be organized and managed using sound economic and managerial principles. This is not to say that pension plans should be treated as either profit centers or as separate aspects of the organizations that sponsor them: either view could lead to suboptimal results. However, pension plans are big business, and they are complex organizations. Although investment management is the core competency needed, there is much more to managing plans than simply managing money.

The path to better pension plan management—and, hence, to better performance—is multidimensional. There are plan goals to be set and alternative plan structures to analyze. There is policy to write and procedures to develop to ensure prudent decision making. Investment activities must be integrated with management activities so that risk can be managed sensibly and so that actual returns justify the risks taken.

This chapter offers a synthesis of the key points developed earlier. We hope this final commentary will be useful in forming a complete picture of how pension plan performance can be improved. We hope that it is useful for all those who want to help their pension plans prepare for the challenges of coming years.

PLAN GOALS AND STRUCTURE

Sensible pension management begins with a clear understanding of the purpose of the plan. What is the sponsor trying to accomplish? What do employees expect?

From the sponsor's perspective, the existence of a pension plan must be justified by its ability to attract and retain high-quality employees and to motivate behavior that the sponsor finds desirable. Different employees may find different plans attractive for a variety of reasons. The highly skilled forty-eight-year-old worker may prefer working for an organization with a DB pension plan because of the higher retirement security it generally offers. On the other hand, the thirty-year-old worker may value the portability and flexibility offered by a DC plan.

Who, then, is the organization trying to hire and retain? What are the costs of replacing a lost employee? What form of compensation is appropriate for managing the organization's human resources?

No plan type—DB, DC, or hybrid—is dominant in all circumstances for all employers and for all employees. Each has attractive and unattractive features. Sponsors must therefore be careful in determining which plan structures they will use. If organization-specific knowledge or longevity or the option to manage the demographics of the workforce are important, the DB structure is probably the best choice. If the labor force values mobility over the insurance aspects of DB plans, or if turnover costs are low because there is little need for organization-specific human capital, the DC structure is probably the best choice. Employers and employees should remember, however, that DB plans have some distinct advantages. In particular, when employees are not knowledgeable about investments, or when employees value the structure of planned savings and insured benefits, DB plans can be a valuable option. Hybrid plans such as cash balance plans can offer a good middle ground, but when converting from a traditional DB plan to a cash balance plan, sponsors should communicate as clearly and transparently as possible about both the advantages of the new plan and also any decrease in expected benefits.

Regardless of the structure and features chosen, no pension plan can be judged a success if it fails to achieve its primary purposes. First, it must fit sensibly into the overall compensation scheme of the employer. Second, it must provide a retirement benefit or asset pool that employees find attractive enough to warrant contracting their human capital to employers. In short, the pension plan must be viewed in its proper context—as a means of contracting between employers and employees.

PLAN INVESTMENT POLICY

The second step toward better performance is the establishment of policies that govern investment and management activities. Policies should be written and complete. The primary purpose of policy is to provide useful guidelines for decision making and to communicate unambiguously to all parties what the plan is trying to do and how it is going about it. Policy should not be unduly restrictive and should not discourage pension plan management from taking actions that are appropriate under whatever circumstances may be present.

DB plan policies can not be set in a vacuum. Central to sound DB plan policy are two factors: the interdependency between the plan and the sponsor, and the way the asset pool and plan liabilities are entwined. To ignore these interactions is to virtually guarantee unanticipated problems with funding and solvency.

Further, special attention must be given to resolving the conflicts of interest that exist between the various parties involved in managing the asset pool. Problems delayed are not problems solved; ignoring potential problems virtually ensures that they will occur to the detriment of the plan. Structuring policies that govern relationships and explicitly recognizing that the asset pool is to be managed for the exclusive benefit of employees, subject to the sponsor's interest in avoiding unreasonably high and unpredictable funding costs, may be painful—at least to those who find their power or perquisites reduced—but it will improve plan efficiency and investment performance. Good policy will encourage pension decision making to be based on sound economics and financial analysis rather than on relationships and avoidance of responsibility.

Policy needs to answer questions that can be anticipated. For example, what will a plan do if there is adverse market action? Will it rebalance to predetermined strategic weights? Will it reduce its exposure to stocks? Most important, will the decision-making process be a knee-jerk reaction resulting from ill-conceived or inadequate policy guidelines, or will it be guided by forward-looking policy that ensures a long-run sound perspective?

Policy for DC plans is every bit as important as it is for DB plans. For employee-directed plans, DC policy should clearly specify how investment alternatives will be selected and monitored, how the sponsor will administer the plan, and how costs to beneficiaries will be evaluated and controlled. In addition, the sponsor's commitment to providing information and education to employees must be specified. Sponsors should also recognize that some employees will not benefit from information and education; in fact, the evidence indicates that many will simply follow whatever the default plan provisions are.

PRUDENT BEHAVIOR

Good policy is a natural extension of prudent behavior. The concept of prudent behavior by pension plan fiduciaries has deep roots in written law and legal precedent, but it continues to evolve. For those who are fiduciaries, figuring out what it means to behave in a prudent manner is critical. This is not an easy task, as prudence and economically rational behavior can sometimes appear to be at odds. For those who are not fiduciaries, the question of what to expect out of fiduciaries is important. At issue is sound decision making supported by good analysis and theory. At issue is accepting responsibility for actions taken or not taken. At issue is good faith and trust and doing one's job well.

Fiduciaries should understand that behaving in a manner that is prudent on the surface may not be prudent in reality. For example, many fiduciaries feel there is safety in numbers, so they tend to mimic what they believe others are doing. This can lead to excessive investment in what are perceived to be high-quality, prudent securities—regardless of the risk-and-return profile that results for the entire portfolio. Likewise, superficial prudence would mean staying away from derivatives, but careful, skillful use of derivatives can be the truly prudent course.

Prudent behavior can be especially difficult for public plan fiduciaries who do not have the guidelines and protections offered under ERISA. In many cases, these fiduciaries are uniquely vulnerable to political pressures encouraging them to go against what most authorities would consider prudent investment practice. Sometimes there may be no satisfactory short-run alternative other than carefully walking the tightrope between what is right for the plan and any of a number of political goals or agendas. Over the long term, however, the public pension fiduciary should lobby for independence with accountability and strive to educate politicians and plan beneficiaries about the realities of sensible pension management.

To be a good fiduciary, there is no substitute for knowledge of investment strategies and alternatives. Similarly, there is no substitute for careful consideration of the relevant issues when making decisions and for careful documentation of the decision-making process.

For organizations that have DC plans, sponsors and those who represent the plan's beneficiaries must not act as if there are no duties to fulfill: there are. Prudent fiduciary behavior clearly implies an obligation to educate employees regarding portfolio choice and to perform adequate due diligence when selecting providers of investment services and investment alternatives. Further, sponsors should ask themselves what the consequences will be if employees decide that the asset accumulations in their pension accounts are not sufficient for retirement.

For sponsors of DB plans, prudent fiduciary behavior means achieving the optimal balance between contributions to the plan and target investment returns. This means that neither the sponsor nor the asset pool should bear excessive risk; rather, the joint risk of the two should be used to determine the level and timing of contributions and the strategic asset allocation. This is the hard part. The prudent hiring, monitoring, and if necessary, replacing of managers and all the attendant tasks of managing the investment pool are hard work, but conceptually these tasks are fairly straightforward.

Those who agree to serve in a fiduciary role, either because it is part of their job or through political appointment, must take their responsibilities seriously. The consequences of not doing so include personal liability and, possibly, disastrous decision making. Determining the appropriate course of action as a fiduciary is not always easy. For example, recall that index investing, an increasingly popular course of action and one that many experts would argue is the most cost efficient and thus the most sensible, still has some ambiguity, in that certain companies represented in an index may be judged individually to be imprudent investments. Moreover, those who follow passive index strategies still have the duty to support proxy choices that are likely to enhance shareholder value and to vote against those that may harm shareholders.

Finally, fiduciaries should accept the responsibility to make decisions and should set policy based on economic factors rather than on accounting fictions. ABO, PBO, pension expense, and other accounting measures are useful in examining various aspects of DB plans, but there are serious limitations to the data provided. Fiduciaries must be aware of the subjective decisions involved in selecting salary growth rates, interest rates, and expected returns, as well as other factors (such as which mortality table to use) that affect the measurement process. Fiduciaries must also be aware that accounting procedures tend to have the effect of smoothing fluctuations in economic factors, thus masking the real economic issues.

INVESTING

The single most important investment management decision to be made is the long-term strategic asset allocation. In many pension plans, not enough attention is devoted to determining this allocation, whereas too much attention is given to "glamorous" areas such as new investment products and strategies that promise, at least to the naive investor, glorious returns at minimal risk.

In making the strategic asset allocation decision, we cannot emphasize too much how important it is for a DB plan to set return goals that reflect the risk tolerance of the plan in light of the sponsor's ability to fund the plan, long-term expectations for capital market returns and risks, and the nature and magnitude of the pension liability. This is an area in which there can never be one absolute "right" answer—even experts will disagree. However, the returns the pension portfolio provides and the risks that it takes in pursuing these returns will be governed primarily by the overall asset allocation of the plan, and secondarily by the departures from that allocation that are the result of investment decision making. Tactical asset allocation, insured asset allocation, and the numerous asset class investment strategies are all useful, but they are merely parts of the picture. The biggest part is the overall exposure the fund takes to the major asset classes; this is where attention should be focused.

For DC plans, the employee/beneficiary typically will be faced with the daunting task of setting the strategic asset allocation. Sponsors cannot simply tell employees what the allocation should be because of the liability that would create. It is not prudent to leave employees who have no special investment expertise floundering on their own, however; in fact, for ERISA-governed plans in the private sector, employers who do not assist employees at least by providing investment education may find that the desired shift of investment risk from the sponsor to the employee turns out to be an illusion. That is, either the courts—or the court of public opinion—may decide that sponsors are responsible, in whole or in part, for the poor or ill-informed choices of employees.

The actual investment performance of pension funds has certainly been subject to criticism in recent years. Some of these criticisms are unfair, as they do not take differences in asset allocation among plans into account. Further, there are several reasons why pensions may naturally underperform seemingly reasonable benchmarks: the size of some plans makes it difficult to maneuver effectively in the short run, and some regulatory incentives inhibit sensible investment decision making. However, as a practical matter, pension plans probably should be able to do better. This does not mean simply going out and taking excessive risks in pursuit of higher returns. Frequently, performance can be improved dramatically by simply tending to the basics of investment management: keeping transaction costs low and management fees at reasonable levels.

We do believe that pension funds, especially larger ones, have an affirmative obligation to improve the performance of the asset pool by being active shareholders. We feel this is a part of their fiduciary responsibilities to plan beneficiaries, and that it is also simply good sense for sponsors, given the costs of not doing so: poor performance or incurring excessive costs on exiting. However, activism must be pursued cautiously. The best way is to insist on good corporate governance at the board level; in general, we caution against getting too involved in the actual business decisions of the company, as this requires an expertise and knowledge of industry and firm-specific success factors that typically is outside the purview of most investment managers. Further, the activist pension fund must continually monitor its motives. The only good motive for shareholder activism is to maximize shareholder wealth because this will benefit plan beneficiaries and the sponsor.

MANAGEMENT

The fifth step to improved performance encompasses all the management activities that are not part of asset allocation or selection. Thus, good management involves managing the plan's investment managers, monitoring and evaluating performance, and controlling the costs of investing. The responsibilities of senior management and boards are clear: investment managers and trading costs directly affect the success of the plan's investment activities.

Selecting, managing, and monitoring investment managers—whether those managers are external or internal—is an important job of senior pension management. Internal managers should be competent and must be compensated appropriately. To do otherwise is either to set up a revolving door leading to high turnover costs and inconsistent investment management if pay is too low, or to put a drag on performance if it is too high. If outside investment managers are used because it is not practical to pay market wages to inside managers, plan management should anticipate an increase in monitoring costs. Those who make this decision should bear in mind how profitable the investment management industry is. Perhaps the appeal of outsourcing the investment management function would be greatly reduced if the magnitude of management fees and the costs of effective monitoring were accurately assessed by sponsors.

As a practical matter, it is highly unlikely that a sponsor really can manage and monitor as many as thirty or forty external managers. The early warning systems, communications, and accountability that are all essential elements of managing external managers become much too cumbersome. Further, the higher the number of managers that are used, the higher the probability that pension funds are at risk of paying active management fees when the combined profile of a multimanager asset pool actually mimics a broad-based market index.

Monitoring internal or external managers requires a comprehensive performance evaluation system that provides senior management and boards with timely, relevant information on how the asset pool has done and on whether or not policy has been followed. Performance measurement requires the user be familiar with the alternative measures of return, including knowing what return measures to use depending on what is being evaluated (e.g., are we evaluating managers or the total portfolio?); adjusting for risk; choosing the right standards for comparison (benchmarking); and breaking investment performance into its component parts for analysis. Although the measures used in these four areas are certainly not without flaws, the totality of the return/risk/benchmark/attribution approach is quite useful in helping interested parties understand how the pension plan is doing. Recent advances in performance measurement are promising, especially with regard to better benchmarking and understanding the problems with and limitations of performance measurement.

Finally, never forget that trading is costly. Investment managers trade because of the investment strategies they follow and because they need to meet the liquidity needs of the pension plan. Controlling the costs of trading begins with measuring them correctly; that is, market impact costs are important. Further, costs should be monitored so that the pension plan does not incur costs that are higher than they have to be to execute the desired trade. For many plans, trading costs can be reduced simply by paying attention to what is going on and by telling investment managers they are being watched.

Soft dollars and directed commissions also are important. Many in the investment management profession have become dependent on soft dollars to pay for training, travel, and a host of services that have only tangential value for investment decision making. In some cases, the services or products that are purchased benefit the pension plan that pays for these services; in many cases this is not true, or the costs of the benefits received are excessive. The simplest way to deal with soft dollars is to avoid them by not permitting directed commissions. If soft dollar arrangements are permitted, however, their use should be governed by policy that places the burden of proving that the costs are reasonable on the firm executing the trade and that specifies that the benefits derived be used for the exclusive benefit of the plan.

RISK MANAGEMENT

Managing risk is not synonymous with eliminating it. Funds that simply wish to eliminate risk are committing to investment returns that are roughly comparable to those provided by Treasury bills. In virtually any reasonable scenario, these returns would not be sufficient either to meet the liability of a DB plan or to provide adequate accumulation of resources in a DC plan. Risks must be taken if one is to keep pace with or, better yet, exceed inflation over long periods of time. Risks must be taken if one expects to accumulate wealth and, hence, future retirement benefits. From the perspective of the DB plan, risks must be taken unless the sponsor is willing to fund 100% of future retirement benefits.

There are some rules of risk management that all pension funds should keep in mind. The first is that there are no free lunches (other than diversification). Reducing risk ultimately means reducing return. The second rule is that risk management often means trading off exposure to one kind of risk against exposure to another kind. Low investment risk increases the sponsor's risk of higher future contributions. High investment risk in pursuit of high returns can result in excessive surplus volatility. The third rule is that any risk management strategy must be understood by those who use it and ultimately justified in terms of its future alternative payoffs. For example, in an effort to reduce the risk of short-term adverse market action, some managers reduce exposures to risky assets but ignore the potential cost of being out of the market if the market should go up. By failing to consider both the up-market and down-market payoffs, these managers confuse market timing strategies with risk reduction strategies. It is an easy mistake to make, but it is a mistake nonetheless. Rule number four might be that derivatives are good—and bad. It is the responsibility of the user to employ derivatives prudently. Derivatives are available, they are useful, they are generally cost efficient. Thus, in some roles, derivatives offer a prudent means of carrying out risk management strategies. However, derivatives must be used only by those who understand the actual contract involved and how the derivative is likely to behave in a variety of market conditions.

THE SUCCESS FACTORS IN PENSION MANAGEMENT

Pension plan management requires many technical skills and at least some quantitative aptitude. It also requires common sense and an understanding of investment basics and financial market history. Sometimes, however, common sense is put aside to pursue the latest fad or some magical investment strategy. Sometimes plan administrators, managers, trustees, or board members and other fiduciaries are intimidated by the complexity and aura of the investment process and delegate far too much authority to others whose interests are not aligned to the interests of the plan, the sponsor, or the employees. Sometimes these decision makers get caught up in an irrational exuberance that somehow the future can be known and risk can be eliminated while attractive returns remain: that black boxes can somehow make sense out of the complex world in which we live. Sometimes they become so fearful of losing their jobs or being viewed as imprudent or incurring undue liability for actions taken (or not taken) that they do too little, or act too late to be effective. The results are insufficient attention to the issues that really matter, unintended risk, subpar performance, and excessive conservatism.

What, then, are the success factors in pension plan management? First, recognize that pension funds are big businesses and require talented people to run them. These people should be highly skilled and compensated accordingly.

Second, there are many complex relationships to be managed. Agency problems and conflicts of interest must be anticipated and managed in the best interests of the plan, the plan's beneficiaries, and the plan's sponsor. Be cognizant of the incentives of those who serve the plan and be careful about policies or decisions that may have unintended consequences—for example, performance incentives that can have the undesirable side effect of encouraging excessive risk taking. Interactions between plan assets and liabilities and between funding and alternative investment returns must be modeled. Decision makers must use their best judgments about what is, after all, in the final analysis, a fairly subjective decision.

Third, pension plans and their sponsors as a general rule are going concerns with long time horizons. Take a systematic, long-term approach to policy development and decision making. Avoid short-term myopia. Give close attention to the seemingly small things that can erode value over long time periods—inflation and trading costs and lack of control—as well as to obviously important matters such as the strategic asset allocation.

Fourth, common sense and technical competence are equally important. Decision makers should have specific beliefs about market efficiency (or inefficiency) and how assets are priced. Inefficient markets may justify active management even with its higher costs. In efficient markets, passive investing should be the strategy of choice. The impenetrable investment strategy that ultimately unravels to the dismay of plan managers, the sponsor, and beneficiaries does so because it was not sensible in the first place: it was not based on any real theory of economic behavior. Remember that financial markets and our understanding of them change over time. Adequate training and continuing education are the cornerstones of maintaining competence at all levels—from plan trustees and corporate boards to pension staff. Even external vendors should be required to demonstrate that they stay current with new thinking and research findings.

Finally, remember that good pension performance and the changes that may be necessary to improve existing performance ultimately come about through people. Pension management requires much of those who are called to the task. Plan managers and decision makers must be part economist, part manager, part lawyer, and part politician. They must understand the history of the financial markets and yet know that today and tomorrow are not the same as yesterday. Pension fund management and, hence, performance, more than many areas of management, rely on the good judgment of those who have the responsibility for the plan.

APPENDIX A
A Guide for the Prudent Fiduciary

Broadly speaking, the responsibilities of a pension plan fiduciary are to exercise care and loyalty. With these two responsibilities in mind, we present what we believe to be the minimum requirements fiduciaries must meet to fulfill their legal, and perhaps ethical, obligations in planning, staffing, and monitoring the plans that they serve.

DUTY OF CARE

1. Participate in and oversee the development of the pension investment policy statement. This statement should include broad guidelines regarding strategic asset allocation, acceptable investment strategies, and permissible types of transactions, or alternatively, the types of transactions that are prohibited (e.g., writing uncovered call options). This statement should also indicate whether the chief investment officer (CIO) is allowed or expected to overlay decisions made by portfolio managers. For example, the statement should address whether or not the CIO is allowed to take positions in futures that increase or reduce the equities exposure of individual managers.
2. Establish a risk tolerance for the pension plan that reflects the circumstances and preferences of both sponsors and beneficiaries. The pension plan fiduciary should actively participate in assessing risk, in setting limits on the total acceptable dollar loss (value at risk), and in developing policies that will keep the plan invested in a way that is consistent with the risk tolerance.
3. Hire a CIO with the appropriate educational credentials and experience to serve as a competent administrator.
4. Decide whether internal or external management of the pension plan will produce the highest risk-adjusted, cost-adjusted investment returns that are consistent with the risk tolerance set for the fund.

5. Select investment managers based on clearly defined, rational criteria, such as historical performance (i.e., performance that yields insight into predictable future behavior), anticipated future investment, strategies, ability to handle administrative tasks, willingness to participate in the monitoring process, compensation, trading style and activity, and use of soft dollars.

6. Establish investment guidelines for each manager. These guidelines should specify the minimum and maximum exposure to each relevant asset. For example, this might limit a manager to owning less than 5% of a company and investing no more than 10% of the managed portfolio in a company.

7. Monitor the performance of investment managers for investment returns as well as for their level of adherence to the previously agreed upon investment guidelines.

8. Ensure that all administrative and clerical functions are performed accurately and in a timely manner.

9. In the case of fiduciaries of defined contribution plans, develop policies regarding investment alternatives and make these available to employees. Fiduciaries should select a preferred list of money managers, monitor the performance of these investment organizations, and educate employees so that they are able to make responsible investment decisions. Fiduciaries of defined contribution plans should also provide investment and performance measurements, and assist employees in interpreting these measurements. Fiduciaries should also facilitate portfolio rebalancing at reasonable intervals.

10. Commit to continuing education to stay current with the latest advances in theory and practice.

DUTY OF LOYALTY

1. Develop methods for resolving conflicts of interest between the sponsoring organization and the pension plan, as well as between the plan and its vendors (e.g., external investment managers), in ways that are not disadvantageous to the pension plan from an ex ante perspective.

2. Develop an approach to exercising shareholder rights. An example of this is proxy voting that works to the advantage of the pension plan from the shareholder's perspective rather than the manager's, regardless of the manager's connection to the sponsoring organization or the pension plan.

3. Learn as much as possible about pension plan governance and investment management to maintain a high level of competence, and be as faithful as possible to the interests of pension plan beneficiaries.

APPENDIX B
Global Investing for Pension Funds

By the end of 2000, U.S. pension funds were allocating 10% of their portfolios to international securities.[1] One reason for this exposure to international investment is quite simple: international securities represent a significant fraction of all investable capital worldwide. As of the end of 2001, foreign equities accounted for about 19% and foreign bonds accounted for about 24% of total investable capital.[2] Thus, pension funds needing a place to invest are virtually forced to look overseas for additional investment opportunities. Another reason for international investment is the potential benefits of international diversification. In addition, some analysts also argue that some overseas markets may not be as efficient as the U.S. marketplace. Thus, there may be occasions for earning positive risk-adjusted excess returns from active global management.

Investing in foreign securities is not the same as investing in U.S. securities. There are at least two questions pension funds should ask when investing outside the United States: does the country of interest have a mature economy that should grow at a modest but relatively stable rate, or is it an emerging economy that could grow explosively but erratically? Are the local markets governed by competitive forces, or are they subject to government regulation and intervention? The answers to these questions are important in selecting exposures and investment strategies.

International investing also has a risk/return profile that is different from investing solely in domestic markets. For example, currency exposure can be an important determinant of realized total return. The risks and returns of foreign equities and bonds are also different from those of their U.S. counterparts—or at least they have been. Significant differences also may exist in the market structure of foreign markets as well as in information availability and regulation. Of course, the fundamentals of the economy of a specific country or region may vary widely.

CURRENCY, RISK, RETURN, AND DIVERSIFICATION

Changes in currency exchange rates can affect the short-run returns from investing in international securities. To some, this foreign-exchange risk offers opportunities: they attempt to forecast currency valuations and thus pursue active (and, it is hoped, profitable) currency management. According to others, currency risk is simply an unsystematic risk to be avoided and thus hedged or eliminated by diversifying. Currency risk may be partially diversified away by holding investments denominated in numerous currencies simultaneously as long as these currencies are not strongly correlated. Derivatives offer the opportunity to hedge currency risk fully at low cost, if such a hedge is desired. Whether to hedge at all is an issue, however, that becomes more and more important as more pension assets are invested overseas. We discuss this in some detail in Chapter 20.

FOREIGN EQUITIES

Non-U.S. equities may be divided into the same categories used for U.S. equities: large and small company equities, value and growth equities, and so forth. There is much more to the story, however.

The conventional wisdom is that diversification into foreign equities makes sense because foreign equities have a positive but far from perfect correlation with domestic securities. There is evidence, however, that with globalization, the correlations are increasing and, hence, the advantages of diversification are diminishing.[3] There is also some evidence that the correlations increase in bear markets, meaning that just when low correlations are needed, they may disappear.[4] That said, even though correlations between country markets may have increased, a global perspective is essential in constructing portfolios. For example, suppose a pension fund decides to increase its exposure to a particular industry. Because of increasing globalization, the fund should consider all the competitors in that industry—not just those that are headquartered in the United States.[5]

In addition, managers should consider international investments in emerging markets as well as in developed markets. One recent study found that emerging-market investors should keep an eye on domestic economic policy. In particular, the study found that the benefits of investment in emerging markets were highest in periods of restrictive U.S. monetary policy.[6]

FOREIGN BONDS

Currency risk is a central issue when investing in foreign bonds. It accounts for as much as half of total bond market risk. The historical record for unhedged foreign bonds in U.S. dollar terms indicates that the returns are (or have been) more volatile than U.S. returns are. Although there seems to be a modest diversification benefit to be gained by adding unhedged foreign bonds to portfolios of U.S. bonds, authorities disagree on the desirability of doing so.

Hedged foreign bonds have performed very well when compared with un-hedged foreign bonds and with U.S. bonds. However, the periods studied are characterized by financial markets that are now less regulated and more inte-grated than they were in the past.[7] In addition, U.S. monetary policy could have affected the historical results. In other words, the seemingly superior historical performance of hedged foreign bond portfolios should be viewed with caution: the environment can change, and as more investors globalize their portfolios, free lunches are not likely to persist. (Indeed, they may not have been really free in the first place.)

Overall, the evidence on the performance of foreign bonds shows neither overwhelmingly good nor overwhelmingly bad results. For pension funds that have currency exposures resulting from benefits payable in non-U.S. currencies, foreign bonds offer a natural hedge. Foreign bonds may also offer the potential to exploit interest rate or currency views and security selection opportunities for those pension funds that believe in active management.

CURRENCY OVERLAYS

A currency overlay is a portfolio management activity that assigns the authority to manage currency risks and returns to an overlay manager. The overlay man-ager may attempt to enhance portfolio returns by taking positions in currencies on the basis of a particular view of how a given currency will do relative to other currencies. However, the overlay manager may attempt to reduce the port-folio's exposure to currency risk by hedging all or a portion of the portfolio's net currency exposure.

The appeal of a currency overlay is twofold. First, there is a specialist, who presumably understands currencies and currency management. Second, there is someone who "sees the big picture" and has the authority to make decisions according to the net exposure a pension fund may face or want.

In one study, currency overlays were compared with portfolios that were formed by jointly selecting currency and asset class weights.[8] The conclusion was that currency overlays are inefficient relative to portfolios that integrate the asset class/currency decisions, indicating that the interaction between assets and currencies is not fully considered in the overlay approach. Overlay managers may be able to add value through active management, but this may be subop-timal compared to a fully integrated approach.

THE REGULATORY AND INFORMATION ENVIRONMENT

Structural issues should be of special interest to pension funds as they globalize their investment portfolios. Deregulation and integration of markets throughout the world have led to generally lower costs of international investing, better information, and more efficient trading mechanisms through computers and elec-tronic communications. However, it is still more costly to trade in most markets outside of the United States—as much as twenty-five to seventy-five basis points more costly.

Another factor that must be considered is that taxes—ordinarily not a problem for U.S. pensions—can be an issue when investing in foreign securities. Withholding taxes on dividends and interest may come into play and may or may not be fully recoverable, depending on the tax treaties in effect with the relevant countries.

Securities regulation may also differ substantially among the different countries. There is no Securities and Exchange Commission (SEC) outside of the United States, although there may be roughly analogous counterparts to the SEC. Accounting standards vary from country to country, making it difficult to interpret whatever financial statements are presented. There may also be restrictions on foreign investment that make certain investment positions unobtainable. For example, in some countries, foreign investors may be prohibited from taking positions in certain securities.

The bottom line for pension funds is that international investing poses new challenges with respect to information, regulation, and structural issues. As a consequence, pension funds and their managers must recognize that the rules for international investing are not the same as those for domestic investing. Investment strategies that rely on timely, high-quality information; speedy trade execution; or low transaction or custody costs may not work in some markets. Thus, international strategies that will achieve the goals of the pension fund are likely to differ from traditional U.S. strategies: they will have to adapt to the countries to which they are being applied.

MANAGEMENT ISSUES

There are also other issues for pension funds that choose to invest internationally. Not the least of these is finding experienced managers. For pensions that prefer passive investing—and there are many funds that favor passive investing abroad to keep transaction costs low—experienced management simply means being conversant with the trading mechanisms and exchange characteristic of the target countries or regions. For pensions that pursue active management strategies, managerial expertise becomes even more important, because countries differ greatly by accounting standards, quality of information provided, and so forth. Traditional security analysis is also likely to be substantially different in different countries because of the difficulty of properly analyzing the effects of demographic, social, and political factors on asset values, and also because of the difficulty of getting high-quality data for use in analysis.

Pension fund decision makers who believe in active management have, in the international market, a larger set of strategic opportunities than is available in the United States. Pensions can attempt country selection strategies (how countries are expected to perform economically relative to other countries) and currency selection strategies (which currencies are expected to do well relative to other currencies). Even proponents of efficient markets may be attracted to emerging markets on the basis of the possibility of inefficiencies resulting from information problems or trading frictions. Of course, information is costly, and inefficient trading systems may interfere with otherwise profitable trades. Moreover, some emerging markets may never emerge, failing to survive long enough and to provide reasonable return for the risk taken. It is worth noting that emerging markets account for only about 3% of the total capital markets.[9] Pension fund managers should think carefully about where they are focusing their time and resources. A lot of return on 3% of a portfolio's assets will not offset a poor strategic asset allocation.

CONCLUSION

Overall, it seems that large and medium-sized pension funds should be thinking along the lines of developing and implementing optimal global investment strategies as opposed to domestic-only strategies. Sponsors of employee-directed plans should include one or more non-U.S. alternatives to employees as well. However, the track record of risk/return data for non-U.S. investing is not as long as it is for U.S. securities. The world has changed rapidly, and given the probable effect of currency on the historical data, we have to be careful not to infer too much from the historical record. The U.S. companies in which pensions invest are increasingly exposed to currency and country risk through their normal operations, as well. Sponsors have more multinational workforces than ever before, and U.S. securities markets, relative to those of the rest of the world, are smaller and less capable of meeting the investment needs of pension funds than they were several years ago. Thus, foreign markets seem to offer reasonable and fertile investment alternatives for U.S. pension funds.

Pension funds should be willing to invest outside the United States. Domestic-only portfolios are likely to be inefficient, providing too little return for the risk taken. To globalize, however, the sponsor needs to take a broader perspective in terms of many of the topics considered in this book. For example, the strategic asset allocation decision now becomes one of choosing not only asset classes but exposures to regions, countries, and possibly sectors within those countries. In addition, the strategic asset allocation now must address a currency component. Performance measurement also takes on additional complexity. For example, returns will normally be stated in terms of the investor's base currency and will be a function both of local investment returns as well as of relative currency movements. Benchmarking must become more robust, as the scope of the benchmark must expand to include countries as well as asset classes. These country exposures make determining the appropriate set of benchmark weights a more difficult task because appropriate weightings can be determined by amount of assets held, the total market capitalization for a given country, or the gross domestic product for a given country.

We offer the following caveats. Remember that the risk/return characteristics of non-U.S. markets are not as well documented as they are for U.S. securities. In the international marketplace, trading is more costly, and information is more uneven in quality and is still more costly. The magnitude of the benefits of diversification is open to debate, and the effect of currency risk is both real and somewhat confusing. Go cautiously, pay attention, do not forget about the bigger issues such as strategic asset allocation, and as always, do not expect a free lunch.

APPENDIX C
An Example of a Multiemployer Hybrid Pension Plan

The Operating Engineers Central Pension Fund (CPF) provides an example of how a hybrid plan can be used to meet a variety of needs. The CPF provides benefits to members of the International Union of Operating Engineers (IUOE). The IUOE represents over 350,000 members.[1]

As a multiemployer pension plan, the CPF is regulated under the Taft-Hartley Act and is overseen by an equal number of union and management trustees. Over 8,000 employers contribute to the plan. In 1993, it was the sixth largest multiemployer plan in the United States and was 148th largest among all U.S. pension plans.

The CPF demonstrates how a pension plan may be structured to meet not only the needs of employers and employees but also the needs of an industry with a homogeneous but mobile workforce. The CPF is a DB plan. The monthly benefits paid to beneficiaries under the terms of the plan, however, are based on a percentage of the contributions made to the plan on the beneficiaries' behalf. The 1993 monthly benefit was 3.3%.

Similar to backloaded plans designed to tie employees to a firm or government organization, CPF benefits are higher for people who remain operating engineers for a long time; this same attribute encourages skill development. Vesting (a 5-year schedule is used even though multiemployer plans may use 10-year schedules) and break-in service requirements help eliminate poor workers. As a DB plan, the employers bear the risk of adverse investment.

Similar to a DC plan, the CPF is easy for participants to understand. In addition, it is easy to calculate the benefit to be paid. Although the employee is tied to his trade, he is not tied to one employer and thus may move from job to job. Unlike DC plans, the account on which benefits are calculated does not deplete, so beneficiaries do not outlive their resources.

APPENDIX D
Measuring Returns

The basics of measuring return are fairly straightforward. However, there are subtleties that become very important when trying to use a return measure to say something about performance. This appendix addresses the essentials of calculating and correctly using measures of return.

TOTAL RETURN

The first step necessary to assess investment performance is the measure of investment return over a single time period. Here there is no disagreement among analysts. The simple measure of single-period investment return for an asset is

Total Return (TR) = Income Yield + Percentage Price (Value) Change,

or

$$TR = [\text{Portfolio Value at End of Period } (Pv_t)/\text{Portfolio Value at Beginning of Period } (Pv_0)] - 1.$$

This assumes no contributions. If there are contributions (C) or distributions (Di) over the period,

$$TR = [(Pv_t - C_t + D_c)/Pv_0] - 1.$$

This equation states that the return on an asset over the first period equals its income yield (the cash flow—i.e., dividends, interest, royalties, or net rent—paid during the period divided by the price of the asset at the beginning of the period) plus the change in price (or value) of the same asset during the period. This yields a total return that appropriately includes the income and capital change components of investment return performance.

As an example, consider a fund that invested $100 in a single stock two years ago. One year later, a dividend of $10 was received (and reinvested) and the price of the stock had increased to $105. Two years later, another $10 dividend is received (and reinvested), but the price of the stock has fallen to $90. The TR in each year is

Year 1: $10/100 + ($105 − 100)/100 = 0.1 + 0.05 = 0.15 or 15%;
Year 2: $10/115 + ($90 − 115)/115 = 0.087 + (−0.217) = −0.13 or −13%.

As this example shows, neither the income nor capital change components are sufficient to describe investment performance; both are necessary to present an accurate picture.

For simplicity, we ignore the complication that arises when the dividend flow occurs in the middle rather than near the end of a period. (Note that an earlier receipt of cash enables the investor to earn more on the reinvested amount.)

Similarly, the above ignores an issue of vital importance for real-world pension funds—the cash flows that occur as a result of payments to beneficiaries and new contributions during the course of the measurement period (this period is generally a year, a quarter, or a month). These intraperiod flows must be accommodated in the calculations if the return component of the conventional performance measures is to be computed in ways that would ultimately allow for the assessment of the quality of investment management. In the following sections on time weighting and dollar weighting, we address the technical aspects of these adjustments.

EVALUATING MANAGERS: THE TIME-WEIGHTED RATE OF RETURN

A significant factor in return performance can be the sponsor's decision to allocate more (or less) money to an asset class or manager. This timing decision can come about for a variety of reasons. Perhaps it is simply the result of additional funding contributions, or perhaps it is to the result of the sponsor's belief that a given manager is doing well and should manage more of the plan's assets. Regardless of motivation, the decision to invest more—or less—with a particular manager, coupled with subsequent market action, may affect the return calculated for a given time period. As a result, the sponsor who uses the wrong measure of return could end up deciding to reward a poor manager or fire a good one.

To achieve insulation from such sponsor decisions, the investment profession agrees that using the Time-Weighted Rate of Return (TWRR) generally is appropriate when evaluating manager performance. For a particular evaluation period, the TWRR for a portfolio is calculated exactly as the total return measure is calculated in the previous section. The unique aspect of TWRR is in how per period returns are linked together to get an annualized return. The use of this measure requires additional information about the value of the portfolio at the time of cash infusion or cash withdrawal.

The annualized TWRR for any n periods within a year given the TR in each period is

$$\text{TWRR} = [(1 + TR_1)(1 + TR_2)\ldots(1 + TR_n)] - 1.$$

For example, consider an investment in a stock of $100. At the end of six months, the investment is worth $125 and there are no dividends. At the end of the second six-month period, the investment is worth $100 and again no dividends are paid. The total returns in each period are

$$TR_1 = 25\%;$$
$$TR_2 = -20\%.$$

The annualized TWRR may be computed as

$$\text{TWRR} = [(1 + 0.25)(1 - 0.2)] - 1 = [(1.25)(0.8)] - 1 = 0.0, \text{ or } 0\%.$$

Thus, the annualized total return for the one-year period is 0%—an intuitively appealing result, as the value at the end of one year is the same as originally invested.

The characteristic of the TWRR in which we are most interested is that, for it to be useful, total return must be calculated every time there is a significant cash flow into or out of the portfolio being measured. By performing this calculation when cash flows occur, TRWW takes the impact of the cash flow out of the evaluation.

EVALUATING THE TOTAL PORTFOLIO: THE DOLLAR-WEIGHTED RATE OF RETURN

The correct way to accommodate and evaluate the performance impact of cash inflows or cash outflows is to use a Dollar-Weighted Rate of Return (DWRR). This is obtained by solving for the internal rate of return of a set of cash flows and end-of-period values, as shown below:

$$V_0 (1 + DWRR)^N + \sum_{t=1}^{n} + C_t (1 + DWRR)^{(n-t)} = V_N,$$

where V_0 is the starting value of the portfolio, C_t is the cash inflow or outflow in period t, and V_N is the ending value of the portfolio.

Assume the initial portfolio value is $100, and two years later it is worth $150. Also assume $10 was contributed at the end of the first year:

$$\$100 (1 + DWRR)^2 + \$10 (1 + DWRR) = \$150.$$

Solving for DWRR, we find

$$DWRR = 17.58\%$$

The DWRR is certainly adequate as long as one is comfortable about estimating the cash-flow timing and about who has control of the inflows and outflows of cash, and it usually is satisfactory for individual managers or funds that do not have large inflows or outflows over a period. However, this computation can be tricky when performed over many time periods because, as inflows and outflows occur, there are many changes in algebraic signs (+ or −). For every change, there is a value of DWRR that solves the mathematical problem. With, say, three sign changes, there will be three answers, so interpretation is often not as simple as it may seem.

Apart from this technical consideration, note that using a DWRR to evaluate a single manager implies that the fund manager being evaluated controls the timing of inflows and outflows. The computed DWRR would be higher or lower if all the dollar values remained the same but the timing of the intermediate cash flow occurred sooner or later. If managers do not control this cash-flow timing, then equally effective managers could have different DWRRs, depending on when funds were contributed or withdrawn by the sponsor. Because plan sponsors generally make the decisions about fund contribution and withdrawal, the manager loses some degree of control over the performance measure relative to the plan sponsor. Thus, the DWRR can produce a somewhat distorted view of investment return for managers. It is, however, generally an appropriate measure for the total pension asset pool—that is, the entire amount under the control of the plan sponsor—or for the entire portion invested in equities, for example. This last observation is conditional, however, on being able to filter out the effect of cash contributions and liquidations used to pay beneficiaries.

COMPARING THE TWRR AND DWRR

To illustrate the difference between the TWRR and the DWRR better, we return to our first example. Suppose that the plan sponsor gives a manager $100. Subsequently, the sponsor observes that a 25% return is produced by the manager in the first period and decides to invest $50 more with the manager at the beginning of period two. Thus, during the second period, $175 has been invested ($125 + 50). The manager then loses 20% of the total so at the end of the period the value is $175 (1 − 0.2), or $140. Recall, the TWRR is 0% per period. However, the DWRR is now calculated as

$$\$100 \ (1 + DWRR)^2 + (\$50)(1 + DWRR)^1 = \$140;$$
$$DWRR = -4.066\% \text{ per period.}$$

Note especially that, because the contribution to the portfolio was made after the period of better investment return (the 25% return that occurred in the first period) and before the period of poorer performance, the DWRR is less than the TWRR. In other words, because the sponsor elected to increase the exposure of the portfolio just before a period of bad performance, the DWRR is lower than the TWRR. If we are trying to evaluate the manager, therefore, the manager should not be penalized for the unfortunate (in this case) timing of the cash inflow.

The primary reason for this difference between the DWRR and the TWRR is that the DWRR implicitly assumes a constant rate of return over the entire evaluation period and the TWRR does not. Thus, intraperiod cash flows affect the DWRR but are excluded as part of the measurement process when using TWRR. Of course, the DWRR is appropriate when the objective is to evaluate how well the entire investment portfolio has performed and to decide whether to invest more (or less)—a decision that presumably is controlled directly by the plan sponsor. The assumption that the plan sponsor has control over the magnitude and timing of inflows and outflows may not always be accurate.

The only drawback to the TWRR is the need to develop intermediate portfolio values; this can be done precisely by frequently generating a complete portfolio valuation. If this is nearly costless, it should be done. For instance, public mutual funds must report portfolio values daily. Thus, an active mutual fund investor can easily compute the TWRR. When there are noticeable costs to valuation, such as the cost of appraisals for nontraded stock or real estate, analysts will sometimes use a proxy to estimate portfolio value. This might be necessary for funds that do not normally compute their values daily. If actual returns are computed only monthly, for example, then a midmonth valuation necessitated by a midmonth cash inflow or outflow might be approximated by using a broad market index as a proxy for the return on the portfolio being evaluated. Thus, if the index rose by $S\%$ from the beginning to the time of the month in which the cash flow occurred, the portfolio value might be treated as if it too rose by (a hypothetical) $S\%$. The computation would then proceed as shown earlier. For example, if the starting value was \$100, \$25 was infused during the period, the ending value was \$150, and the market rose by 5% between the period's start and the cash flow, the return would be

$$[(105 - 100)/100] + [(150 - 130)/130] = 21.4\%.$$

over the period.

Generally speaking, the shorter the measurement interval is—for example, months versus years—and the smaller the cash inflows and outflows are relative to the portfolio's starting size, the closer the DWRR and the TWRR will be. Indeed, with monthly measurement periods and with contributions or outflows that are, say, equal to 10% or less of the starting value, there generally will be only very small differences between the two measures. These differences may not be large enough to warrant the data collection effort necessary to compute TWRR. Nonetheless, it is generally more precise to use the TWRR to evaluate the manager of a fund.

In reality, most pension plans that compute returns periodically use consultants to do this. The consultants obtain the basic data from the pension plan's master trustee—the trust company that is responsible for keeping track of the holdings, dividends, interest, receipts, and cash flows—once a quarter. The consultants then use approximation techniques to estimate the TWRR. Because consultants presumably do all evaluations in the same way, all interested parties hope and pray (given the data limitations, they may be unable to do much more) that what biases exist are systematic, affecting all evaluated portfolios in the same way. Note that with the trend among money management firms and consultants to comply with the AIMR GIPS, the data gathering and computational issues that once were barriers to the correct way of dealing with these issues are disappearing.

RETURNS OVER MANY PERIODS

Once a single-period measure of returns is computed (e.g., once annualized returns have been computed), the question arises of how to combine single-period returns to make up a multiple-period measure. There are two alternatives. The first approach is using an arithmetic average. The second is to use a geometric average. The arithmetic average is

$$TRa_{it} = \Sigma TR_{it}/T,$$

where TRa_{it} is the arithmetic average of the returns on the ith portfolio over periods 1 through T, R_{it} is the return in each period t, and T is the number of periods. In this formulation, the average will be given in the same time dimension in which each period's return is computed. If the periods are months, for instance, the average will be in terms of months. To put the average of monthly returns into annual terms, multiply by the result by 12.

If portfolio returns were 5%, 10%, 15%, and − 10% in each of four quarters, the average quarterly return would be

$$(5 + 10 + 15 - 10)/4 = 5\%$$

per quarter. To calculate the annual return, simply add the quarterly returns or multiply the average quarterly return by four—either way, the annual return is 20%.

Note that although the computed annual return is 20%, the true return is not. Suppose that at the beginning of the first quarter, the portfolio value was $100. A 20% return would indicate that the portfolio's value at the end of the year would be $120, but this is not the case. The portfolio rises by 5% in the first quarter, and its dollar value increases by 5%. If the starting value were $100, its value would be $105 at the end of the first quarter. The portfolio rises by 10% in the second quarter, and its new dollar value is $105(1 + 0.10) = $115.50. In the third quarter it rises by 15%, so its dollar value rises to $115(1 + 0.15) = $132.25. In the final quarter it falls by 10%, so its ending dollar value is only $132.25(1 − 0.10) = $119.03. This is less than the $120 suggested by the arithmetically determined annual return. Thus, the arithmetic mean computation can lead to the overstatement of the dollar value that is truly there.

To remedy this problem, use the geometric mean return. The geometric average for a single period such as one year is

$$Rg_{it} = (V_T/V_0) - 1,$$

where Rg_{it} is the geometric average return for the ith portfolio, V_T is the value at the end of the period, and V_0 is the value at the beginning of the period. The annual geometric mean in the example above is

$$Rg = (\$119.02/100) - 1 = .1902, \text{ or } 19.02\%.$$

As long as all the returns are the same for each measurement interval, the arithmetic mean will equal the geometric mean. When the returns differ, the geometric mean will be less than the arithmetic mean. Indeed, the higher the period-to-period variability, the lower the geometric mean relative to the arithmetic mean. When assessing historical investment performance, the geometric mean is more useful because it will not allow for an implied overstatement of the dollar values at the end of the evaluation period. When projecting historical investment performance into the future, the arithmetic mean coupled with the standard deviation is generally more useful in avoiding understatement of the per period return.

To illustrate, suppose Portfolio A experienced a return of 10% in each of two years, and suppose Portfolio B had a 20% return in year 1 and a 0% return in the second year. To confirm the appropriateness of the geometric mean in this example, consider a dollar investment. If $100 were invested in Portfolio A, it would be worth $110 after one year and $121 after two years. If the same $100 were invested in Portfolio B, it would be worth only $120 after two years. The arithmetic mean does not reveal this difference in terms of dollar amounts, but the geometric mean does. Thus, the geometric mean return reflects changes in dollar values better than the arithmetic mean does. The arithmetic mean return for Portfolio A is $(0.10 + 0.10)/2$, or 10% per year; the arithmetic mean for Portfolio B is also 10%. The geometric mean return for Portfolio A is

$$(121/100)^{1/2} - 1 = 10\%,$$

whereas the geometric mean return for Portfolio B is lower:

$$(120/100)^{1/2} - 1 = 9.5\%.$$

As noted, when a return estimate is combined with an independent risk measure, as in forming expectations of future performance, the arithmetic mean return is generally used. This is partly by convention and partly because the geometric mean itself changes with the variability of outcomes and, hence, is not truly independent of customarily used measures of risk. For instance, suppose Portfolio C has a 30% return in one year and a -10% return in the next. It is much more volatile than Portfolio A and somewhat more volatile than Portfolio B, although it has the same arithmetic mean return. Its geometric mean return is only 8.2%, however. Using a geometric mean return in conjunction with a risk measure is, in some sense, double-counting, as the geometric mean return declines with volatility, other things being equal.

APPENDIX E
Adjusting for Risk

Two conceptually different measures of risk are used to evaluate portfolio performance. The first of these is the time series variance of total portfolio returns. The second is a measure related to systematic or market risk, rather than to total portfolio risk.

TOTAL RISK

The measure of total risk most commonly used for portfolio evaluation purposes is the time series variance, or the standard deviation of returns. This tool measures the dispersion around the arithmetic mean of the time series returns. In doing so, it captures the volatility of returns over time relative to the average per period return. The variance is

$$\text{Var}(\text{TR}_p) = \sum_{t=1}^{T}(\text{TR}_{pt} - \text{TR}a_{pt})^2/(T - 1),$$

where TR_{pt} is the total return on portfolio p during period t, $\text{TR}a_{pt}$ is the arithmetic mean total return, and T is the number of observations. The standard deviation $\text{SD}(\text{TR}_p)$ is merely the square root of the above quantity. Nearly every statistics textbook describes this measure.

MARKET RISK

Sometimes total risk may not be the appropriate measure to use. Instead, the appropriate measure may be the systematic or market risk to which a portfolio is exposed. The systematic risk is the portion of the total risk that cannot be eliminated by holding a diversified portfolio. Conceptually, the total risk of an asset comprises both systematic (or market) risk and unsystematic or diversifiable (nonmarket) risk. Using market risk means that a portfolio manager will not be penalized by attributing total risk to the portfolio manager when the manager is not responsible for—or may be prohibited from—eliminating non-systematic or nonmarket risk. Unsystematic risk can generally be eliminated only by broad investment strategy decisions that are customarily made by the plan sponsor, not the money manager.

A common approach to estimating systematic or market risk is to use what is known as the market model. The market model is a regression estimate of the relationship between the periodic return on a portfolio and the return on a broad-based market index. The regression equation takes the following form:

$$R_{pt} - R_{ft} = \alpha_p + \beta_p(R_{mt} - R_{ft}) + \varepsilon_{pt},$$

where R_{ft} is the tth-period return on the risk-free asset, R_{pt} is the tth-period return on the market portfolio, α_p is the regression intercept, β_p is the estimate of systematic risk of the portfolio (formally this was known as $\{Cov[(R_{pt} - R_{ft}),(R_{mt} - R_{tt})]/Var(R_{mt})\}$), and ε_{pt} is a random-error term with a mean of zero and a finite variance. In equations such as this, the β estimate indicates the volatility of the portfolio relative to the market portfolio. If the β_p were estimated as 2.0, then with a risk-free rate of 6% and a market return of 14%, the portfolio would be expected to have a return of

$$0.06 + 2.0(0.14 - 0.06) = 0.22, \text{ or } 22\%.$$

The expected risk premium of $2.0(0.14-0.06) = 16\%$ for a portfolio with a β_p of 2.0, twice the expected risk premium of the market portfolio $(0.14 - 0.06 = 8\%)$.

For performance measurement, of chief concern are the statistically estimated parameters α_p, β_p, and Var(ep)—the variance of the portfolio's return variance not explained by the variable R_{mt}. In general, these parameters can be well measured when such a model is estimated over five years or so of monthly data, yielding sixty observations. Twenty observations at least are necessary for this calculation to have any serious economic content. There is a trade-off, however: the more observations, the stronger the statistical inference. The longer the time period, though, the more probable that the current investment policies are unlike those that prevailed at the start of the time period. There is no easy resolution to this trade-off; common sense, however, helps. If there have been no policy changes, go for length. If there have been investment policy changes, use only data available since the last change and accept the fact that the statistics will, because of the low number of observations, be a bit suspect. Finally, the market parameters used will change over time. Thus, the risk-free rate (R_{ft}) is likely to vary over time, and α_p and β_p will be slightly biased measures of the true variables. The result is that the analyst must use his or her judgment regarding the likelihood of changes in any fundamental market parameters.

APPENDIX F
Example of an Equity Swap Hedge

Consider a pension fund that holds €40,000,000 in large capitalization German stocks. The fund manager has no concerns or view about the value of the euro, but he or she is worried about the performance of the German stock market over the next two years. To hedge, the manager may enter into an equity swap.

The swap will commit the pension fund to pay the change in the German DAX equity index to a counterparty (effectively "passing through" the change in value from the DAX index). In return, the investor will receive a money market–based return tied to the LIBOR.

The terms of the swap are

Currency	Euro
Notional amount	Variable
Initial notional amount	€40,000,000
Stock index	DAX
Spread to dealer	0
Index interest rate	6-month LIBOR
Payment frequency	Semiannual
Maturity	2 years

After the swap is established, assume the following pattern of interest rates and changes in the DAX:

Time (months)	DAX	% Change	LIBOR
0	3400	—	3%
6	3740	10%	2.5%
12	3600	−3.7%	2.25%
18	3500	−2.8%	3%
24	3250	−7.1%	3.5%

Cash Flows (from pension fund's perspective)

Time (months)	% Change from Index	Index Receipt (pay)	Interest Receipt (payment)	Net Receipt	Notional Amount
0	—	—	—	—	40,000,000
6	10.0%	(4,000,000)	600,000	(3,400,000)	44,000,000
12	−3.7%	1,647,059	550,000	2,197,059	42,352,941
18	−2.8%	1,176,471	476,471	1,652,941	41,176,471
24	−7.1%	2,941,176	617,647	3,558,824	38,235,294

The "Net Receipt" column shows the proceeds the pension fund will receive (or pay) as a consequence of the swap. In this example, the pension fund may appear to have made a profitable swap in the second through fourth periods (and an unprofitable one in the first period) because the falling DAX results in payments to the fund from the equity side of the swap in addition to the LIBOR-linked payments. Remember, however, that the portfolio of German stocks held by the pension fund is losing value in these periods (assuming it correlates with the DAX index), as well. Thus, the swap is simply is offsetting the losses in the portfolio in these periods; the hedge is working. Note also that, as it is structured, the swap exposes the investor to currency risk. If desired, this risk may be hedged with a currency swap or with other derivatives.

APPENDIX G
Manager Selection

I. GENERAL PROVISIONS OF MANAGER SELECTION REQUEST FOR PROPOSAL

1. Summary Cover Sheet

- Name of the firm
- Address of the firm
- Name, telephone number, and title of individual with authority to commit the firm
- Name, telephone number, and title of proposed account manager, if different from above
- Year of SEC registration
- Product type
- Equity
- Fixed Income
- Cash
- Real Estate
- Other
- Date of Submission
- Time-Stamped Date of Receipt

2. Description of Organization

- Submit an organization chart indicating the reporting relationships of the entity responsible for this proposed relationship and the most senior management of the organization.
- Indicate the location of your firm's offices and indicate the staff size in the following categories:
- Professionals
- Portfolio managers
- Research analysts
- Economists

- Traders
- Client service
- Marketing
- Administration (including accounting and record keeping)
- Nonprofessionals
- Describe joint ventures or other affiliations of your firm requiring a commitment of capital, a commitment of personnel, or the acceptance of liability
- Provide copies of the most current SEC filings and audited financial statements; please note material changes since the preparation of these documents.

3. Qualifications and Experience of Key Personnel

- List the key personnel for whom no substitutions will be made without prior written consent; provide biographies of key personnel that include
  - Education
  - Complete professional history including duration of term in present position
  - Current position and responsibilities
  - Current client responsibilities where relevant number of accounts and total size of accounts by class of assets being managed (e.g., equity, fixed, cash, balanced)
  - Provide a list of investment management clients indicating the clients for whom more than $25 million is being managed.
  - List clients obtained within the last three years and client contacts
  - List clients who have terminated in the last three years and client contact where available; list significant new hires and terminations within the last three years for the entity responding to this proposal.

4. Business Arrangements

- Provide proposed management fee schedule including
  - Start-up fees
  - Annual fees and method of computation and payment schedule
  - Quarterly presentations before Investment Committee
  - Proposed arrangement for brokerage services
  - Provide total commission costs over the last twelve months
  - List brokers executing at least 10% of dollar volume over the last twelve months
  - List total value of "soft dollar" services purchased over the last twelve months
  - Specify procedures for handling transfer of assets
  - Provide sample reports for accounting and auditing purposes
  - Provide a specimen contract.

II. TECHNICAL REQUIREMENTS: FIXED INCOME MANAGEMENT

1. Please submit the holdings of a representative $25 million portfolio assuming investment in the most recent quarter. If respondent is proposing a commingled fund, please submit the holding of the fund as of the most recent quarter end. List representative buys and sells or, if a commingled fund is proposed, list all transactions. Calculate the following summary statistics for the portfolio:

   - Market-weighted duration
   - Market-weighted average maturity
   - Market-weighted average quality rating
   - Cash and cash equivalents as a percentage of portfolio assets
   - Number of issues and proportion of market value represented by the largest ten holdings
   - Holding period return in most recent quarter
   - Capital appreciation over the period.

2. Please submit performance of fixed-income holdings for each of the last twenty quarters and annual time-weighted rates of return net of all fees and management costs. Calculate the following summary statistics:

   - Market-weighted duration
   - Market-weighted average maturity
   - Market-weighted average quality rating
   - Cash and cash equivalents as a percent of portfolio assets
   - Number of issues and proportion of market value represented by the largest ten holdings; standard deviation of returns in excess of the risk-free rate over the last twenty quarters
   - The ratio of the arithmetic mean return in excess of the risk rate (twenty quarters) divided by the standard deviation of returns (twenty quarters). Level of portfolio turnover measured as the lesser of purchases and sales each quarter as a percentage of average assets over the period
   - Income yield over the holding period, capital appreciation over the holding period
   - Level of turnover over the period measured as the lesser of purchases and sales divided by the average market value of assets over the period.

3. For each of the last twenty quarters, provide detailed proportional asset allocations quality rating with the duration computed for the portion of the portfolio assigned each quality rating.

4. Provide a detailed description of management style:

- Specify decision rules for making buys
- Specify decision rules for making sells
- Specify screens or filter rules to subset the universe of securities considered
- Provide technical and summary descriptions of portfolio optimization algorithms.

5. Provide a detailed description of resources:

- Is software used to implement decision rules owned or leased? If leased, name the vendor.
- What provisions are in place to ensure the maintenance of the software?
- What electronic databases are used to support portfolio management?
- What is the source of bond pricing used by your firm? Under what conditions can bond pricing be overridden by dealer quotes?

6. Provide samples of client reports and indicate the frequency of these reports:

- List reports and other research routinely provided clients without additional charge.
  - Who will represent your firm at quarterly client meetings?

III. TECHNICAL REQUIREMENTS: EQUITY MANAGEMENT

1. Please submit the holdings of a representative $25 million portfolio assuming investment in the most recent quarter. If respondent is proposing a commingled fund, please submit the holding of the fund as of the most recent quarter end. List representative buys and sells. If a commingled fund is proposed, list all transactions. Calculate the following summary statistics for the portfolio:

- Market price/earnings ratio and portfolio beta
- Proportional investment by broad industry grouping
- Proportional investment by exchange or security market
- Average market capitalization
- Number of issues and proportion of market value represented by the largest holdings
- Holding period return in most recent quarter.

2. Please submit performance of equity holdings for each of the last twenty quarters and annual time-weighted rates of return, net of all fees and management costs.

- Calculate summary statistics as in 1 above:
  - Market price/earnings
  - Portfolio beta
  - Proportional investment by industry group and market

- Average market capitalization
- Holding period income yield
- Holding period capital appreciation
- Cash and cash equivalents as a percent of portfolio assets
- Number of issues and proportion of market value represented by the largest ten holdings
- Standard deviation of returns in excess of the risk-free rate over the last twenty quarters
- The ratio of the arithmetic mean return in excess of the risk-free rate (twenty quarters) divided by the standard deviation of returns (twenty quarters)
- Level of portfolio turnover measured as the lesser of purchases and sales each quarter as a percent of average assets over the period

3. Provide a detailed description of management style.

   - Specify decision rules for making buys
   - Specify decision rules for making sells
   - Screen filters to subset the universe of securities considered
   - Technical and summary description of optimization algorithms.

4. Provide a detailed description of resources.

   - Is software used to implement decision rules owned or leased? If leased, name the vendor.
   - What provisions are in place to ensure the maintenance of the software?
   - What electronic databases are used to support portfolio management?
   - What is the source of equity pricing for thinly traded issues used by your firm? Under what conditions can equity pricing be overridden by dealer quotes?

5. Provide samples of client reports and indicate the frequency of these reports.

   - List reports and other research routinely provided clients without additional charge.
     - Who will represent your firm at quarterly client meetings?

Notes

Preface

1. Logue and Rader, 1998, winner, The Clarence Arthur Kulp/Elizur Wright Memorial Award for outstanding original contribution to the literature of risk and insurance, American Risk and Insurance Association, August, 2000
2. United Nations (2001, p. 680–81).
3. Retirement Confidence Survey (2002, p. 5).
4. A common metaphor is that retirement income is based on a three-legged stool: the three legs are social security, pension income, and personal savings.
5. Federal Reserve System (2004, p. 76).

Chapter 1

1. McDonnell et al. (1997, Table 13.2).

Chapter 2

1. This is a simple example to show the basic point. Because capital gains taxes are lower than ordinary income taxes, and because capital gains taxes themselves can be deferred, the person may face an after-tax interest rate of greater than 7%. If the after-tax interest rate is 8.5%, the investments grow to $921,167, of about 75% of the value of the qualified fund.
2. In addition, lawmakers may believe that pension plans increase savings and hence lead to greater economic growth.
3. For a formal analysis of some of the issues discussed here, see Laibson, Repetto, and Tobacman (1998).
4. Ippolito (1997).

Chapter 3

1. Through early 2003, the S&P 500 was down over 40%, and other indexes had fallen by over 70%.

2. Gustman and Steinmeier (1995).

3. The trend toward DC plans is discussed in greater length in Chapter 11.

4. Hustead (1998).

5. Ippolito (1995).

6. Petersen (1994).

7. McDonnell et al. (1997, Table 21.14), as updated through June 28, 2002.

8. McDonnell et al. (1997, Tables 21.9 and 21.2), as updated through June 28, 2002.

9. For an introduction, see Allen et al. (2003).

10. See Allen et al. (2003).

11. McDonnell et al. (1997, Table 21.13), as updated through June 28, 2002.

Chapter 4

1. For example, in 2003 the PBGC took over US Airways' pilot pension plan. Under the plan, pilots would receive $50,000 to $70,000 per year on retirement at age sixty. The PGBC, however, will pay only about $28,600 per year for people who retire at age sixty. See Arndt and Zellner (2003). Emerging from bankruptcy, US Airways did establish a follow-on DC plan to help close the gap for the pilots. This follow-on plan was approved by the PBGC, which reviews follow-on plans to ensure they are not abusive of the pension insurance system (Pension Benefit Guaranty Corporation, 2003).

2. Rebecca Duseau of Adams Partners contributed much to the development of this chapter.

3. 26 Mass (9 Pick.) 446 (1830).

4. This section relies heavily on Droms (1992).

5. ERISA, §404 (a)(1)(B).

6. Crawford (1995).

7. Del Guercio (1996).

8. For an excellent discussion of problems with this requirement, see Fischel and Langbein (1988).

9. Watson (1994).

10. Lurie (2002).

11. See Nofsinger (1998).

12. Lurie (1997).

13. See, for instance, Dyer (1995).

14. Blake (2001).

15. Gigot (2001).

16. See Ochs (1995).

Chapter 5

1. There are several texts available that are more detailed and are updated regularly as laws and regulations change. Two examples are Krass (2003) and Allen et al. (2003).

2. ERISA § 501.

3. ERISA § 102.

4. See 29 C.F.R. §2520.102-2(c) for details.

5. 29 C.F.R. §2520.102-3 lists the required contents of the SPD.

6. 29 C.F.R. §2520.102-3(t)(2).

7. ERISA 103(b).

8. 29 C.F.R. §2520.103-1(b)(5).

9. ERISA § 104(b).

10. 29 C.F.R. §2520.104b-10(d)(3).

11. Because contributions to the pension plan can be tax deductible, private companies are often happy to make these contributions. In fact, not only does the government require minimum contributions, it also sets maximum contributions. See IRC Sec. 404(a).

12. To start, see the Internal Revenue Code (IRC) Sec. 412.

13. These smoothing issues will also arise in Chapter 11's discussion of financial accounting for DB pension plans.

14. IRC Sec. 412(l).

15. See Walsh (2003).

16. Minimum age and service requirements are covered in IRC Sec. 410(a)(1).

17. IRC Sec. 410(a)(3).

18. IRC Sec. 410(a)(2).

19. IRC Sec. 401(a)(26).

20. See IRC Sec. 401(m)(4)(A).

21. IRC Sec. 411(a)(12).

22. Of course, Congress could retain these provisions before that date. For a helpful summary of the pension effects of EGTRRA see Levinson (2001) or Lurie (2001).

23. IRC Sec. 410(a)(1)(B)(I).

24. IRC 416(g). EGTRRA defined a "key employee" as an officer earning more than $130,000, a 5% owner, or a 1% owner with compensation of greater than $150,000. See IRC 416(I)(1).

25. IRC Sec. 414(q)(1).

26. See 26 C.F.R. §1.410(b)-2.

27. See 26 C.F.R. §1.410(b)-4.

28. See 26 C.F.R. §1.410(b)-5.

29. See 26 C.F.R. §1.401(a)(4)-1.

30. See 26 C.F.R. §1.401(a)(4)-4.

31. See 26 C.F.R. §1.401(a)(4)-5.

32. See 26 C.F.R. §1.401(a)(4)-2(c) and 26 C.F.R. §1.401(a)(4)-3(c).

33. See 26 C.F.R. §1.401(a)(4)-2(b)(2).

34. This is known as "permitted disparity." See 26 C.F.R. §1.401(l)-1.

35. For the background to SOX, see Blumenthal (2002, p. 1–22).

36. Pub. L. No. 107-204 Sec. 302(a)(3).

37. Pub. L. No. 107-204 Sec. 302(a)(4).

38. Pub. L. No. 107-204 Sec. 301.

39. Emshwiller and Smith (2001).

40. Chen and Francis (2002).

41. Pub. L. No. 107-204 Sec. 306.

42. Pub. L. No. 107-204 Sec. 306(2).

Chapter 6

1. Malkiel and Radisich (2001).

2. Blume and Siegel (1992).

3. Loftus (1998).

Chapter 7

1. Sharpe (1990).

2. The data in this paragraph is from Dimson et al. (2000).

3. Ibbotson and Associates (2003, p. 33, 43).

4. American Association of Individual Investors (2003), using the Standard & Poor's 500 index for stocks and the Lehman Brothers aggregate index for bonds.

5. From 1926 to 2002, U.S. stocks; Ibbotson and Associates (2003, p. 111).

6. See Mehra (2003), a review of the literature since the publication of Mehra and Prescott (1985).

7. Arnott and Bernstein (2002).

8. Ibbotson and Chen (2003).

9. Mehra (2003).

10. Bodie (1995).

11. Samuelson (1990).

12. Cambell et al. (2001).

13. Pagliari et al. (2001).

14. Christie (2001).

15. Christie (2003).

16. Malkiel (2002).

17. Purcell and Crowley (1999).

18. Liang (2001).

Chapter 8

1. For the first elaboration of the integration notion, see Treynor (1977).

2. Bodie et al. (1987).

3. Feldstein and Morck (1983).

4. Bulow et al. (1987).

5. Ambachtscheer (1995).

6. Standard & Poor's (2003).

7. Wilshire Associates (2002).

8. See Copeland and Weston (1988).

9. Bulow (1982) and Bulow and Scholes (1983).

10. Ippolito (1985).

11. Ippolito (1986).

12. Berkowitz and Rowe (1990).

13. See, for example, Ezra (1988).

14. Barrett (1988).

15. One way to match a bond portfolio to the plan liabilities is to match the cash throw-off of the bonds with the obligations that must be paid. There are other more complex ways to achieve bond portfolio dedication, but cash-flow matching is the simplest. Cash-flow matching would ensure that the promised payments—the legal claims—of the plan beneficiaries were safe.

16. An alternative hybrid pension fund management strategy might distinguish between the present value of vested liabilities and all other liabilities, and then treat the funding of these two pools differently.

Chapter 9

1. Brinson et al. (1986). See also Blake et al. (1999).

2. Ambachtsheer (1988).

3. Solnick and McLeavey (2003).

4. Sharpe (1990).

5. Tschampion et al. (forthcoming).
6. Tschampion et al. (forthcoming).
7. Bronson et al. (forthcoming).
8. See, for example, Haugen (1990) and Elton and Gruber (1992).
9. Note that pension funds do not simply match the durations of assets and liabilities. Rather, they must adjust for scale differences by setting asset durations equal to liability durations multiplied by the ratio of liabilities to assets. They must also adjust for differences in the convexity—the rate of change in the assets' or liabilities' sensitivities to changes in interest rates.
10. For a good discussion of how this may be done, see Leibowitz et al. (1994).
11. Sharpe (1976) and Harrison and Sharpe (1983).
12. Weinberg (1995).
13. Black and Dewhurst (1981); Tepper (1981).
14. Stewart (2003).
15. Myers (1994) and Tigue (1994).
16. Bodie et al. (1987).
17. Petersen (1996).
18. Harris (2002).
19. Ippolito (1988).
20. Sharpe (1990) and Sharpe and Perold (1988).
21. Arnott (1990).
22. Arnott and Lovell (1990).
23. Sharpe (1990).
24. MacBeth and Emanuel (1993).

Chapter 10

1. See Wardlow (1995) for an overview.
2. Two outstanding articles dealing with the details in masterful ways are Revsine (1989) and Stickney (1995).
3. Indeed, during the 1980s, many corporate raiders carefully evaluated the magnitude of a target company's pension surplus—the difference between the value of assets and the ABO—before trying to acquire a company. After acquisition, they bought a pension plan termination annuity equal to the value of the ABO and withdrew the after-tax amount of the recoverable surplus.
4. See Weinberg (1995).
5. See Stickney (1995).
6. See, for example, the commentary in Arnott and Bernstein (1988).
7. This is roughly termed "duration matching." The most common measure of duration is

$$\Sigma \; \{[t \times C_t]/[1 + (Y/2)]^t\}/P,$$

where t is time, 1,2,3, and so forth; C_t is the cash flow in each period t; Y is the yield on the bond; and P is the bond's price. In theory and under some very specific circumstances, two instruments with the same duration should experience nearly identical changes in value whenever Y, the yield, changes.
8. Ibbotson Associates (2003, p. 33).
9. See Sanes and Zurack (1987).

Chapter 11

1. For example, between 1990 and 1998 (the latest year for which data is available), the fraction of full-time public employees participating in a DB plan was constant at about 90%. The percentage participating in a DC plan increased but remained relatively small: about 10% in 1990 and 15% in 1998. McDonnell et al. (1997, Table 4.1, as revised May 2001). Notice that in 1998, 90% of full-time public employees participated in DB plans and 15% participated in DC plans. The sum is more than 100% because some employees participated in more than one plan.

2. For example, in medium and large private establishments, DB participation fell from 59% to 50% between 1991 and 1997. DC participation grew from 48% to 57%.

3. DC assets increased from $700 billion in 1990 to $2.3 trillion in 2001. Board of Governors of the Federal Reserve System (2002, p. 113).

4. For example, Gustman and Steinmeier (1992), Kruse (1995), Ippolito (1995), Perdue (2001), Friedberg and Owyang (2002).

5. It was in 1981 that the Treasury Department clarified the rules under which 401(k) plans would be tax qualified.

6. See Ippolito (1997, Chapter 7).

7. For example, see Clowes (2000, Chapter 13), and Ippolito (2002).

8. See, for example, Friedberg and Owyang (2002).

9. Dini and Goar (2002).

10. Advisory Opinion dated December 14, 2001. Letter to Mr. William A. Schmidt and Mr. Eric Berger from Louis Campagna, Chief, Division of Fiduciary Interpretations.

11. Jacobius (2000).

12. Madrian and Shea (2001), Choi et al. (2002).

13. Benartzi and Thaler (2001).

14. HR Investment Consultants, cited by Brenner (1996).

15. This section based on Tschampion et al. (forthcoming).

16. See Kaiser (1990).

17. The federal inflation-indexed bonds introduced in early 1997 may be attractive to some individuals, depending on their pricing, because they offer a partial offset to inflation-induced interest rate changes.

18. Profit Sharing and 401(k) Council of America (2003).

19. Benartzi and Thaler (2002).

Chapter 12

1. This chapter reproduces, with permission, material from Baker, Logue, and Rader (2002).

2. Profit Sharing and 401(k) Council of America (2003).

3. Schultz (2001).

4. Sulds and Rabin (2002).

5. See Pugh, Oswald, and Jahera (2000), p. 167.

6. Rosen (1990).

7. Chang (1990).

8. Park and Song (1995).

9. Scholes and Wolfson (1990).

10. Chang (1990).

11. Park and Song (1995).

12. A similar argument holds for the case of executive stock options. A recent study found that the efficiency costs can be substantial in that context. See Meulbroek (2001).

13. Benartzi (2001).

Chapter 13

1. An example of a multiemployer hybrid plan is given in Appendix C.

2. Bodie, Marcus, and Merton (1988).

3. IBM's experience with both this PEP plan and a subsequent cash balance plan will be discussed later in this chapter.

4. See Matthews (1990) and Thomas (1991).

5. Schultz and MacDonald (1998).

6. Schultz and MacDonald (1998).

7. Schultz (1999).

8. Schultz (1998).

9. Myers (2002).

10. *Kathi Cooper et al. v. The IBM Personal Pension Plan and IBM Corporation.*

11. *Eaton et al. v. Onan Corporation.*

12. 67 Fed. Reg. No. 238, December 11, 2002.

13. Schultz and MacDonald (1998).

14. *Berger et al. v. Xerox Corporation Retirement Income Guarantee Plan.*

15. *Berger et al. v. Xerox*, p. 11.

Chapter 14

1. McDonnell et al. (1997), Tables 11.1, 18.2, 19.3.

2. Ibbotson Associates (2003, p. 33).

3. Ibbotson Associates (2003, p. 33).

4. See Treynor (1965).

5. Roll and Ross (1994).

6. Halpern and Lakonishok (1990).

7. Lehmann and Modest (1987).

8. See Elton and Gruber (1995) for a good discussion.

9. See Lehmann and Modest (1987) and Roll and Ross (1994).

10. See Bailey, Richards, and Tierney (1990).

11. including Fama (1972); Brinson, Hood, and Beebower (1986); and Bodie, Kane, and Marcus (1995).

12. This section is based on Christopherson and Williams (1997).

13. See, for example, Fama and French (1992) and Chen, Roll, and Ross (1986).

14. Sharpe (1992).

15. Fama and French (1996).

16. Fama and French (1992).

Chapter 15

1. See Jensen (1969).

2. See, for example, Dunn and Theisen (1983).

3. See, for example, Ippolito (1989).

4. See, for example, Grinblatt and Titman (1989a, 1989b).

5. See Goetzmann and Ibbotson (1994).
6. Kahn and Rudd (1995).
7. Elton et al. (1993).
8. See Malkiel (1995) and Brown and Goetzmann (1995).
9. Malkiel (1995).
10. Brown and Goetzmann (1995).
11. Christopherson, Ferson, and Glassman (1996).
12. Olsen (1999).
13. See, for example, the approach developed in Admati and Ross (1985), which uses managers' expectations of security returns and risks.
14. See Arnott and Lovell (1990).
15. Berkowitz, Finney, and Logue (1988).
16. Ippolito and Turner (1987).
17. Lakonishok, Schleifer, and Vishny (1992).
18. See, for example, Ferson and Khang (2002).
19. Berkowitz, Finney, and Logue (1988).
20. See, for example, Lakonishok, Schleifer, and Vishny (1992).
21. Del Guercio (1996).
22. See, for example, Haugen (1995).
23. McCarthy and Turner (1989).

Chapter 16

1. See Lowenstein (1996).
2. See Solnik, Boucrelle, and Le Fur (1996) for a good discussion of currency risk factors.
3. Leibowitz, Kogleman, and Bader (1994).
4. See Haugen (1990).
5. Haugen (1990).
6. See Solnik, Boucrelle, and Le Fur (1996).
7. Froot (1993).
8. Siegel (1994).
9. See Gastineau and Bhatia (1996).
10. See Nederlof (1996).
11. Smithson (1996).
12. Beder (1995).
13. See Nederlof (1996).
14. Sharpe (2002).

Chapter 17

1. *Institutional Investor* (1999). In a 1998 survey, a similar result was obtained: 44.7% of pension plan sponsors used derivatives; Levich, Hayt, and Ripston (1999).
2. See Hill (1993).
3. For a good treatment of these, see Arditti (1996) and Hull (1997).
4. This example was adapted from an example in McMillan (1993).
5. This example was adapted from an example in Polsky (1996).

Chapter 18

1. Reichenstein (1994).
2. Kujaca (1996).

3. Olsen (1999).
4. Gould (1990).
5. Brown, Harlow, and Starks (1996).
6. Elton, Gruber, and Blake (2003).
7. Ellis (1993).
8. Bensman (1996).
9. Rohrer (1995).

Chapter 19

1. Williams (2002).
2. Perold (1988).
3. Leinweber (1993).
4. On organized exchanges in the United States, stock prices traditionally went up or down in increments of eighths or sixteenths. In 2001, however, the New York Stock Exchange and the NASDAQ converted to penny increments.
5. Berkowitz, Logue, and Noser (1988).
6. Wagner (1993).
7. Bergsman (1996).

Chapter 20

1. See Barberis and Thaler (2003) for a good summary of this literature.
2. Tversky (1990).
3. See Odean (1998, 1999).
4. Benartzi and Thaler (1995).
5. Statman (1999).
6. Statman (1999).
7. Wood (1997).
8. O'Barr and Conley (1992).
9. Choi et al. (2002).
10. Thaler and Benartzi (forthcoming).
11. Benartzi and Thaler (forthcoming).
12. Barberis and Thaler (2003).
13. See Shleifer and Vishney (1997) and D'Avolio (2002) for example.

Chapter 21

1. Securities and Exchange Commission Division of Corporate Finance (2003).
2. Guidera (2002).
3. Millstein (1994).
4. See Monks and Minow (1995).
5. Pound (1992), p. 7.
6. See, for instance, Pound (1992), Sametz (1995), and Roe (1995).
7. See Gertner (1990).
8. See Elson (1996) for a discussion of board compensation.
9. See, for example, Black (1992) and Skowronski and Pound (1993).
10. See Black (1992).
11. Karpoff, Malatesta, and Walkling (1996), and Wahal (1996).
12. Smith (1996).

13. Gillan and Starks (1996).
14. Prevost and Rao (2000).
15. Strickland, Wiles, and Zenner (1996).
16. Opler and Sokobin (1995).
17. Caton, Goh, and Donaldson (2001).
18. Admati, Pfleiderer, and Zechner (1994).
19. See Roe (1995).
20. Monks and Minow (1995).
21. See Romano (1995).
22. Monks and Minow (1995).
23. Sametz (1995).
24. Longstreth (1995).
25. Longstreth (1995).

Appendix B

1. UBS Asset Management (2002).
2. Diermeier and Singer (2002).
3. Malkiel (2002).
4. A recent study, however, indicates that correlations decline in extreme bull markets; Longin and Solnik (2001).
5. Solnik (2002).
6. Conover et al. (2002).
7. Rosenberg (1995).
8. Jorion (1994).
9. Diermeier and Singer (2002).

Works Cited

Admati, Anat R., Paul Pfleiderer, and Josef Zechner. 1994. Large shareholder activism, risk sharing and financial market equilibrium. *Journal of Political Economy,* vol. 102, 6: 1097–1130.

Admati, Anat R., and Stephen A. Ross. 1985. Measuring investment performance in a rational expectations equilibrium model. *Journal of Business,* vol. 58, 1: 1–26.

Allen, Everett T., Joseph J. Melone, Jerry S. Rosenbloom, and Dennis F. Mahoney. 2003. *Pension planning: Pension, profit sharing, and other deferred compensation plans,* 9th ed. New York: McGraw-Hill/Irwin.

Ambachtsheer, Keith P. 1988. *Telling the prospective returns story. The Ambachtsheer letter.* Toronto: Keith P. Ambachtsheer and Associates.

———. 1995. Total quality management. In *Investment policy, seminar proceedings.* Charlottesville, VA: AIMR, 41–53.

American Association of Individual Investors. 2003. *The individual investor's guide to the top mutual funds,* 22nd ed. Chicago, IL: American Association of Individual Investors.

Arditti, Fred D. 1996. *Derivatives.* Boston, MA: Harvard Business School Press.

Arndt, Michael, and Wendy Zellner. 2003. How to fix the airlines. *Business Week,* April 14, p. 74.

Arnott, Robert D. 1990. Managing the asset mix: decisions and consequences. Paper presented at the Fourth Annual Allocation Congress, Boca Raton, FL.

Arnott, Robert D., and Peter L. Bernstein. 1988. The right way to manage your pension fund. *Harvard Business Review,* vol. 67, 1: 95–102.

———. 2002. What risk premium is "normal"? *Financial Analysts Journal,* vol. 58, 2: 64.

Arnott, Robert D., and Robert M. Lovell, Jr. 1990. Monitoring and rebalancing the portfolio. In *Managing investment portfolios: A dynamic process,* 2nd ed., ed. John L. Maginn and Donald L. Tuttle. Boston, MA: Warren, Gorham and Lamont, 13-1–13-42.

Bailey, Jeffrey V., Thomas M. Richards, and David E. Tierney. 1990. Benchmark portfolios and the manager/plan sponsor relationship. In *Current topics in investment management,* ed. Frank J. Fabozzi and T. Dessa Fabozzi. New York: HarperCollins.

Baker, Gus, Dennis E. Logue, and Jack S. Rader. 2002. On compensation, pension plans and company stock: perspectives following Enron. *AFP Exchange,* vol. 22, 3: 34–37.

Barberis, Nicholas, and Richard Thaler. 2003. A survey of behavioral finance. In *Handbook of the economics of finance,* ed. George Constantinides, Milt Harris, and Rene Stulz. Amsterdam: Elsevier, 1052–1121.

Barrett, W. Brian. 1988. Term structure modeling for pension liability discounting. *Financial Analysts Journal,* vol. 44, 6: 63–67.

Beder, Tanya Styblo. 1995. VAR: Seductive but dangerous. *Financial Analysts Journal,* vol. 51, 5: 12–24.

Benartzi, Shlomo 2001. Excessive extrapolation and the allocation of 401(k) accounts to company stock. *Journal of Finance,* vol. 56, 5: 1747–1764.

Benartzi, Shlomo, and Richard H. Thaler. 1995. Myopic loss aversion and the equity premium puzzle. *Quarterly Journal of Economics,* 110: 75–92.

———. 2001. Naive Diversification strategies in defined contribution savings plans. *American Economic Review,* vol. 91, 1: 79–98.

———. 2002. How much is investor autonomy worth? *Journal of Finance,* vol. 57, 4: 1593–1616.

———. Forthcoming. Sell more tomorrow: Using behavioral economics to increase employee diversification. UCLA working paper.

Bensman, Miriam. 1996. Doing without style. *Institutional Investor,* vol. 30, 2: 79–85.

Berger v. Xerox Retirement Income Guaranty Plan, 2002 WL 31165120 (SD Ill 2002).

Bergsman, Steve. 1996. Soft dollars: Where do we go from here? *Pension Management,* vol. 32, 5: 24–26, 53.

Berkowitz, Stephen A., Louis D. Finney, and Dennis E. Logue. 1988. Pension plans vs. mutual funds: is the client victim or culprit? *California Management Review,* vol. 30, 3: 74–91.

Berkowitz, Stephen A., Dennis E. Logue, and Eugene A. Noser. 1988. The total cost of transactions on the NYSE. *Journal of Finance,* vol. 43, 1: 97–112.

Berkowitz, Stephen A., and Douglas L. Rowe. 1990. Pension plans. In *Handbook of modern finance,* ed. Dennis E. Logue. Boston, MA: Warren, Gorham and Lamont, 33-1–33-27.

Black, Bernard S. 1992. Institutional investors and corporate governance: The case for institutional voice. *Journal of Applied Corporate Finance,* vol. 5, 3: 19–32.

Black, Fischer, and Moray P. Dewhurst. 1981. A new investment strategy for pension funds. *Journal of Portfolio Management,* vol. 7, 4: 26–34.

Blake, David, Bruce N. Lehmann, and Allan Timmermann. 1999. Asset allocation dynamics and pension fund performance. *Journal of Business,* vol. 72, 4: 429–461.

Blake, Rich. 2001. Bracing for a backlash: Remember when employees were crowing over their 401(k)s? Now they're suing over them. A wave of class-action litigation has only just begun. *Institutional Investor,* vol. 35, 11: 67.

Bloomenthal, Harold S. 2002. *Sarbanes-Oxley Act in perspective.* St. Paul, MN: West Group.

Blume, Marshall E., and Jeremy J. Siegel. 1992. The theory of security pricing and market structure. *Financial markets, Institutions and Instruments* 1: 3–57.

Board of Governors of the Federal Reserve System. 2004. *Flow of Funds Accounts of the United States: Flows and Outstandings Fourth Quarter 2003.* Washington, DC: Federal Reserve Statistical Release.

Bodie, Zvi. 1995. On the risks of stocks in the long run. *Financial Analysts Journal,* 51, 3: 18–22.

Bodie, Zvi, Alex Kane, and Alan J. Marcus. 1995. *Essentials of Investments,* 2nd ed. Burr Ridge, IL: Irwin Professional Publishing.

Bodie, Zvi, Jay O. Light, Randall Morck, and Robert A. Taggart, Jr. 1987. Funding and capital allocation in corporate pension plans: an empirical investigation. In *Issues in pension economics,* ed. Zvi Bodie, John B. Shoven, and David A. Wise. Chicago: University of Chicago Press, 15–44.

Bodie, Zvi, Alan J. Marcus, and Robert C. Merton. 1988. Defined benefit versus defined contribution benefit plans: What are the real trade offs? *Pensions in U.S. economy,* ed. Zvi Bodie, John B. Shoven, and David A. Wise. Chicago: University of Chicago Press, 139–160.

Brenner, Lynn. 1996. Facing up to total plan costs. *CFO,* vol. 12, 4: 51–56.

Brinson, Gary P., L. Randolph Hood, and Gilbert L. Beebower. 1986. Determinants of portfolio performance. *Financial Analysts Journal,* vol. 45, 2: 39–44.

Bronson, James W., Matthew H. Scanlan, and Jan R. Squires. Forthcoming. Managing individual investor portfolios. In *Managing investor portfolios: A dynamic process,* 3rd ed. Charlottesville, VA: AIMR.

Brown, Keith C., W. V. Harlow, and Laura T. Starks. 1996. Of tournaments and temptations: An analysis of managerial incentives in the mutual fund industry. *Journal of Finance,* vol. 51, 1: 85–110.

Brown, Stephen J., and William Goetzmann. 1995. Performance persistence. *Journal of Finance,* vol. 50, 2: 679–698.

Bulow, Jeremy L. 1982. What are corporate pension liabilities? *Quarterly Journal of Economics,* vol. 97, 3: 435–452.

Bulow, Jeremy L. Randall Morck, and Laurence Summers. 1987. How does the market value unfunded pension liabilities. In *Issues in pension economics,* ed. Zvi Bodie, John B. Shoven, and David A. Wise. Chicago: University of Chicago Press, 81–103.

Bulow, Jeremy L., and Myron Scholes. 1983. Who owns the assets in a defined benefit pension plan? In *Financial aspects of the United States pension system,* ed. Zvi Bodie and John B. Shoven. Chicago: University of Chicago Press, 17–32.

Cambell, John Y., Martin Lettau, Burton Malkiel, and Yexiao Xu. 2001. Have individual stocks become more volatile? An empirical investigation of idiosyncratic risk. *Journal of Finance,* vol. 56, 1: 1–44.

Caton, Gary L., Jeremy Goh, and Jeffrey Donaldson. 2001. The effectiveness of institutional activism. *Financial Analysts Journal,* vol. 57, 4: 21–26.

Chang, Saeyoung. 1990. Employee stock ownership plans and shareholder wealth: an empirical investigation. *Financial Management,* vol. 19, 1: 48–58.

Chen, Kathy, and Theo Francis. 2002. Questioning the books: Enron official failed to warn participants of 401(k) plan. *Wall Street Journal,* February 6, 2002.

Chen, Nai-Fu, Richard Roll, and Stephen A. Ross. 1986. Economic forces and the stock market. *Journal of Business,* vol. 59, 3: 383–404.

Choi, James, David Laibson, Brigitte Madrian, and Andrew Metrick. 2002. Defined contribution pensions: Plan rules, participant decisions, and the path of least resistance. In *Tax policy and the economy,* Vol. 16, ed. James M. Poterba. Cambridge, MA: MIT Press, 67–113.

Christie, Rebecca. 2001. Bond dealers fight treasury advisers' call for end to sale of inflation-indexed securities. *Wall Street Journal,* June 15, 2001.

———. 2003. Treasury counts TIPS to cut costs—inflation-indexed securities are widening investor pool, saving money, agency says. *Wall Street Journal,* June 2, 2003.

Christopherson, Jon A., Wayne E. Ferson, and Debra A. Glassman. 1996. Conditioning manager alphas on economic information: another look at the persistence of performance. NBER Working Paper 5830.

Christopherson, Jon A., and C. Nola Williams. 1997. Equity style: What it is and why it matters. In *The handbook of equity style management,* 2nd ed., ed. T. Daniel Coggin, Frank J. Fabozzi, and Robert D. Arnott. Hoboken, NJ: John Wiley & Sons, 1–19.

Clowes, Michael J. 2000. *The money flood: How pension funds revolutionized investing.* New York: John Wiley & Sons.

Code of Federal Regulations (C.F.R.).

Conover, C. Mitchell, Gerald R. Jensen, and Robert R. Johnson. 2002. Emerging markets: When are they worth it? *Financial Analysts Journal,* vol. 58, 2: 86–95.

Copeland, Thomas E., and J. Fred Weston. 1988. *Financial theory and corporate policy.* Reading, MA: Addison-Wesley.

Crawford, George. 1995. A fiduciary duty to use derivatives? *Stanford Journal of Law, Business and Finance,* vol. 1, 1: 307–332.

D'Avolio, Gene. 2002. The market for borrowing stock. *Journal of Financial Economics,* vol. 66, 2–3: 271–306.

Diermeier, Jeffrey J., and Brian D. Singer. 2002. Quarterly focus: Echoes of the bubble; return of diversification under globalization. Newsletter, UBS Global Asset Management.

Del Guercio, Diane. 1996. The distorting effects of the prudent-man laws on institutional equity investments. *Journal of Financial Economics,* vol. 40, 1: 31–62.

Dimson, Elroy, Paul Marsh, and Mike Staunton. 2000. *The Millennium Book: A Century of Investment Returns.* London: ABN-AMRO and London Business School.

Dini, Justin and Jinny Goar. 2002. Advice and dissent: While the firestorm about company stock dominates the debate over 401(k)s, the financial services industry is waging a related—and just as critical—battle over investment advice. *Institutional Investor,* vol. 36, 3: 57.

Droms, William G. 1992. Fiduciary responsibilities of investment managers and trustees. *Financial Analysts Journal,* vol. 48, 4: 58–64.

Dunn, Patricia C., and Rolf D. Theisen. 1983. How consistently do active managers win? *Journal of Portfolio Management,* vol. 9, 4: 47–50.

Dyer, Jack. 1995. Fiduciaries less rigorous with 401(k) plans. *Pensions and Investments,* vol. 23, 11: 10.

Eaton et al. v. Onan Corporation, 117 F Supp 812 (SD Ind 2002).

Ellis, Charles D. 1993. *Investment policy: How to win the loser's game,* 2nd ed. Burr Ridge, IL: Irwin Professional Publishing.

Elson, Charles M. 1996. Director compensation and the management-captured board—the history of a symptom and a cure. *Southern Methodist University Law Review,* vol. 50, 1: 127–174.

Elton, Edwin J., and Martin J. Gruber. 1992. Optimal investment strategies with investor liabilities. *Journal of Banking and Finance,* vol. 16, 5: 869–890.

———. 1995. Evaluation of portfolio performance. In *Modern portfolio theory and investment analysis.* Hoboken, NJ: John Wiley & Sons, 630–371.

Elton, Edwin J., Martin J. Gruber, and Christopher R. Blake. 2003. Incentive fees and mutual funds. *Journal of Finance,* vol. 58, 2: 779–804.

Elton, Edwin J., Martin J. Gruber, Sanjiv Das, and Matthew Hlavka. 1993. Efficiency with costly information: A reinterpretation of the evidence from manager portfolios. *Review of Financial Studies,* vol. 6, 1: 1–23.

Employee retirement income security act of 1974, as amended, (ERISA) U.S. Code, Title 29, Chapter 18.

Emshwiller John, and Rebecca Smith. 2001. Enron jolt: Investments, assets generate big loss—part of charge tied to 2 partnerships interests Wall Street. *Wall Street Journal,* October 17, 2001.

Ezra, D. Don. 1980. How actuaries determine the unfunded pension liability. *Financial Analysts Journal,* vol. 36, 4: 43–50.

———. 1988. Economic values: A pension pentateuch. *Financial Analysts Journal,* vol. 44, 2: 58–67.

Fama, Eugene F. 1972. Components of investment performance. *Journal of Finance,* vol. 27, 3: 551–567.

Fama, Eugene F., and Kenneth R. French. 1992. The cross-section of expected stock returns. *Journal of Finance,* vol. 47, 2: 427–466.

Fama, Eugene F., and Kenneth R. French. 1996. Multifactor explanations of asset pricing anomalies. *Journal of Finance,* vol. 51, 1: 55–84.

Federal Register.

Federal Reserve System. 2004. *Flow of funds accounts of the United States: Flows and outstandings fourth quarter 2003.* Washington, DC: Board of Governors of the Federal Reserve System.

Feldstein, Martin, and Randall Morck. 1983. Pension funds and the value of equities. *Financial Analysts Journal,* vol. 39, 5: 29–39.

Ferson, Wayne, and Kenneth Khang. 2002. Conditional performance measurement using portfolio weights: evidence for pension funds. *Journal of Financial Economics,* vol. 65, 2: 249–282.

Fischel, Daniel, and John H. Langbein. 1988. ERISA's fundamental contradiction: The exclusive benefit rule. *University of Chicago Law Review,* vol. 55, 4: 1105–1160.

Friedberg, Leora, and Michael T. Owyang. 2002. Not your father's pension plan: The rise of 401(k) and other defined contribution plans. *Federal Reserve Bank of St. Louis Review,* vol. 84, 1: 23–34.

Froot, K. A. 1993. Currency hedging over long horizons. Working Paper 4355. Cambridge, MA: National Bureau of Economic Research.

Gastineau, Gary L., and Sanjiv Bhatia. 1996. Risk management: An overview. In AIMR Conference Proceedings: Risk Management. Charlottesville, VA: AIMR, 1–4.

Gertner, Marc. 1990. DOL enhances enforcement of pension investments. *Pension World,* vol. 26, 12: 18–20.

Ghilarducci, Teresa, Garth Mangum, Jeffrey S. Peterson, and Peter Phillips. 1995. *Portable pension plans for casual labor markets: Lessons from the Operating Engineers Central Pension Fund.* Westport, CT: Quorum Books.

Gigot, Thomas S. 2001. 401(k) plan litigation under ERISA. *Journal of Pension Planning and Compliance,* vol. 27, 3: 63.

Gillan, Stuart L., and Laura T. Starks. 1996. Shareholder activism and institutional investors: The effects of corporate-governance related proposals. Working paper, University of Texas.

Goetzmann, William N., and Roger Ibbotson. 1994. Do winners repeat? Patterns in mutual fund behavior. *Journal of Portfolio Management,* vol. 20, 2: 9–18.

Gould, Floyd J. 1990. Efficient markets, investment management selection and the loser's game. In *Current topics in investment management,* ed. Frank J. Fabozzi and T. Dessa Fabozzi. New York: Harper & Row, 49–56.

Grinblatt, Mark, and Sheridan Titman. 1989a. Mutual fund performance: an analysis of quarterly holdings. *Journal of Business,* vol. 62, 3: 393–416.

———. 1989b. Portfolio performance evaluation: old issues and new insights. *Review of Financial Studies,* vol. 2, 3: 393–421.

Guidera, Jerry. 2002. Shareholder activists win two big ones. *Wall Street Journal,* May 9, 2002.

Gustman, Alan L., and Thomas L. Steinmeier. 1992. The stampede toward defined contribution pension plans: Fact of fiction? *Industrial Relations,* vol. 31, 2: 361–369.

———. 1995. *Pension incentives and job mobility.* Kalamazoo, MI: W.E. Upjohn Institute for Employment Research.

Halpern, Paul, and Josef Lakonishok. 1990. Why the difference in performance measurement? *Investing,* vol. 4, 1: 37.

Harris, Jennifer D. 2002. *Survey Report: 2001 Survey of State and Local Government Employee Retirement Systems.* Washington, DC: Public Pension Coordinating Council.

Harrison, I. Michael, and William F. Sharpe. 1983. Optimal funding and asset allocation risks for defined benefit pension plans. In *Financial aspects of the United States pension system,* ed. Zvi Bodie and John B. Shoven. Chicago: University of Chicago Press, 91–103.

Harvard v. Amory, 26 Mass (9 Pick.) 446 (1830).

Haugen, Robert. 1990. Pension investing and corporate risk management. In *Managing institutional assets,* edited by Frank J. Fabozzi. New York: Harper & Row.

———. 1995. *The new finance: The case against efficient markets.* Englewood Cliffs, NJ: Prentice-Hall.

Hill, Joanne M. 1993. Adding value with equity derivatives: Part II. In *Derivative strategies for managing portfolio risk.* Charlottesville, VA: AIMR, 62–73.

Hirschman, Albert. 1970. *Exit, Voice, and Loyalty.* Cambridge, MA: Harvard University Press.

Hull, John C. 1997. *Options, futures, and other derivatives,* 3rd ed. Englewood Cliffs, NJ: Prentice-Hall.

Hustead, Edwin C. 1998. Trends in retirement income plan administrative expenses. In *Living with defined contribution pensions,* ed. Olivia S. Mitchell and Sylvester J. Schieber. Philadelphia: University of Pennsylvania Press, 166–177.

Ibbotson Associates. 2003. *Stock, Bonds, Bills, and Inflation.* Chicago, IL: Ibbotson Associates.

Ibbotson, Roger G., and Peng Chen. 2003. Long-run stock returns: Participating in the real economy. *Financial Analysts Journal,* vol. 59, 1: 88.

Institutional Investor. 1999. Mainstreaming derivatives, vol. 33, 8: 160.

Internal Revenue Code (IRC).

Ippolito, Richard A. 1985. The labor contract and true economic pension liabilities. *American Economic Review,* vol. 75, 6: 1031–1043.

———. 1986. *Pension, Economics and Public Policy.* Homewood, IL: Dow Jones/Irwin.

———. 1988. The role of risk in a tax arbitrage pension portfolio. Washington, DC: Pension Benefit Guaranty Corporation Working Paper.

———. 1989. Efficiency with costly information: a study of mutual fund performance. *Quarterly Journal of Economics,* vol. 104, 1: 4–23.

———. 1995. Toward explaining the growth of defined contribution plans. *Industrial Relations,* 34: 1–20.

———. 1997. *Pension plans and employee performance: Evidence, analysis, and policy.* Chicago: University of Chicago Press.

———. 2002. The reversion tax's perverse result. *Regulation,* vol. 25, 1: 46–53.

Ippolito, Richard A., and John Turner. 1987. Turnover fees and pension plan performance. *Financial Analysts Journal,* vol. 43, 6: 16–26.

Jacobius, Arlene. 2000. Hitting the target: Top-notch education campaign honored. *Pas-sions & Investments,* vol. 28, 3: 29.

Jensen, Michael C. 1969. Risk, the pricing of capital assets, and the evaluation of in-vestment portfolios. *Journal of Business,* vol. 42, 2: 167–247.

Jorion, Phillippe. 1994. Mean/variance analysis of currency overlays. *Financial Analysts Journal,* vol. 50, 3: 48–56.

Kaiser, Ronald W. 1990. Individual investors. In *Managing investment portfolios: A dy-namic process,* ed. John L. Maginn and Donald L. Tuttle, 2nd ed. Boston, MA: Warren, Gorham and Lamont, 1990, 3-3–3-46.

Kahn, Ronald N., and Andrew Rudd. 1995. Does historical performance predict future performance? *Financial Analysts Journal,* vol. 51, 6: 43–52.

Karpoff, Jonathan M., Paul H. Malatesta, and Ralph A. Walkling. 1996. Corporate gov-ernance and shareholder initiatives: empirical evidence. *Journal of Financial Econom-ics,* vol. 42, 3: 365–395.

Kathi Cooper et al., v. The IBM Personal PensionPlan and IBM Corporation, 274 F Supp 3d 1010 (SD Ill 2003).

Krass, Stephen J. 2003. *The pension answer book.* New York: Aspen Publishers.

Kruse, Douglas L. 1995. Pension substitution in the 1980s: Why the shift toward Defined Contribution? *Industrial Relations,* vol. 34, 2: 218–241.

Kujaca, James A. 1996. *The trillion dollar promise.* Burr Ridge, IL: Irwin Professional Publishing.

Laibson, David I., Andrea Repetto, and Jeremy Tobacman. 1998. Self-control and savings for retirement. *Brookings Papers on Economic Activity,* vol. 1998, 1: 91–196.

Lakonishok, Josef, Andrei Shleifer, and Robert W. Vishny. 1992. The structure and per-formance of the money management industry. *Brookings Papers on Economic Activ-ity: Microeconomics,* vol. 1992, 339–391.

Lehmann, Bruce, and David M. Modest. 1987. Mutual fund performance evaluation: A comparison of benchmarks and benchmark comparisons. *Journal of Finance,* vol. 42, 2: 223–265.

Leibowitz, Martin L., Stanley Kogelman, and Lawrence N. Bader. 1994. Funding ratio return. *Journal of Portfolio Management,* vol. 21, 1: 39–47.

Leinweber, David J. 1993. Using information from trading in trading and portfolio man-agement. In *Execution techniques, true trading costs and the microstructure of mar-kets.* Charlottesville, VA: AIMR, 24–34.

Levich, Richard M., Gregory S. Hayt, and Beth A. Ripston. 1999. 1998 survey of de-rivatives and risk management practices by U.S. institutional investors. New York University Working Paper.

Levinson, Gerald M. 2001. New tax law aptly named "Little ERISA." *Journal of Pension Planning and Compliance,* vol. 27, 3: 78–86.

Liang, Bing. 2001. Hedge fund performance: 1990–1999. *Financial Analysts Journal,* vol. 57, 1: 11–18.

Loftus, John S. 1998. Enhanced Equity Indexing. In *Selected topics in equity portfolio management,* ed. Frank J. Fabozzi. Hoboken, NJ: John Wiley & Sons.

Logue, Dennis E., and Jack S. Rader. 1998. *Managing pension plans: A comprehensive guide to improving plan performance.* Boston, MA: Harvard Business School Press.

Longin, Francois, and Bruno Solnik. 2001. Extreme correlation of international equity markets. *Journal of Finance,* vol. 56, 2: 649–676.

Longstreth, Bevis. 1995. Corporate governance: There's danger in new orthodoxies. *Jour-nal of Portfolio Management,* vol. 21, 3: 47–52.

Lowenstein, Roger. 1996. How pension funds lost in the market boom. *Wall Street Journal.* February 1, 1996.

Lurie, Alvin D. 1997. ETI's, a scheme for the rescue of city and country with pension funds. *Journal of Pension Planning and Compliance,* vol. 22, 4: 1.

———. 2001. The 2001 tax law: A Congressional vanishing act, but with real magic for retirement plans. *Compensation and Benefits Management,* vol. 17, 4: 1–9.

———. 2002. Calling on all pension funds to come to the aid of their cities. *Journal of Pension Planning and Compliance,* vol. 28, 2: 58.

MacBeth, James D., and David C. Emanuel. 1993. Tactical asset allocation: Pros and cons. *Financial Analysts Journal,* vol. 49, 6: 30–43.

Madrian and Shea. 2001. Preaching to the converted and converting those taught: Financial education in the workplace. University of Chicago Working Paper.

Malkiel, Burton G. 1995. Returns from investing in equity mutual funds: 1971–1991. *Journal of Finance,* vol. 50, 2: 549–572,

———. 2002. How much diversification is enough? In *AIMR conference proceedings: Equity portfolio construction.* Charlottesville, VA: AIMR, 18–28.

Malkiel, Burton G., and Alexander Radisich. 2001. The growth of index funds and the pricing of equity securities, *Journal of Portfolio Management,* vol. 27, 2: 9–21.

Matthews, Gregory E. 1990. The Cinderella of qualified plans—target benefits. *Trust and Estates,* vol. 129, 11: 23–30.

McCarthy, David D., and John A. Turner. 1989. Pension rates of return in large and small plans. In *Trends in pensions,* ed. John A. Turner and Daniel J. Beller. Washington DC: Government Printing Office, 235–285.

McDonnell, Ken, Paul Fronstin, Kelly Olsen, Pamela Ostuw, Jack VanDerhei, and Paul Yakoboski. 1997. *EBRI databook on employee benefits,* 4th ed. Washington, DC: Employee Benefit Research Institute.

McMillan, Henry M. 1993. Asset/liability management: Implications for derivative strategies. In *Derivative strategies for managing portfolio risk.* Charlottesville, VA: AIMR, 35–44.

Mehra, Rajnish. 2003. The equity premium: Why is it a puzzle? *Financial Analysts Journal,* vol. 59, 1: 54–69.

Mehra, Rajnish, and Edward Prescott. 1985. The equity premium: A puzzle. *Journal of Monetary Economics,* vol. 15, 2: 145–161.

Meulbroek, Lisa K. 2001. The efficiency of equity-linked compensation: Understanding the full cost of awarding executive stock options. *Financial Management,* vol. 20, 2: 5–44.

Millstein, Ira M. 1994. Distinguishing "ownership" and "control" in the 1990s. Paper presented at Institutional Shareholder Services Conference.

Monks, Robert A.G., and Nell Minow. 1995. *Corporate governance.* Cambridge: Basil Blackwell.

Myers, Randy. 1994. Pension bonds? *Institutional Investor,* vol. 28, 8: 73–74.

Myers, Stewart C. 2002. Expert report. In *Kathi Cooper et al. v. The IBM Personal Pension Plan and IBM Corporation.* Cambridge, MA: The Brattle Group.

Nederlof, Maarten. 1996. Risk management programs. In *AIMR conference proceedings: Risk management.* Charlottesville, VA: AIMR, 15–23.

Nofsinger, John R. 1998. Why targeted investing does not make sense! *Financial Management,* vol. 27, 3: 87–96.

O'Barr, William M., and John M. Conley. 1992. Managing relationships: The culture of institutional investing, *Financial Analysts Journal,* vol. 48, 5: 21–27.

Ochs, Joyce. 1995. Staying out of trouble. *Pension management,* vol. 31, 9: 16–19.

Odean, Terrance. 1998. Are investors reluctant to realize their losses? *Journal of Finance,* vol. 53, 5: 1775–1798.

———. 1999. Do investors trade too much? *American Economic Review,* vol. 89, 5: 1279–1298.

Olsen, Russell L. 1999. *The independent fiduciary.* Hoboken, NJ: John Wiley & Sons.

Opler, Tim C., and Jonathan Sokobin. 1995. Does coordinated institutional activism work? An analysis of the activities of the council of institutional investors. Working paper. Columbus: Charles A. Dice Center for Research in Financial Economics, Ohio State University.

Pagliari, Joseph, Frederich Lieblich, Mark Schaner, and James Webb. 2001. Twenty years of the NCREIF property index. *Real Estate Economics,* vol. 29, 1: 1–27.

Park, Sangsoo, and Moon H. Song. 1995. Employee stock ownership plans, firm performance and monitoring by outside blockholders. *Financial Management,* vol. 24, 4: 52–65.

Pension Benefit Guaranty Corporation. 2003. *PBGC will not object to "follow-on" pension plan for US Airways pilots.* Washington DC: PBGC (Press Release) March 28, 2003.

Perdue, Pamela D. 2001. Going, going, gone: The continuing decline of the traditional defined benefit plan. *Journal of Pension Planning & Compliance,* vol. 26, 4: 1–12.

Perlman, Lawrence. 1993. A perspective on the new shareholder activism. *Journal of Applied Corporate Finance,* vol. 6, 2: 35–38.

Perold, Andre F. 1988. The implementation shortfall: Paper versus reality. *Journal of Portfolio Management,* vol. 14, 3: 4–9.

Petersen, Mitchell A. 1994. Cash flow variability and firm's pension choice: A role for operating leverage. *Journal of Financial Economics,* 36: 361–383.

———. 1996. Allocating assets and discounting cash flows: pension plan finance. In *Pensions, savings and capital markets,* ed. P.A. Fernandez et al.. Washington, DC: Department of Labor, 1–26.

Polsky, Lisa K. 1996. Integrating risk management and strategy. In *AIMR conference proceedings: Risk management.* Charlottesville, VA: AIMR, 8–14.

Pound, John. 1992. Raiders, targets and politics: the history and future of American corporate control. *Journal of Applied Corporate Finance,* vol. 5, 3: 6–18.

Prevost, Andrew K., and Ramesh P. Rao. 2000. Of what value are shareholder proposals sponsored by public pension funds? *Journal of Business,* vol. 73, 2: 177–204.

Profit Sharing and 401(k) Council of America. 2003. *46th annual survey of profit sharing and 401(k) plans.* Chicago, IL: PSCA, 30.

Pugh, William N., Sharon L. Oswald, and John S. Jahera Jr. 2000. The effect of ESOP adoptions on corporate performance: Are there really performance changes? *Managerial and Decision Economics,* vol. 21, 5: 167–180.

Purcell, Dave, and Paul Crowley. 1999. The reality of hedge funds. *Journal of Investing,* vol. 8, 3: 26–44.

Reichenstein, William. 1994. Why the corporate pension fund is not just another SBU. *Journal of Applied Corporate Finance,* vol. 6, 4: 103–108.

Reilly, Frank K. And David J. Wright. Forthcoming. An analysis of risk-adjusted performance for global market assets. *Journal of Portfolio Management.*

Retirement Confidence Survey. 2004. *The 2003 retirement confidence survey summary of findings.* Washington, DC: Retirement Confidence Survey.

Revsine, Laurence. 1989. Understanding Financial Accounting Standard 87. *Financial Analysts Journal,* vol. 45, no. 1: 61–68.

Roe, Mark J. 1995. The modern corporation and private pensions: Strong managers, weak owners. *Journal of Applied Corporate Finance,* vol 8, 2: 111–119.

Rohrer, Julie. 1995. Cash and carry. *Institutional Investor,* vol. 29, 4: 139–140.

Roll, Richard, and Stephen A. Ross. 1994. On the cross-sectional relation between expected returns and betas. *Journal of Finance,* vol. 49, 1: 101–122.

Romano, Roberta. 1995. The politics of public pension funds. *The Public Interest,* 119: 42–53.

Rosen, Corey. 1990. The record of employee ownership. *Financial Management,* vol. 19, 1: 39–48.

Rosenberg, Michael R. 1995. International fixed income investing: theory and practice. In *The handbook of fixed income securities,* ed. Frank J. Fabozzi and T. Dessa Fabozzi. Burr Ridge, IL: Irwin Professional Publishing, 1045–1076.

Sametz, Arnold W. 1995. An expanded role for private pensions in U.S. corporate governance. *Journal of Applied Corporate Finance,* vol. 8, 2: 97–110.

Samuelson, Paul A. 1990. Asset allocation can be dangerous to your wealth. *Journal of Portfolio Management,* vol. 16, 3: 5–8.

Sanes, Steven P., and Mark A. Zurack. 1987. Pension plans, portfolio insurance and FASB Statement No. 87: "An old risk in a new light." *Financial Analysts Journal,* vol. 43, 1: 10–13.

Scholes, Myron S., and Mark A. Wolfson. 1990. Employee ownership plans and corporate restructuring: Myths and realities. *Financial Management,* vol. 19, 1: 12–28.

Schultz, Ellen E. 1998. Ins and outs of "cash-balance" plan: employees will need to know what effects the new setup could have on their pensions. *Wall Street Journal.* December 4, 1998.

———. 1999. Actuaries become red-faced over recorded pension talk. *Wall Street Journal,* May 5, 1999.

———. 2001. Employers fight limits on firm's stock in 401(k)s. *Wall Street Journal,* December 21, 2001.

Schultz, Ellen E., and Elizabeth MacDonald. 1998. Retirement wrinkle: Employers win big with a pension shift; employees often lose. *Wall Street Journal.* December 4, 1998.

Securities and Exchange Commission Division of Corporate Finance. 2003. *Staff report: Review of the proxy process regarding the nomination and election of directors.* Washington, DC: Securities and Exchange Commission Division of Corporate Finance, July 15, 2003.

Sharpe, William F. 1976. Corporate pension funding policy. *Journal of Financial Economics,* vol. 4, 2: 183–193.

———.1990. Asset allocation. In *Managing investment portfolios: A dynamic process,* 2nd ed., ed. John L. Maginn and Donald L. Tuttle. New York: Warren Gorham and Lamont, 7-1-7-70.

———. 1992. Asset allocation: Management style and performance measurement. *Journal of Portfolio Management,* vol. 18, 2: 7–19.

———. 2002. Budgeting and monitoring pension fund risk. *Financial Analysts Journal,* vol. 58, 5: 74–86.

Sharpe, William F., and Andre F. Perold. 1988. Dynamic strategies for asset allocation. *Financial Analysts Journal,* 44: 16–27.

Shleifer, A., and R. Vishney. 1997. The limits of arbitrage. *Journal of Finance,* vol. 52, 35–55.

Siegel, Jeremy J. 1994. *Stocks for the long run.* Burr Ridge, IL: Irwin Professional Publishing.

Skowronski, Walter, and John Pound. 1993. Building relationships with major share-holders: A case study of lockheed. *Journal of Applied Corporate Finance,* vol. 6, 2: 39–47.

Smith, Michael. P. 1996. Shareholder activism by institutional investors: Evidence from CalPERS. *Journal of Finance,* vol. 51, 1: 227–252.

Smithson, Charles. 1996. Calculating and using VAR. *Risk Magazine,* vol. 9, 1: 25.

Solnik, Bruce. 2002. Global considerations for portfolio construction. In *AIMR conference proceedings: Equity portfolio construction.* Charlottesville, VA: AIMR, 29–37.

Solnik, Bruno, Cyril Boucrelle, and Yann Le Fur. 1996. International market correlation and volatility. *Financial Analysts Journal,* vol. 52, 5: 17–34.

Solnick, Bruno, and Dennis McLeavey. 2004. *International investments,* 5th ed. Boston, MA: Pearson Addison Wesley.

Standard & Poor's. 2003. *S&P 500 pension analysis shows market decline continues to erode pensions.* Standard & Poor's. Press release.

Statman, Meir. 1999. Behavioral finance: Past battles and future engagements. *Financial Analysts Journal,* vol. 55, 6: 18–27.

Stewart, G. Bennett, III. 2003. Pension roulette: Have you bet too much on equities? *Harvard Business Review,* vol. 81, 6: 104–110.

Stickney, Clyde P. 1995. Analyzing post retirement benefit disclosures. *Journal of Financial Statement Analysis,* vol. 1, 1: 15–25.

Strickland, Dean, Kenneth Wiles, and Mark Zenner. 1996. A requiem for the USA: Is small shareholder monitoring effective? *Journal of Financial Economics,* vol. 42, 2: 319–338.

Sulds, Jonathan L., and Richard J. Rabin. 2001. New wave of 401(k) litigation. *Pensions and Investments,* vol. 30, 24: 11.

Tepper, Irwin. 1981. Taxation and corporate pension policy. *Journal of Finance,* vol. 36, 1: 1–13.

Thaler, Richard, and Shlomo Benartzi. Forthcoming. Save more tomorrow: Using behavioral economics to increase employee savings. *Journal of Political Economy.*

Thomas, James M. 1991. Target benefit plans blend best of both worlds. *Pension World,* vol. 27, 5: 16–17.

Tigue, Patricia. 1994. Pension obligation bonds: Benefits and risks. *Government Finance Review,* vol. 10, 2: 30–32.

Treynor, Jack L. 1965. How to rate management of investment funds. *Harvard Business Review,* vol. 43, 1: 63–75.

———. 1977. The principles of corporate pension finance. *Journal of Finance,* vol. 32: 627–638.

Tschampion, R. Charles, Laurence B. Siegel, Dean J. Takahashi and John L. Maginn. Forthcoming. Managing institutional investor portfolios. In *Managing investment portfolios: A dynamic process,* 3rd ed. Charlottesville, VA: AIMR.

Tversky, Amos. 1990. The psychology of risk. In AIMR conference proceedings: *Quantifying the market risk premium phenomenon for investment decision making.* Charlottesville, VA: AIMR, 73–77.

UBS Asset Management. *2002 international pension fund indicators 2001: A perspective on pension fund investment worldwide.* New York: UBS Asset Management.

United Nations. 2001. *World population prospects: The 2000 revision.* New York: United Nations.

Wagner, Wayne H. 1993. Defining and measuring trading costs. In *AIMR conference proceedings: Execution techniques, true trading costs and the microstructure of markets.* Charlottesville, VA: AIMR, 15–23.

Wahal, Sunil. 1996. Pension fund activism and firm performance. *Journal of Financial and Quantitative Analysis,* vol. 31, 1: 1–23.

Walsh, Mary Williams. 2003. Discord over efforts at valuing pensions *New York Times,* May 1, 2003.

Wardlow, Penelope S. 1995. GASB's new pensions package. *Journal of Accountancy,* vol. 180, no. 1: 56–58.

Watson, Ronald. 1994. Does targeting investment make sense? *Financial Management,* vol. 23, 4: 69–74.

Weinberg, Neil. 1995. Votes today, taxes tomorrow. *Forbes,* June 5, 1995.

Williams, Fred. 2002. What's the difference?: In commission recapture, ignorance may not be bliss. *Pensions and Investments,* vol. 30, 21: 3.

Wilshire Associates. 2002. *2002 Wilshire report on state retirement systems: Funding levels and asset allocation.* Santa Monica, CA: Wilshire Associates.

Wood, Arnold. 1995. Behavioral risk: Anecdotes and disturbing evidence. *Journal of Investing,* vol. 6, 1: 8–12.

Index

Note: page numbers followed by "*t*" refer to tables